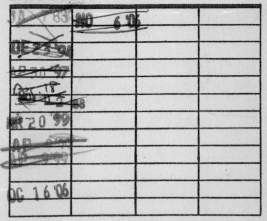

Isaiah Berlin: Selected Writings
Edited by Henry Hardy

*

AGAINST THE CURRENT

By the same author

*

KARL MARX
THE AGE OF ENLIGHTENMENT
FOUR ESSAYS ON LIBERTY
VICO AND HERDER
RUSSIAN THINKERS
CONCEPTS AND CATEGORIES

AGAINST
the
CURRENT

ESSAYS IN THE HISTORY OF IDEAS

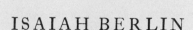

ISAIAH BERLIN

Edited and
with a Bibliography by
Henry Hardy

With an Introduction by
Roger Hausheer

THE VIKING PRESS   NEW YORK

First published in 1980 by The Viking Press
625 Madison Avenue, New York, N.Y. 10022

LIBRARY OF CONGRESS CATALOGING IN PUBLICATION DATA
Berlin, Isaiah, Sir.
Against the current.
Bibliography: p. Includes index.
Contents: The counter-enlightenment.—The origi-
nality of Machiavelli.—The divorce between the sciences
and the humanities. [etc.]
1. Philosophy—Addresses, essays, lectures.
I. Hardy, Henry. II. Title.
B29.B445   109   79-22928
ISBN 0-670-10944-4

Printed in the United States of America
Set in Caslon

Contents

Author's Note

I have nothing of my own to add to the essays on the history of ideas contained in this book, but I should be exceedingly remiss if I did not take this opportunity of offering my thanks to Mr Roger Hausheer for providing so sympathetic and luminous an account of my views on the topics discussed in these essays. No author could wish for a more understanding, scrupulous or civilised critic. I should like to express my sincere thanks to this most promising young scholar.

ISAIAH BERLIN

September 1978

Editor's Preface

This is the third[1] of four volumes in which I have brought together, and prepared for reprinting, most of the essays so far published by Isaiah Berlin which had not hitherto been made available in a collected form. His many writings were scattered, often in obscure places, most were out of print, and only half a dozen essays had previously been collected and reissued.[2] These four volumes, together with a complete bibliography of what he has published to date, reprinted in the present volume,[3] will make much more of his work readily accessible than before. This it clearly deserves.

A few passages – chiefly translations – have been rewritten by the author for this collection. Otherwise, apart from necessary corrections, and the addition of missing references, the essays are reprinted in their original form.

The essays in the present volume are contributions to the history of ideas. For various reasons, I have omitted eight essays in this field which, other things being equal, would have belonged here. These are 'Political Ideas in the Twentieth Century' and 'John Stuart Mill and the Ends of Life', which have already been reissued in *Four Essays on Liberty*; 'The Philosophical Ideas of Giambattista Vico' and 'Herder and Enlightenment', which have been revised and published as a book, *Vico and Herder*; 'Socialism and Socialist Theories', which is written for a purpose and in a style which confines it to its encyclopedic context; 'European Unity and Its Vicissitudes' and 'L'apoteosi della volontà romantica: la rivolta contro il tipo di un mondo ideale', whose contents are due to be absorbed into the author's projected book on the intellectual origins of romanticism; and 'The

---

[1] The first was *Russian Thinkers* (London and New York, 1978); the second *Concepts and Categories: Philosophical Essays* (London, 1978; New York, 1979).

[2] *Four Essays on Liberty* (London and New York, 1969) and *Vico and Herder* (London and New York, 1976). Other collections have appeared only in translation.

[3] See pp. 356–73 below.

Bent Twig: A Note on Nationalism', which by and large covers the same ground as an essay on the same topic reprinted here, 'Nationalism: Past Neglect and Present Power'. Details of these pieces can be found in the bibliography already mentioned.[1]

The details of the original publication of the essays that are included here are as follows. 'The Counter-Enlightenment' appeared in the *Dictionary of the History of Ideas* (New York, 1968–73: Scribner's);[2] 'The Originality of Machiavelli' was published in Myron P. Gilmore (ed.), *Studies on Machiavelli* (Florence, 1972: Sansoni); 'The Divorce between the Sciences and the Humanities' was the second Tykociner Memorial Lecture, published by the University of Illinois in 1974; 'Vico's Concept of Knowledge' appeared as 'A Note on Vico's Concept of Knowledge' in Giorgio Tagliacozzo and Hayden V. White (eds), *Giambattista Vico: An International Symposium* (Baltimore, 1969: Johns Hopkins Press); 'Vico and the Ideal of the Enlightenment' was published in *Social Research* 43 (1976);[3] 'Montesquieu' appeared in the *Proceedings of the British Academy* 41 (1955); 'Hume and the Sources of German Anti-Rationalism' was a contribution to G. P. Morice (ed.), *David Hume: Bicentennial Papers* (Edinburgh, 1977: Edinburgh University Press);[4] 'Herzen and his Memoirs' is the introduction to Alexander Herzen, *My Past and Thoughts*, translated by Constance Garnett (London, 1968: Chatto and Windus; New York, 1968: Knopf); 'The Life and Opinions of Moses Hess' was the Lucien Wolf Memorial Lecture (Cambridge, 1959: Heffer, for the Jewish Historical Society of England); 'Benjamin Disraeli, Karl Marx and the Search for Identity' appeared in *Transactions of the Jewish Historical Society of England 22 (1968–9)* (London, 1970: Jewish Historical Society of England); 'The "Naïveté" of Verdi' was published in *Atti del I Congresso internazionale di studi verdiani, 1966* (Parma, 1969: Istituto di Studi Verdiani); 'Georges Sorel' was a Creighton Lecture published first in *The Times Literary Supplement*, 31 December 1971, and then in an expanded form in Chimen Abramsky (ed.), *Essays in Honour of E. H. Carr*

---

[1] They are, respectively, items 37, 74, 79, 98, 38, 73, 128 and 143. The bibliography should also be consulted for the many smaller pieces in this area, including book reviews.

[2] With a bibliography not here reproduced.

[3] Its last section, 'The Workings of Providence', is not reprinted here.

[4] The 'Additional Bibliographical Material' appended to this article has not been reproduced here.

EDITOR'S PREFACE

(London, 1974: Macmillan); and 'Nationalism: Past Neglect and Present Power' appeared in *Partisan Review* 45 (1978). I am grateful to the publishers concerned for allowing me to reprint these essays. 'The Counter-Enlightenment', 'The Divorce between the Sciences and the Humanities' and 'Nationalism: Past Neglect and Present Power' have been left without references (with the exception of passages quoted in footnotes and one long passage), as they originally appeared. Translations, unless otherwise stated, are by Isaiah Berlin. My 'A Bibliography of Isaiah Berlin' first appeared in *Lycidas* (the magazine of Wolfson College, Oxford) No 3 (1975) – additions and corrections ibid. No 4 (1976) – and has been revised and updated for inclusion here.

I have received very generous help from a number of people in editing this volume. Roger Hausheer has not only written the introduction, but has helped extensively with German sources, especially Hamann and Hess, and has read the proofs. David Robey has helped with Machiavelli, Edward Larrissy with Blake, Robert Shackleton with Montesquieu, Robert Wokler with Rousseau, Barry Stroud with Hume, Aileen Kelly with Herzen, Lord Blake and Vernon Bogdanor with Disraeli, Terrell Carver with Marx, and Jeremy Jennings with Sorel. I could not have managed without the assistance of these scholars, and I record my great gratitude to them. Isaiah Berlin continues, with undiminished courtesy, to do his best to answer my virtually endless queries, and Pat Utechin, his secretary, has again provided invaluable help and support. Finally I should like to thank Anne Wilkinson and Jim Hardy for their kindness in reading the proofs.

HENRY HARDY

February 1979

Introduction

Roger Hausheer

Two extravagances: to exclude Reason, to admit only
Reason.

Blaise Pascal

A man of clear ideas errs grievously if he imagines that
whatever is seen confusedly does not exist: it belongs to
him, when he meets with such a thing, to dispel the mist,
and fix the outlines of the vague form which is looming
through it.

J. S. Mill

In our time, what is at issue is the very nature of man, the
image we have of his limits and possibilities as man. History
is not yet done with its exploration of the limits and
meanings of 'human nature'.

C. Wright Mills

I

Isaiah Berlin's essays in the history of ideas are not written from a
point of view. They are not intended directly to illustrate or support
(or for that matter attack or undermine) any single historical or political
theory, doctrine or ideology; they range from such wholly diverse
figures as Marx, Disraeli and Sorel to topics as apparently remote
from one another as nationalism and the theory of knowledge; they
are wholly exploratory and undogmatic, raising more tentative but
often deeply unsettling questions than they claim to answer; and
above all, they represent an utterly independent, scrupulously open-
minded, but deeply passionate search for truth. Less, perhaps, than
any other thinker does Berlin suppose himself in possession of some
simple truth, and then proceed to interpret and rearrange the world
in the light of it. Yet his essays are not scattered leaves, blown by the

four winds. Nor are they mere occasional pieces, standing in isolation from one another, significant only in the context of their original publication. For in so far as they proceed from a central vision of man and his capacities, and their transformation through historical time – a vision which is richly ramified, complex, and incapable of completion – they are bound lightly and naturally together at many hidden and unexpected levels. Time and again, Berlin raises and illuminates, in the light of vividly concrete historical examples, major issues with which he has dealt in a more abstract manner in his philosophical essays; issues which are not only at the core of his lifelong preoccupation with ideas, but of great intrinsic interest and importance in themselves, and at the forefront of attention today.

His essays sail manfully against the current in at least two ways. Many of them are devoted to intellectual figures of great originality who have either been largely ignored or else regarded with patronising disdain, both by their contemporaries and by later generations of scholars. Indeed, to help rescue from oblivion or neglect, and render historical justice to, thinkers who have been ignored, misrepresented or misunderstood, partly at least because they have dared to oppose the ruling intellectual orthodoxies of their time, is not the least of Berlin's services to scholarship. His essays on Vico, Hess and Sorel, to take but three examples, would be memorable for this alone. But what makes these essays so strikingly original and exciting is the sense we are given of the gradual birth of seminal new ideas, of the emergence since the mid-eighteenth century of some of the great cardinal notions of the modern world. For in examining the ideas of philosophers, thinkers, and men of vision like Vico, Hamann and Herder, Herzen and Sorel, Berlin displays a uniquely perceptive sensitivity to the deeper stirrings and movements, the dark, uneasy, brooding seasons of the human spirit beneath the bland rationalistic surface of the thought of an age, when a small but at times passionate voice of opposition, overlooked, misinterpreted or ridiculed by its contemporaries, utters in an often fragmentary or semi-articulate form novel ideas about man and his nature which are destined to grow into a world-transforming movement in a later day. From the doctrines of many of these thinkers some of their most powerful inspiration is drawn, directly or indirectly, by the many and various movements of protest which have grown up against some of the monolithic orthodoxies of our own time. And while Berlin is only too keenly aware of the insane excesses to which the views of some of these antinomian thinkers – in particular, perhaps, Hamann, Herder and Sorel — may contribute, and have as a matter of fact contributed, yet the penetrating and painful insights they afford us cannot just be brushed aside. At every step forward in our collective development, Berlin seems to say, we must pause to listen sympathetically to the voices crying out in tortured dissent, or just raised to utter criticism, whether cautiously reasoned or wildly inchoate : we ignore them at our peril, for they may tell us something vital about ourselves; and, in so doing, point towards a larger and more generous (and perhaps more truthful) conception of what men are and can be.

Many of the subjects of his essays, therefore, are agonised men in the grips of a vision so novel and complex that they themselves are unable fully to comprehend and formulate it; they search and grope instinctively, not wholly aware of what it is that they are doing, searching for, attempting to express. This gives rise to the reflection that there may be many levels of intentional action, and that some of the insights of a man of original intellectual vision, and the full implications and consequences of these, may never become transparently clear, either to himself or to others, in his own lifetime; for if he has left some record of what he has thought or felt, the full significance and impact of what he was searching for — what, in effect, his under-lying, evolving, still fully to be clarified aims were — may emerge only centuries after his death, when a sophisticated vocabulary and appropriate methods have grown up around the constellation of problems which he was among the very first to touch upon. The classic and most striking case of this is Vico. But in some degree it is surely true of most great writers and thinkers of richly suggestive vision, in so far as they have opened new and permanent doors of insight, perception and understanding.

II

At the heart of all Berlin's writings there is a cluster of perennial philosophical problems. The nature of self, will, freedom, human identity, personality and dignity; the manner and degree in which these can be abused, offended against, insulted, and their proper boundaries (whatever these may be) transgressed; the consequences, both probable and actual, of failing to understand them for what they are, and above all of torturing them into conformity with conceptual systems and models which deny too much of their essential nature; the distinction between 'inner' human nature as opposed to 'external' physical nature, and between the basic categories and methods proper to their investigation – all these problems are touched upon, and our understanding of them enlarged and deepened, by the essays in this volume. Again, the burning issue of philosophical monism, the doctrine that all reality, and all the branches of our knowledge of it, form a rational, harmonious whole, and that there is ultimate unity or harmony between human ends, is discussed and criticised from many angles by close scrutiny of the cardinal doctrines of some of those thinkers who did most to undermine it. Berlin's preoccupation with the emergence of pluralism, both in the realms of ethical, political and aesthetic values, and in the sphere of human knowledge, so central to his writings in political theory, philosophy of history, and, to a lesser but still important degree, epistemology, is apparent in his choice and treatment of individual thinkers and currents of thought in his essays in the history of ideas. His major excavations in this field have helped bring to light ruined monuments and fragments, strange chunks of intellectual masonry, which seem at times to hint at the shadowy outlines of a phenomenology of European consciousness since the mid-eighteenth century – namely the emergence of novel types of transforming insight and general outlook, with their associated concepts and categories, at certain times and places and in certain thinkers or groups of thinkers – and thereby to throw light upon some of the questions that have troubled him most deeply, not just as an academic philosopher or as a professional scholar, but as a human being.

III

The history of ideas is a comparatively new field of study: it still craves recognition in a largely hostile world, though there are encouraging signs of a gradual change of heart even in the English-speaking world. There is a growing feeling that investigation of what men have thought and felt, and of the basic ideas in terms of which they have seen themselves and framed their aspirations, may provide a more luminous source of light in the study of man than the established social, political and psychological sciences, for all that many of these have developed an apparatus of specialised terminology and the use of empirical, quantitative methods. For in so far as they tend to view men, both as individuals and groups, as the proper objects of the generalising empirical sciences, as so much passive, inexpressive material moulded by impersonal forces obedient to statistical or causal laws, these sciences tend to leave out, or at least play down, something of central importance : namely that men are defined precisely by their possession of an inner life, of purposes and ideals, and of a vision or conception, however hazy or implicit, of who they are, where they have come from, and what they are at. And indeed, it is just their possession of an inner life in this sense that distinguishes them from animals and natural objects. The history of ideas, because it attempts (among other things) to trace the birth and development of some of the ruling concepts of a civilisation or culture through long periods of mental change, and to reconstruct the image men have of themselves and their activities, in a given age and culture, probably makes a wider variety of demands upon its practitioners than almost any other discipline ; or, at least, demands which are special, and often painful. The sharp logical skills of conceptual analysis required in the criticism of ideas, the rich stores of assimilated learning, the vast powers of sympathetic, reconstructive imagination akin to those of the creative artist – the capacity to 'enter into' and understand from 'inside' forms of life wholly different from his own – and the almost magical power of intuitive divination – these capacities, all ideally possessed by the historian of ideas, rarely come together in one man. This doubtless explains in part why there has never been more than a handful of genuine historians of ideas, and why the history of ideas itself, as a reputable discipline with universally accepted credentials of its own, should still have to battle for recognition.

Yet the great difficulties posed by the cultivation of a field of knowledge, and the consequent rarity of high achievement, are not in themselves alone sufficient to explain its comparative neglect. Are there, perhaps, deeper and less obvious reasons for its ambiguous status? Is it that by burrowing away in the foundations of some of our deepest assumptions it may excavate things long and conveniently forgotten, or taken to be more solid, more fixed and final, than they are? Or reopen painful questions about turnings taken in the course of our collective development, questions some of which may take on a new and disturbing significance today? Before our eyes, the granite bedrock of some of our most familiar and cherished beliefs may dissolve into shifting sand. At all events, many of Berlin's essays have called into question, implicitly or explicitly, some of the most ancient and most deeply held assumptions of men, at any rate in the western world. And though the analogy is far from perfect, the history of ideas at its best may be able to do for a culture what psychoanalysis claims to be able to do for the individual: to analyse and lay bare the origins and nature not, it is true, of motivation and hidden springs of behaviour, but of the often implicit, deeply embedded, formative ideas, concepts and categories − some of which are more provisional and open to historical change than could have seemed possible before the last half of the eighteenth century − by means of which we order and interpret a major part of our experience, above all in the peculiarly human spheres of moral, aesthetic and political activity; and in so doing enlarge both our self-knowledge and our sense of the scope of our creative liberty.

Berlin's life has been spent in the study of philosophy and the examination, criticism and exposition of general ideas. If we are to understand the peculiar status the history of ideas holds for him, as well as the unique nature of his own contribution to it, we must know something of the philosophical background out of which his interests grew. Berlin has himself often repeated the sharp-eyed insight that, in the western tradition at least, from Plato to our own day, the overwhelming majority of systematic thinkers of all schools, whether rationalists, idealists, phenomenalists, positivists or empiricists, have, despite their many radical differences, proceeded on one central unargued assumption: that reality, whatever mere appearances may indicate to the contrary, is in essence a rational whole where all things ultimately cohere. They suppose that there exists (at least in principle) a body of discoverable truths touching all conceivable questions, both theoretical and practical; that there is, and can be, only one correct method or set of methods for gaining access to these truths; and that these truths, as well as the methods used in their discovery, are universally valid. Their procedure usually takes the following form: they first identify a privileged class of indubitable entities or incorrigible propositions, claiming an exclusive logical or ontological status for these, and assigning appropriate methods for their discovery; and finally, with a gusto that has deep psychological roots in the instinct for both order and destruction, reject as 'not real', confused or, at times, 'nonsense' what cannot be translated into the type of entity or proposition which they have chosen as the impregnable model. Descartes with his doctrine of clear and distinct ideas, or Leibniz with his notion of a *mathesis universalis*, or latter-day positivists with their atomic propositions and protocol sentences, or phenomenalists and sense-data theorists with their sense-*qualia*, all exemplify this reductionist tendency. Thinkers of this kind are prone, on the basis of their doctrines, to seek to carry out a radical revision of reality, in theory or in practice, relegating much that seems prima facie meaningful or important to their philosophical bonfire; often enough, things of priceless value have been consumed by the flames, and much of what remains has been fearfully mutilated or distorted.

It is against this background that we must view, on the one hand, Berlin's attitude to one of the most influential philosophical currents of his time, that associated with the neo-positivism of Russell and his disciples, and, on the other, his absorbed preoccupation with humane studies and, above all, with the history of ideas. In a number of essays – 'Logical Translation', 'Verification', 'Empirical Propositions and Hypothetical Statements'[1] – written when he was still teaching and working in the field of general philosophy, Berlin set out to square accounts with logical positivism by offering a critique of some of the central doctrines upon which it rests. These essays, while they represent a kind of valedictory to a particular way of doing philosophy, contain at the same time the seeds of a covert manifesto. Berlin's keen sense of the irreducibly wide variety of kinds of experience and types of proposition, and of the impossibility of expressing them in or translating them out into one type of proposition, or of analysing all the contents of the universe in terms of one basic kind of entity or 'stuff', is here given free expression in the spheres of logic and epistemology. Things are as they are, and we do well not to analyse away what makes them uniquely themselves.

What makes these essays so particularly fascinating and important is twofold: they are written from within the ranks of the philosophical tendency which he criticises, and, in so far as they reveal certain very deep-rooted attitudes and convictions on his own part, they point towards, and help enlarge our understanding of, both his intense interest in the history of ideas and his conception of philosophy's role. While these essays constitute a fundamental critique of one of the major schools of modern philosophy, and a radical break with it, they are above all the expression of the deep and unsilenceable misgivings of a sympathetic insider, of someone who has fully grasped – perhaps too fully – the aims and methods of the intellectual movement he criticises,

[1] Reprinted in *Concepts and Categories* (London, 1978; New York, 1979), the second volume of this series.

and who, try as he will, cannot accept them. Indeed, it is tempting to see an analogy between Berlin's reaction to the philosophy of Hume, Russell, Ayer, the early Wittgenstein, Carnap, the Vienna Circle and the main strains of neo-positivism, with their reductionist methods of ironing and flattening out, and the rejection by philosophers like Vico of Descartes and the rationalists of his time, or the attitude of visionaries and thinkers like Hamann and Herder to the doctrines of the French Enlightenment. For these, too, were thinkers who understood perfectly the goals and methods of their opponents, and to whom Berlin has subsequently turned and devoted a deep and sympathetic understanding. Yet he is entirely free of their partisan vehemence, remote from their at times alarmingly obscurantist tendencies, and far from blind to the great cardinal merits of the opposition: he acknowledges the great achievements of logical positivism in clearing the ground of much metaphysical nonsense, and time and again in his writings he pays passing tribute to the great triumphs of the natural sciences, which he sees as the most successful single endeavour of the human intellect in modern times; and just as often he reiterates the conviction that all phenomena that are properly tractable by the quantitative methods of the empirical sciences, without violence to or denial of their innermost natures, should be brought under the umbrella of causal or statistical laws.

The inadequacy of simple reductionist frameworks is most keenly felt in that vast, amorphous, volatile area which comprises spiritual, moral, aesthetic and political experience. Here, more than anywhere else, it is deeply misleading and often injurious to apply simple reductionist concepts; and under one aspect, Berlin's entire philosophical *oeuvre* may be seen as a long battle, now overt, now covert, but always subtle, resourceful and determined, against the facile application of inadequate models and concepts in the field of human studies. Men should never be blinded by the distorting spectacles of theory to what they know immediately to be true of themselves. Many of his essays offer a sensitive and subtle investigation of the impingement, for example, of our increasingly exact and sophisticated knowledge of the natural, external world upon the inner, moral and spiritual worlds of human experience. The pieces on Vico's theory of knowledge, the essays on Hamann and Hume, and Sorel, and the essay on nationalism, may be seen to connect in this regard with some of the major concerns of 'Historical Inevitability'.[1] For again and again Berlin warns

[1] Reprinted in *Four Essays on Liberty* (London and New York, 1969).

against two fatal dangers : that of subscribing to all-embracing systems which, while they may afford novel and genuine insight, are yet one-sided and over-simple, incapable of doing justice to enough of the facts while turning all or most attention to those they have brought to light, and seeing all else in terms of them; and that of transferring methods and procedures from one discipline, where they have been enormously successful, to another where they are not at home, in which their application distorts or even destroys the facts.

There is perhaps no more illuminating flash of self-disclosure in Berlin's writings than the passage in his essay on his friend John Austin[1] where, after depicting the originality and power of Austin's intellect, his boldness and philosophical fertility, his astonishing capacity for breaking up problems into tiny pieces, he tells us that Austin commanded his affection and respect above all for this passing comment : 'They all *talk* about determinism and *say* they believe in it. I've never met a determinist in my life, I mean a man who really did believe in it as you and I believe that men are mortal. Have you?' Philosophers ruminating in their studies, or natural scientists conducting experiments in their laboratories, might claim to be determinists in theory, but their moral conduct and their practical lives, the words they utter and the judgements they make, belie their surface professions.

For Berlin, philosophy cannot yield *a priori* knowledge of man's nature or of the universe; nor by logical translation can it afford us certain and incorrigible empirical knowledge. Thus where Ayer persisted in the path of logical positivism, buttressing, developing and refining his central doctrines, and Austin, like the later Wittgenstein, turned to a close and detailed analysis of the concepts of ordinary language, Berlin was drawn increasingly, in his search for answers to some of the central questions of philosophy, to a concrete historical study of some of the major intellectual developments in western culture since the eighteenth century. This led him to explore and deepen the notion that a large part of the thought and experience of a period is organised by what Collingwood termed 'constellations of absolute presuppositions'.

---

[1] 'Austin and the Early Beginnings of Oxford Philosophy', in Sir Isaiah Berlin and others, *Essays on J. L. Austin* (Oxford, 1973), to be included in the last volume of this series.

What exactly is the role of philosophy for Berlin? He has himself answered this question in a series of important and penetrating essays. 'The Purpose of Philosophy', 'Does Political Theory Still Exist?', and 'The Concept of Scientific History',[1] taken together, reveal (among many other things) his conception of the positive and vital place of philosophy in all mental activity, and above all of the history of ideas as a type of philosophical endeavour which may yield a genuine form of knowledge, or self-knowledge, which is entirely *sui generis*, illuminating and liberating, and discoverable only by the systematic study of the intellectual history of men – of cultures, civilisations, intellectual and political movements, and so forth. Berlin distinguishes a class of questions which are properly philosophical in the sense that there is no universally accredited, ready-made method or set of methods for discovering answers to them; they may differ greatly from one another, some appearing to be questions about matters of fact or value, others about methods of inquiry and the words and symbols which they use; yet what they all have in common is that they do not 'carry within their own structure clear indications of the techniques of their solution'. They are distinguishable from the two remaining (and to some extent overlapping) classes of questions – the empirical questions of common sense and the natural sciences on the one hand, and the formal ones of mathematics, logic and other deductive disciplines on the other – by being unanswerable by the systematic application of specialised skills or procedures. For Berlin the history of thought is largely the story of the sorting out of issues into one or another of these two classes of questions. But while one constellation of inter-related questions after another has torn itself away from the parent body of philosophy to become an independent, adult, empirical science or formal discipline, the number of irreducible, unanswerable philosophical questions – and here Berlin diverges very sharply from all those philosophers, perhaps the majority, who seek to make these questions vanish by a powerful philosophical solvent – has not diminished, nor do they grow less pressing.

The nature of some of these questions may be made more clear if we remember the crucial distinction, dwelt on by Kant, between the content of experience and the concepts and categories in terms of which we organise and interpret it. For Kant, as Berlin points out,

[1] Reprinted in *Concepts and Categories* (see p. xix, note 1 above).

the fundamental categories through which we perceive the external world were universal and immutable, common to all rational, sentient beings. Once they had been discovered and duly analysed, certain fundamental truths about men would be fixed for all time. The vital step taken by Kant was given a revolutionary turn by a succession of thinkers who were more preoccupied with historical and aesthetic questions than with those of epistemology and logic. They grasped, and made a very great deal of, something to which Kant paid little serious systematic attention, namely that, while some of the basic categories and 'spectacles' through which we see the world did indeed seem unchanging, others did change, sometimes quite radically, from age to age and culture to culture. The basic empirical content of what a culture saw and heard, thought and felt, might change but little if at all, but some of the models in terms of which it was perceived and organised – the spectacles through which it was viewed – might be transformed. Many of these basic categories and models are as old as humanity itself, while others are more volatile and transient, so that the investigation of their emergence takes on a historical aspect. The study and systematic critical discussion of such models is of the first importance, for it is a question of nothing less than the entire framework of our experience itself; many of these models collide with one another; and some are rendered obsolete by their failure to account for a sufficient number of facets of experience, to be replaced by others which, while they may be more accommodating, often close some of the doors opened by the models they replace. The adequacy of our fundamental presuppositions – how much of our experience they include, how much they leave out, how much they illuminate and how much obscure – should be of central concern to both philosophers and historians of ideas.

The history of ideas, then, is a comparatively late-born and highly sophisticated child of advanced civilisation. At the earliest, it may be thought to have come into being during the last half of the eighteenth century, a close relative of historicism, pluralism and relativism, and of the various historically based comparative disciplines: anthropology, philology, linguistics, etymology, aesthetics, jurisprudence, sociology, ethnology. Its central preoccupation consists in a large-scale extension of the ancient injunction 'know thyself' to the collective historical whole, the civilisation or culture, in which the individual self is embedded, and of which it is in no small measure a product. It is above all else concerned to tell us who and what we are, and by what stages and often tortuous paths we have become what we are. It stresses the continuity of ideas and emotions, of thought and practice, of philosophy, politics, art and literature, rather than artificially prising them apart, as usually happens with the more specialised branches of the humane studies. The central objects of its inquiry are the all-pervading, ruling, formative concepts and categories peculiar to a culture or period – or indeed a literary school or a political movement, an artistic genius or a seminal thinker, in so far as these have been the first to raise issues and advance ideas which have passed into the common outlook of subsequent generations. For Berlin does not deal only with great thinkers: the history of ideas is not the story of a succession of great philosophers, where one system of ideas or theories begets another, as if by a process of parthenogenesis; rather, he is interested in the emergence of ideas, in many types of intellectual personality, varied, original, eccentric, often dissident and outside the mainstream of their time, in opposition to the orthodox dogmas and received presuppositions which they help to overturn.

What the history of ideas is able to offer as a branch of philosophy, and as a relatively new source of genuine knowledge and enlightenment, is insight into the origins of, and literally world-transforming shifts in, the basic conceptual patterns in terms of which we understand ourselves and acquire our identity as human beings. These underlying, ubiquitous presuppositions, precisely because they are of a high degree of generality and themselves serve as the means whereby we order a very large part – the human part – of our experience, have usually remained submerged and unexamined: the task of the historian of ideas is to try to get outside them, to make them the objects of reflection and systematic study, thereby bringing them out into the light where they can be openly criticised and evaluated. Many of our values and ideals, properly analysed and examined, their origins and evolution properly traced and described, will be revealed for what they are: not timeless, objective, unshakeable, self-evident truths derived from the eternal and immutable essence of human nature, but the late and fragile blossoms of a long, untidy, often painful and tragic, but ultimately intelligible historical process of cultural change. The criteria applied in such critical discussion must themselves in turn be subjected to scrutiny, and what exactly they are for Berlin is a question to which we will turn later.

In one sense, then, Berlin's entire *oeuvre* is a long and sustained rejection of a view of philosophy and truth, and of the methods of

inquiry into man's true capacities and condition, which, in the western
tradition at least, has been central for more than two thousand years;
a view the shortcomings of which struck him early on in life, and
which he has continued to expose with resourcefulness and vigour,
under a wide variety of aspects and with a wealth of concrete historical
detail, thereby shedding light from many unexpected angles upon
some of the most pressing problems of our own time.

v

Perhaps the profoundest and most far-reaching shift in general ideas
since the Reformation, and one still powerfully active in our world
today, is the revolt, which first became articulate in the second third
of the eighteenth century, at first in Italy and then with gathering
force in the German-speaking world, of a succession of antinomian
thinkers against the central rationalist and scientific traditions of the
west. To this literally world-transforming current of ideas, from
which so many modern movements of thought and feeling derive – in
particular European romanticism, nationalism, relativism, pluralism,
and the many currents of voluntarism of which existentialism is the
most recent expression in our own time – Berlin has devoted some of
his finest and most illuminating essays. In his article 'The Counter-
Enlightenment' Berlin examines the main ideas of some of these
thinkers. In the case of Vico, whose apparent isolation from this
group of thinkers in time and place makes his lonely anticipation of
most of their central doctrines all the more extraordinary, the arch-
enemies were, on the one hand, Descartes with his doctrine of clear
and distinct ideas, his contempt for historical and humane studies
generally, and his attempts to assimilate all forms of knowledge to that
of one kind, namely mathematics; and, on the other, the natural law
theorists with their cardinal assumption of a fixed, universal human
nature, identical in all places and times. For Hamann and Herder, and
the many later thinkers directly or indirectly influenced by their
radical innovations, the insidious enemies were the more fanatical and
dogmatic *philosophes* of the French Enlightenment, whose central
doctrines were held to be devitalising distortions of the truth, masking
more than they illuminated. Despite their many differences, the
thinkers of the French Enlightenment held in common a stock of
fundamental presuppositions which went almost wholly unchallenged:

that human nature is the same in all times and places; that universal human goals, true ends and effective means, are at least in principle discoverable; that methods similar to those of Newtonian science, which had proved so successful in bringing to light the regularities of inanimate nature, should be discovered and applied in the field of morals, politics, economics, and in the sphere of human relationships in general, thus eradicating vice and suffering and what Helvétius termed 'interested error'. What all these rationalist thinkers shared was the belief that somewhere, by some means, a single, coherent, unified structure of knowledge concerning questions of both fact and value was in principle available. They sought all-embracing schemas, universal unifying frameworks, within which everything that exists could be shown to be systematically – i.e. logically or causally – interconnected, vast structures in which there should be no gaps left open for spontaneous, unattended developments, where everything that occurs should be, at least in principle, wholly explicable in terms of immutable general laws. It is this proud and shining column, which Berlin identifies as the central mainstay of the rational and scientific edifices of western thought, which some of the thinkers in this volume undermined and caused to totter.

As Berlin is careful to point out, there had indeed been dissent from this central assumption on the part of a sceptical and relativist tradition stretching back to antiquity; and in the modern era thinkers from Bodin to Montesquieu, by emphasising the vast variety of customs, *mores*, institutions, general outlooks and beliefs, had administered a series of gentle shocks to the supporting pillar. Yet none of these had sufficed to bring the structure crashing down. In this respect, Berlin's treatment of Montesquieu is particularly valuable. He does not deny that the great French thinker is quite rightly thought of as one of the true fathers of the French Enlightenment. Despite Montesquieu's use of metaphysical concepts such as natural law and natural purpose, his approach was essentially empirical and naturalistic; he believed, above all, in the direct evidence yielded by observation. His central doctrines were absorbed into the texture of nineteenth-century liberal thought and practice, what had once seemed novel and arresting became commonplace, and successive social and political thinkers looked back on him as a distinguished predecessor with nothing new to say to them. Yet looking back at him with the accumulated experience of the first half of the twentieth century, Berlin feels more disposed to emphasise the sceptical note running through all his writings, that lack of enthusiasm for all sweeping and simplistic projects for large-scale change which upset and irritated a good many of his more optimistic contemporaries with their starker, simpler, more rationalistic vision. For while he himself claimed that he had founded a new science in the spirit of Descartes, he knew in his heart that the very nature of his material was resistant to such methods, and his practice belies his professions. Unlike so many of his contemporaries, he could never bring himself to regard concrete specific detail as mere material for illustrating general rules or laws. He respects, and indeed delights in, the irreducibly unique and particular for its own sake; and is deeply distrustful of the concept of man in general. For Montesquieu each type of society possesses an inner spirit or dynamic principle which informs all its most diverse ramifications. It is the duty of statesmen and law-givers to understand this inner spirit or organising force, and to rule or legislate in conformity with it. Different societies have different needs and pursue different goals: what is good for one in one situation and at one stage of development is not necessarily equally good for others in different conditions; hence there are and can be no universal, final solutions to human problems, and no ultimate rational standards or criteria for adjudicating between human ends. There was something essentially subversive of Enlightenment dogma in this attitude, and his distrust of rapid, simple, sweeping solutions to complex problems, managed by rationalistic philosophers in the light of universalistic theories, brings Montesquieu closer to Vico and Herder than to Voltaire and the *Encyclopédie*. And indeed, as Berlin brings out so clearly, there is a contradiction at the heart of his social and political thought: although he is a pluralist rather than a monist and is not obsessed by some single ruling principle, and although he is indeed unique in his time for his inexhaustible awareness of the varieties of forms of life and society, he nevertheless believes that, no matter how much the means and secondary ends of men may vary, their ultimate, fundamental ends are the same: satisfaction of basic material needs, security, justice, peace and so forth. Berlin thus puts his finger on an irreconcilable tension in Montesquieu's thought between the belief that to each society belong its own peculiar customs, moral outlooks, modes of life on the one hand, and the belief in justice as a universal, eternal standard and the passion for legality on the other. Berlin offers a convincing explanation by suggesting that both attitudes spring from an intense fear of despotism and arbitrariness. At all events, the contradiction remains unresolved, and Montesquieu's thought represents for Berlin a sharp divergence from the ideals at the core of the Enlightenment, though not a dramatic break with them.

The capacity of pluralist notions to upset is further explored in the learned and ingenious essay on Machiavelli. Here Berlin advances the thesis that for some four hundred years Machiavelli has caused sharp disagreement between scholars and civilised men, and deeply troubled Christian and liberal consciences, not because of his alleged immorality and Satanism, but because, by advancing an alternative system of morality to that prevalent in his own day and since, he was perhaps the very first thinker to cast doubts, at any rate by implication, upon the very validity of all monist constructions as such. In Berlin's interpretation of him, Machiavelli is not, as most commentators have asserted, a mere political technician, interested only in operational means and indifferent to ultimate ends; nor is he a detached, objective political scientist, simply observing and offering a neutral description of the ways of men. Far from divorcing ethics from politics, as Croce and others have maintained, Machiavelli looks beyond the officially Christian ethics of his time (and, by implication, beyond other related moral outlooks, Stoic or Kantian or even utilitarian), which are essentially concerned with the individual, to a more ancient tradition, that of the Greek *polis* or of republican Rome – an essentially collective or communal morality according to which to be a human being and to have values and purposes is identical with being a member of a community. On this view, the ultimate ends of life for the individual are inseparable from the collective life of the *polis*. Men can attain to moral health and lead full, productive, public lives only in the service of a strong, united, successful community. Machiavelli does not, therefore, reject Christian morality in favour of some amoral science of means, but in the name of a realm of ends which are essentially social and collective rather than individual and personal. What matters to him before all else is the welfare and glory of his *patria*. His position implies that there are two equally ultimate, mutually exclusive ethical codes between which men must make an absolute choice. This suggestion that there may be a collision between ultimate values with no means of rational arbitration between them, and the consequent conclusion that there is no one single path to human fulfilment, individual or collective, has proved deeply disturbing. It entails that the need for choice between ultimate, conflicting values, far from being a rare and anomalous experience in the lives of men, is in fact an intrinsic element in the human condition itself. To have made men aware of this, however vaguely, was one of Machiavelli's major achievements: he was, as Berlin remarks, 'in spite of himself, one of the makers of pluralism'.

VI

The earliest sustained attack on universal, rationalist schemas came from Vico, Hamann and Herder. In his book *Vico and Herder*, Berlin has examined the major original ideas of two of these thinkers. Many of the essays in the present volume are a commentary and enlargement upon them. Vico, a thinker of tortured genius born before his time, struggled all his life to express a handful of revolutionary ideas about man, history and society. The significance of his doctrines has become apparent only in the centuries since his death, and, as Berlin suggests, some of the most important among them are coming into their own for the first time in the present day. He was probably the first thinker ever to formulate explicitly the thesis that there is no universal, immutable human nature; he revived the ancient doctrine that men truly understand only what they themselves have made, and gave it a revolutionary twist by applying it to history: we understand historical processes, which everywhere bear the stamp of human will, ideals and purposes, as it were from 'inside', by a species of sympathetic insight, in a way in which we cannot understand the 'senseless' 'external' operations of nature, which we did not ourselves make; building, perhaps, on the dim insights of French jurists and universal historians, he virtually created the concept of a culture, all the activities of which bear a distinctive mark and evince a common pattern; he developed the closely connected notion that a culture progresses through an intelligible succession of phases of development which are not connected with each other by mechanical causality, but are interrelated as expressions of the continuously evolving purposive activities of men; he saw human activities as being in the first place forms of self-expression, conveying a total vision of the world; and, perhaps most exciting of all, he created the notion of a new type of knowledge, the reconstructive imagination, or *fantasia*, the knowledge we acquire of other men at other times and places through entering into their general outlooks, their ways of seeing themselves and their goals – a form of knowledge which is neither wholly contingent nor deducible *a priori*.

In 'Vico and the Ideal of the Enlightenment', Berlin draws out some of the implications of Vico's views for the Utopian notion, which in one guise or another has played a prominent role in western political thought, of an ideal, static, rational society in which all human values and all conceivable paths to human fulfilment will exist side by side, not merely without loss to one another, but in a state of mutual enhancement. For Vico, the outlooks, activities and goals of men are necessarily those of a particular stage of social and cultural development. Each stage in what he calls the *storia ideale eterna* is linked to those before and after in an unaltering cyclical pattern. Since the earlier stages of the creative historical process are an essential part of our own origins, we are able to recreate and understand the past by discovering its potentialities in our own minds. But unlike idealist metaphysicians such as Hegel, who believe that nothing of value gets lost in the transition from one cultural phase to another, and unlike rationalist thinkers who believe that all values must by definition fit neatly into the completed jig-saw of the final perfect solution to all human problems, Vico's doctrine entails a less sanguine vision. Social development and cultural change bring absolute losses as well as gains. Some forms of valuable experience may vanish for ever, a unique, integral part of the sunken world that gave them birth, not to be replaced by similar forms of equal value. Inspired singers, of whom Homer is for Vico the most memorable example, in all their primitive vigour and concrete imaginative force, cannot – conceptually cannot – spring from the same stage of culture as the critical philosophers, with their intellectual analysis and bloodless abstractions. Thus for Vico the idea of perfection, of an order in which all true values will be fully realised, is excluded not for purely empirical reasons – ignorance, human weakness, lack of technical means – but because it is conceptually incoherent *a priori*.

In the other two essays on Vico, Berlin's concern with pluralism in the sphere of knowledge emerges very clearly. They turn upon Vico's seminal distinction between two very different types of human knowledge, which start from radically different presuppositions, and lead to profoundly divergent results. In Vico's view, the entire realm of 'external', non-human, physical nature is not continuous with the 'internal' human world of morality, art, language, forms of expression, thought and feeling. Corresponding to these two distinct provinces, there are two independent methods of inquiry: there is what Vico terms *scienza* or knowledge *per caussas*, the only perfect knowledge of which we are capable, that, namely, of the products of human creation

– mathematics, music, poetry, law – which are intelligible through and through precisely because they are artefacts of the human mind; and there is *coscienza*, the knowledge of the external world acquired by the observer from 'outside', in terms of causal uniformities and compresences, which, because it can only tell us how things are or happen, but never why or for what intelligible reason or in pursuit of what purpose, must for ever contain an area of impenetrable opacity. Vico's great originality consisted in applying the category of *scienza* to human history which men themselves 'make', and in instituting an 'anthropological historicism' which required a systematic science of mind which would be identical with the history of its development and growth. This could be traced only through investigation of the changing symbols – words, monuments, works of art, laws and customs, and the like – in which mind expressed itself. Memory and imagination, and the potential dispositions (most of which lie unactivated) of one's own mind, provide the basic tools of this type of understanding, upon which all humane studies ultimately rest: we know at first hand what it is to feel fear, love, hate, to belong to a family or a nation, to understand a facial expression or a human situation or a joke, to appreciate a work of art, to form and live by ideals, and to have an inexhaustible (and developing) variety of other kinds of immediate 'inner' experience besides.

This type of 'direct' knowledge is neither inductive nor deductive nor hypothetico-deductive. It is *sui generis* and can be described and analysed only in terms of itself. It cannot be yielded by nor translated into a Cartesian or a Newtonian or any similar system which correlates things and events from 'outside' in terms of causal regularities. This we know from our own experience: a familiar activity or an intimate aspect of our lives, which we have hitherto seen from inside in terms of human goals and aspirations, can be alienated from us by being, as it were, 'objectified': it is suddenly seen as alien and external to ourselves, a causal product of forces beyond our control – sociological, biological, physical. And the converse of this: an activity or a work of art or a person, a code of rules or an institution, can become an intimate part of ourselves because, by a process of imaginative penetration, we see it from 'inside' in the light of human ends and values. This is the ill-defined and shifting boundary where rational explanation in terms of human ideals and intentions comes into contact (and conflict) with causal explanation in terms of the 'senseless' non-human regularities of physical nature. It has been the scene of battles in the past; it is likely to be the scene of even greater battles in the future; few modern writers have done more than Berlin to sharpen our awareness of its vital importance.

The species of knowing uncovered by Vico was the seed of the doctrines of *Einfühlung* and *Verstehen* later developed by Herder, and after him by the great German historicists, Troeltsch, Dilthey, Meinecke and Max Weber, and it had implications for epistemology and the philosophy of mind which were major preoccupations of a great deal of nineteenth-century thought. It is to a discussion of one of the most important of these that 'The Divorce between the Sciences and the Humanities' is devoted. An intrinsic part of the optimistic belief in steady general progress is the notion that all methods of investigation and research, all modes of knowing and understanding, are systematically interconnected; that the presuppositions and methods of all forms of intellectual discovery can be ultimately derived from a small handful of principles of the highest imaginable degree of abstraction; and that the entire sphere of human knowledge grows all of a piece, since each segment of it interlocks with and enlarges every other. Yet if Vico's distinction between 'inner' and 'outer' knowledge is valid, and if, as his cardinal doctrines imply, reality is not a unified, timeless, immutable structure of which a logically perfect language could give a direct transcription undistorted by the 'extraneous' influence of time and place – a model measured against which all natural languages could be shown to be more or less inadequate approximations; if, moreover, the forms of speech and the myths, poetry and religion of so-called primitive men are not, as Voltaire and the *Encyclopédistes* typically believed, the first childlike stammering of truths more clearly and more fully formulated by later rational thinkers, but rather the unique expression of their total vision of life, the embodiment of their response to the problems generated by their own peculiar world – a response which is just as authentic as and ultimately incommensurable with that of later more enlightened ages to their own problems; then it follows that all knowledge is not of one single unified kind, a great organic corpus which, despite periodical lapses into barbarism, grows steadily from age to age by irreversible increments, developing gradually towards an unchanging state of ultimate perfection. The unbridgeable gulf between the natural sciences and humane studies,[1] and the breach blown in the ideal of steady progress

[1] For so it seemed to Vico; but it may not be, for if Kuhn's account of scientific development is correct, that too is Vichian.

in all branches of human knowledge, have very far-reaching consequences indeed.

In the essay on the sources of German anti-rationalism, Berlin
examines the notions of perhaps the most radical antinomian thinker
in this volume, J. G. Hamann. As a young man Hamann, a protégé
of the leading figures of the Berlin *Aufklärung*, Mendelssohn and
Nicolai, had been a successful publicist and apostle of enlightenment.
But after undergoing a transforming inner experience, and returning
to the pietist faith of his earlier years, he set out to attack the ideals and
values at the core of the rationalist tradition, and transmuted them into
something like their opposites. He represents the most uncompromising backlash of human dignity and the ideals of warmth, love and
spontaneity against the spirit-crushing abstractions of the systematisers
and 'terribles simplificateurs' of eighteenth-century France. In waging
this terrible battle he and his comrade-in-arms, Jacobi, pressed into
service two of the central doctrines (one of them in a much modified
form) of the sober empiricist philosopher, David Hume. There can be few
more paradoxical chapters in the history of modern European thought.

The doctrine that the sole path to knowledge was afforded by the
natural, empirical sciences; that all statements with a claim to truth
must be in principle publicly testable by any rational being; that there
were and could be no other sources of genuine knowledge, transcendent or non-rational – these principal tenets of the French Enlightenment encountered increasing opposition from the mid-eighteenth
century onwards, even in France itself. The reaction against dry
rationalism, materialism and ethical naturalism expressed itself at first
in a wave of sentiment and feeling in both literature and manners:
Diderot accorded a large and important place to emotion in the life
of men, and Rousseau, above all, was a major liberator of feeling and
natural passion. Outside France, von Muralt, Bodmer and Breitinger
in Switzerland, and Lowth, Blackwell and the Wartons in England,
had all in their various ways rebelled against the desiccating spirit of
excessive rationalism. Yet this rebellion was largely confined to the
spheres of literature, manners and the arts: the foundations on which
the major dogmas of the Enlightenment rested remained untouched.
The really violent and devastating attack, which shook these major
assumptions once and for all, was launched by a band of dark, tortured
and deeply disturbing thinkers from the remoter corners of the German-speaking world: the story of the far-reaching consequences and
repercussions of what Berlin calls 'this German backlash against the

French cultural domination of the western world', both sinister and liberating, is very largely the history of modern thought.

Both by temperament and conviction Hamann was an enemy of tidy, all-embracing schemas: he believed that abstract networks of general laws, while they might help us (like tools or weapons) to dominate and exploit areas of reality, must blunt our sense of the vivid freshness of immediate experience, and blind us to the unique, bizarre, unpredictable and often wildly chaotic data of life as we live it. Scientific theories had at best an instrumental value: they could not yield unassailable knowledge of any kind. True knowledge is given to us immediately only by the senses, and by spontaneous imagination, instinct and insight. Direct perception, the immediate, incontrovertible sense of reality, Hamann calls *Glaube* or faith. He attributed this doctrine of faith or belief to Hume. For he rightly perceived that Hume's epistemology rests upon primitive belief in reality unsupported by *a priori* demonstration; but in a manner which would certainly have alarmed Hume, he modified the doctrine to apply to non-empirical spheres as well: without the fundamental human capacity for *Glaube* men cannot think or act, believe in an external world or history, or in the existence of other persons or of God. The faculty of faith is no more open to refutation by reason than is the evidence of the senses; though it may on occasion deceive, it is not shored up by an elaborate apparatus of proof. Above all, the artificial utilitarian contraptions of scientists, which do not express the inner nature of men or of God, have nothing to say to it. No man can love, or see his innermost nature expressed in, the web of lifeless categories spun by the rationalist Spinoza or the de-spiritualised play of cause and effect of the vast materialist machines constructed by Holbach or Helvétius. Poets, lovers and the devout alone are able to enter into and acquire full knowledge of the objects of their intense devotion. The data of immediate acquaintance are concrete and unique: any attempt to 'reorganise' them into artificial patterns distorts them, and transforms them into something other and poorer than themselves. Indeed, there is an almost uncannily modern ring about Hamann's views on the relationship between thought, experience and language. When he proclaims that he is less interested in the traditional philosophical question 'What is reason?' and more concerned with asking 'What is language?' because it is the latter which is the source 'of all the paralogisms and antinomies which are laid at the door of the former', and when he declares that 'by it [language] all things are made', he foreshadows the

INTRODUCTION

doctrines of Austin and the later Wittgenstein. And when, speaking of artificial conceptual systems, he asserts that 'our creatures are merciless mutilators of nature', and goes on to ask, more in irony than in earnest, whether there exist 'simple natural points to which everything can be reduced', or whether 'everything consists of mathematical lines', he is uttering criticisms remarkably similar to those made by ordinary language philosophers today against the neo-positivism of Russell and his followers. For Hamann, the words of common human speech are bearers of human meanings; as such, they do not distort direct perception to the same degree as abstract formulas, general propositions, rules and laws. They are either a form of expression, of communication between immortal souls, or else they are the artificial, oppressive instruments of the classifying sciences. Sooner or later, too great an enthusiasm for systems of idealised figments at the expense of direct vision mediated by ordinary language will lead to the construction of great bureaucratic machines. Men will come to be treated as mechanical objects of administration, emptied of inner life and meaning, mere external husks and shells. In this, Hamann is one of the earliest and most clairvoyant of those who darkly foresaw what Max Weber later called 'das Gehäuse der Hörigkeit', 'the House of Bondage', and what followers of the Frankfurt School today deplore as 'die verwaltete Welt' – the world, including men and nature, conceived of as a mechanical system to be manipulated for utilitarian ends by teams of rational experts.

In Herder, Berlin sees the originator of three major ideas which were not only highly novel in his own day, but which are still vitally alive in ours. All three break with the central western tradition which stretches back to antiquity and are wholly incompatible with the central values and cardinal doctrines, moral, historical and aesthetic, of the Enlightenment. They are populism, or the belief that men can realise themselves fully only when they belong to an identifiable group or culture with roots in tradition, language, custom, common historical memories; expressionism, or the notion that all men's works 'are above all voices speaking', forms of expression or communication which convey a total view or vision of life; and finally pluralism, the recognition of a potentially infinite variety of cultures and systems of values, all equally ultimate and incommensurable with one another, rendering logically incoherent the belief in a universally valid, ideal path to human fulfilment sought with varying degrees of success by all men at all places and times.

Looking about him in the modern world, Berlin perceives how vital these formative ideas are, and how their importance is likely to increase. They are all ideas which can engage the whole man, head and heart, and they are likely to have consequences commensurate with their appeal. The deep need for roots and self-expression felt by all men needs no stressing in an age of disruption and nationalism. The article on nationalism deals with some of these cardinal themes. Again, the sense of suffocation, of a desiccation of the spirit, felt by so many young people in the technological civilisations of the west, stems at least in part from the inability to fulfil that craving for self-expression, individual or collective, which Herder was the first to point to as one of the deepest and most enduring needs of men. From the hippies and the flower children to Heidegger, Habermas and the School of Frankfurt, the fundamental message has been the same; and all could claim Herder as their patron saint. The essay on Sorel, too, enlarges upon some of these burning issues. And again, in an age of narrow dogmatic ideologies which claim absolute allegiance, the notion that the ends of life are many, changing, equally ultimate and therefore liable to come into mortal conflict, is guaranteed a long life. Many later thinkers, and perhaps none more than Herzen, took up and developed this idea. Indeed, in a sense he built his life around them, suffered and lived through them. Nothing would have horrified these two thinkers more than to see a robust class of men (of whatever social formation) with terribly simple purposes and needs, and equally simple conceptions of the ends of life, large in numbers, highly organised and wielding great powers, impose their impoverished outlook on a much more variegated, rich, fragile and creative group of human beings.

VII

One of these three seminal ideas originated by Herder lies at the heart of Berlin's essays on Moses Hess and on Marx and Disraeli, and it illuminates the critical pages he has written on nationalism: the idea that one of the fundamental needs of men, as basic as those for food, shelter, procreation, security and communication, is to belong to identifiable communal groups, each possessing its own unique language, traditions, historical memories, style and outlook. Only if a man truly *belongs* to such a community, naturally and unselfconsciously, can he enter into the living stream and lead a full, creative, spontaneous life, at home in the world and at one with himself and his fellow men; enjoying a recognised status within such a natural unit or group, which itself must command full unqualified recognition in the world at large; and thereby acquiring a vision of life, an image of himself and his condition in a community where concrete, immediate, spontaneous human relations may flower undistorted by neurotic self-questioning about one's true identity, and free from the crippling wounds inflicted by the real or imaginary superiority of others.

Frustration of the need to belong to such a community entails consequences of various disturbing kinds, and it is to a sensitive exploration of the main among them that Berlin turns in these two essays. For him the newly liberated Jews of the late eighteenth and the nineteenth centuries offer a kind of paradigm case. Escaping as many of them did from the narrow, familiar, self-enclosed world of the ghetto into the wider, freer, more exciting but stranger and more dangerous gentile world, their identity was suddenly called in question. Who were they? Some among them – the more pliable and easy-going – shed their past with no apparent trouble and merged unobtrusively into their new environment; others – those whose very sense of self, intimately bound up with their passionate desire to do and be something in the world, would not allow them to forget their origins – could not perform this act of facile self-transformation. Troubled, and more often agonised and wounded, by not being automatically accepted as members of the worlds they sought to enter, they hit upon various more or less conscious solutions to their problems of self-identity.

These solutions to the search for status, recognition, 'belonging', tended to take one of two main forms: conscious demands for equality of status (or at times superiority) on the part of members of a hitherto submerged or oppressed group, nationality, community; or their self-identification with some other group or movement untainted by the defects and weaknesses of their own original condition. The first of these stratagems entailed full, self-assertive and often aggressive acceptance of their own original identity; the second, the acquisition of a new personality, new values and habits, remote from the inferior status which had inflicted wounds upon their *amour propre*. And those who adopt the latter course, Berlin tells us, 'are liable to develop either exaggerated resentment of, or contempt for, the dominant majority, or else over-intense admiration or indeed worship for it, or, at times, a combination of the two, which leads both to original insights and – born of overwrought sensibilities – a neurotic distortion of the facts'.

Berlin's thesis is that the two masterful, creative personalities, Marx and Disraeli, with their passionate desire to dominate, lead or change the society of their day, fall into the latter class, while the mild and honest Hess, less capable of either self-deception or imaginative construction, but with his gift of simple direct perception, took the former course.

Disraeli, an outsider in British society, sought above all else power and recognition: in his perfervid imagination the British aristocracy was translated into the realms of mythology; he made himself its leader, basing his own claims to aristocracy upon the antiquity of his race, which he stressed again and again in his writings; he saw himself as leading it into a coalition with the exploited masses against the sworn enemies of all true distinction, the crude, utilitarian, materialistic middle classes; he detested equality and mediocrity, and believed that imagination, intuition and traditional values were superior to all forms of scientific calculation, reason and analysis. So powerful was the myth he thus created that by its spell he was able to bind together his heterogeneous followers, affecting British political thought and practice 'for many fateful decades'. Yet this act of comprehensive psychological self-transformation, which so many of Disraeli's biographers have seen as a piece of cynically skilful sleight-of-hand, could triumph against the odds and carry conviction only if it were wholly genuine. Berlin maintains that Disraeli really did see himself as a peer of the dukes and baronets whom he led against the Manchester manufacturers and Benthamites; he was himself largely taken in by his own fictions. By grasping the innermost impulse at the heart of Disraeli's vision, the search for a persona, for an identity which would enable him to stand somewhere and be someone in the world, Berlin has offered a deeper, more coherent, and much more sympathetically convincing understanding of Disraeli than most of his biographers. By penetrating to the deepest root of a man's being, to his sense of self – of who he is, where he comes from, and where he belongs – Berlin has helped render intelligible a specific, particularly bizarre and puzzling case. Still more, he has generalised it to yield fruitful insight into some of those very urgent problems which preoccupy social psychologists, theorists of education, sociologists and politicians today. For in Disraeli Berlin sees an early, highly gifted and articulate, and therefore paradigmatic, example of what was later to become increasingly common: the 'alienated' man wholly out of his element — a victim of social dis-integration and the dissolutions of traditional ties and bonds brought about by the scientific revolution and centralising industrialism — whose life is a long, and often bitter and unsuccessful, search for identity.

Unlike Disraeli, Marx makes scant reference to his Jewish origins, and is open to the suspicion of having to a large degree suppressed them. Indeed, there is evidence in his writings of a strong strain of anti-Semitism. Berlin's thesis is that Marx, despite the depth and originality of his central ideas, failed to give a satisfactory account of nationalism, and systematically underestimated its importance as an independent force, not least because of his own not openly avowed, and probably not even wholly conscious, embarrassment at his own origins. He too, on this view, like Disraeli, sought to identify himself with a social group of which he was not by origin a member. He chose the universal class of exploited proletarians, who were wholly free of the stigma with which he was himself marked. The proletariat of whom he speaks, and with whom he had so little direct contact, is as much a figment, an abstract category or an imaginary ideal, as Dis-raeli's aristocracy. They are not, as Berlin says, real workers, miners and factory operatives, men of flesh and blood, owing allegiance to their nation and bound by a thousand ties of tradition and local loyalty; rather they are made the vehicle for the wounded feelings of humanity in general, and at times of Marx himself. Hence the appeal so often made by Marx's words to others like himself, the rootless, alienated, cosmopolitan intellectuals, whose revulsion at the cruelty and injustice of their world goes hand in hand with a sense of wounded dignity and a desperate search for identity. As Berlin is careful to point out, the fact that some at least of Marx's doctrines may have sprung in part from a response to a deep psychological need does not itself invalidate them in any way. But it may help to explain why theories, which on other grounds may have been shown to be inadequate, fail to live up to the claims originally made for them. The doctrines and lives of both Marx and Disraeli were those of men who could not accept their origins, and hence themselves, for what they were. Many of their ideas evolved not in the first place as tools of objective analysis and descrip-tion, but as comforting myths to rally oppressed and insulted spirits, not least those of the authors of the doctrines themselves.

When Berlin turns from these two masterful, myth-making figures, with their gift of piercing original insight coupled with self-inflicted blindness, to Moses Hess, he leaves the intense, dramatic, highly-coloured world of neurotic distortion for an altogether calmer and more relaxed element where things are seen with perhaps less depth and intensity, but with more sense of balance and proportion.

Marxist critics have portrayed Hess as a minor precursor of Marx whose importance was wholly eclipsed by the great master. In this essay Berlin establishes the claims of Hess to be taken seriously as a social thinker in his own right who possesses a gift of prophetic insight superior to that of his revolutionary contemporaries, Marx and Engels. Moses Hess, 'the father of German communism', as Berlin calls him, represents one of the most memorable examples of the triumph of direct moral insight and immediate, lived experience over doctrine and dogma. A morally sensitive and honest man, revolted by the spectacle of exploitation and injustice and attracted by abstract schemes for universal human improvement, Hess came to see that it is not only impossible, but highly undesirable, for a man to seek to root out and deny his true identity, bound up as it is with the historical memories, customs, language and traditions of his people, in the name of rationalistic universal principles which take no account of what is concrete and unique. There is a simple directness and humanity about Hess, an almost childlike freshness of perception and freedom from conceptual chains, which contrasts so strongly with the at times almost neurotic obsession with dogmatic abstractions, so remote from lived experience, that characterises the more depressing facets of Marx's intellectual make-up. It is as though both Marx and Disraeli feel compelled to bend and distort reality into conformity with their own creative wills, while Hess is pleased to see things simply, as they are. In an illuminating aside, Berlin wonders how deeply Marx's life and outlook might have been altered, had he received as a child a religious education similar to that accorded to Moses Hess by his grandfather, a pious Jew, rather than assimilating the rationalistic dogmas of Voltaire and the French Enlightenment. Unlike Marx, the later Hess did not underestimate the importance of nationalism as a basic, independent historical force. He came to reject cosmopolitanism as suppressing natural differences between groups of men, and, like Herder, believed that such natural differentiation of mankind into separate races and nations, far from being a lamentable error which must at all costs be eliminated, was an inexhaustible source of creative variety. With equal firmness, he condemned the Hegelian distinction between dominant 'historic' nations on the one hand, and submerged inactive peoples on the other, whom the former, by dint of their 'superiority', had a right to conquer and absorb. From a highly abstract, schematised view of history as a process leading necessarily to a new, rational, harmonious world order, where humane communist principles would drive out greed and private property – a process in which the Jews, after fulfilling their appointed historic mission as the ethical people, would disappear as an identifiable group – Hess, impelled by an incorruptible sense of reality, by an immediate, 'unfiltered' perception of the facts, was driven to the essentially Herderian view that the Jews were not merely held together by religious bonds but constituted a nation like any other and that, in order to attain to a full sense of settled identity, they needed a state of their own. He is thus one of the founding fathers of Zionism.

He was convinced all his life that equality and justice were desirable for their own sake, and his socialism rested upon essentially moral premises : these goods could be secured only by the conscious purposive action of men convinced of their intrinsic moral value. In his view, certain very general human values were permanently and universally valid : the free expression of natural human feeling and affection, social justice, individual liberty, membership of and identification with a historically continuous community. If men could be persuaded by rational argument that this was so, they would change their practice accordingly. It was this 'Utopian socialism' which Marx and Engels mocked. For them, and others under the spell of Hegelian historicism, the processes of history followed unchanging and objectively discoverable patterns : a man whose eyes had been opened to these would identify himself with, and support, that 'historical' value or group which was destined to triumph at that particular stage ; to act otherwise, to fight against the innermost immutable nature of things, was to be irrational and court inevitable destruction. Hess refused to believe in the comforting doctrine that the universe itself was fighting on the side of his cherished values. He did not believe in the inevitability of class conflict, and transforming revolution, or in the dictatorship of the proletariat or the violent expropriation of property. And, as Berlin points out, though the lives of entire nations have been transformed by the revolution to which Marx and Engels dedicated their lives, violent expropriation of the property-owning classes and institution of the dictatorship of the proletariat, or of its representative, the Communist Party, have not of themselves automatically secured social justice, individual liberty, economic equality, and social harmony.

Wherever the achievement of these goods has been most closely approached, it has been, more often than not, the work of men consciously pursuing goals which seemed to them intrinsically valuable, the realisation of which depended solely upon their own dedicated individual effort and not upon the inexorable impersonal forces of history. Nor could Hess bring himself to believe that the central values of socialism must necessarily conflict with some of the most sacred values of tradition: love of place, a deep sense of one's individual and collective past, national memories and symbols, and so on. As Berlin says, Hess retained a freshness of vision and an incapacity 'to commit acts of violence against his own nature'. 'He was saved by his moral insight which remained uncontaminated by personal vanity or dogma.' In this essay Berlin offers an exceptionally sensitive account of a man who, in the name of abstract theory and rationalistic schemes of amelioration, represses and denies his deepest feelings about himself and his identity – until, little by little, the truth becomes too strong for the artificial bonds restraining it, and bursts forth in all its vigour, with a powerful attendant sense of liberation.

VIII

The central themes of human dignity and identity, and of the search for a sense of being at home in a familiar world, recur in the highly suggestive essay on nationalism. Here Berlin discusses the typical forms it takes and some of its major sources, and touches upon one of the most puzzling features of nineteenth-century political thought and prophecy, namely its failure to give a true estimate of the decisive role nationalism was to play in shaping the modern world.

As a coherent doctrine nationalism seems to emerge for the first time in the last third of the eighteenth century in the writings of Herder. For Herder and those German thinkers influenced by him, the arch-enemy was French universalism and materialism. Berlin sees Herder's thought as representing on the one hand a comprehensive rejection of the doctrine that universal rational rules governing theory and practice could be discovered, and, on the other, a German reaction to the condescending, patronising attitude of the politically and culturally dominant French. This natural response of wounded pride is an early and typical case of a phenomenon which was to become increasingly common in the nineteenth century, growing into a world-wide movement in our own day, with consequences the full scope and nature of which are still being painfully revealed. To be made an object of contempt, amused condescension, or patronising tolerance by proud, successful and powerful neighbours, Berlin tells us, 'is one of the most traumatic experiences that individuals or societies can suffer'. The exaggerated and at times pathological response on the part of those whose dignity is insulted is to raise up their own real or imaginary virtues against those of their tormentors. The Germans, unable to look back on a long tradition of military, economic and political dominance, or to point to a succession of high achievements in art, literature and science, discovered in themselves superior moral and spiritual depth, a noble and selfless love of truth and the inner life of the spirit, which they contrasted with the hedonistic, worldly, superficial and morally empty French. In comparison with the polished and decadent French they felt themselves to be young, vigorous and untried, the true bearers of the future. This strong Messianic note was first sounded by the Germans, then by the Slavs, and today has become a common element in the rhetoric of the decolonialised and emergent nations. Yet the great social and political thinkers of the nineteenth century did not foresee this development. This is particularly true of Marx and Engels, for whom nationalism, like religion, was one of the weapons wielded by the reactionary bourgeoisie against the exploited masses. It could not survive the demise of capitalism, and would disappear for ever once the revolution had established the dictatorship of the proletariat. As Berlin points out, the systematic failure on the part of Marxist theorists, particularly in Germany, to understand the true nature of Fascism and National Socialism, interpreting it as the last throes of capitalism, was due to an ideologically distorted view of the facts, and led in many cases to the loss of their own lives. Why a thinker of such originality, depth and power as Marx should have failed to pay due attention to a factor which subsequently transformed the world, Berlin does not here attempt to explain. But the answer to this question is implicit in the essay on Marx and Disraeli.

The fundamental issue of human dignity is further illuminated by the essay on Sorel. Despite the outwardly erratic course taken by his political allegiances, Sorel's principal ideas and his central vision of human nature are vitally relevant today. Indeed, as Berlin presents him, he seems more modern and to speak to us more directly than a good many of his more celebrated, solid and sober contemporaries. He was not a systematic thinker, purveying a political doctrine whose outlines were fixed and final. He loathed system and condemned it in others. Yet his ideas are of value not only for their intrinsic power but because what was once confined to small groups of intellectuals has become a world-wide set of attitudes today.

Sorel firmly rejected two of the central tenets of western social and political theory, namely the Greek doctrine of salvation by knowledge and the Judaeo-Christian doctrine of historical theodicy. In his view natural science is not an ontology, it cannot give us an account of the ultimate nature and structure of the world; rather it is an instrument or a weapon developed by man in his constant struggle against hostile natural forces. It cannot therefore solve the great questions of human life, whether metaphysical, moral or political. These fall outside its scope. Indeed, one of the greatest of modern evils arises when men and their spiritual and material needs are treated as objects exhaustively analysable by science. Then men are reduced by scientific experts and rational bureaucrats to functioning parts in a machine, robbed of their true human essence as free creative agents. Sorel's view of the nature of science, and of its misapplication to the lives of human beings, is strongly reminiscent of the darker apprehensions of Hamann, though unlike the German antinomian he regards science as a triumph of human intellect and effort and as an indispensable machine in the battle to resist blind nature. But it must be seen for what it is, and not overstep its proper boundaries. It does not itself contain the key to human perfection and fulfilment. To identify scientific and technical progress with spiritual and moral progress only betrays a hopeless blindness of the spirit.

Sorel was equally sceptical of the belief that history, despite all its apparent chaos and abrupt reversals, was moving by inevitable steps towards some universally desirable consummation. Like Hess, he believed in absolute and freely chosen moral values, ends pursued for their own intrinsic worth; and like Hess, he rejected the belief that history prescribed the goals to be pursued by rational men at any given stage, and guaranteed their ultimate achievement. Nothing could secure the values sacred to men save their own unremitting effort. The two absolutes Sorel most consistently believed in were morality and science in the sense discussed.

It is by going to the heart of Sorel's writings, and seizing their *idée maîtresse*, that Berlin is able to show how this enigmatic and confusing writer is not merely intelligible, but deeply original and important.

For at the centre of Sorel's vision is the belief that man is first and foremost an active, creative being. Diverging from the classical tradition, Sorel sees men as seekers not in the first place of happiness, peace, salvation, security or knowledge, but of creative work. The free exercise of the will, the imposition of an inwardly conceived pattern upon the external recalcitrant material of nature, self-realisation and self-expression, both individual and collective, through free, spontaneous, creative work – these are the ends of life which correspond most closely to man's innermost essence. This view goes naturally with a hatred of hedonism and of materialist values generally. With great subtlety and penetration, Berlin uses this insight both to make sense of Sorel and his bewildering political *voltes-face*, and to point to a truth about human nature largely neglected by famous and influential moral and political thinkers in the mainstream of western thought, a truth which goes a very long way to explaining, and rendering intelligible, the wave of radical unrest experienced the world over during the past decade.

Indeed, surveying the modern world, Berlin detects at the heart of the most disparate movements, from the nationalist tide in the Third World to the radical unrest among the disaffected young in the industrial technocracies, what may be the early stirrings of a reaction destined to grow into a world-transforming movement. It is the reaction of some irreducible core of free, creative, spontaneous human nature, of some elementary sense of identity, dignity and worth, against all that patronises and diminishes men, and threatens to rob them of themselves. This is but a modern expression, taking novel but recognisable forms, of the great battle begun by Hamann and Herder against the central values of the eighteenth- and nineteenth-century faith in liberal rationalism, cosmopolitanism, science, progress and rational organisation: a battle waged throughout the nineteenth century by the great unsettling rebels, Fourier, Proudhon, Stirner, Kierkegaard, Carlyle, Nietzsche, Tolstoy, Sorel; and continued in the twentieth by existentialists, anarchists and irrationalists, and all the varying strains of contemporary rebellion and revolt. For all their deep differences, these thinkers, groups and movements are brothers beneath the skin: they fight in the name of some direct inward knowledge of self and free causal agency, and an irreducible sense of specific concrete identity. Rational and benevolent colonial masters and technocratic specialists and experts, no matter how altruistic and honourable their intentions, precisely because they view men as in the first place heteronomous objects to be administered, regimented and controlled, not free and unpredictably self-transforming causal agents, must necessarily fail to respect and understand this fundamental human craving, and often enough ignore, crush or eradicate it. Rebellion against regimentation takes the form of a demand to do and be something in the world, to be one's own master, free of external interference – an independent self, whether individual or collective, not dictated to or organised by others. The long and heated contest, which stretches back at least to the middle of the eighteenth century, has never been more alive than it is today.

Unexpected light is thrown on some of these themes by the essay on Verdi. By applying to him the distinction first drawn by Schiller between naïve and sentimental artists, Berlin brings out something essential in Verdi which is easily overlooked. The 'naïve' artist is whole and undivided, at one with himself and his world; he is not self-conscious, and his art is a natural and undistorted expression of what he directly sees and feels, for its own sake and not in pursuit of any ulterior purpose. The 'sentimental' artist, on the other hand, has fallen from the primordial state of unity and harmony, which he seeks, often with a desperate sense of urgency, to restore through his works; but he pursues an ideal which is ultimately unattainable in any finite medium. In Verdi Berlin sees the last great 'naïve' artist of genius, at least in the world of music. He is a most memorable and vivid example of the Herderian ideal of 'belonging' which haunts Berlin's pages. Verdi speaks directly and unselfconsciously in his works to all men as men, in terms of primal human passions and emotions. He is as an artist wholly free of neurosis, self-questioning and decadence. His works are not a symptom of reaction or rebellion, nor does he come armed with a manifesto or a programme or an ideology. Or rather, if he does have an ideology, Berlin tells us, 'it is that of vast numbers of mankind across large stretches of history: this is, indeed, one of the central meanings of the term "humanism"'. These are very revealing words. They remind us that Berlin has shown little interest in decadent writers, that he is not naturally drawn to figures like Dostoevsky, Kafka or Beckett. Those who depict marginal states of mind, rarefied, exotic or 'abnormal' types of experience, moods too far removed from the hard and timeless core of basic human passions and emotions, relationships and needs, are not of the first interest to him. A thinker like Hamann, for example, may seem to most a queer eccentric visionary; Sorel, erratic, unsteady, unhinged; yet there is nothing sick

or decadent about them. On the contrary, they are in pursuit of an
ideal of wholeness, creative vigour and rounded humanity. Berlin is
preoccupied above all with writers and thinkers who express, or are
in search of, some human centre of gravity, some ideal of the rounded
fullness of life in all its variety. Indeed, there are moments when one
feels that one can hear at the back of many of these essays a disconsolate
voice lamenting the irreparable loss of 'normality', of some 'natural'
condition in which men feel easy and at home, surrounded by trusted
and familiar things, divided neither within their own breasts, nor
against one another, nor from nature.

IX

With Herzen, we come to a thinker who most nearly anticipated the
kind of radical pluralism which Berlin has himself expounded with
such eloquence and persuasiveness in a steady stream of articles, essays
and books. One of the chief influences on Herzen as a young man at
the University of Moscow was that of Hegel. He did not, however,
remain an orthodox Hegelian for long, but transformed Hegel's doctrines into something peculiarly his own. The chief result was scepticism of the capacity of any single doctrine or coherent conceptual
schema to explain life and offer solutions to general human problems.
Like Sorel, he seems to speak directly to us about our own predicament; and his complex sense of reality and of the critical moral and
political issues of his time gives his utterances a concrete sharpness,
freshness and durability which marks them off from those of the
majority of professional social thinkers in the nineteenth century, who
tended to offer general solutions derived by rational methods from
highly abstract principles.

Herzen's powers of observation, analysis and exposition remained
unblunted by the yearning for cut and dried systems of exact classification. Berlin points to a 'curious combination of idealism and scepticism' in Herzen. On the one hand, he was able to understand only too
well what could turn men into fanatic revolutionaries; on the other,
he displayed an almost clairvoyant awareness of the terrifying consequences of their doctrines. While he was filled with revulsion at the
arbitrariness, cruelty and injustice of the systems they sought to overthrow, he saw that the worlds called into being in their place by a
bitter desire for revenge and retribution would breed their own terrible

excesses. Above all, he feared for the fate of individual liberty, and upheld the claims of private life and art, human decency and dignity, against the fanatically egalitarian doctrines of the new liberators. He was terrified that individuals would be tamed, subdued and oppressed both by majorities and in the name of empty abstractions. He was deeply sceptical of all-embracing historical schemas which claimed to be able to guarantee an ideal order laid up for humanity in the future, the realisation of which justified the suffering and sacrifice of present generations. He believed, like Stirner, that individual human beings should not be sacrificed on the altar of abstractions whether in the name of progress, justice, humanity, the state, the nation, history itself, or any other fictitious metaphysical entity. He was above all a troubled rationalist who could not bring himself to believe in the existence of a fixed human nature obedient to invariant laws. The core of his outlook is the belief that the perennial, basic human problems are not soluble at all; that men can only do their best in the situation in which they find themselves, with no *a priori* guarantee of ultimate success; that men are themselves changed by the efforts they make to solve the problems of their age or culture, thereby creating new men and new problems; and that therefore the future problems and needs of men, and their solution and satisfaction, cannot in principle be anticipated, still less provided for in advance; finally, that an indissoluble part of the definition of human nature consists in a cluster of concepts like free-will, choice, purpose, effort, struggle, entailing as they do the opening up of new and unpredictable paths to human fulfilment.

For Herzen the agony of choice could not be avoided. In a universe which is not a rational cosmos but chaotic and open to unforeseeable change there could be no absolute values or universal ideals. The choice between values is an absolute choice. That is to say, there can be no empirical explanation of it of the kind offered by the generalising natural sciences in terms of inductive knowledge of the objective pattern of human needs and values; nor is it susceptible of deductive justification in the light of some *a priori*, intuitive or theological knowledge of the true nature of man and the ends of life; for either of these would empty it of its inherent significance: it is simply a choice. A man chooses as he does for his own reasons, which are his own property and for which in the end he alone is responsible. Herzen's position has become increasingly attractive with time, particularly to a generation of men who have grown sceptical of all attempts to find final solutions to human problems; and it has been defended and developed with great ingenuity and conviction by Berlin, and presented as one of the most sane, adult and mature philosophies of our times.

But does it lead to ethical relativism and subjectivism? Does the kind of radical pluralism preached by Herzen and advocated by Berlin dissolve the ancient notion of the moral unity of the human race? In the absence of a set of overarching, universal, objective standards, is mere anarchy of values the result? Is the door opened to the raising up of any and every conceivable form of human action or behaviour to the status of a moral end? What safeguards, if any, can this general attitude offer against the kind of systematic bestiality and madness of, for example, the Third Reich? To answer this question one must look more closely at Berlin's concept of human nature.

X

What is the basic idea of human nature which, according to Berlin, always underlies and determines moral, political and social, and perhaps epistemological theories as well? Pervading all the statements Berlin has made on this major topic there are a number of assumptions. The first is that, in the absence of any fixed, final, divinely revealed or deductively or empirically guaranteed knowledge of man's true nature, of its manifest and latent needs and capacities, its elasticity and scope for self-development, we do well to accept a minimal account of what man is in order not to foreclose the possible (and even likely) emergence of entirely novel and unforeseeable forms of life and self-fulfilment, in individuals and groups, whereby our conception of human nature will be enlarged. For if his essays in the history of ideas reveal anything, it is precisely that new, richer and deeper forms of collective self-knowledge, of what men are and can be, do in fact emerge from the historical interaction of men with men – collectively and individually, with their own past, with other nations and cultures, and with their physical environment. And as these essays show, this process does not occur according to some set of *a priori* principles or following discoverable empirical laws: it is a branching out in new directions, essentially untidy, hesitant, sometimes violent, unpredictable in advance, and guaranteed neither to stand still nor to proceed in any assignable direction.

Yet this process is not random, or haphazard, or chaotic, nor is it devoid of rational significance. For in so far as it expresses the intelligible purposive response of sentient rational creatures in certain vital respects identical with ourselves, confronted by and devising solutions to the problems of their total environment, we can enter into and understand the process in that special sense which Vico was the first to grasp and articulate. Moreover, since our own image or conception of man and his nature is in large measure a historical product of this ceaseless exploration or search, of the slow and unpredictable growth of new, more adequate, more sophisticated models of human nature, these essays, which excavate and examine some of the major epoch-making additions to our central concept of man, may be seen as significant and remarkably sensitive contributions to an experimental, open-ended, undogmatic phenomenology of modern western man. Berlin will almost certainly dislike this term, with its strong Hegelian overtones, but it does capture something of the peculiar nature of his contribution to the search for self-understanding, and it establishes a link with a thinker from whom he is nothing like as remote as many suppose. He does indeed reject with both hands the Hegelian vision of human history as a logically necessary process of development passing through preordained stages to an ultimate rational goal where all human interests, capacities and values will coexist in frictionless harmony; nor is he any less hostile to Hegel's conception of moral ends as that system of deductively discoverable principles and rules of action prescribed by Reason to men at a specific stage of historical development, to disregard which is a mark of irrationality or blindness or immaturity on the part of the agent. Yet at the same time he makes much of three essentially Hegelian views. He has often repeated in his writings that Hegel showed with considerable imaginative genius that the history of thought and culture is a changing pattern of liberating ideas which form general attitudes and outlooks, which then eventually grow old and antiquated; their inadequacy to the texture of the lived experience of self-conscious men becomes increasingly apparent until finally they come to be felt as a constricting straitjacket which must be broken at all costs; new, emancipating conceptions emerge, which form new, more satisfying general outlooks, and these, in their turn, gradually grow into prison-houses of the spirit. Again, Berlin's work in the history of ideas derives much of its value from the fact that he seems to hold a quasi-Hegelian view of history as an intelligible process of intellectual growth and self-correction – a collective learning-process – in which the concepts of civilisation, society, develop-

1

ment, growth, barbarism, maturity and so forth are central to an understanding of human nature as it is revealed, not timelessly once and for all as some unchanging universal essence, but as it changes and grows through time. And finally, closely connected with this, and with much of what Vico wrote, Berlin makes much of the view that there is a specific faculty of imaginative historical judgement, different from the skills required by the methods of deduction and induction, whereby the gifted historian knows what does not go with what, what can and what cannot – conceptually cannot – belong to a specific epoch or stage of development of a culture or a civilisation; it is this which gives its meaning to such typically social-historical notions as the anachronistic, the normal, the typical and so forth.

Berlin is, therefore, not a cultural relativist in the manner of, for example, Spengler or Westermarck. Unlike such relativists, who maintained that one age or civilisation must be wholly opaque to another, Berlin believes that it is possible for men of learning and imagination to enter into and understand cultures and ages remote from their own. Nor is Berlin a subjectivist – he believes in the objective standards of judgement derived from understanding the life and activities of individual societies; these values form part of objective historical structures, and their discovery and understanding require imagination controlled by exact scholarship; provided they fit the circumstances and suit the instincts of a given society, and are not self-destructive or in conflict with some very small handful of fundamental values, failure to recognise which would entail denial that the relevant agents are human beings, then there is nothing to be said against them; above all, they cannot be appealed against from some single over-arching standard of values. Nor, therefore, is Berlin a moral relativist. He has often asserted that too great a divergence in behaviour from at least a small handful of moral norms results in denial of humanity to the agent: it is, he says, 'clear that ability to recognise universal – or almost universal – values enters into our analysis of such fundamental concepts as "man", "rational", "sane", "natural"'.

If Berlin has an ontology, it is the doctrine that that which most undeniably exists, and of which we have the most direct incorrigible knowledge, are human beings in specific historical circumstances – ourselves and others, concrete, individual, unique, self-directing, and in varying degrees responsible and free, possessed of inner lives made up of thoughts, feelings and emotions, consciously forming purposes and principles, and pursuing these in our outward lives; and that to attempt to reduce these to the less intelligible, because merely causal or statistical, terms and laws of the natural sciences – or, for that matter, to transform them into functional components of any abstract system, metaphysical, teleological or mechanistic – however convenient this may be for practical purposes, diabolic, human or divine, is ultimately to deny too much of what all men know immediately and most vividly to be the truth about themselves, and often enough to confine, stunt and mutilate them, with consequences some of which these essays make all too plain.

Nowhere in his writings has Berlin claimed that the thesis of determinism is demonstrably false; only that if it is true, and if its validity becomes widely accepted by men, reflecting itself not only in their theoretical professions but in their daily thought and practice, then this would entail a radical revision, or even the final demise, of some of the most basic categories in terms of which men have conceived of themselves as human; that words like freedom, choice, responsibility, moral deserts, praise, blame, remorse, regret, and many more besides, would either take on a wholly novel meaning, or else be emptied of significance altogether. And Berlin's assertion that this is so, and his evident belief that in certain vital respects – those, namely, in virtue of which we identify a creature as human – men should not be treated by science as purely natural objects, does not spring from the dogmatic conviction that they cannot as a matter of fact be so treated. Rather the reverse, for it is the very fear that the categories and methods of the empirical, quantitative sciences can be, and have in fact been, extended into the sphere of what had hitherto been supposed to be properly and uniquely human forms of experience, often with a disquieting degree of success and with results that are difficult to describe and evaluate, that gives Berlin's monitory strictures their point. It may well be, he seems to be saying, that we can go on applying quantitative causal methods in realm after realm of experience; but if we find the quality and contents of much (or all) of human activity radically altered by such extension, and if in the process much (or all) of what is human – what we understand most fully from within in the Vichian sense – is either destroyed or transformed into something less intelligible because purely causal, statistical, external, then in the name of what, to what end, in pursuit of what value or ideal above and beyond the kingdom of human concerns themselves, as we are directly acquainted with these from personal experience and from knowledge of others and of history, do we proceed to do this? In the name of truth? But no full account of the truth can exclude the data of direct experience, of our immediate knowledge of what it is to be a human being. In the name of efficiency or organisation? But these, too, are not autonomous ends; they stand and fall with the existence of identifiable human beings. This burning central issue, raised implicitly or explicitly by so much of what Berlin has said and written, clearly troubles him very deeply. It is an issue which lies at the heart of much contemporary disquiet.

Berlin's works may seem to many to offer a vision of life shot through with pessimism; and indeed, it cannot be denied that in his conception of man and the ends of life there is a powerful element of tragedy: avenues to human realisation may intersect and block one another; things of inestimable intrinsic value and beauty around which an individual or a civilisation may seek to build an entire way of life can come into mortal conflict; and the outcome is eradication of one of the protagonists and an absolute unredeemable loss. The overall tendency of Berlin's writings has been to enlarge and deepen our sense of such inevitable conflict and loss, and of the consequent necessity for absolute choices. He has blown breaches in all the harmonising, tranquillising visions which, while they diminish tension and agony, at the same time lower vitality and vigour and cause men to forget their essential humanity. He is constantly calling us back to our essential freedom and responsibility. His writings, scattered as so many of them have been through a variety of inaccessible journals and periodicals, when taken together, offer one of the most complete, cogent, formidable and satisfying accounts of the radical liberal humanist conception of man and his predicament that has ever been formulated, and as such should be made widely available to the age. Growing interest in them is, to use his own memorable words on the works of Verdi, 'a symptom of sanity in our time'.

ROGER HAUSHEER

The Counter-Enlightenment

OPPOSITION to the central ideas of the French Enlightenment, and of its allies and disciples in other European countries, is as old as the movement itself. The proclamation of the autonomy of reason and the methods of the natural sciences, based on observation as the sole reliable method of knowledge, and the consequent rejection of the authority of revelation, sacred writings and their accepted interpreters, tradition, prescription, and every form of non-rational and transcendent source of knowledge, was naturally opposed by the churches and religious thinkers of many persuasions. But such opposition, largely because of the absence of common ground between them and the philosophers of the Enlightenment, made relatively little headway, save by stimulating repressive steps against the spreading of ideas regarded as dangerous to the authority of church or state. More formidable was the relativist and sceptical tradition that went back to the ancient world. The central doctrines of the progressive French thinkers, whatever their disagreements among themselves, rested on the belief, rooted in the ancient doctrine of natural law, that human nature was fundamentally the same in all times and places; that local and historical variations were unimportant compared with the constant central core in terms of which human beings could be defined as a species, like animals, or plants, or minerals; that there were universal human goals; that a logically connected structure of laws and generalisations susceptible of demonstration and verification could be constructed and replace the chaotic amalgam of ignorance, mental laziness, guesswork, superstition, prejudice, dogma, fantasy, and, above all, the 'interested error' maintained by the rulers of mankind and largely responsible for the blunders, vices and misfortunes of humanity.

It was further believed that methods similar to those of Newtonian physics, which had achieved such triumphs in the realm of inanimate nature, could be applied with equal success to the fields of ethics, politics and human relationships in general, in which little progress had been made; with the corollary that once this had been effected, it would sweep away irrational and oppressive legal systems and economic policies the replacement of which by the rule of reason would rescue men from political and moral injustice and misery and set them on the path of wisdom, happiness and virtue. Against this, there persisted the doctrine that went back to the Greek sophists, Protagoras, Antiphon and Critias, that beliefs involving value-judgements, and the institutions founded upon them, rested not on discoveries of objective and unalterable natural facts, but on human opinion, which was variable and differed between different societies and at different times; that moral and political values, and in particular justice and social arrangements in general, rested on fluctuating human convention. This was summed up by the sophist quoted by Aristotle who declared that whereas fire burned both here and in Persia, human institutions change under our very eyes. It seemed to follow that no universal truths, established by scientific methods, that is, truths that anyone could verify by the use of proper methods, anywhere, at any time, could in principle be established in human affairs.

This tradition reasserted itself strongly in the writings of such sixteenth-century sceptics as Cornelius Agrippa, Montaigne, and Charron, whose influence is discernible in the sentiments of thinkers and poets in the Elizabethan and Jacobean age. Such scepticism came to the aid of those who denied the claims of the natural sciences or of other universal rational schemas and advocated salvation in pure faith, like the great Protestant reformers and their followers, and the Jansenist wing of the Roman church. The rationalist belief in a single coherent body of logically deduced conclusions, arrived at by universally valid principles of thought and founded upon carefully sifted data of observation or experiment, was further shaken by sociologically minded thinkers from Bodin to Montesquieu. These writers, using the evidence of both history and the new literature of travel and exploration in newly discovered lands, Asia and the Americas, emphasised the variety of human customs and especially the influence of dissimilar natural factors, particularly geographical ones, upon the development of different human societies, leading to differences of institutions and outlook, which in their turn generated wide differences of belief and behaviour. This was powerfully reinforced by the revolutionary doctrines of David Hume, especially by his demonstration that no logical links existed between truths of fact and such *a priori* truths as those of logic or mathematics, which tended to weaken or dissolve the hopes of those who, under the influence of Descartes and his followers, thought that a single system of knowledge, embracing all provinces and answering all questions, could be established by unbreakable chains of logical argument from universally valid axioms, not subject to refutation or modification by any experience of an empirical kind.

Nevertheless, no matter how deeply relativity about human values or the interpretation of social, including historical, facts entered the thought of social thinkers of this type, they too retained a common core of conviction that the ultimate ends of all men at all times were, in effect, identical: all men sought the satisfaction of basic physical and biological needs, such as food, shelter, security, and also peace, happiness, justice, the harmonious development of their natural faculties, truth, and, somewhat more vaguely, virtue, moral perfection, and what the Romans had called *humanitas*. Means might differ in cold and hot climates, mountainous countries and flat plains, and no universal formula could fit all cases without Procrustean results, but the ultimate ends were fundamentally similar. Such influential writers as Voltaire, d'Alembert and Condorcet believed that the development of the arts and sciences was the most powerful human weapon in attaining these ends, and the sharpest weapon in the fight against ignorance, superstition, fanaticism, oppression and barbarism, which crippled human effort and frustrated men's search for truth and rational self-direction. Rousseau and Mably believed, on the contrary, that the institutions of civilisation were themselves a major factor in the corruption of men and their alienation from nature, from simplicity, purity of heart and the life of natural justice, social equality, and spontaneous human feeling; artificial man had imprisoned, enslaved and ruined natural man. Nevertheless, despite profound differences of outlook, there was a wide area of agreement about fundamental points: the reality of natural law (no longer formulated in the language of orthodox Catholic or Protestant doctrine), of eternal principles by following which alone men could become wise, happy, virtuous, and free. One set of universal and unalterable principles governed the world for theists, deists and atheists, for optimists and pessimists, puritans, primitivists and believers in progress and the richest fruits of science and culture; these laws governed inanimate and animate nature, facts and events, means and ends, private life and public, all societies, epochs and civilisations; it was solely by departing from them that men fell into crime, vice, misery. Thinkers might differ about what these laws were, or how to discover them, or who were qualified to expound them; that these laws were real, and could be known, whether with certainty, or only probability, remained the central dogma of the entire Enlightenment. It was the attack upon this that constitutes the most formidable reaction against this dominant body of belief.

II

A thinker who might have had a decisive role in this counter-movement, if anyone outside his native country had read him, was the Neapolitan philosopher Giambattista Vico. With extraordinary originality Vico maintained, especially in the last work of his life, the *Scienza nuova*, that the Cartesians were profoundly mistaken about the role of mathematics as the science of sciences; that mathematics was certain only because it was a human invention. It did not, as they supposed, correspond to an objective structure of reality; it was a method and not a body of truths; with its help we could plot regularities – the occurrence of phenomena in the external world – but not discover why they occurred as they did, or to what end. This could be known only to God, for only those who make things can truly know what they are and for what purpose they have been made. Hence we do not, in this sense, know the external world – nature – for we have not made it; only God, who created it, knows it in this fashion. But since men are directly acquainted with human motives, purposes, hopes, fears, which are their own, they can know human affairs as they cannot know nature.

According to Vico, our lives and activities collectively and individually are expressions of our attempts to survive, satisfy our desires, understand each other and the past out of which we emerge. A utilitarian interpretation of the most essential human activities is misleading. They are, in the first place, purely expressive; to sing, to dance, to worship, to speak, to fight, and the institutions which embody these activities, comprise a vision of the world. Language, religious rites, myths, laws, social, religious, juridical institutions, are forms of self-expression, of wishing to convey what one is and strives for; they obey intelligible patterns, and for that reason it is possible to reconstruct the life of other societies, even those remote in time and place and utterly primitive, by asking oneself what kind of framework of human

4

ideas, feelings, acts could have generated the poetry, the monuments, the mythology which were their natural expression. Men grow individually and socially; the world of men who composed the Homeric poems was plainly very different from that of the Hebrews to whom God had spoken through their sacred books, or that of the Roman Republic, or medieval Christianity, or Naples under the Bourbons. Patterns of growth are traceable.

Myths are not, as enlightened thinkers believe, false statements about reality corrected by later rational criticism, nor is poetry mere embellishment of what could equally well be stated in ordinary prose. The myths and poetry of antiquity embody a vision of the world as authentic as that of Greek philosophy, or Roman law, or the poetry and culture of our own enlightened age — earlier, cruder, remote from us, but with its own voice, as we hear it in the *Iliad* or the Twelve Tables, belonging uniquely to its own culture, and with a sublimity which cannot be reproduced by a later, more sophisticated culture. Each culture expresses its own collective experience, each step on the ladder of human development has its own equally authentic means of expression.

Vico's theory of cycles of cultural development became celebrated, but it is not his most original contribution to the understanding of society or history. His revolutionary move is to have denied the doctrine of a timeless natural law the truths of which could have been known in principle to any man, at any time, anywhere. Vico boldly denied this doctrine, which has formed the heart of the western tradition from Aristotle to our own day. He preached the notion of the uniqueness of cultures, however they might resemble each other in their relationship to their antecedents and successors, and the notion of a single style that pervades all the activities and manifestations of societies of human beings at a particular stage of development. Thereby he laid the foundations at once of comparative cultural anthropology and of comparative historical linguistics, aesthetics, jurisprudence; language, ritual, monuments, and especially mythology, were the sole reliable keys to what later scholars and critics conceived as altering forms of collective consciousness. Such historicism was plainly not compatible with the view that there was only one standard of truth or beauty or goodness, which some cultures or individuals approached more closely than others, and which it was the business of thinkers to establish and men of action to realise. The Homeric poems were an unsurpassable masterpiece, but they could only spring from a brutal, stern, oligarchical, 'heroic' society, and later civilisations, however superior in other respects, did not and could not produce an art necessarily superior to Homer. This doctrine struck a powerful blow at the notion of timeless truths and steady progress, interrupted by occasional periods of retrogression into barbarism, and drew a sharp line between the natural sciences, which dealt with the relatively unaltering nature of the physical world viewed from 'outside', and humane studies, which viewed social evolution from 'inside' by a species of empathetic insight, for which the establishment of texts or dates by scientific criticism was a necessary, but not a sufficient, condition.

Vico's unsystematic works dealt with many other matters, but his importance in the history of the Enlightenment consists in his insistence on the plurality of cultures and on the consequently fallacious character of the idea that there is one and only one structure of reality which the enlightened philosopher can see as it truly is, and which he can (at least in principle) describe in logically perfect language – a vision that has obsessed thinkers from Plato to Leibniz, Condillac, Russell and his more faithful followers. For Vico, men ask different questions of the universe, and their answers are shaped accordingly : such questions, and the symbols or acts that express them, alter or become obsolete in the course of cultural development ; to understand the answers one must understand the questions that preoccupy an age or a culture ; they are not constant nor necessarily more profound because they resemble our own more than others that are less familiar to us. Vico's relativity went further than Montesquieu's. If his view was correct, it was subversive of the very notion of absolute truths and of a perfect society founded on them, not merely in practice but in principle. However, Vico was little read, and the question of how much influence he had had before his *New Science* was revived by Michelet a century after it was written is still uncertain.

If Vico wished to shake the pillars on which the Enlightenment of his times rested, the Königsberg theologian and philosopher, J. G. Hamann, wished to smash them. Hamann was brought up as a pietist, a member of the most introspective and self-absorbed of all the Lutheran sects, intent upon the direct communion of the individual soul with God, bitterly anti-rationalist, liable to emotional excess, preoccupied with the stern demands of moral obligation and the need for severe self-discipline. The attempt of Frederick the Great in the middle years of the eighteenth century to introduce French culture and a degree of rationalisation, economic and social as well as military, into

East Prussia, the most backward part of his provinces, provoked a peculiarly violent reaction in this pious, semi-feudal, traditional Protestant society (which also gave birth to Herder and Kant). Hamann began as a disciple of the Enlightenment, but, after a profound spiritual crisis, turned against it, and published a series of polemical attacks written in a highly idiosyncratic, perversely allusive, contorted, deliberately obscure style, as remote as he could make it from the, to him, detestable elegance, clarity, and smooth superficiality of the bland and arrogant French dictators of taste and thought. Hamann's theses rested on the conviction that all truth is particular, never general: that reason is impotent to demonstrate the existence of anything and is an instrument only for conveniently classifying and arranging data in patterns to which nothing in reality corresponds; that to understand is to be communicated with, by men or by God. The universe for him, as for the older German mystical tradition, is itself a kind of language. Things and plants and animals are themselves symbols with which God communicates with his creatures. Everything rests on faith; faith is as basic an organ of acquaintance with reality as the senses. To read the Bible is to hear the voice of God, who speaks in a language which he has given man the grace to understand. Some men are endowed with the gift of understanding his ways, of looking at the universe, which is his book no less than the revelations of the Bible and the fathers and saints of the church. Only love – for a person or an object – can reveal the true nature of anything. It is not possible to love formulas, general propositions, laws, the abstractions of science, the vast system of concepts and categories – symbols too general to be close to reality – with which the French *lumières* have blinded themselves to concrete reality, to the real experience which only direct acquaintance, especially by the senses, provides.

Hamann glories in the fact that Hume had successfully destroyed the rationalist claim that there is an *a priori* route to reality, insisting that all knowledge and belief ultimately rest on acquaintance with the data of direct perception. Hume rightly supposes that he could not eat an egg or drink a glass of water if he did not believe in their existence; the data of belief – what Hamann prefers to call faith – rest on grounds and require evidence as little as taste or any other sensation. True knowledge is direct perception of individual entities, and concepts are never, no matter how specific they may be, wholly adequate to the fullness of the individual experience. 'Individuum est ineffabile', wrote Goethe to Lavater in the spirit of Hamann, whom

Goethe profoundly admired. The sciences may be of use in practical matters; but no concatenation of concepts will give one an understanding of a man, of a work of art, of what is conveyed by gestures, symbols, verbal and non-verbal, of the style, the spiritual essence, of a human being, a movement, a culture; nor for that matter of the Deity, which speaks to one everywhere if only one has ears to hear and eyes to see. What is real is individual, that is, is what it is in virtue of its uniqueness, its differences from other things, events, thoughts, and not in virtue of what it has in common with them, which is all that the generalising sciences seek to record. 'Feeling alone', said Hamann, 'gives to abstractions and hypotheses hands, feet, wings'; and again 'God speaks to us in poetical words, addressed to the senses, not in abstractions for the learned', and so must anyone who has something to say that matters, who speaks to another person.

Hamann took little interest in theories or speculations about the external world; he cared only for the inner personal life of the individual, and therefore only for art, religious experience, the senses, personal relationships, which the analytic truths of scientific reason seemed to him to reduce to meaningless ciphers. 'God is a poet, not a mathematician', and it is men who, like Kant, suffer from a 'gnostic hatred of matter' that provide us with endless verbal constructions – words that are taken for concepts, and worse still, concepts that are taken for real things. Scientists invent systems, philosophers rearrange reality into artificial patterns, shut their eyes to reality, and build castles in the air. 'When *data* are given you, why do you seek for *ficta*?' Systems are mere prisons of the spirit, and they lead not only to distortion in the sphere of knowledge, but to the erection of monstrous bureaucratic machines, built in accordance with the rules that ignore the teeming variety of the living world, the untidy and asymmetrical inner lives of men, and crush them into conformity for the sake of some ideological chimera unrelated to the union of spirit and flesh that constitutes the real world. 'What is this much lauded reason with its universality, infallibility . . . certainty, over-weening claims, but an *ens rationis*, a stuffed dummy . . . endowed with divine attributes?' History alone yields concrete truth, and in particular the poets describe their world in the language of passion and inspired imagination. 'The entire treasure of human knowledge and happiness lies in images'; that is why the language of primitive man, sensuous and imaginative, is poetical and irrational. 'Poetry is the native language of mankind, and gardening is more ancient than agriculture, painting than writing, song than recitation, proverbs than rational conclusions, barter than trade.' Originality, genius, direct expression, the Bible or Shakespeare fashion the colour, shape, living flesh of the world, which analytical science, revealing only the skeleton, cannot begin to do.

Hamann is first in the line of thinkers who accuse rationalism and scientism of using analysis to distort reality : he is followed by Herder, Jacobi, Möser, who were influenced by Shaftesbury, Young, and Burke's anti-intellectualist diatribes, and they, in their turn, were echoed by romantic writers in many lands. The most eloquent spokesman of this attitude is Schelling, whose thought was reproduced vividly by Bergson at the beginning of this century. He is the father of those anti-rationalist thinkers for whom the seamless whole of reality in its unanalysable flow is misrepresented by the static, spatial metaphors of mathematics and the natural sciences. That to dissect is to murder is a romantic pronouncement which is the motto of an entire nineteenth-century movement of which Hamann was a most passionate and implacable forerunner. Scientific dissection leads to cold political dehumanisation, to the straitjacket of lifeless French rules in which the living body of passionate and poetical Germans is to be held fast by the Solomon of Prussia, Frederick the Great, who knows so much and understands so little. The arch-enemy is Voltaire, whom Herder called a 'senile child' with a corrosive wit in place of human feeling.

The influence of Rousseau, particularly of his early writings, on this movement in Germany, which came to be called *Sturm und Drang*, was profound. Rousseau's impassioned pleas for direct vision and natural feeling, his denunciation of the artificial social roles which civilisation forces men to play against the true ends and needs of their natures, his idealisation of more primitive, spontaneous human societies, his contrast between natural self-expression and the crippling artificiality of social divisions and conventions which rob men of dignity and freedom, and promote privilege, power and arbitrary bullying at one end of the human scale, and humiliating obsequiousness at the other, and so distort all human relations, appealed to Hamann and his followers.

But even Rousseau did not seem to them to go far enough. Despite everything, Rousseau believed in a timeless set of truths which all men could read, for they were engraved on their hearts in letters more durable than bronze, thereby conceding the authority of natural law, a vast, cold, empty abstraction. To Hamann and his followers all rules or precepts are deadly ; they may be necessary for the conduct of day-to-day life, but nothing great was ever achieved by following them. English critics were right in supposing that originality entailed breaking rules, that every creative act, every illuminating insight, is obtained by ignoring the rules of despotic legislators. Rules, he declared, are vestal virgins: unless they are violated there will be no issue. Nature is capable of wild fantasy, and it is mere childish presumption to seek to imprison her in the narrow rationalist categories of 'puny' and desiccated philosophers. Nature is a wild dance, and so-called practical men are like sleep-walkers who are secure and successful because they are blind to reality; if they saw reality as it truly is, they might go out of their minds.

Language is the direct expression of the historical life of societies and peoples: 'every court, every school, every profession, every corporation, every sect has its own language'; we penetrate the meaning of this language by the 'passion' of 'a lover, a friend, an intimate', not by rules, imaginary universal keys which open nothing. The French *philosophes* and their English followers tell us that men seek only to obtain pleasure and avoid pain, but this is absurd. Men seek to live, create, love, hate, eat, drink, worship, sacrifice, understand, and they seek this because they cannot help it. Life is action. It is knowable only by those who look within themselves and perform the 'hell-ride [*Höllenfahrt*] of self-knowledge', as the great founders of pietism – Spener, Francke, Bengel – have taught us. Before a man has liberated himself from the deathly embrace of impersonal, scientific thought which robs all it touches of life and individuality, he cannot understand himself or others, or how or why we come to be what we are.

While Hamann spoke in irregular, isolated flashes of insight, his disciple Herder attempted to construct a coherent system to explain the nature of man and his experience in history. While profoundly interested in the natural sciences and eagerly profiting by their findings, particularly in biology and physiology, and conceding a good deal more to the French than the fanatical Hamann was willing to do, Herder in that part of his doctrine which entered into the texture of the thought of the movements that he inspired deliberately aimed against the sociological assumptions of the French Enlightenment. He believed that to understand anything was to understand it in its individuality and development, and that this required a capacity which he called *Einfühlung* ('feeling into') the outlook, the individual character of an artistic tradition, a literature, a social organisation, a people, a culture, a period of history. To understand the actions of individuals, we must understand the 'organic' structure of the society in terms of which alone the minds and activities and habits of its members can be understood. Like Vico, he believed that to understand a religion, or a work of art, or a national character, one must 'enter into' the unique conditions of its life: those who have been storm-tossed on the waves of the North Sea (as he was during his voyage to the west) can fully understand the songs of the old Skalds as those who have never seen grim northern sailors coping with the elements never will; the Bible can truly be understood only by those who attempt to enter into the experience of primitive shepherds in the Judaean hills. To grade the merits of cultural wholes, of the legacy of entire traditions, by applying a collection of dogmatic rules claiming universal validity, enunciated by the Parisian arbiters of taste, is vanity and blindness. Every culture has its own unique *Schwerpunkt* ('centre of gravity'), and unless we grasp it we cannot understand its character or value. From this springs Herder's passionate concern with the preservation of primitive cultures which have a unique contribution to make, his love of almost every expression of the human spirit, work of the imagination, for simply being what it is. Art, morality, custom, religion, national life grow out of immemorial tradition, are created by entire societies living an integrated communal life. The frontiers and divisions drawn between and within such unitary expressions of collective imaginative response to common experience are nothing but artificial and distorting categorisations by the dull, dogmatic pedants of a later age.

Who are the authors of the songs, the epics, the myths, the temples, the *mores* of a people, the clothes they wear, the language they use? The people itself, the entire soul of which is poured out in all they are and do. Nothing is more barbarous than to ignore or trample on a cultural heritage. Hence Herder's condemnation of the Romans for crushing native civilisations, or of the church (despite the fact that he was himself a Lutheran clergyman) for forcibly baptising the Balts, and so forcing them into a Christian mould alien to their natural traditions, or of British missionaries for doing this to the Indians and other inhabitants of Asia, whose exquisite native cultures were being ruthlessly destroyed by the imposition of alien social systems, religions, forms of education that were not theirs and could only warp their natural development. Herder was no nationalist: he supposed that different cultures could and should flourish fruitfully side by side like so many peaceful flowers in the great human garden; nevertheless, the seeds of nationalism are unmistakably present in his fervid attacks on hollow cosmopolitanism and universalism (with which he charged the French *philosophes*); they grew apace among his aggressive nineteenth-century disciples.

Herder is the greatest inspirer of cultural nationalism among the nationalities oppressed by the Austro-Hungarian, Turkish and Russian empires, and ultimately of direct political nationalism as well, much as he abhorred it, in Austria and Germany, and by infectious reaction, in other lands as well. He rejected the absolute criteria of progress then fashionable in Paris: no culture is a mere means towards another; every human achievement, every human society is to be judged by its own internal standards. In spite of the fact that in later life he attempted to construct a theory of history in which the whole of mankind, in a somewhat vague fashion, is represented as developing towards a common *Humanität* which embraces all men and all the arts and all the sciences, it is his earlier, relativistic passion for the individual essence and flavour of each culture that most profoundly influenced the European imagination. For Voltaire, Diderot, Helvétius, Holbach, Condorcet, there is only universal civilisation, of which now one nation, now another, represents the richest flowering. For Herder there is a plurality of incommensurable cultures. To belong to a given community, to be connected with its members by indissoluble and impalpable ties of common language, historical memory, habit, tradition and feeling, is a basic human need no less natural than that for food or drink or security or procreation. One nation can understand and sympathise with the institutions of another only because it knows how much its own mean to itself. Cosmopolitanism is the shedding of all that makes one most human, most oneself. Hence the attack upon what is regarded as the false mechanical model of mankind used by scientifically minded French *philosophes* (Herder makes an exception for Diderot alone, with whose writings, wayward and imaginative and full of sudden insights, he felt a genuine affinity), who understand only machine-like, causal factors, or the arbitrary will of individual kings and legislators and commanders, sometimes wise and virtuous and altruistic, at other times self-interested or corrupt or stupid or vicious. But the forces that shape men are far more complex, and differ from age to age and culture to culture and cannot be contained in these simple cut and dried formulas. 'I am always frightened when I hear a whole nation or period characterised in a few short words; for what a vast multitude of differences is embraced by the word "nation", or "the Middle Ages", or "ancient and modern times".' Germans can be truly creative only among Germans; Jews only if they are restored to the ancient soil of Palestine. Those who are forcibly pulled up by the roots wither in a foreign environment when they survive at all: Europeans lose their virtue in America, Icelanders decay in Denmark. Imitation of models (unlike unconscious, unperceived, spontaneous influences by one society on another) leads to artificiality, feeble imitativeness, degraded art and life. Germans must be Germans and not third-rate Frenchmen; life lies in remaining steeped in one's own language, tradition, local feeling; uniformity is death. The tree of (science-dominated) knowledge kills the tree of life.

So, too, Herder's contemporary, Justus Möser, the first historical sociologist, who wrote about the old life of his native region of Osnabrück in western Germany, said that 'every age had its own style', every war has its own particular tone, the affairs of state have a specific colouring, dress and manner have inner connections with religion and the sciences; that *Zeitstil* and *Volksstil* are everything; that there is a 'local reason' for this or that institution that is not and cannot be universal. Möser maintained that societies and persons could be understood only by means of a 'total impression', not by isolation of element from element in the manner of analytical chemists; this, he tells us, is what Voltaire had not grasped when he mocked the fact that a law which applied in one German village was contradicted by another in a neighbouring one: it is by such rich variety, founded upon ancient, unbroken tradition, that the tyrannies of uniform systems, such as those of Louis XIV or Frederick the Great, were avoided; it is so that freedoms were preserved.

Although the influence was not direct, these are the very tones one hears in the works of Burke and many later romantic, vitalistic, intuitionist, and irrationalist writers, both conservative and socialist, who defend the value of organic forms of social life. Burke's famous onslaught on the principles of the French revolutionaries was founded upon the selfsame appeal to the 'myriad strands' that bind human beings into a historically hallowed whole, contrasted with the utilitarian model of society as a trading company held together solely by contractual obligations, the world of 'economists, sophisters and calculators' who are blind and deaf to the unanalysable relationships that make a family, a tribe, a nation, a movement, any association of human beings held together by something more than a quest for mutual advantage, or by force, or by anything that is not mutual love, loyalty, common history, emotion and outlook. This emphasis in the last half of the eighteenth century on non-rational factors, whether connected with specific religious beliefs or not, which stresses the value of the individual, the peculiar (*das Eigentümliche*), the impalpable, and appeals to ancient historical roots and immemorial custom, to the wisdom of simple, sturdy peasants uncorrupted by the sophistries of subtle 'reasoners', has strongly conservative and, indeed, reactionary implications. Whether stated by the enthusiastic populist Herder with his acute dislike for political coercion, empires, political authority, and all forms of imposed organisation; or by Möser, moderate Hanoverian conservative; or by Lavater, altogether unconcerned with politics; or by Burke, brought up in a different tradition, respectful towards church and state and the authority of aristocracies and élites sanctified by history, these doctrines clearly constitute a resistance to attempts at a rational reorganisation of society in the name of universal moral and intellectual ideals.

At the same time abhorrence of scientific expertise inspired radical protest in the works of William Blake, of the young Schiller, and of populist writers in eastern Europe. Above all, it contributed to literary turbulence in Germany in the second third of the eighteenth century: the plays of such leaders of the *Sturm und Drang* as Lenz, Klinger, Gerstenberg and Leisewitz are outbursts against every form of organised social or political life. What provoked them may have been the asphyxiating philistinism of the German middle class, or the cruel injustices of the small and stuffy courts of stupid and arbitrary German princelings; but what they attacked with equal violence was the entire tidy ordering of life by the principles of reason and scientific knowledge advocated by the progressive thinkers of France, England and Italy. Lenz regards nature as a wild whirlpool into which a man of feeling and temperament will throw himself if he is to experience the fullness of life; for him, for Schubart and for Leisewitz art and, in particular, literature are passionate forms of self-assertion which look on all acceptance of conventional forms as but 'delayed death'. Nothing is more characteristic of the entire *Sturm und Drang* movement than Herder's cry 'I am not here to think, but to be, feel, live!', or 'heart! warmth! blood! humanity! life!' French reasoning is pale and ghostly. It is this that inspired Goethe's reaction in the 70s to Holbach's *Système de la nature* as a repulsive, 'Cimmerian, corpse-like' treatise, which had no relation to the marvellous, inexhaustibly rich vitality of the Gothic cathedral at Strasbourg, in which, under Herder's guidance, he saw one of the noblest expressions of the German spirit in the Middle Ages, of which the critics of the Augustan age understood nothing. Heinse in his fantasy *Ardinghello und die glückseligen Inseln* leads his central characters, after a bloodstained succession of wild experiences of more than 'Gothic' intensity, to an island where there is total freedom in personal relations, all rules and conventions have finally been flung to the winds, where man in an anarchist-communist society can at last stretch himself to his full stature as a sublime creative artist. The inspiration of this work is a violent, radical individualism, which represents an early form, not unlike the contemporary erotic fantasies of the Marquis de Sade, of a craving for escape from imposed rules and laws whether of scientific reason or of political or ecclesiastical authority, royalist or republican, despotic or democratic.

By an odd paradox, it is the profoundly rational, exact, unromantic Kant, with his lifelong hatred of all forms of *Schwärmerei*, who is in part, through exaggeration and distortion of at least one of his doctrines, one of the fathers of this unbridled individualism. Kant's moral doctrines stressed the fact that determinism was not compatible with morality, since only those who are the true authors of their own acts, which they are free to perform or not perform, can be praised or blamed for what they do. Since responsibility entails power of choice, those who cannot freely choose are morally no more accountable than stocks and stones. Thereby Kant initiated a cult of moral autonomy, according to which only those who act and are not acted upon, whose actions spring from a decision of the moral will to be guided by freely adopted principles, if need be against inclination, and not from the inescapable causal pressure of factors beyond their control – physical, physiological, psychological (such as emotion, desire, habit) – can properly be considered to be free or, indeed, moral agents at all. Kant acknowledged a profound debt to Rousseau who, particularly in the 'profession of faith of the Savoyard vicar' in the fourth book of his *Émile*, spoke of man as an active being in contrast with the passivity of material nature, a possessor of a will which makes him free to resist the temptations of the senses. 'I am a slave through my vices and free through my remorse'; it is the active will, made known directly by 'conscience', which for Rousseau is 'stronger than reason [i.e. prudential argument] which fights against it', that enables man to choose the good; he acts, if need be, against 'the law of the body', and so makes himself worthy of happiness. But although this doctrine of the will as a capacity not determined by the causal stream is directed against the sensationalist positivism of Helvétius or Condillac, and has an affinity to Kant's free moral will, it does not leave the objective framework of natural law which governs things as well as persons, and prescribes the same immutable, universal goals to all men.

This emphasis upon the will at the expense of contemplative thought and perception, which function within the predetermined grooves of the categories of the mind that man cannot escape, enters deeply into the German conception of moral freedom as entailing resistance to nature and not harmonious collusion with her, overcoming of natural inclination, and rising to Promethean resistance to coercion, whether by things or by men. This, in its turn, led to the rejection of the doctrine that to understand is to accept the view that knowledge demonstrates the rational necessity and therefore the value of what, in his irrational state, may have seemed to man mere obstacles in his path. This conception, opposed as it is to reconciliation with reality, in its later, romantic form favoured the ceaseless fight, at times ending in tragic defeat, against the forces of blind nature, which cares nothing for human ideas, and against the accumulated weight of authority and tradition – the vast incubus of the uncriticised past, made concrete in the oppressive institutions of the present. Thus, when Blake denounces Newton and Locke as the great enemies, it is because he accuses them of seeking to imprison the free human spirit in constricting, intellectual machines; when he says, 'A Robin Red breast in a Cage/Puts all Heaven in a Rage', the cage is none other than Newtonian physics, which crushes the life out of the free, spontaneous life of the untrammelled human spirit. 'Art is the Tree of Life . . . Science is the Tree of Death'; Locke, Newton, the French *raisonneurs*, the reign of cautious, pragmatic respectability and Pitt's police were all, for him, parts of the same nightmare. There is something of this, too, in Schiller's early play *Die Räuber* (written in 1781), where the violent protest of the tragic hero Karl Moor, which ends in failure, crime and death, cannot be averted by mere knowledge, by a better understanding of human nature or of social conditions or of anything else; knowledge is not enough. The doctrine of the Enlightenment that we can discover what men truly want and can provide technical means and rules of conduct for their greatest permanent satisfaction and that this is what leads to wisdom, virtue, happiness is not compatible with Karl Moor's proud and stormy spirit, which rejects the ideas of his milieu, and will not be assuaged by the reformist gradualism and belief in rational organisation advocated by, say, the *Aufklärung* of the previous generation. 'Law has distorted to a snail's pace what could have been an eagle's flight.' Human nature is no longer conceived of as, in principle, capable of being brought into harmony with the natural world: for Schiller some fatal Rousseauian break between spirit and nature has occurred, a wound has been inflicted on humanity which art seeks to avenge, but knows it cannot fully heal.

Jacobi, a mystical metaphysician deeply influenced by Hamann, cannot reconcile the demands of the soul and the intellect: 'The light is in my heart: as soon as I try to carry it to my intellect, it goes out.' Spinoza was for him the greatest master since Plato of the rational vision of the universe; but for Jacobi this is death in life: it does not answer the burning questions of the soul whose homelessness in the chilly world of the intellect only self-surrender to faith in a transcendent God will remedy.

Schelling was perhaps the most eloquent of all the philosophers who represented the universe as the self-development of a primal, non-rational force that can be grasped only by the intuitive powers of men of imaginative genius – poets, philosophers, theologians or statesmen. Nature, a living organism, responds to questions put by the man of genius, while the man of genius responds to the questions put by nature, for they conspire with each other; imaginative insight alone, no matter whose – an artist's, a seer's, a thinker's – becomes conscious of the contours of the future, of which the mere calculating intellect and analytic capacity of the natural scientist or the politician, or any other earthbound empiricist, has no conception. This faith in a peculiar, intuitive, spiritual faculty which goes by various names – reason, understanding, primary imagination – but is always differentiated from the critical analytic intellect favoured by the Enlightenment, the contrast between it and the analytic faculty or method that collects, classifies, experiments, takes to pieces, reassembles, defines, deduces, and establishes probabilities, becomes a commonplace used thereafter by Fichte, Hegel, Wordsworth, Coleridge, Goethe, Carlyle, Schopenhauer and other anti-rationalist thinkers of the nineteenth century, culminating in Bergson and later anti-positivist schools.

This, too, is the source of that stream in the great river of romanticism which looks upon every human activity as a form of individual self-expression, and on art, and indeed every creative activity, as a stamping of a unique personality, individual or collective, conscious or unconscious, upon the matter or the medium in and upon which it functions, seeking to realise values which are themselves not given but generated by the process of creation itself. Hence the denial, both in theory and in practice, of the central doctrine of the Enlightenment, according to which the rules in accordance with which men should live and act and create are pre-established, dictated by nature herself. For Joshua Reynolds, for example, the 'great style' is the realisation of the artist's vision of eternal forms, prototypes beyond the confusions of ordinary experience, which his genius enables him to discern and which he seeks to reproduce, with all the techniques at his command, on his canvas or in marble or bronze. Such mimesis or copying from ideal patterns is, for those who derive from the German tradition of revolt against French classicism, not true creation. Creation is creation of ends as well as means, of values as well as their embodiments; the vision that I seek to translate into colours or sounds is generated by me, and peculiar to me, unlike anything that has ever been, or will be, above all not something that is common to me and other men seeking to realise a common, shared, universal, because rational, ideal. The notion that a work of art (or any other work of man) is created in accordance with rules dictated by objective nature, and therefore binding for all practitioners of it, as Boileau or the Abbé Batteux had taught, is rejected *in toto*. Rules may be an aid here or there, but the least spark of genius destroys them, and creates its own practice, which uncreative craftsmen may imitate, and so be saying nothing of their own. I create as I do, whether I am an artist, a philosopher, a statesman, not because the goal that I seek to realise is objectively beautiful, or true, or virtuous, or approved by public opinion, or demanded by majorities or tradition, but because it is my own.

What this creative self may be differs according to doctrine. Some regard it as a transcendent entity to be identified with a cosmic spirit, a divine principle to which finite men aspire as sparks do to the great central flame; others identify it with their own individual, mortal, flesh-and-blood selves, like Byron, or Hugo, or other defiantly romantic writers and painters. Others again identified the creative self with a super-personal 'organism' of which they saw themselves as elements or members — nation, or church, or culture, or class, or history itself, a mighty force of which they conceived their earthly selves as emanations. Aggressive nationalism, self-identification with the interests of the class, the culture or the race, or the forces of progress — with the wave of a future-directed dynamism of history, something that at once explains and justifies acts which might be abhorred or despised if committed from calculation of selfish advantage or some other mundane motive – this family of political and moral conceptions is so many expressions of a doctrine of self-realisation based on defiant rejection of the central theses of the Enlightenment, according to which what is true, or right, or good, or beautiful, can be shown to be valid for all men by the correct application of objective methods of discovery and interpretation, open to anyone to use and verify. In its full romantic guise, this attitude is an open declaration of war upon the very heart of the rational and experimental method which Descartes and Galileo had inaugurated, and which for all their doubts and qualifications even such sharp deviationists as Montesquieu, or Hume and Rousseau and Kant, fully and firmly accepted. For the truly ardent opponents of classicism, values are not found but made, not discovered but created; they are to be realised because they are mine, or ours, whatever the nature of the true self is pronounced to be by this or that metaphysical doctrine.

The most extravagant of the German romantics, Novalis or Tieck, looked on the universe not as a structure that can be studied or described by whatever methods are most appropriate, but as a perpetual activity of the spirit and of nature which is the selfsame spirit in a dormant state; of this constant upward movement the man of genius is the most conscious agent, who thus embodies the forward activity that advances the life of the spirit most significantly. While some, like Schelling and Coleridge, conceive this activity as the gradual growth into self-consciousness of the world spirit that is perpetually moving towards self-perfection, others conceive the cosmic process as having no goal, as a purposeless and meaningless movement, which men, because they cannot face this bleak and despair-inducing truth, seek to hide from themselves by constructing comforting illusions in the form of religions that promise rewards in another life, or metaphysical systems that claim to provide rational justification both for what there is in the world and for what men do and can do and should do; or scientific systems that perform the task of appearing to give sense to a process that is, in fact, purposeless, a formless flux which is what it is, a brute fact, signifying nothing. This doctrine, elaborated by Schopenhauer, lies at the root of much modern existentialism and of the cultivation of the absurd in art and thought, as well as of the extremes of egoistic anarchism driven to their furthest lengths by Stirner, and by Nietzsche (in some of his moods), Kierkegaard (Hamann's most brilliant and profound disciple) and modern irrationalists.

The rejection of the central principles of the Enlightenment –

universality, objectivity, rationality, and the capacity to provide permanent solutions to all genuine problems of life or thought, and (not less important) accessibility of rational methods to any thinker armed with adequate powers of observation and logical thinking – occurred in various forms, conservative or liberal, reactionary or revolutionary, depending on which systematic order was being attacked. Those, for example, like Adam Müller or Friedrich Schlegel, and, in some moods, Coleridge or Cobbett, to whom the principles of the French Revolution or the Napoleonic organisation came to seem the most fatal obstacles to free human self-expression, adopted conservative or reactionary forms of irrationalism and at times looked back with nostalgia towards some golden past, such as the pre-scientific ages of faith, and tended (not always continuously or consistently) to support clerical and aristocratic resistance to modernisation and the mechanisation of life by industrialism and the new hierarchies of power and authority. Those who looked upon the traditional forces of authority or hierarchical organisation as the most oppressive of social forces – Byron, for example, or George Sand, or, so far as they can be called romantic, Shelley or Büchner – formed the 'left wing' of the romantic revolt. Others despised public life in principle, and occupied themselves with the cultivation of the inner spirit. In all cases the organisation of life by the application of rational or scientific methods, any form of regimentation or conscription of men for utilitarian ends or organised happiness, was regarded as the philistine enemy.

What the entire Enlightenment has in common is denial of the central Christian doctrine of original sin, believing instead that man is born either innocent and good, or morally neutral and malleable by education or environment, or, at worst, deeply defective but capable of radical and indefinite improvement by rational education in favourable circumstances, or by a revolutionary reorganisation of society as demanded, for example, by Rousseau. It is this denial of original sin that the church condemned most severely in Rousseau's *Émile*, despite its attack on materialism, utilitarianism and atheism. It is the powerful reaffirmation of this Pauline and Augustinian doctrine that is the sharpest single weapon in the root-and-branch attack on the entire Enlightenment by the French counter-revolutionary writers de Maistre, Bonald and Chateaubriand, at the turn of the century.

One of the darkest of the reactionary forms of the fight against the Enlightenment, as well as one of the most interesting and influential, is to be found in the doctrines of Joseph de Maistre and his followers and allies, who formed the spearhead of the counter-revolution in the early nineteenth century in Europe. De Maistre held the Enlightenment to be one of the most foolish, as well as the most ruinous, forms of social thinking. The conception of man as naturally disposed to benevolence, cooperation and peace, or, at any rate, capable of being shaped in this direction by appropriate education or legislation, is for him shallow and false. The benevolent Dame Nature of Hume, Holbach and Helvétius is an absurd figment. History and zoology are the most reliable guides to nature : they show her to be a field of unceasing slaughter. Men are by nature aggressive and destructive; they rebel over trifles – the change to the Gregorian calendar in the mideighteenth century, or Peter the Great's decision to shave the boyars' beards, provoke violent resistance, at times dangerous rebellions. But when men are sent to war, to exterminate beings as innocent as themselves for no purpose that either army can grasp, they go obediently to their deaths and scarcely ever mutiny. When the destructive instinct is evoked men feel exalted and fulfilled. Men do not come together, as the Enlightenment teaches, for mutual cooperation and peaceful happiness; history makes it clear that they are never so united as when given a common altar upon which to immolate themselves. This is so because the desire to sacrifice themselves or others is at least as strong as any pacific or constructive impulse. De Maistre felt that men are by nature evil, self-destructive animals, full of conflicting drives, who do not know what they want, want what they do not want, do not want what they want, and it is only when they are kept under constant control and rigorous discipline by some authoritarian élite – a church, a state, or some other body from whose decisions there is no appeal – that they can hope to survive and be saved. Reasoning, analysis, criticism shake the foundations and destroy the fabric of society. If the source of authority is declared to be rational, it invites questioning and doubt; but if it is questioned it may be argued away; its authority is undermined by able sophists, and this accelerates the forces of chaos, as in France during the reign of the weak and liberal Louis XVI. If the state is to survive and frustrate the fools and knaves who will always seek to destroy it, the source of authority must be absolute, so terrifying, indeed, that the least attempt to question it must entail immediate and terrible sanctions : only then will men learn to obey it. Without a clear hierarchy of authority – awe-inspiring power – men's incurably destructive instincts will breed chaos and mutual extermination. The supreme power – especially the church – must never seek to explain or justify itself in rational terms; for what one man can demonstrate, another may be able to refute. Reason is the thinnest of walls against the raging seas of violent emotion: on so insecure a basis no permanent structure can ever be erected. Irrationality, so far from being an obstacle, has historically led to peace, security and strength, and is indispensable to society: it is rational institutions – republics, elective monarchies, democracies, associations founded on the enlightened principles of free love – that collapse soonest; authoritarian churches, hereditary monarchies and aristocracies, traditional forms of life, like the highly irrational institution of the family, founded on lifelong marriage – it is they that persist.

The *philosophes* proposed to rationalise communication by inventing a universal language free from the irrational survivals, the idiosyncratic twists and turns, the capricious peculiarities of existing tongues; if they were to succeed, this would be disastrous, for it is precisely the individual historical development of a language that belongs to a people that absorbs, enshrines and encapsulates a vast wealth of half-conscious, half-remembered collective experience. What men call superstition and prejudice are but the crust of custom which by sheer survival has shown itself proof against the ravages and vicissitudes of its long life; to lose it is to lose the shield that protects men's national existence, their spirit, the habits, memories, faith that have made them what they are. The conception of human nature which the radical critics have promulgated and on which their whole house of cards rests is an infantile fantasy. Rousseau asks why it is that man, who was born free, is nevertheless everywhere in chains; one might as well ask, says de Maistre, why it is that sheep, who are born carnivorous, nevertheless everywhere nibble grass. Men are not made for freedom, nor for peace. Such freedom and peace as they have had were obtained only under wisely authoritarian governments that have repressed the destructive critical intellect and its socially disintegrating effects. Scientists, intellectuals, lawyers, journalists, democrats, Jansenists, Protestants, Jews, atheists, these are the sleepless enemy that never ceases to gnaw at the vitals of society. The best government the world has ever known was that of the Romans: they were too wise to be scientists themselves: for this purpose they hired the clever, volatile, politically incapable Greeks. Not the luminous intellect, but dark instincts govern man and societies; only élites which understand this, and keep the people from too much secular education that is bound to make them over-critical and discontented, can give to men as much happiness and justice and freedom as, in this vale of tears, men can expect to have. But at the back of everything must lurk the potentiality of force, of coercive power.

In a striking image de Maistre says that all social order in the end rests upon one man, the executioner. Nobody wishes to associate with this hideous figure, yet on him, so long as men are weak, sinful, unable to control their passions, constantly lured to their doom by evil temptations or foolish dreams, rest all order, all peace, all society. The notion that reason is sufficient to educate or control the passions is ridiculous. When there is a vacuum, power rushes in; even the blood-stained monster Robespierre, a scourge sent by the Lord to punish a country that had departed from the true faith, is more to be admired — because he did hold France together and repelled her enemies, and created armies that, drunk with blood and passion, preserved France — than liberal fumbling and bungling. Louis XIV ignored the clever reasoners of his time, suppressed heresy, and died full of glory in his own bed. Louis XVI played amiably with subversive ideologists who had drunk at the poisoned well of Voltaire, and died on the scaffold. Repression, censorship, absolute sovereignty, judgements from which there is no appeal, these are the only methods of governing creatures whom de Maistre described as half men, half beasts, monstrous centaurs at once seeking after God and fighting Him, longing to love and create, but in perpetual danger of falling victims to their own blindly destructive drives, held in check by a combination of force and traditional authority and, above all, a faith incarnated in historically hallowed institutions that reason dare not touch. Nation and race are realities; the artificial creations of constitution-mongers are bound to collapse. 'Nations', said de Maistre, 'are born and die like individuals . . . They have a common soul, especially visible in their language.' And since they are individuals, they should endeavour to remain 'of one race'. So too Bonald, his closest intellectual ally, regrets that the French nation has abandoned its ideal of racial purity, thus weakening itself. The question of whether the French are descended from Franks or Gauls, whether their institutions are Roman or German in origin, with the implication that this could dictate a form of life in the present, although it has its roots in political controversies in the sixteenth, seventeenth and early eighteenth centuries, now takes the colour of mystical organicism, which transcends, and is proof against, all forms of discursive reasoning. Natural growth alone is real for de Maistre. Only time, only history, can create authority that men can worship and obey: mere military dictatorship, a work of individual human hands, is brutal force without spiritual power: he calls it *bâtonocratie*, and predicts the end of Napoleon. In similar strain Bonald denounced individualism whether as a social doctrine or an intellectual method of analysing historical phenomena. The inventions of man, he declared, are precarious aids compared to divinely ordained institutions that penetrate man's very being, language, family, the worship of God. By whom were they invented? Whenever a child is born there are father, mother, family, God; this is the basis of all that is genuine and lasting, not the arrangements of men drawn from the world of shopkeepers, with their contracts, or promises, or utility, or material goods. Liberal individualism inspired by the insolent self-confidence of mutinous intellectuals has led to the inhuman competition of bourgeois society in which the strongest and the fastest win and the weak go to the wall. Only the church can organise a society in which the ablest are held back so that the whole of society can progress and the weakest and least greedy also reach the goal.

These gloomy doctrines became the inspiration of monarchist politics in France, and together with the notion of romantic heroism and the sharp contrast between creative and uncreative, historic and unhistorical individuals and nations, duly inspired nationalism, imperialism, and finally, in their most violent and pathological form, Fascist and totalitarian doctrines in the twentieth century.

The failure of the French Revolution to bring about the greater portion of its declared ends marks the end of the French Enlightenment as a movement and a system. Its heirs and the counter-movements that, to some degree, they stimulated and affected in their turn, romantic and irrational creeds and movements, political and aesthetic, violent and peaceful, individualist and collective, anarchic and totalitarian, and their impact, belong to another page of history.

The Originality of Machiavelli

THERE is something surprising about the sheer number of interpretations of Machiavelli's political opinions.[1] There exist, even now, over a score of leading theories of how to interpret *The Prince* and *The Discourses* – apart from a cloud of subsidiary views and glosses. The bibliography of this is vast and growing faster than ever.[2] While there may exist no more than the normal extent of disagreement about the meaning of particular terms or theses contained in these works, there is a startling degree of divergence about the central view, the basic political attitude of Machiavelli.

This phenomenon is easier to understand in the case of other thinkers whose opinions have continued to puzzle or agitate mankind – Plato, for example, or Rousseau, or Hegel, or Marx. But then it might be said that Plato wrote in a world and in a language that we cannot be sure we understand; that Rousseau, Hegel, Marx were

[1] The first draft of this paper was read at a meeting of the British section of the Political Studies Association in 1953. I should like to take this opportunity of offering my thanks to friends and colleagues to whom I sent it for their comments. They include A. P. d'Entrèves, Carl J. Friedrich, Felix Gilbert, Myron Gilmore, Louis Hartz, J. P. Plamenatz, Laurence Stone and Hugh Trevor-Roper. I have greatly profited from their criticisms, which have saved me from many errors; for those that are left I am, of course, alone responsible.

[2] The full list now contains more than three thousand items. The bibliographical surveys that I have found most valuable are P. H. Harris, 'Progress in Machiavelli Studies', *Italica* 18 (1941), 1–11; Eric W. Cochrane, 'Machiavelli: 1940–1960', *Journal of Modern History* 33 (1961), 113–36; Felix Gilbert, *Machiavelli and Guicciardini* (Princeton, 1965); Giuseppe Prezzolini, *Machiavelli anticristo* (Rome, 1954), trans. into English as *Machiavelli* (New York, 1967; London, 1968); De Lamar Jensen (ed.), *Machiavelli: Cynic, Patriot, or Political Scientist?* (Boston, 1960); and Richard C. Clark, 'Machiavelli: Bibliographical Spectrum', *Review of National Literatures* 1 (1970), 93–135.

prolific theorists, whose works are scarcely models of clarity or consistency. But *The Prince* is a short book: its style is usually described as being singularly lucid, succinct and pungent – a model of clear Renaissance prose. *The Discourses* is not, as treatises on politics go, of undue length, and it is equally clear and definite. Yet there is no consensus about the significance of either; they have not been absorbed into the texture of traditional political theory; they continue to arouse passionate feelings; *The Prince* has evidently excited the interest and admiration of some of the most formidable men of action of the last four centuries, especially of our own, men not normally addicted to reading classical texts.

There is evidently something peculiarly disturbing about what Machiavelli said or implied, something that has caused profound and lasting uneasiness. Modern scholars have pointed out certain real or apparent inconsistencies between the (for the most part) republican sentiment of *The Discourses* (and *The Histories*) and the advice to absolute rulers in *The Prince*; indeed there is a difference of tone between the two treatises, as well as chronological puzzles: this raises problems about Machiavelli's character, motives and convictions which for three hundred years and more have formed a rich field of investigation and speculation for literary and linguistic scholars, psychologists and historians.

But it is not this that has shocked western feeling. Nor can it be only Machiavelli's 'realism' or his advocacy of brutal or unscrupulous or ruthless policies that has so deeply upset so many later thinkers, and driven some of them to explain or explain away his advocacy of force and fraud. The fact that the wicked are seen to flourish or that immoral courses appear to pay has never been very remote from the consciousness of mankind. The Bible, Herodotus, Thucydides, Plato, Aristotle – to take only some of the fundamental works of western culture – the characters of Jacob or Joshua or David, Samuel's advice to Saul, Thucydides' Melian dialogue or his account of at least one ferocious but rescinded Athenian resolution, the philosophies of Thrasymachus and Callicles, Aristotle's advice to tyrants in the *Politics*, Carneades' speeches to the Roman Senate as described by Cicero, Augustine's view of the secular state from one vantage point, and Marsilio's from another – all these had cast enough light on political realities to shock the credulous out of uncritical idealism.

The explanation can scarcely lie in Machiavelli's tough-mindedness alone, even though he did perhaps dot the i's and cross the t's more sharply than anyone before him.[1] Even if the initial outcry – the reactions of, say, Pole or Gentillet – is to be so explained, this does not account for the reactions of those acquainted with the views of Hobbes or Spinoza or Hegel or the Jacobins and their heirs. Something else is surely needed to account both for the continuing horror and for the differences among the commentators. The two phenomena may not be unconnected. To indicate the nature of the latter phenomenon let me cite only the best known rival interpretations of Machiavelli's political views produced since the sixteenth century.

According to Alberico Gentili[2] and Garrett Mattingly,[3] the author of *The Prince* wrote a satire, for he certainly cannot literally have meant what he said. For Spinoza,[4] Rousseau,[5] Ugo Foscolo,[6] Luigi Ricci (who introduces *The Prince* to the readers of The World's Classics)[7] it is a cautionary tale; for whatever else he was, Machiavelli was a passionate patriot, a democrat, a believer in liberty, and *The Prince* must have been intended (Spinoza is particularly clear on this) to warn men of what tyrants could be and do, the better to resist them. Perhaps the author could not write openly with two rival powers – those of the church and of the Medici – eyeing him with equal (and not unjustified) suspicion. *The Prince* is therefore a satire (though no work seems to me to read less like one).

For A. H. Gilbert[8] it is anything but this – it is a typical piece of its period, a mirror for princes, a genre exercise common enough in the Renaissance and before (and after) it, with very obvious borrowings and 'echoes'; more gifted than most of these, and certainly more

---

[1] His habit of putting things *troppo assolutamente* had already been noted by Guicciardini. See 'Considerazioni intorno ai *Discorsi* del Machiavelli', book 1, chapter 3, p. 8 in *Scritti politici e ricordi*, ed. Roberto Palmarocchi (Bari, 1933).

[2] Alberico Gentili, *De legationibus libri tres* (London, 1585), book 3, chapter 9, pp. 101–2.

[3] Garrett Mattingly, 'Machiavelli's *Prince*: Political Science or Political Satire?', *American Scholar* 27 (1958), 482–91.

[4] Benedictus de Spinoza, *Tractatus politicus*, chapter 5, section 7.

[5] *Du contrat social*, book 3, chapter 6, note.

[6] *I sepolchri*, 156–8: 'che, temprando lo scettro a' regnatori,/gli allòr ne sfronda, ed alle genti svela/di che lagrime grondi e di che sangue . . .'.

[7] Luigi Ricci, preface to Niccolò Machiavelli, *The Prince* (London, 1903).

[8] Allan H. Gilbert, *Machiavelli's Prince and its Forerunners* (Durham, North Carolina, 1938).

hard-boiled (and influential); but not so very different in style, content, or intention.

Giuseppe Prezzolini[1] and Hiram Haydn,[2] more plausibly, regard it as an anti-Christian piece (in this following Fichte and others)[3] and see it as an attack on the church and all her principles, a defence of the pagan view of life. Giuseppe Toffanin,[4] however, thinks Machiavelli was a Christian, though a somewhat peculiar one, a view from which Roberto Ridolfi,[5] his most distinguished living biographer, and Leslie Walker (in his English edition of *The Discourses*)[6] do not wholly dissent. Alderisio,[7] indeed, regards him as a sincere Catholic, although he does not go quite so far as Richelieu's agent, Canon Louis Machon, in his *Apology for Machiavelli*,[8] or the anonymous nineteenth-century compiler of *Religious Maxims faithfully extracted from the works of Niccolò Machiavelli* (referred to by Ridolfi in the last chapter of his biography).[9]

For Benedetto Croce[10] and all the many scholars who have followed him, Machiavelli is an anguished humanist, and one who, so far from seeking to soften the impression made by the crimes that he describes, laments the vices of men which make such wicked courses politically

---

[1] op. cit. (p. 25, note 2 above).

[2] Hiram Haydn, *The Counter-Renaissance* (New York, 1950).

[3] e.g. the Spaniards Pedro de Ribadeneira, *Tratado de la Religión* (Madrid, 1595), and Claudio Clemente (pseudonym of Juan Eusebio Nieremberg), *El Machiavelismo degollado* (Alcalá, 1637).

[4] Giuseppe Toffanin, *La fine dell'umanesimo* (Turin, 1920).

[5] Roberto Ridolfi, *Vita di Niccolò Machiavelli* (Rome, 1954), trans. by Cecil Grayson as *The Life of Niccolò Machiavelli* (London and Chicago, 1963).

[6] *The Discourses of Niccolò Machiavelli*, trans. with introduction and notes in 2 vols by Leslie J. Walker (London, 1950).

[7] Felice Alderisio, *Machiavelli : l'Arte dello Stato nell'azione e negli scritti* (Turin, 1930).

[8] As quoted by Prezzolini, op. cit. (p. 25, note 2 above), English version, p. 231.

[9] op. cit. (note 5 above), Italian version, p. 382; English version, p. 235.

[10] Croce ascribes to Machiavelli 'un'austera e dolorosa coscienza morale', *Elementi di politica* (Bari, 1925), p. 62. The idea that Machiavelli actually wishes to denounce naked power politics—what Gerhard Ritter in a volume of that name has called *Die Dämonie der Macht* — goes back to the sixteenth century (see Burd's still unsuperseded edition of *The Prince* (Oxford, 1891), pp. 31 ff.).

unavoidable – a moralist who 'occasionally experiences moral nausea'[1] in contemplating a world in which political ends can be achieved only by means that are morally evil, and thereby the man who divorced the province of politics from that of ethics. But for the Swiss scholars Walder, Kaegi and von Muralt[2] he is a peace-loving humanist, who believed in order, stability, pleasure in life, in the disciplining of the aggressive elements of our nature into the kind of civilised harmony that he found in its finest form among the well-armed Swiss democracies of his own time.[3]

For the neo-stoic Justus Lipsius and a century later for Algarotti (in 1759) and Alfieri[4] (in 1786) he was a passionate patriot, who saw in Cesare Borgia the man who, if he had lived, might have liberated Italy from the barbarous French and Spaniards and Austrians who were trampling over her and had reduced her to misery and poverty, decadence and chaos. Garrett Mattingly[5] could not credit this because it was obvious to him, and he did not doubt that it must have been no less obvious to Machiavelli, that Cesare was incompetent, a mountebank, a squalid failure; while Eric Vögelin seems to suggest that it is not Cesare, but (of all men) Tamerlane who was hovering before Machiavelli's fancy-laden gaze.[6]

For Cassirer,[7] Renaudet,[8] Olschki[9] and Keith Hancock,[10] Machiavelli is a cold technician, ethically and politically uncommitted, an objective analyst of politics, a morally neutral scientist, who (Karl

---

[1] op. cit. (p. 28, note 10 above), p. 66; see Cochrane's comment, op. cit. (p. 25, note 2 above), p. 115, note 9.

[2] For references see Cochrane, ibid., p. 118, note 19.

[3] 'The Swiss are most free [*liberissimi*] because the best armed [*armatissimi*].' *The Prince*, chapter 12.

[4] Vittorio Alfieri, *Del principe e delle lettere*, book 2, chapter 9. *Opere*, vol. 4, ed. Alessandro Donati (Bari, 1927), pp. 172–3.

[5] op. cit. (p. 27, note 3 above).

[6] Eric Vögelin, 'Machiavelli's *Prince*: Background and Formation', *Review of Politics* 13 (1951), 142–68.

[7] Ernst Cassirer, *The Myth of the State* (London and New Haven, Connecticut, 1946), chapter 12.

[8] Augustin Renaudet, *Machiavel: étude d'histoire des doctrines politiques* (Paris, 1942).

[9] Leonardo Olschki, *Machiavelli the Scientist* (Berkeley, California, 1945).

[10] W. K. Hancock, 'Machiavelli in Modern Dress: an Enquiry into Historical Method', *History* 20 (1935–6), 97–115.

Schmid[1] tells us) anticipated Galileo in applying inductive methods to social and historical material, and had no moral interest in the use made of his technical discoveries – equally ready to place them at the disposal of liberators and despots, good men and scoundrels. Renaudet describes his method as 'purely positivist', Cassirer, as concerned with 'political statics'. But for Federico Chabod he is not coldly calculating at all, but passionate to the point of unrealism;[2] Ridolfi, too, speaks of *il grande appassionato*,[3] and De Caprariis[4] thinks him positively visionary.

For Herder he is, above all, a marvellous mirror of his age, a man sensitive to the contours of his time, who faithfully described what others did not admit or recognise, an inexhaustible mine of acute contemporary observation; and this is accepted by Ranke and Macaulay, Burd and, in our day, Gennaro Sasso.[5] For Fichte he is a man of deep insight into the real historical (or super-historical) forces that mould men and transform their morality – in particular, a man who rejected Christian principles for those of reason, political unity and centralisation. For Hegel he is the man of genius who saw the need for uniting a chaotic collection of small and feeble principalities into a coherent whole; his specific nostrums may excite disgust, but they are accidents due to the conditions of their own time, now long past; yet, however obsolete his precepts, he understood something more important – the demands of his own age – that the hour had struck for the birth of the modern, centralised, political state, for the formation of which he 'established the truly necessary fundamental principles'.[6]

[1] Karl Schmid, 'Machiavelli', in Rudolf Stadelmann (ed.), *Grosse Geschichtsdenker* (Tübingen/Stuttgart, 1949); see the illuminating review of Leonard von Muralt, *Machiavellis Staatsgedanke* (Basel, 1945) by A. P. d'Entrèves, *English Historical Review* 62 (1947), 96–9.

[2] In his original article of 1925 ('Del "Principe" di Niccolò Machiavelli', *Nuova rivista storica* 9 (1925), 35–71, 189–216, 437–73; repr. as a book (Milan/Rome/Naples, 1926)) Chabod develops Croce's view in a direction closer to the conclusions of this article. See the English collection of Chabod's essays on Machiavelli, *Machiavelli and the Renaissance*, trans. David Moore, introduction by A. P. d'Entrèves (London, 1958), pp. 30–125 ('*The Prince*: Myth and Reality') and *Scritti su Machiavelli* (Turin, 1964), pp. 29–135.

[3] op. cit. (p. 28, note 5 above), Italian version, p. 364.

[4] For reference see Cochrane, op. cit. (p. 25, note 2 above), p. 120, note 28.

[5] Gennaro Sasso, *Niccolò Machiavelli* (Naples, 1958).

[6] If Machiavelli's *Prince* is viewed in its historical context – of a divided, invaded, humiliated Italy – it emerges not as a disinterested 'summary of moral and political principles, appropriate to all situations and therefore to

The thesis that Machiavelli was above all an Italian and a patriot, speaking above all to his own generation, and if not solely to Florentines, at any rate only to Italians, and must be judged solely, or at least mainly, in terms of his historical context, is a position common to Herder and Hegel, Macaulay and Burd, De Sanctis and Oreste Tommasini.[1] Yet for Herbert Butterfield[2] and Raffaello Ramat[3] he suffers

none', but 'as a most magnificent and true conception on the part of a man of genuine political genius, a man of the greatest and noblest mind' (*Die Verfassung Deutschlands*, in *Schriften zur Politik und Rechtsphilosophie* (*Sämtliche Werke*, ed. Georg Lasson, vol. 7), 2nd ed. (Leipzig, 1923), p. 113). See p. 135 of the same work for Hegel's defence of 'die Gewalt eines Eroberers' conceived as a unifier of German lands. He regarded Machiavelli as a forerunner in an analogous Italian situation.

[1] Especially Tommasini in his huge compendium, *La vita e gli scritti di Niccolò Machiavelli nella loro relazione col Machiavellismo* (vol. 1, Rome/Turin/Florence, 1883; vol. 2, Rome, 1911). In this connection Ernst Cassirer makes the valid and relevant point that to value – or justify – Machiavelli's opinions solely as a mirror of their times is one thing; to maintain that he was himself consciously addressing only his own countrymen and, if Burd is to be believed, not even all of them, is a very different one, and entails a false view of him and the civilisation to which he belonged. The Renaissance did not view itself in historical perspective. Machiavelli was looking for – and thought that he had found – timeless, universal truths about social behaviour. It is no service either to him or to the truth to deny or ignore the unhistorical assumptions which he shared with all his contemporaries and predecessors. The praise lavished upon him by the German historical school from Herder onwards, including the Marxist Antonio Gramsci, for the gifts in which they saw his strength – his realistic sense of his own times, his insight into the rapidly changing social and political conditions of Italy and Europe in his time, the collapse of feudalism, the rise of the national state, the altering power relationships within the Italian principalities and the like – might have been galling to a man who believed he had discovered eternal verities. He may, like his countryman Columbus, have mistaken the nature of his own achievement. If the historical school (including the Marxists) is right, Machiavelli did not do, and could not have done, what he set out to do.

But nothing is gained by supposing he did not set out to do it; and plenty of witnesses from his day to ours would deny Herder's assertion, and maintain that Machiavelli's goal – the discovery of the permanent principles of a political science – was anything but Utopian; and that he came nearer than most to attaining them.

[2] Herbert Butterfield, *The Statecraft of Machiavelli* (London, 1955).

[3] Raffaello Ramat, '*Il Principe*', in *Per la storia dello stile rinascimentale* (Messina/Florence, 1953), pp. 75–118.

from an equal lack of scientific and historical sense. Obsessed by classical authors, his gaze is on an imaginary past; he deduces his political maxims in an unhistorical and *a priori* manner from dogmatic axioms (according to Lauri Huovinen)[1] – a method that was already becoming obsolete at the time in which he was writing; in this respect his slavish imitation of antiquity is judged to be inferior to the historical sense and sagacious judgement of his friend Guicciardini (so much for the discovery in him of inklings of modern scientific method).

For Bacon[2] (as for Spinoza, and later for Lassalle) he is above all the supreme realist and avoider of Utopian fantasies. Boccalini[3] is shocked by him, but cannot deny the accuracy or importance of his observations; so is Meinecke[4] for whom he is the father of *Staatsräson*, with which he plunged a dagger into the body politic of the west, inflicting a wound which only Hegel would know how to heal (this is Meinecke's optimistic verdict half a century ago, apparently withdrawn after the Second World War).

[1] Lauri Huovinen, *Das Bild vom Menschen im politischen Denken Niccolò Machiavellis* (*Annales Academiae Scientiarum Fennicae*, series B, vol. 74 (Helsinki, 1951), No 2).

[2] 'We are much beholden to Machiavelli and other writers of that class, who openly and unfeignedly declare and describe what men do, and not what they ought to do.' Bacon goes on to qualify this by explaining that to know the good one must investigate the evil, and ends by calling such approaches 'corrupt wisdom' (*De augmentis*, book 7, chapter 2, and book 8, chapter 2: quoted from *The Works of Francis Bacon*, ed. Spedding, Ellis and Heath (London, 1857–74), vol. 5, pp. 17 and 76). Compare Machiavelli's aphorism in a letter to Guicciardini, No 179 in the Alvisi edition (Niccolò Machiavelli, *Lettere familiari*, ed. Edoardo Alvisi (Florence, 1883)): 'io credo che questo sarebbe il vero modo ad andare in Paradiso, imparare la via dell'Inferno per fuggirla.' A. P. d'Entrèves has kindly drawn my attention to this characteristic passage; so far as I know there is no reason for supposing that Bacon had any knowledge of it. Nor, it may be, had T. S. Eliot when he wrote 'Lord Morley . . . intimates that Machiavelli . . . saw only half of the truth about human nature. What Machiavelli did not see about human nature is the myth of human goodness which for liberal thought replaces the belief in Divine Grace' ('Niccolò Machiavelli', in *For Lancelot Andrewes* (London, 1970), p. 50).

[3] Traiano Boccalini, *Ragguagli di Parnaso*, centuria prima, No 89.

[4] Friedrich Meinecke, *Die Idee der Staatsräson in der neueren Geschichte*, 2nd ed. (Munich/Berlin, 1927), trans. by Douglas Scott as *Machiavellism* (London, 1957).

But for König[1] he is not a tough-minded realist or cynic at all, but an aesthete seeking to escape from the chaotic and squalid world of the decadent Italy of his time into a dream of pure art, a man not interested in practice who painted an ideal political landscape; much (if I understand this view correctly) as Piero della Francesca painted an ideal city; *The Prince* is to be read as an idyll in the best neoclassical, neopastoral, Renaissance style (yet De Sanctis in the second volume of his *History of Italian Literature* denies it a place in the humanist tradition on account of Machiavelli's hostility to imaginative visions).

For Renzo Sereno[2] it is a fantasy indeed but of a bitterly frustrated man, and its dedication is the 'desperate plea'[3] of a victim of 'Fortune's great and steady malice'.[4] A psychoanalytic interpretation of one queer episode in Machiavelli's life is offered in support of his thesis.

For Macaulay he is a political pragmatist and a patriot who cared most of all for the independence of Florence, and acclaimed any form of rule that would ensure it.[5] Marx calls the *History of Florence* a 'masterpiece', and Engels (in the *Dialectics of Nature*) speaks of Machiavelli as one of the 'giants' of the Enlightenment, a man free from *petit-bourgeois* outlook. Soviet criticism is more ambivalent.[6]

---

[1] René König, *Niccolò Machiavelli : Zur Krisenanalyse einer Zeitenwende* (Zurich, 1941).

[2] Renzo Sereno, 'A Falsification by Machiavelli', *Renaissance News* 12 (1959), 159–67.

[3] ibid., p. 166.

[4] *The Prince*, dedication (trans. by Allan Gilbert in Machiavelli, *The Chief Works and Others*, 3 vols (Durham, North Carolina, 1965), vol. 1, p. 11: all quotations in this essay from Machiavelli's writings are given in this version, unless otherwise stated).

[5] For an extended modern development of this, see Judith Janoska-Bendl, 'Niccolò Machiavelli: Politik ohne Ideologie', *Archiv für Kulturgeschichte* 40 (1958), 315–45.

[6] The only extended treatment of Machiavelli by a prominent Bolshevik intellectual known to me is in Kamenev's short-lived introduction to the Russian translation of *The Prince* (Moscow, 1934), reprinted in English as 'Preface to Machiavelli', *New Left Review* No 15 (May–June 1962), 39–42. This unswervingly follows the full historicist-sociological approach criticised by Cassirer. Machiavelli is described as an active publicist, preoccupied by the 'mechanism of the struggles for power' within and between the Italian principalities, a sociologist who gave a masterly analysis of the 'sociological' jungle that preceded the formation of a 'powerful, national, essentially bourgeois'

For the restorers of the short-lived Florentine republic he was evidently nothing but a venal and treacherous toady, anxious to serve any master, who had unsuccessfully tried to flatter the Medici in the hope of gaining their favour. George Sabine (in his well-known text-book)[1] views him as an anti-metaphysical empiricist, a Hume or Popper before his time, free from obscurantist, theological and metaphysical preconceptions. For Antonio Gramsci[2] he is above all a revolutionary innovator who directs his shafts against the obsolescent feudal aristocracy and papacy and their mercenaries: his *Prince* is a myth which signifies the dictatorship of new, progressive forces: ultimately the coming role of the masses and of the need for the emergence of new politically realistic leaders – *The Prince* is 'an anthropomorphic symbol' of the hegemony of the 'collective will'.

Like Jakob Burckhardt[3] and Friedrich Meinecke,[4] C. J. Friedrich[5] and Charles Singleton[6] maintain that he has a developed conception of the state as a work of art; the great men who have founded or maintain human associations are conceived as analogous to artists whose aim is beauty, and whose essential qualification is understanding of their material – they are moulders of men, as sculptors are moulders of marble or clay.[7] Politics, in this view, leaves the realm of ethics,

---

Italian state. His almost 'dialectical' grasp of the realities of power, and freedom from metaphysical and theological fantasies, establish him as a worthy forerunner of Marx, Engels, Lenin and Stalin. These opinions were brought up at Kamenev's trial and pilloried by Vyshinsky, the prosecutor. See on this Chimen Abramsky, 'Kamenev's Last Essay', *New Left Review* No 15 (May–June 1962), 34–38; and, on the peculiar fate of Machiavelli in Russia, Jan Malarczyk, *Politicheskoe uchenia Makiavelli v Rossii, v russkoi dorevolyutsionnoi i sovetskoi istoriografii (Annales Universitatis Mariae Curie-Sklodkowska*, vol. 6, No 1, section G, 1959 (Lublin, 1960)).

[1] George H. Sabine, *A History of Political Theory* (London, 1951).
[2] Antonio Gramsci, *Note sul Machiavelli*, in *Opere*, vol. 5 (Turin, 1949).
[3] Jakob Burckhardt, *The Civilization of the Renaissance in Italy*, trans. S. G. C. Middlemore (London, 1929), part 1, chapter 7, pp. 104 ff.
[4] op. cit. (p. 32, note 4 above).
[5] C. J. Friedrich, *Constitutional Reason of State* (Providence, Rhode Island, 1957).
[6] Charles S. Singleton, 'The Perspective of Art', *Kenyon Review* 15 (1953), 169–89.
[7] See Joseph Kraft, 'Truth and Poetry in Machiavelli', *Journal of Modern History* 23 (1951), 109–21.

and approaches that of aesthetics. Singleton argues that Machiavelli's originality consists in his view of political action as a form of what Aristotle called 'making' – the goal of which is a non-moral artefact, an object of beauty or use external to man (in this case a particular arrangement of human affairs) – and not of 'doing' (where Aristotle and Aquinas had placed it), the goal of which is internal and moral – not the creation of an object, but a particular kind – the right way – of living or being.

This position is not distant from that of Villari, Croce and others, inasmuch as it ascribes to Machiavelli the divorce of politics from ethics. Singleton transfers Machiavelli's conception of politics to the region of art, which is conceived as being amoral. Croce gives it an independent status of its own : of politics for politics' sake.

But the commonest view of him, at least as a political thinker, is still that of most Elizabethans, dramatists and scholars alike, for whom he is a man inspired by the Devil to lead good men to their doom, the great subverter, the teacher of evil, *le docteur de la scélératesse*, the inspirer of St Bartholomew's Eve, the original of Iago. This is the 'murderous Machiavel' of the famous four-hundred-odd references in Elizabethan literature.[1] His name adds a new ingredient to the more ancient figure of Old Nick. For the Jesuits he is 'the devil's partner in crime', 'a dishonourable writer and an unbeliever', and *The Prince* is, in Bertrand Russell's words, 'a handbook for gangsters' (compare with this Mussolini's description of it as a *'vade mecum* for statesmen', a view tacitly shared, perhaps, by other heads of state). This is the view common to Protestants and Catholics, Gentillet and François Hotman, Cardinal Pole, Bodin and Frederick the Great, followed by the

[1] Edward Meyer, *Machiavelli and the Elizabethan Drama* (Litterarhistorische Forschungen I: Weimar, 1897). See on this Christopher Morris, 'Machiavelli's Reputation in Tudor England', *Il pensiero politico* 2 (1969), 416–33, especially p. 423. See also Mario Praz, 'Machiavelli and the Elizabethans', *Proceedings of the British Academy* 13 (1928), 49–97; Napoleone Orsini, 'Elizabethan Manuscript Translations of Machiavelli's *Prince*', *Journal of the Warburg Institute* 1 (1937–8), 166–9; Felix Raab, *The English Face of Machiavelli* (London, 1964; Toronto, 1965); J. G. A. Pocock, 'Machiavelli, Harrington and English Political Ideologies in the Eighteenth Century', in *Politics, Language and Time* (London, 1972), pp. 104–47; and, most famous of all, Wyndham Lewis, *The Lion and the Fox* (London, 1951). Zera S. Fink in *The Classical Republicans* (Evanston, 1945), J. G. A. Pocock and Felix Raab stress his positive influence in seventeenth-century England, with Bacon and Harrington at the head of his admirers.

authors of all the many anti-Machiavels, among the latest of whom are Jacques Maritain[1] and Leo Strauss.[2]

There is prima facie something strange about so violent a disparity of judgements.[3] What other thinker has presented so many facets to the students of his ideas? What other writer – and he not even a recognised philosopher – has caused his readers to disagree about his purposes so deeply and so widely? Yet, I must repeat, Machiavelli does not write obscurely; nearly all his interpreters praise him for his terse, dry, clear prose.

What is it that has proved so arresting to so many? Let me deal with some obvious answers. It is no doubt astonishing to find a thinker so free from what we have been taught to regard as being the normal intellectual assumptions of his age. Machiavelli does not so much as mention natural law, the basic category in terms of which (or rather the many varieties of which) Christians and pagans, teleologists and materialists, jurists, theologians and philosophers, before and indeed for many decades after him, discussed the very topics to which he applied his mind. He was of course not a philosopher or a jurist: nevertheless, he was a political expert, a well-read man of letters. The influence of the old Stoic-Christian doctrine was not, by his time, what it had once been in Italy, especially among the early humanists. Still, having set himself to generalise about the behaviour of men in society in a novel fashion, Machiavelli might have been expected, if not to refute or reject explicitly, at least to deliver a glancing blow at some of the assumptions which, he clearly thinks, have led so many to their doom. He does, after all, tell us that his path has never before been trodden by any man, and this, in his case, is no mere cliché: there is, therefore, something extraordinary in the fact that he completely

[1] Jacques Maritain, 'The End of Machiavellianism', *Review of Politics* 4 (1942), 1–33.

[2] Leo Strauss, *Thoughts on Machiavelli* (Glencoe, Illinois, 1958).

[3] One of the best and liveliest accounts of the mass of conflicting theories about *The Prince* is provided by E. W. Cochrane in the article cited above on p. 25, note 2, to which this catalogue owes a great deal. For earlier conflicts see Pasquale Villari's standard and in some ways still unsuperseded *The Life and Times of Niccolò Machiavelli*, trans. Linda Villari (London, 1898), and the earlier works cited by him, e.g. Robert von Mohl, 'Die Machiavelli-Literatur', in *Die Geschichte und Literatur der Staatswissenschaften* (Erlangen, 1855–8), vol. 3, pp. 519–91, and J. F. Christius, *De Nicolao Machiavelli libri tres* (Leipzig, 1731). For later works see above, p. 25, note 2.

ignores the concepts and categories – the routine paraphernalia – in terms of which the best-known thinkers and scholars of his day were accustomed to express themselves. And, indeed, Gentillet in his *Contre-Machiavel* denounces him precisely for this. Only Marsilio before him had dared do this : and Neville Figgis thinks it a dramatic break with the past.[1]

The absence of Christian psychology and theology – sin, grace, redemption, salvation – need cause less surprise : few contemporary humanists speak in such terms. The medieval heritage has grown very thin. But, and this is more noteworthy, there is no trace of Platonic or Aristotelian teleology, no reference to any ideal order, to any doctrine of man's place in nature in the great chain of being, with which the Renaissance thinkers are deeply concerned – which, say, Ficino or Pico or Poggio virtually take for granted. There is nothing here of what Popper has called 'essentialism', *a priori* certainty directly revealed to reason or intuition about the unalterable development of men or social groups in certain directions, in pursuit of goals implanted in them by God or by nature. The method and the tone are empirical. Even Machiavelli's theory of historical cycles is not metaphysically guaranteed.

As for religion, it is for him not much more than a socially indispensable instrument, so much utilitarian cement : the criterion of the worth of a religion is its role as a promoter of solidarity and cohesion – he anticipates Saint-Simon and Durkheim in stressing its crucial social importance. The great founders of religions are among the men he most greatly admires. Some varieties of religion (e.g. Roman paganism) are good for societies, since they make them strong or spirited ; others on the contrary (e.g. Christian meekness and unworldliness) cause decay or disintegration. The weakening of religious ties is a part of general decadence and corruption : there is no need for a religion to rest on truth, provided that it is socially effective.[2] Hence his veneration of those who set their societies on sound spiritual foundations – Moses, Numa, Lycurgus.

There is no serious assumption of the existence of God and divine law ; whatever our author's private convictions, an atheist can read Machiavelli with perfect intellectual comfort. Nor is there piety towards authority, or prescription – nor any interest in the role of the

[1] John Neville Figgis, *Studies of Political Thought from Gerson to Grotius*, 2nd ed. (Cambridge, 1916).

[2] *Discourses* I 12.

individual conscience, or in any other metaphysical or theological issue. The only freedom he recognises is political freedom, freedom from arbitrary despotic rule, i.e. republicanism, and the freedom of one state from control by other states, or rather of the city or *patria*, for 'state' may be a premature term in this connection.[1]

There is no notion of the rights of, or obligation to, corporations or non-political establishments, sacred or secular – the need for absolute centralised power (if not for sovereignty) is taken for granted. There is scarcely any historical sense: men are much the same everywhere, and at all times, and what has served well for the ancients – their rules of medicine, or warfare, or statecraft – will surely also work for the moderns. Tradition is valued chiefly as a source of social stability. Since there is no far-off divine event to which creation moves and no Platonic ideal for societies or individuals, there is no notion of progress, either material or spiritual. The assumption is that the blessings of the classical age can be restored (if fortune is not too unpropitious) by enough knowledge and will, by *virtù* on the part of a leader, and by appropriately trained and bravely and skilfully led citizens. There are no intimations of an irrevocably determined flow of events; neither *fortuna* nor *necessità* dominates the whole of existence; there are no absolute values which men ignore or deny to their inevitable doom.

It is, no doubt, this freedom from even such relics of the traditional metaphysics of history as linger on in the works of even such perfectly secular humanists as Egidio and Pontano, not to mention earlier authors of 'mirrors for princes', as well as Machiavelli's constant concern with the concrete and practical issues of his day, and not any mysterious presentiment of the coming scientific revolution, that gives him so modern a flavour. Yet it is plainly not these characteristics that have proved so deeply fascinating and horrifying to his readers

---

[1] See on this much-discussed issue the relevant theses of J. H. Whitfield in *Machiavelli* (Oxford, 1947), especially pp. 93–5, and J. H. Hexter in '*Il principe* and *lo stato*', *Studies in the Renaissance* 4 (1957), 113–35, and the opposed views of Fredi Chiapelli in *Studi sul linguaggio del Machiavelli* (Florence, 1952), pp. 59–73, Francesco Ercole in *La politica di Machiavelli* (Rome, 1926) and Felix Gilbert, op. cit. (p. 25, note 2 above), pp. 328–30. For an earlier version of Gilbert's anti-Ercole thesis see his 'The Concept of Nationalism in Machiavelli's *Prince*', *Studies in the Renaissance* 1 (1954), 38–48. H. C. Dowdall goes further and seems to maintain that it is, in effect, by inventing the word 'state' that Machiavelli founded modern political science ('The Word "State"', *Law Quarterly Review* 39 (1923), 98–125).

from his day to our own. 'Machiavelli's doctrine', wrote Meinecke, 'was a sword thrust in the body politic of Western humanity, causing it to cry out and to struggle against itself.'[1]

What was it that was so upsetting in the views of Machiavelli? What was the 'dagger' and the 'unhealed wound' of which Meinecke speaks, 'the most violent mutilation suffered by the human practical intellect'[2] which Maritain so eloquently denounced? If it is not Machiavelli's (ruthless, but scarcely original) realism, nor his (relatively original, but by the eighteenth century pretty widespread) empiricism that proves so shocking during all these centuries, what was it?

'*Nothing*,' says one of his commentators:[3] *The Prince* is a mere tabulation of types of government and rulers, and of methods of maintaining them. It is this and no more. All the 'feeling and controversy' occasioned by it evidently rest on an almost universal misreading of an exceptionally clear, morally neutral text.

I cite this not uncommon view for fairness's sake. My own answer to the question will be clearer if before offering it I state (in however brief and over-simplified a form) what I believe Machiavelli's positive beliefs to have been.

II

Like the Roman writers whose ideals were constantly before his mind, like Cicero and Livy, Machiavelli believed that what men — at any rate superior men — sought was the fulfilment and the glory that come from the creation and maintenance by common endeavour of a strong and well-governed social whole. Only those will accomplish this who know the relevant facts. If you make mistakes and live in a state of delusion, you will fail in whatever you undertake, for reality misunderstood — or worse still, ignored or scorned — will always defeat you in the end. We can achieve what we want only if we understand firstly ourselves, and then the nature of the material with which we work.

Our first task, therefore, is the acquisition of such knowledge. This, for Machiavelli, was mainly psychological and sociological: the best

[1] op. cit. (p. 32, note 4 above), p. 61 (English version, p. 49).
[2] op. cit. (p. 36, note 1 above), p. 3.
[3] Jeffrey Pulver, *Machiavelli: The Man, His Work, and His Times* (London, 1937), p. 227.

source of information is a mixture of shrewd observation of contemporary reality together with whatever wisdom may be gleaned from the best observers of the past, in particular the great minds of antiquity, the sages whose company (as he says in his celebrated letter to Vettori) he seeks when he gets away from the trivial occupations of his daily life; these noble spirits, in their humanity, treat him kindly and yield answers to his questions; it is they who have taught him that men are in need of firm and energetic civil government. Different men pursue different ends, and for each pursuit need an appropriate skill. Sculptors, doctors, soldiers, architects, statesmen, lovers, adventurers each pursue their own particular goals. To make it possible for them to do so, governments are needed, for there is no hidden hand which brings all these human activities into natural harmony. (This kind of approach is wholly typical of the humanism of Machiavelli's country and his time.) Men need rulers because they require someone to order human groups governed by diverse interests and bring them security, stability, above all protection against enemies, to establish social institutions which alone enable men to satisfy their needs and aspirations. They will never attain to this unless they are individually and socially healthy; only an adequate education can make them physically and mentally sturdy, vigorous, ambitious and energetic enough for effective cooperation in the pursuit of order, power, glory, success.

Techniques of government exist – of that he has no doubt – although the facts, and therefore the methods of dealing with them, may look different to a ruler and to his subjects: this is a matter of perspective: 'those who draw maps of countries put themselves low down on the plains to observe the nature of mountains ... and to observe that of low places put themselves high up on mountain tops'.[1] What is certain is that unless there is a firm hand at the helm, the ship of state will founder. Human society will collapse into chaos and squalor unless a competent specialist directs it; and although Machiavelli himself gives reasons for preferring freedom and republican rule, there are situations in which a strong prince (the Duke of Valentino, even a Medici, if his plea had any sincerity to it) is preferable to a weak republic.

All this Aristotle and the later Stoics would have endorsed. But from the fact that there is such a thing as an art of government, indispensable to the attainment of goals that men in fact seek, it does not follow that Machiavelli did not care to what uses it was applied, and merely produced a handbook of scientific political 'directives' that was

[1] *The Prince*, dedication.

40

morally neutral, *wertfrei*. For he makes it all too plain what it is that he himself desires.

Men must be studied in their behaviour as well as in their professions. There is no *a priori* route to the knowledge of the human material with which a ruler must deal. There is, no doubt, an unchanging human nature the range of whose response to changing situations can be determined (there is no trace in Machiavelli's thought of any notion of systematic evolution or of the individual or society as a self-transforming entity); one can obtain this knowledge only by empirical observation. Men are not as they are described by those who idealise them – Christians or other Utopians – nor by those who want them to be widely different from what in fact they are and always have been and cannot help being. Men (at least his own countrymen for and about whom he was writing) seem to him for the most part to be 'ungrateful, wanton, false and dissimulating, cowardly and greedy . . . arrogant and mean, their natural impulse is to be insolent when their affairs are prospering and abjectly servile when adversity hits them.'[1] They care little for liberty – the name means more to them than the reality – and they place it well below security, property or desire for revenge. These last the ruler can provide to a reasonable degree. Men are easily corrupted, and difficult to cure. They respond both to fear and to love, to the cruel Hannibal and to the just and humane Scipio. If these emotions cannot be combined, fear is the more reliable : provided always that it does not turn to hate, which destroys the minimum of respect that subjects must retain for those who govern them.

Society is, normally, a battlefield in which there are conflicts between and within groups. These conflicts can be controlled only by the judicious use of both persuasion and force. How is this done? As in medicine, architecture or the art of war, we can obtain systematic knowledge of the required technique if only we will look at the practice (and the theory) of the most successful societies we know, namely those of classical times.

Machiavelli's theories are certainly not based on the scientific principles of the seventeenth century. He lived a hundred years before Galileo and Bacon, and his method is a mixture of rules of thumb, observation, historical knowledge and general sagacity, somewhat like

---

[1] This celebrated passage from the seventeenth chapter of *The Prince* is here given in Prezzolini's vivid rendering: see his 'The Christian Roots of Machiavelli's Moral Pessimism', *Review of National Literatures* 1 (1970), 26–37 : 27.

the empirical medicine of the pre-scientific world. He abounds in precepts, in useful maxims, practical hints, scattered reflections, especially historical parallels, even though he claims to have discovered general laws, eternally valid *regole generali*. An example of a triumph or a failure in the ancient world, a striking saying by an ancient author, carries more weight with him (as Butterfield and Ramat correctly note) than historical analysis of the type that was becoming common even in his own day, and of which Guicciardini was a master.

Above all he warns one to be on one's guard against those who do not look at men as they are, and see them through spectacles coloured by their hopes and wishes, their loves and hatreds, in terms of an idealised model of man as they want him to be, and not as he is and was and will be. Honest reformers, however worthy their ideals, like the worthy leader of the Florentine republic, Piero Soderini, whom Machiavelli served, or the far more gifted Savonarola (towards whom his attitude oscillates sharply), foundered and caused the ruin of others, largely because they substituted what should be for what is; because at some point they fell into unrealism.

They were men of very different quality. Savonarola had a strong will, whereas Soderini was, in Machiavelli's view, small-minded and indecisive. But what they had in common was an inadequate grasp of how to use power. At the crucial moment they both showed their lack of a sense of *verità effettuale* in politics, of what works in practice, of real power, of the big battalions. Machiavelli's texts contain frequent warnings against unreliable sources of information, émigrés for example, whose minds are distorted by their wishes and cannot attain to an objective view of the facts, and others whose reason (this is a humanist commonplace) is darkened by the passions that distort their vision.

What has led and will lead such statesmen to their doom? Often enough only their ideals. What is wrong with ideals? That they cannot be attained. How does one know this? This is one of the foundations upon which Machiavelli's claim to be a thinker of the first order ultimately rests. Machiavelli has a clear vision of the society which he wishes to see realised on earth, or if this sounds too grandiose for so concrete and applied a thinker, the society which he wishes to see attained in his own country, perhaps even in his own lifetime; at any rate within the predictable future. He knows that such an order can be created, because it, or something sufficiently close to it, has been realised in Italy in the past, or in other countries – the Swiss or German cities for example, or the great centralised states in his own time. It is not merely that he wishes to create or restore such an order in Italy, but that he sees in it the most desirable condition that can, as both history and observation teach, be attained by men.

The data of observation are drawn mainly from contemporary Italy; as for history, it is for him what had been recorded by the great historians, the writers whom he most admires, Romans, Greeks, the authors of the Old Testament. Where have men risen to their full height? In Periclean Athens, and in the greatest period of human history – the Roman Republic before its decline, when Rome ruled the world. But he thinks well, too, of the reigns of the 'good' emperors, from Nerva to Marcus Aurelius. He does not feel that he needs to demonstrate that these were golden hours in the life of humanity; this, he believes, must be self-evident to anyone who contemplates these epochs and compares them with the bad periods – the last years of the Roman Republic, the collapse that followed, the barbarian invasion, the medieval darkness (although he may not have thought of it in these terms), the divisions of Italy, the weakness, the poverty, the misery, the defencelessness of the faction-ridden Italian principalities of his own day before the trampling armies of the great, well organised national states of the north and the west.

He does not trouble to argue this at length: it seems to him perfectly obvious (as it must have done to most men of his age) that Italy was both materially and morally in a bad way. He did not need to explain what he meant by vice, corruption, weakness, lives unworthy of human beings. A good society is a society that enjoys stability, internal harmony, security, justice, a sense of power and of splendour, like Athens in its best days, like Sparta, like the kingdoms of David and Solomon, like Venice as it used to be, but, above all, like the Roman Republic. 'Truly it is a marvellous thing to consider to what greatness Athens came in the space of a hundred years after she freed herself from the tyranny of Pisistratus. But above all, it is very marvellous to observe what greatness Rome came to after she freed herself from her kings.'[1]

The reason for this is that there were men in these societies who knew how to make cities great. How did they do it? By developing certain faculties in men, of inner moral strength, magnanimity, vigour, vitality, generosity, loyalty, above all public spirit, civic sense,

[1] *Discourses* II 2.

dedication to the security, power, glory, expansion of the *patria*. The ancients developed these qualities by all kinds of means, among which were dazzling shows and bloodstained sacrifices that excited men's senses and aroused their martial prowess, and especially by the kind of legislation and education that promoted the pagan virtues. Power, magnificence, pride, austerity, pursuit of glory, vigour, discipline, *antiqua virtus* – this is what makes states great. Agesilaus and Timoleon, Brutus and Scipio, are his heroes; not Pisistratus or Julius Caesar who extinguished republican regimes and destroyed their spirit by exploiting human weaknesses. But there is no need to stay within Graeco-Roman confines; Moses and Cyrus are as deserving of respect as Theseus and Romulus – stern, sagacious and incorruptible men who founded nations and were rightly honoured by them.

What was done once can be done again. Machiavelli does not believe in the irreversibility of the historical process or the uniqueness of each of its phases. The glories of antiquity can be revived if only men vigorous and gifted and realistic enough can be mobilised for the purpose. In order to cure degenerate populations of their diseases, these founders of new states or churches may be compelled to have recourse to ruthless measures, force and fraud, guile, cruelty, treachery, the slaughter of the innocent, surgical measures that are needed to restore a decayed body to a condition of health. And, indeed, these qualities may be needed even after a society has been restored to health ; for men are weak and foolish and perpetually liable to lapse from the standards that alone can preserve them on the required height. Hence they must be kept in proper condition by measures that will certainly offend against current morality. But if they offend against this morality, in what sense can they be said to be justified? This seems to me to be the nodal point of Machiavelli's entire conception. In one sense they can be justified, and in another not ; these senses must be distinguished more clearly than he found it necessary to do, for he was not a philosopher, and did not set himself to the task of examining, or even spelling out, the implications of his own ideas.

Let me try to make this clearer. It is commonly said, especially by those who follow Croce, that Machiavelli divided politics from morals – that he recommended as politically necessary courses which common opinion morally condemns : e.g. treading over corpses for the benefit of the state. Leaving aside the question of what was his conception of the state, and whether he in fact possessed one,[1] it seems to

1 See p. 38, note 1 above.

me that this is a false antithesis. For Machiavelli the ends which he advocates are those to which he thinks wise human beings, who understand reality, will dedicate their lives. Ultimate ends in this sense, whether or not they are those of the Judaeo-Christian tradition, are what is usually meant by moral values.

What Machiavelli distinguishes is not specifically moral from specifically political values;[1] what he achieves is not the emancipation of politics from ethics or religion, which Croce and many other commentators regard as his crowning achievement; what he institutes is something that cuts deeper still – a differentiation between two incompatible ideals of life, and therefore two moralities. One is the morality of the pagan world: its values are courage, vigour, fortitude in adversity, public achievement, order, discipline, happiness, strength, justice, above all assertion of one's proper claims and the knowledge and power needed to secure their satisfaction; that which for a Renaissance reader Pericles had seen embodied in his ideal Athens, Livy had found in the old Roman Republic, that of which Tacitus and Juvenal lamented the decay and death in their own time. These seem to Machiavelli the best hours of mankind and, Renaissance humanist that he is, he wishes to restore them.

Against this moral universe (moral or ethical no less in Croce's than in the traditional sense, that is, embodying ultimate human ends however these are conceived) stands in the first and foremost place, Christian morality. The ideals of Christianity are charity, mercy, sacrifice, love of God, forgiveness of enemies, contempt for the goods of this world, faith in the life hereafter, belief in the salvation of the individual soul as being of incomparable value – higher than, indeed wholly incommensurable with, any social or political or other terrestrial goal, any economic or military or aesthetic consideration. Machiavelli lays it down that out of men who believe in such ideals, and practise them, no satisfactory human community, in his Roman sense, can in principle be constructed. It is not simply a question of the unattainability of an ideal because of human imperfection, original sin, or bad luck, or ignorance, or insufficiency of material means. It is not, in other words, the inability in practice on the part of ordinary human

---

[1] For which he is commended by De Sanctis, and (as Prezzolini points out, op. cit., p. 25, note 2 above) condemned by Maurice Joly in the famous *Dialogue aux enfers entre Machiavel et Montesquieu* (Brussells, 1864), which served as the original of the forged *Protocols of the Learned Elders of Zion* (London, 1920).

beings to rise to a sufficiently high level of Christian virtue (which may, indeed, be the inescapable lot of sinful men on earth) that makes it, for him, impracticable to establish, even to seek after, the good Christian state. It is the very opposite: Machiavelli is convinced that what are commonly thought of as the central Christian virtues, whatever their intrinsic value, are insuperable obstacles to the building of the kind of society that he wishes to see; a society which, moreover, he assumes that it is natural for all normal men to want – the kind of community that, in his view, satisfies men's permanent desires and interests.

If human beings were different from what they are, perhaps they could create an ideal Christian society. But he is clear that human beings would in that event have to differ too greatly from men as they have always been; and it is surely idle to build for, or discuss the prospects of, beings who can never be on earth; such talk is beside the point, and only breeds dreams and fatal delusions. What ought to be done must be defined in terms of what is practicable, not imaginary; statecraft is concerned with action within the limits of human possibility, however wide; men can be changed, but not to a fantastic degree. To advocate ideal measures, suitable only for angels, as previous political writers seem to him too often to have done, is visionary and irresponsible and leads to ruin.

It is important to realise that Machiavelli does not wish to deny that what Christians call good is, in fact, good, that what they call virtue and vice are in fact virtue and vice. Unlike Hobbes or Spinoza (or eighteenth-century *philosophes* or, for that matter, the first Stoics), who try to define (or redefine) moral notions in such a way as to fit in with the kind of community that, in their view, rational men must, if they are consistent, wish to build, Machiavelli does not fly in the face of common notions – the traditional, accepted moral vocabulary of mankind. He does not say or imply (as various radical philosophical reformers have done) that humility, kindness, unworldliness, faith in God, sanctity, Christian love, unwavering truthfulness, compassion, are bad or unimportant attributes; or that cruelty, bad faith, power politics, sacrifice of innocent men to social needs, and so on, are good ones.

But if history, and the insights of wise statesmen, especially in the ancient world, verified as they have been in practice (*verità effettuale*), are to guide us, it will be seen that it is in fact impossible to combine Christian virtues, for example meekness or the search for spiritual salvation, with a satisfactory, stable, vigorous, strong society on earth. Consequently a man must choose. To choose to lead a Christian life is to condemn oneself to political impotence: to being used and crushed by powerful, ambitious, clever, unscrupulous men; if one wishes to build a glorious community like those of Athens or Rome at their best, then one must abandon Christian education and substitute one better suited to the purpose.

Machiavelli is not a philosopher and does not deal in abstractions, but what his thesis comes to is of central concern to political theory: that a fact which men will not face is that these two goals, both, evidently, capable of being believed in by human beings (and, we may add, of raising them to sublime heights), are not compatible with one another. What usually happens, in his view, is that since men cannot bring themselves resolutely to follow either of these paths wherever they may lead ('men take certain middle ways that are very injurious; indeed, they are unable to be altogether good or altogether bad'),[1] they try to effect compromises, vacillate, fall between two stools, and end in weakness and failure.

Anything that leads to political ineffectiveness is condemned by him. In a famous passage in the *Discourses* he says that Christian faith has made men 'weak', easy prey to 'wicked men', since they 'think more about enduring their injuries than about avenging them'.[2] The general effect of Christian teaching has been to crush men's civic spirit, and make them endure humiliations uncomplainingly, so that destroyers and despots encounter too little resistance. Hence Christianity is in this respect compared unfavourably with Roman religion, which made men stronger and more 'ferocious'.

Machiavelli modifies this judgement on Christianity in at least two passages in the *Discourses*. In the first he observes that Christianity has had this unfortunate effect only because it was misinterpreted in a spirit of *ozio* – quietism or indolence – for there is surely nothing in Christianity which forbids 'the betterment and the defence of our country'.[3] In the second passage he declares that 'If religion of this sort had been kept up among the princes of Christendom, in the form in which its giver founded it, Christian states and republics would be more united, much more happy than they are',[4] but the decadent Christianity of the church of Rome has had the opposite effect – the

[1] *Discourses* I 26.
[2] ibid. II 2.
[3] ibid.
[4] ibid. I 12.

papacy has destroyed 'all piety and all religion' in Italy, and her unity too.

Even if these passages are taken literally, and are not viewed as pieces of minimum lip-service to avert clerical censorship or persecution, what they assert is that if the church had developed a patriotic and thoroughly militant outlook, on the lines of Roman *antiqua virtus*, and had made men virile, stern, devout and public-spirited, it would have produced more satisfactory social consequences. What it has done is to lead, on the one hand, to corruption and political division – the fault of the papacy – and on the other, to other-worldliness and meek endurance of suffering on earth for the sake of the eternal life beyond the grave. It is this last strain that dissolves the social fabric and helps bullies and oppressors.

In his political attack on the church of Rome, shared by Guicciardini and others in his time, Machiavelli might have found enthusiastic allies in the Reformation (there is no evidence, so far as I know, that news of the 'monks' quarrel' had ever reached his ears). His demand for a Christianity which did not put the blessings of a pure conscience and faith in heaven above earthly success, and exalted love of glory and self-assertion above meekness and resignation, might have been more difficult to meet. Machiavelli finds nothing to criticise in pagan Roman religion at its most vigorous; he demands a similar religion – not necessarily wholly unchristian, but muscular enough to be, for practical purposes, not less effective. It does not seem unreasonable to conclude from this (as Fichte[1] and Prezzolini[2] tell us) that he is an implacable critic of truly Christian institutions, rather than their champion. In this he is followed by all those later thinkers who share with him either his conception of man and his natural needs (eighteenth-century materialists, Nietzsche, social Darwinists) or (like Rousseau and some nineteenth-century positivists) his civic ideals.

It is important to note that Machiavelli does not formally condemn Christian morality, or the approved values of his own society. Unlike systematic moralists like Hobbes or Spinoza he does not attempt to redefine terms to conform with an egoistic rationalism, so that such Christian virtues as, say, pity, humility, self-sacrifice, obedience are shown to be weaknesses or vices. He transposes nothing: the things men call good are indeed good. Words like *buono, cattivo, onesto, inu-*

[1] *Fichte's Werke*, ed. Immanuel Hermann Fichte (Berlin, 1971), vol. 11, pp. 411–13.
[2] op. cit. (p. 25, note 2 above), English version, p. 43.

mano etc. are used by him as they were in the common speech of his time, and indeed of our own. He merely says that the practice of these virtues makes it impossible to build a society which, once it is contemplated, in the pages of history or by the political imagination, will surely awaken in us – in any man – a great longing.

One of the crucial passages is to be found in the tenth chapter of the first book of the *Discourses* : he is distinguishing between the good and the bad Roman emperors on the lines of Tacitus or Dio, and adds 'if a prince is of human birth, he will be frightened away from any imitation of wicked times and will be fired with an immense eagerness [*immenso desiderio*] to follow the ways of good ones' – 'good' in some non-Christian sense, evidently. Whitfield thinks that he is not pessimistic or cynical. Perhaps not cynical – that is a fine point: the line between cynicism (and indeed pessimism too) and an unflinching realism is at times not easy to draw. But Machiavelli is not, in the usual sense of the word, hopeful. Yet like every humanist thinker from his own day to ours, he believes that if only the truth were known – the real truth, not the fairy tales of shallow moralists – it would help to make men understand themselves and make them go farther.

He believes also that the qualities that men need in order to revive these *buoni tempi* are not compatible with those that are urged upon them by Christian education. He does not seek to correct the Christian conception of a good man. He does not say that saints are not saints, or that honourable behaviour is not honourable or to be admired ; only that this type of goodness cannot, at least in its traditionally accepted forms, create or maintain a strong, secure and vigorous society, that it is in fact fatal to it. He points out that in our world men who pursue such ideals are bound to be defeated and to lead other people to ruin, since their view of the world is not founded upon the truth, at least not upon *verità effettuale* – the truth that is tested by success and experience – which (however cruel) is always, in the end, less destructive than the other (however noble).

If the two passages mentioned above[1] are to be taken literally, Christianity, at least in theory, could have taken a form not incompatible with the qualities that he celebrates ; but, not surprisingly, he does not pursue this line of thought. History took another turn. The idea of such a Christian commonwealth – if he gave it a serious thought – must have seemed to him as Utopian as a world in which all

[1] See p. 47, notes 3 and 4 above.

or even most men are good. Christian principles have weakened men's civic virtues. Speculation on the form that Christianity might have taken, or could, in unlikely circumstances, still take, can for him only be an idle (and dangerous) pastime.

Christians as he knew them in history and his own experience, that is, men who in their practice actually follow Christian precepts, are good men, but if they govern states in the light of such principles, they lead them to destruction. Like Prince Myshkin in Dostoevsky's *The Idiot*, like the well-meaning *Gonfalonieri* of the Florentine Republic, like Savonarola, they are bound to be defeated by the realists (the Medici or the Pope or King Ferdinand of Spain) who understand how to create lasting institutions; build them, if need be, on the bones of innocent victims. I should like to emphasise again that he does not explicitly condemn Christian morality: he merely points out that it is, at least in rulers (but to some degree in subjects too), incompatible with those social ends which he thinks it natural and wise for men to seek. One can save one's soul, or one can found or maintain or serve a great and glorious state; but not always both at once.

This is a vast and eloquent development of Aristotle's *obiter dictum* in the *Politics* that a good man may not be identical with a good citizen (even though Aristotle was not thinking in terms of spiritual salvation). Machiavelli does not explicitly rate either way of life above the other. When he says 'hate is incurred as much by means of good deeds as of bad',[1] he means by 'good deeds' what any man brought up to live by Christian values means. Again, when he says that good faith, integrity are 'praiseworthy'[2] even if they end in failure, he means by 'praiseworthy' that it is right to praise them, for of course what is good (in the ordinary sense) *is* good. When he praises the 'chastity, affability, courtesy, and liberality'[3] of Scipio or Cyrus or Timoleon, or even the 'goodness' of the Medici Pope Leo X, he speaks (whether he is sincere or not) in terms of values that are common to Cicero and Dante, to Erasmus and to us. In the famous fifteenth chapter of *The Prince* he says that liberality, mercy, honour, humanity, frankness, chastity, religion, and so forth, are indeed virtues, and a life lived in the exercise of these virtues would be successful if men were all good. But they are not; and it is idle to hope that they will become so. We must take men as we find them, and seek to improve them along possible, not impossible, lines.

[1] *The Prince*, chapter 19.   [2] ibid., chapter 18.
[3] ibid., chapter 14.

This may involve the benefactors of men – the founders, educators, legislators, rulers – in terrible cruelties. 'I am aware that everyone will admit that it would be most praiseworthy for a prince to exhibit such of the above-mentioned qualities as are considered good. But because no ruler can possess or fully practise them, on account of human conditions that do not permit it',[1] he must at times behave very differently in order to compass his ends. Moses and Theseus, Romulus and Cyrus all killed; what they created lasted, and was glorious; '. . . any man who under all conditions insists on making it his business to be good will surely be destroyed among so many who are not good. Hence a prince . . . must acquire the power to be not good, and understand when to use it and when not to use it, in accord with necessity.'[2] 'If all men were good, this maxim [to break faith if interest dictates] would not be good, but . . . they are bad.'[3] Force and guile must be met with force and guile.

The qualities of the lion and the fox are not in themselves morally admirable, but if a combination of these qualities will alone preserve the city from destruction, then these are the qualities that leaders must cultivate. They must do this not simply to serve their own interest, that is, because this is how one can become a leader, although whether men become leaders or not is a matter of indifference to the author – but because human societies in fact stand in need of leadership, and cannot become what they should be, save by the effective pursuit of power, of stability, *virtù*, greatness. These can be attained when men are led by Scipios and Timoleons or, if times are bad, men of more ruthless character. Hannibal was cruel, and cruelty is not a laudable quality, but if a sound society can be built only by conquest, and if cruelty is necessary to it, then it must not be evaded.

Machiavelli is not sadistic; he does not gloat on the need to employ ruthlessness or fraud for creating or maintaining the kind of society that he admires and recommends. His most savage examples and precepts apply only to situations in which the population is thoroughly corrupt, and needs violent measures to restore it to health, e.g. where a new prince takes over, or a revolution against a bad prince must be made effective. Where a society is relatively sound, or the rule is traditional and hereditary and supported by public sentiment, it would be quite wrong to practise violence for violence's sake, since its results would be destructive of social order, when the purpose of government is to create order, harmony, strength. If you are a lion and a fox you

[1] ibid., chapter 15.   [2] ibid.   [3] ibid., chapter 18.

51

can afford virtue – chastity, affability, mercy, humanity, liberality, honour – as Agesilaus and Timoleon, Camillus, Scipio and Marcus did. But if circumstances are adverse, if you find yourself surrounded by treason, what can you do but emulate Philip and Hannibal and Severus?

Mere lust for power is destructive: Pisistratus, Dionysius, Caesar were tyrants and did harm. Agathocles, the tyrant of Syracuse, who gained power by killing his fellow citizens, betraying his friends, being 'without fidelity, without mercy, without religion',[1] went too far, and so did not gain glory; 'his outrageous cruelty and inhumanity together with his countless wicked acts'[2] led to success, but since so much vice was not needed for it, he is excluded from the pantheon; so is the savage Oliverotto da Fermo, his modern counterpart, killed by Cesare Borgia. Still, to be altogether without these qualities guarantees failure; and that makes impossible the only conditions in which Machiavelli believed that normal men could successfully develop. Saints might not need them; anchorites could perhaps practise their virtues in the desert; martyrs will obtain their reward hereafter; but Machiavelli is plainly not interested in these ways of life and does not discuss them. He is a writer about government; he is interested in public affairs; in security, independence, success, glory, strength, vigour, felicity on earth, not in heaven; in the present and future as well as the past; in the real world, not an imaginary one. And for this, given unalterable human limitations, the code preached by the Christian church, if it is taken seriously, will not do.

Machiavelli, we are often told, was not concerned with morals. The most influential of all modern interpretations – that of Benedetto Croce, followed to some extent by Chabod, Russo and others – is that Machiavelli, in Cochrane's words,[3] 'did not deny the validity of Christian morality, and he did not pretend that a crime required by political necessity was any less a crime. Rather he discovered . . . that this morality simply did not hold in political affairs and that any policy based on the assumption that it did would end in disaster. His factual, objective description of contemporary political practices, then, is a sign not of cynicism or of detachment, but of anguish.'

This account, it seems to me, contains two basic misinterpretations. The first is that the clash is one between 'this [i.e. Christian] morality' and 'political necessity'. The implication is that there is an incompatibility between, on the one hand, morality – the region of ultimate

[1] *The Prince*, chapter 8. [2] ibid. [3] op. cit. (p. 25, note 2 above), p. 115.

values sought after for their own sakes – values recognition of which alone enables us to speak of 'crimes' or morally to justify and condemn anything; and on the other, politics – the art of adapting means to ends – the region of technical skills, of what Kant was to call 'hypothetical imperatives', which take the form 'If you want to achieve *x* do *y* (e.g. betray a friend, kill an innocent man)', without necessarily asking whether *x* is itself intrinsically desirable or not. This is the heart of the divorce of politics from ethics which Croce and many others attribute to Machiavelli. But this seems to me to rest on a mistake.

If ethics is confined to, let us say, Stoic, or Christian or Kantian or even some types of utilitarian ethics, where the source and criterion of value are the word of God, or eternal reason, or some inner sense or knowledge of good and evil, of right and wrong, voices which speak directly to individual consciousness with absolute authority, this might have been tenable. But there exists an equally time-honoured ethics, that of the Greek *polis*, of which Aristotle provided the clearest exposition. Since men are beings made by nature to live in communities, their communal purposes are the ultimate values from which the rest are derived, or with which their ends as individuals are identified. Politics – the art of living in a *polis* – is not an activity which can be dispensed with by those who prefer private life: it is not like seafaring or sculpture which those who do not wish to do so need not undertake. Political conduct is intrinsic to being a human being at a certain stage of civilisation, and what it demands is intrinsic to living a successful human life.

Ethics so conceived – the code of conduct, or the ideal to be pursued by the individual – cannot be known save by understanding the purpose and character of his *polis*: still less be capable of being divorced from it, even in thought. This is the kind of pre-Christian morality which Machiavelli takes for granted. 'It is well known', says Benedetto Croce,[1] 'that Machiavelli discovered the necessity and the autonomy of politics, politics which is beyond moral good and evil, which has its own laws against which it is futile to rebel, which cannot be exorcised and banished from the world with holy water.' Beyond good and evil in some non-Aristotelian, religious or liberal-Kantian sense; but not beyond the good and evil of those communities, ancient or modern, whose sacred values are social through and through. The art of colonisation or of mass murder (let us say) may also have their 'own laws against which it is futile to rebel' for those who wish to practise them

[1] op. cit. (p. 28, note 10 above), p. 60.

successfully. But if or when these laws collide with those of morality, it is possible and indeed morally imperative to abandon such activities.

But if Aristotle and Machiavelli are right about what men are (and should be – and Machiavelli's ideal is, particularly in the *Discourses*, drawn in vivid colours), political activity is intrinsic to human nature, and while individuals here and there may opt out, the mass of mankind cannot do so; and its communal life determines the moral duties of its members. Hence in opposing the 'laws of politics' to 'good and evil' Machiavelli is not contrasting two 'autonomous' spheres of acting – the 'political' and the 'moral': he is contrasting his own 'political' ethics to another conception of it which governs the lives of persons who are of no interest to him. He is indeed rejecting one morality – the Christian – but not in favour of something that cannot be described as a morality at all, but only as a game of skill, an activity called political, which is not concerned with ultimate human ends, and is therefore not ethical at all.

He is indeed rejecting Christian ethics, but in favour of another system, another moral universe – the world of Pericles or of Scipio, or even of the Duke Valentino, a society geared to ends just as ultimate as the Christian faith, a society in which men fight and are ready to die for (public) ends which they pursue for their own sakes. They are choosing not a realm of means (called politics) as opposed to a realm of ends (called morals), but opt for a rival (Roman or classical) morality, an alternative realm of ends. In other words the conflict is between two moralities, Christian and pagan (or as some wish to call it, aesthetic), not between autonomous realms of morals and politics.

Nor is this a mere question of nomenclature, unless politics is conceived as being concerned not (as it usually is) with means, skills, methods, technique, 'know-how', Croce's *pratica* (whether or not governed by unbreakable rules of its own), but with an independent kingdom of ends of its own, sought for their own sake, a substitute for ethics.[1] When Machiavelli said (in a letter to Francesco Vettori) that he loved his native city more than his own soul, he revealed his basic moral beliefs, a position with which Croce does not credit him.[2]

---

[1] Meinecke, Prezzolini (op. cit. (p. 25, note 2 above), English version, p. 43) and Ernesto Landi, 'The Political Philosophy of Machiavelli', trans. Maurice Cranston, *History Today* 14 (1964), 550–5, seem to me to approach this position most closely.

[2] Benedetto Croce, 'Per un detto del Machiavelli', *La critica* 28 (1930), 310–12.

The second thesis in this connection which seems to me mistaken is the idea that Machiavelli viewed the crimes of his society with anguish. (Chabod in his excellent study, unlike Croce and some Croceans, does not insist on this.) This entails that he accepts the dire necessities of the *raison d'état* with reluctance, because he sees no alternative. But there is no evidence for this: there is no trace of agony in his political works, any more than in his plays or letters.

The pagan world that Machiavelli prefers is built on recognition of the need for systematic guile and force by rulers, and he seems to think it natural and not at all exceptional or morally agonising that they should employ these weapons wherever they are needed. Nor is the distinction he draws that between the rulers and the ruled. The subjects or citizens must be Romans too: they do not need the *virtù* of the rulers, but if they also cheat, Machiavelli's maxims will not work; they must be poor, militarised, honest and obedient; if they lead Christian lives, they will accept too uncomplainingly the rule of mere bullies and scoundrels. No sound republic can be built of such materials as these. Theseus and Romulus, Moses and Cyrus, did not preach humility or a view of this world as but a temporary resting place to their subjects.

But it is the first misinterpretation that goes deepest, that which represents Machiavelli as caring little or nothing for moral issues. This is surely not borne out by his own language. Anyone whose thought revolves round central concepts such as the good and the bad, the corrupt and the pure, has an ethical scale in mind in terms of which he gives moral praise and blame. Machiavelli's values are not Christian, but they are moral values.

On this crucial point Hans Baron's criticism of the Croce-Russo thesis[1] seems to me correct. Against the view that for Machiavelli politics were beyond moral criticism Baron cites some of the passionately patriotic, republican and libertarian passages in the *Discourses* in which the (moral) qualities of the citizens of a republic are favourably compared with those of the subjects of a despotic prince. The last chapter of *The Prince* is scarcely the work of a detached, morally neutral observer, or of a self-absorbed man, preoccupied with his own inner personal problems, who looks on public life 'with anguish' as the graveyard of moral principles. Like Aristotle's or Cicero's, Machiavelli's

---

[1] Hans Baron, 'Machiavelli: the Republican Citizen and the Author of "The Prince"', *English Historical Review* 76 (1961), 217–53, *passim*.

morality was social and not individual : but it is a morality no less than theirs, not an amoral region, beyond good or evil.

It does not, of course, follow that he was not often fascinated by the techniques of political life as such. The advice given equally to conspirators and their enemies, the professional appraisal of the methods of Oliverotto or Sforza or Baglioni, spring from typical humanist curiosity, the search for an applied science of politics, fascination by knowledge for its own sake, whatever the implications. But the moral ideal, that of the citizen of the Roman Republic, is never far away. Political skills are valued solely as means – for their effectiveness in recreating conditions in which sick men recover their health and can flourish. And this is precisely what Aristotle would have called the moral end proper to man.

This leaves still with us the thorny problem of the relation of *The Prince* to the *Discourses*. But whatever the disparities, the central strain which runs through both is one and the same. The vision – the dream – typical of many writers who see themselves as tough-minded realists – of the strong, united, effective, morally regenerated, splendid and victorious *patria*, whether it is saved by the *virtù* of one man or many – remains central and constant. Political judgements, attitudes to individuals or states, to *fortuna*, and *necessità*, evaluation of methods, degree of optimism, the fundamental mood – these vary between one work and another, perhaps within the same exposition. But the basic values, the ultimate end – Machiavelli's beatific vision – does not vary.

His vision is social and political. Hence the traditional view of him as simply a specialist on how to get the better of others, a vulgar cynic who says that Sunday school precepts are all very well, but in a world full of evil men you too must lie, kill and so on, if you are to get somewhere, is incorrect. The philosophy summarised by 'eat or be eaten, beat or be beaten' – the kind of wordly wisdom to be found in, say, Mazzei[1] or Giovanni Morelli,[2] with whom he has been compared – is not what is central in him. Machiavelli is not specially concerned with the opportunism of ambitious individuals; the ideal before his eyes is a shining vision of Florence or of Italy; in this respect he is a typically impassioned humanist of the Renaissance, save that his ideal is not artistic or cultural but political, unless the state – or regenerated Italy – is considered, in Burckhardt's sense, as an artistic goal. This is very

[1] Ser Lapo Mazzei, *Lettere di un notaro a un mercante del secolo XIV*, ed. Cesare Guasti, 2 vols (Florence, 1880).

[2] Giovanni di Pagolo Morelli, *Ricordi*, ed. Vittore Branca (Florence, 1956).

different from mere advocacy of tough-mindedness as such, or of a realism irrespective of its goal.

Machiavelli's values, I should like to repeat, are not instrumental but moral and ultimate, and he calls for great sacrifices in their name. For them he rejects the rival scale – the Christian principles of *ozio* and meekness – not, indeed, as being defective in itself, but as inapplicable to the conditions of real life; and real life for him means not merely (as is sometimes alleged) life as it was lived around him in Italy – the crimes, hypocrisies, brutalities, follies of Florence, Rome, Venice, Milan. This is not the touchstone of reality. His purpose is not to leave unchanged or to reproduce this kind of life, but to lift it to a new plane, to rescue Italy from squalor and slavery, to restore her to health and sanity.

The moral ideal for which he thinks no sacrifice too great – the welfare of the *patria* – is for him the highest form of social existence attainable by man; but attainable, not unattainable; not a world outside the limits of human capacity, given human beings as we know them, that is, creatures compounded out of those emotional, intellectual and physical properties of which history and observation provide examples. He asks for men improved but not transfigured, not superhuman; not for a world of ideal beings unknown on this earth, who, even if they could be created, could not be called human.

If you object to the political methods recommended because they seem to you morally detestable, if you refuse to embark upon them because they are, to use Ritter's word, 'erschreckend', too frightening, Machiavelli has no answer, no argument. In that case you are perfectly entitled to lead a morally good life, be a private citizen (or a monk), seek some corner of your own. But, in that event, you must not make yourself responsible for the lives of others or expect good fortune; in a material sense you must expect to be ignored or destroyed.

In other words you can opt out of the public world, but in that case he has nothing to say to you, for it is to the public world and to the men in it that he addresses himself. This is expressed most clearly in his notorious advice to the victor who has to hold down a conquered province. He advises a clean sweep: new governors, new titles, new powers and new men; he should 'make the rich poor, the poor rich, as David did when he became king: "the poor he filled with good things and the rich he sent away empty". Besides this, he should build new cities, overthrow those already built, change the inhabitants from one place to another; and in short he should leave nothing in that province untouched, and make sure that no rank or position or office or wealth is held by anyone who does not acknowledge it as from you.'[1] He should take Philip of Macedon as his model, who 'grew in these ways until he became lord of Greece'.

Now Philip's historian informs us — Machiavelli goes on to say — that he transferred the inhabitants from one province to another 'as herdsmen transfer their herds' from one place to another. Doubtless, Machiavelli continues,

> These methods are very cruel, and enemies to all government not merely Christian but human, and any man ought to avoid them and prefer to live a private life rather than to be a king who brings such ruin on men. Notwithstanding, a ruler who does not wish to take that first good way of lawful government, if he wishes to maintain himself, must enter upon this evil one. But men take certain middle ways that are very injurious; indeed, they are unable to be altogether good or altogether bad.[2]

This is plain enough. There are two worlds, that of personal morality and that of public organisation. There are two ethical codes, both ultimate; not two 'autonomous' regions, one of 'ethics', another of 'politics', but two (for him) exhaustive alternatives between two conflicting systems of value. If a man chooses the 'first good way', he must, presumably, give up all hope of Athens and Rome, of a noble and glorious society in which human beings can thrive and grow strong, proud, wise and productive; indeed, they must abandon all hope of a tolerable life on earth: for men cannot live outside society; they will not survive collectively if they are led by men who (like Soderini) are influenced by the first, 'private' morality; they will not be able to realise their minimal goals as men; they will end in a state of moral, not merely political, degradation. But if a man chooses, as Machiavelli himself has done, the second course, then he must suppress his private qualms, if he has any, for it is certain that those who are too squeamish during the remaking of a society, or even during its pursuit and maintenance of its power and glory, will go to the wall. Whoever has chosen to make an omelette cannot do so without breaking eggs.

Machiavelli is sometimes accused of too much relish at the prospect of breaking eggs — almost for its own sake. This is unjust. He thinks these ruthless methods are necessary — necessary as means to provide

[1] *Discourses* I 26.   [2] ibid.

good results, good in terms not of a Christian, but of a secular, humanistic, naturalistic morality. His most shocking examples show this. The most famous, perhaps, is that of Giovanpaolo Baglioni, who caught Julius II during one of his campaigns, and let him escape, when in Machiavelli's view he might have destroyed him and his cardinals and thereby committed a crime 'the greatness of which would have transcended every infamy, every peril that could have resulted from it'.[1]

Like Frederick the Great (who called Machiavelli 'the enemy of mankind' and followed his advice),[2] Machiavelli is, in effect, saying 'Le vin est tiré: il faut le boire.' Once you embark on a plan for the transformation of a society you must carry it through no matter at what cost: to fumble, to retreat, to be overcome by scruples, is to betray your chosen cause. To be a physician is to be a professional, ready to burn, to cauterise, to amputate; if that is what the disease requires, then to stop half-way because of personal qualms, or some rule unrelated to your art and its technique, is a sign of muddle and weakness, and will always give you the worst of both worlds. And there are at least two worlds: each of them has much, indeed everything, to be said for it; but they are two and not one. One must learn to choose between them, and having chosen, not look back.

There is more than one world, and more than one set of virtues: confusion between them is disastrous. One of the chief illusions caused by ignoring this is the Platonic-Hebraic-Christian view that virtuous rulers create virtuous men. This according to Machiavelli is not true. Generosity is a virtue, but not in princes. A generous prince will ruin the citizens by taxing them too heavily, a mean prince (and Machiavelli does not say that meanness is a good quality in private men) will save the purses of the citizens and so add to public welfare. A kind ruler – and kindness is a virtue – may let intriguers and stronger characters dominate him, and so cause chaos and corruption.

Other writers of 'mirrors for princes' are also rich in such maxims, but they do not draw the implications; Machiavelli's use of such generalisations is not theirs; he is not moralising at large, but illustrating a specific thesis: that the nature of men dictates a public morality which is different from, and may come into collision with, the virtues of men who profess to believe in, and try to act by, Christian precepts. These may not be wholly unrealisable in quiet times, in private life.

[1] ibid. I 27.
[2] It is still not clear how much of this Frederick owed to his mentor Voltaire.

But they lead to ruin outside this. The analogy between a state and people and an individual is a fallacy: 'a state and a people are governed in a different way from an individual';[1] 'not individual good but common good is what makes cities great'.[2]

One may disagree with this. One may argue that the greatness, glory and wealth of a state are hollow ideals, or detestable, if the citizens are oppressed and treated as mere means to the grandeur of the whole. Like Christian thinkers, or like Constant and the liberals, or like Sismondi and the theorists of the welfare state, one may prefer a state in which citizens are prosperous even though the public treasury is poor, in which government is neither centralised nor omnipotent, nor, perhaps, sovereign at all, but the citizens enjoy a wide degree of individual freedom; one may contrast this favourably with the great authoritarian concentrations of power built by Alexander or Frederick the Great or Napoleon, or the great autocrats of the twentieth century.

If so, one is simply contradicting Machiavelli's thesis: he sees no merit in such loose political textures. They cannot last. Men cannot long survive in such conditions. He is convinced that states which have lost the appetite for power are doomed to decadence and are likely to be destroyed by their more vigorous and better armed neighbours; and Vico and modern 'realistic' thinkers have echoed this.

Machiavelli is possessed by a clear, intense, narrow vision of a society in which human talents can be made to contribute to a powerful and splendid whole. He prefers republican rule in which the interests of the rulers do not conflict with those of the ruled. But (as Macaulay perceived) he prefers a well-governed principate to a decadent republic: and the qualities he admires and thinks capable of being welded into – indeed, indispensable to – a durable society, are not different in *The Prince* and the *Discourses*: energy, boldness, practical skill, imagination, vitality, self-discipline, shrewdness, public spirit, good fortune, *antiqua virtus, virtù* – firmness in adversity, strength of character, as celebrated by Xenophon or Livy. All his more shocking maxims – those responsible for the 'murd'rous Machiavel' of the

---

[1] '. . . una repubblica e un popolo si governa altrimenti che un privato', *Legazioni all'Imperatore*, quoted by L. Burd, op. cit. (p. 28, note 10 above), p. 298, note 17.

[2] *Discourses* II 2. This echoes Francesco Patrizzi's 'aliae sunt regis virtutes, aliae privatorum', in *De regno et regis institutione*, quoted by Felix Gilbert in 'The Humanist Concept of the Prince and *The Prince* of Machiavelli', *Journal of Modern History* 11 (1939), 449–83: 464, note 34.

Elizabethan stage – are descriptions of methods of realising this single end : the classical, humanistic and patriotic vision that dominates him.

Let me cite a round dozen of his most notoriously wicked pieces of advice to princes. You must employ terrorism or kindness, as the case dictates. Severity is usually more effective, but humanity, in some situations, brings better fruit. You may excite fear but not hatred, for hatred will destroy you in the end. It is best to keep men poor and on a permanent war footing, for this will be an antidote to the two great enemies of active obedience – ambition and boredom – and the ruled will then feel in constant need of great men to lead them (the twentieth century offers us only too much evidence for this sharp insight). Competition – divisions between classes – in a society is desirable, for it generates energy and ambition in the right degree.

Religion must be promoted even though it may be false, provided it is of a kind which preserves social solidarity and promotes manly virtues, as Christianity has historically failed to do. When you confer benefits (he says, following Aristotle), do so yourself; but if dirty work is to be done, let others do it, for then they, not the prince, will be blamed, and the prince can gain favour by duly cutting off their heads; for men prefer vengeance and security to liberty. Do what you must do in any case, but try to represent it as a special favour to the people. If you must commit a crime do not advertise it beforehand, since otherwise your enemies may destroy you before you destroy them. If your action must be drastic, do it in one fell swoop, not in agonising stages. Do not be surrounded by over-powerful servants – victorious generals are best got rid of, otherwise they may get rid of you.

You may be violent and use your power to overawe, but you must not break your own laws, for that destroys confidence and disintegrates the social texture. Men should either be caressed or annihilated; appeasement and neutralism are always fatal. Excellent plans without arms are not enough or else Florence would still be a republic. Rulers must live in the constant expectation of war. Success creates more devotion than an amiable character; remember the fate of Pertinax, Savonarola, Soderini. Severus was unscrupulous and cruel, Ferdinand of Spain is treacherous and crafty: but by practising the arts of both the lion and the fox they escaped both snares and wolves. Men will be false to you unless you compel them to be true by creating circumstances in which falsehood will not pay. And so on.

These examples are typical of 'the devil's partner'. Now and then doubts assail our author: he wonders whether a man high-minded enough to labour to create a state admirable by Roman standards will be tough enough to use the violent and wicked means prescribed; and conversely, whether a sufficiently ruthless and brutal man will be disinterested enough to compass the public good which alone justifies the evil means. Yet Moses and Theseus, Romulus and Cyrus, combined these properties.[1] What has been once, can be again: the implication is optimistic.

All these maxims have one property in common: they are designed to create or resurrect or maintain an order which will satisfy what the author conceives as men's most permanent interests. Machiavelli's values may be erroneous, dangerous, odious; but he is in earnest. He is not cynical. The end is always the same: a state conceived after the analogy of Periclean Athens, or Sparta, but above all the Roman Republic. Such an end, for which men naturally crave (of this he thinks that history and observation provide conclusive evidence), 'excuses' any means; in judging means, look only to the end: if the state goes under, all is lost. Hence the famous paragraph in the forty-first chapter of the third book of *The Discourses* where he says, 'when it is absolutely a question of the safety of one's country, there must be no consideration of just or unjust, of merciful or cruel, of praiseworthy or disgraceful; instead, setting aside every scruple, one must follow to the utmost any plan that will save her life and keep her liberty.' The French have reasoned thus: and the 'majesty of their king and the power of their kingdom' have come from it. Romulus could not have founded Rome without killing Remus. Brutus would not have preserved the Republic if he had not killed his sons. Moses and Theseus, Romulus, Cyrus and the liberators of Athens had to destroy in order to build. Such conduct, so far from being condemned, is held up to admiration by the classical historians and the Bible. Machiavelli is their admirer and faithful spokesman.

What is there, then, about his words, about his tone, which has caused such tremors among his readers? Not, indeed, in his own lifetime – there was a delayed reaction of some quarter of a century, but after that it becomes one of continuous and mounting horror. Fichte, Hegel, Treitschke 'reinterpreted' his doctrines and assimilated them to their own views. But the sense of horror was not thereby greatly mitigated. It is evident that the effect of the shock which he administered was not a temporary one: it has lasted almost to our own day.

[1] Hugh Trevor-Roper has drawn my attention to the irony of the fact that the heroes of this supreme realist are all, wholly or in part, mythical.

Leaving aside the historical problem of why there was no immediate contemporary criticism, let us consider the continuous discomfort caused to its readers during the four centuries that have passed since *The Prince* was placed upon the Index. The great originality and the tragic implications of Machiavelli's theses seem to me to reside in their relation to a Christian civilisation. It was all very well to live by the light of pagan ideals in pagan times; but to preach paganism more than a thousand years after the triumph of Christianity was to do so after the loss of innocence – and to be forcing men to make a conscious choice. The choice is painful because it is a choice between two entire worlds. Men have lived in both, and fought and died to preserve them against each other. Machiavelli has opted for one of them, and he is prepared to commit crimes for its sake.

In killing, deceiving, betraying, Machiavelli's princes and republicans are doing evil things, not condonable in terms of common morality. It is Machiavelli's great merit that he does not deny this.[1] Marsilio, Hobbes, Spinoza, and, in their own fashion, Hegel and Marx, did try to deny it. So did many a defender of the *raison d'état*, imperialist and populist, Catholic and Protestant. These thinkers argue for a single moral system : and seek to show that the morality which justifies, and indeed demands, such deeds, is continuous with, and a more rational form of, the confused ethical beliefs of the uninstructed morality which forbids them absolutely.

From the vantage point of the great social objectives in the name of which these (prima facie wicked) acts are to be performed, they will be seen (so the argument goes) as no longer wicked, but as rational – demanded by the very nature of things – by the common good, or man's true ends, or the dialectic of history – condemned only by those who cannot or will not see a large enough segment of the logical, or theological, or metaphysical, or historical pattern; misjudged, denounced only by the spiritually blind or short-sighted. At worst, these 'crimes' are discords demanded by the larger harmony, and therefore, to those who hear this harmony, no longer discordant.

Machiavelli is not a defender of any such abstract theory. It does not occur to him to employ such casuistry. He is transparently honest

[1] This is recognised by Jacques Maritain (see his *Moral Philosophy* (London, 1964), p. 199) who conceded that Machiavelli 'never called evil good or good evil'. *Machtpolitik* is shown to be what it is: the party with the big battalions; it does not claim that the Lord is on its side: no *Dei gesta per Francos*.

and clear. In choosing the life of a statesman, or even the life of a citizen with enough civic sense to want your state to be as successful and as splendid as possible, you commit yourself to rejection of Christian behaviour.[1] It may be that Christians are right about the wellbeing of the individual soul, taken outside the social or political context. But the well-being of the state is not the same as the well-being of the individual – they 'are governed in a different way'. You will have made your choice: the only crimes are weakness, cowardice, stupidity, which may cause you to draw back in midstream and fail.

Compromise with current morality leads to bungling, which is always despicable, and when practised by statesmen involves men in ruin. The end 'excuses' the means, however horrible these may be in terms of even pagan ethics, if it is (in terms of the ideals of Thucydides or Polybius, Cicero or Livy) lofty enough. Brutus was right to kill his children: he saved Rome. Soderini did not have the stomach to perpetrate such deeds and ruined Florence. Savonarola, who had sound ideas about austerity and moral strength and corruption, perished because he did not realise that an unarmed prophet will always go to the gallows.

If one can produce the right result by using the devotion and affection of men, let this be done by all means. There is no value in causing suffering as such. But if one cannot, then Moses, Romulus, Theseus, Cyrus are the exemplars, and fear must be employed. There is no sinister Satanism in Machiavelli, nothing of Dostoevsky's great sinner, pursuing evil for evil's sake. To Dostoevsky's famous question 'Is everything permitted?', Machiavelli (who for Dostoevsky would surely have been an atheist) answers 'Yes, if the end – that is, the pursuit of a society's basic interests in a specific situation – cannot be realised in any other way.'

This position has not been properly understood by some of those who claim to be not unsympathetic to Machiavelli. Figgis, for example,[2] thinks that he permanently suspended 'the *habeas corpus* acts of the whole human race', that is to say, that he advocated methods of terrorism because for him the situation was always critical, always

---

[1] At the risk of exhausting the patience of the reader, I must repeat that this is a conflict not of pagan statecraft with Christian morals, but of pagan morals (indissolubly connected with social life and inconceivable without it) with Christian ethics, which, whatever its implication for politics, can be stated independently of it, as, e.g., Aristotle's or Hegel's ethics cannot.

[2] op. cit. (p. 37, note 1 above), p. 76.

desperate, so that he confused ordinary political principles with rules needed, if at all, only in extreme cases.

Others – perhaps the majority of his interpreters – look on him as the originator or at least a defender of what later came to be called 'raison d'état', 'Staatsräson', 'ragion di stato' – the justification of immoral acts when undertaken on behalf of the state in exceptional circumstances. More than one scholar has pointed out, reasonably enough, that the notion that desperate cases require desperate remedies – that 'necessity knows no law' – is to be found not only in antiquity but equally in Aquinas and Dante and other medieval writers long before Bellarmino or Machiavelli.

These parallels seem to me to rest on a deep but characteristic misunderstanding of Machiavelli's thesis. He is not saying that while in normal situations current morality – that is, the Christian or semi-Christian code of ethics – should prevail, yet abnormal conditions can occur, in which the entire social structure in which alone this code can function becomes jeopardised, and that in emergencies of this kind acts which are usually regarded as wicked and rightly forbidden are justified.

This is the position of, among others, those who think that all morality ultimately rests on the existence of certain institutions – say Roman Catholics who regard the existence of the church and the papacy as indispensable to Christianity – or nationalists who see in the political power of a nation the sole source of spiritual life. Such persons maintain that extreme and 'frightful' measures needed for protecting the state or the church or the national culture in moments of acute crisis may be justified, since the ruin of these institutions may fatally damage the indispensable framework of all other values. This is a doctrine in terms of which both Catholics and Protestants, both conservatives and communists, have defended enormities which freeze the blood of ordinary men.

But this is not Machiavelli's position. For the defenders of the *raison d'état*, the sole justification of these measures is that they are exceptional – that they are needed to preserve a system the purpose of which is precisely to preclude the need for such odious measures, so that the sole justification of such steps is that they will end the situations that render them necessary. But for Machiavelli these measures are, in a sense, themselves quite normal. No doubt they are called for only by extreme need; yet political life tends to generate a good many such needs, of varying degrees of 'extremity'; hence Baglioni, who shied away from the logical consequences of his own policies, was clearly unfit to rule.

The notion of *raison d'état* entails a conflict of values which may be agonising to morally good and sensitive men. For Machiavelli there is no conflict. Public life has its own morality, to which Christian principles (or any absolute personal values) tend to be a gratuitous obstacle. This life has its own standards: it does not require perpetual terror: but it approves, or at least permits, the use of force where it is needed to promote the ends of political society.

Sheldon Wolin[1] seems to me right in insisting that Machiavelli believes in permanent 'economy of violence' – the need for a consistent reserve of force always in the background to keep things going in such a way that the virtues admired by him and by the classical thinkers to whom he appeals, can be protected and allowed to flower. Men brought up within a community in which such force, or its possibility, is used rightly, will live the happy lives of Greeks or Romans during their finest hours. They will be characterised by vitality, genius, variety, pride, power, success (Machiavelli scarcely ever speaks of arts or sciences); but it will not, in any clear sense, be a Christian commonwealth. The moral conflict which this situation raises will trouble only those who are not prepared to abandon either course: those who assume that the two incompatible lives are in fact reconcilable.

But to Machiavelli the claims of the official morality are scarcely worth discussing: they are not translatable into social practice: 'If all men were good . . .', but he feels sure that men can never be improved beyond the point at which considerations of power are relevant. If morals relate to human conduct, and men are by nature social, Christian morality cannot be a guide for normal social existence. It remained for someone to state this. Machiavelli did so.

One is obliged to choose: and in choosing one form of life, give up the other. That is the central point. If Machiavelli is right, if it is in principle (or in fact: the frontier seems dim) impossible to be morally good and do one's duty as this was conceived by common European, and especially Christian ethics, and at the same time build Sparta or Periclean Athens or the Rome of the Republic or even of the Antonines, then a conclusion of the first importance follows: that the belief that the correct, objectively valid solution to the question of how men should live can in principle be discovered, is itself in principle not

[1] Sheldon S. Wolin, *Politics and Vision* (London, 1960), pp. 220–24.

true. This was a truly *erschreckend* proposition. Let me try to put it in its proper context.

One of the deepest assumptions of western political thought is the doctrine, scarcely questioned during its long ascendancy, that there exists some single principle which not only regulates the course of the sun and the stars, but prescribes their proper behaviour to all animate creatures. Animals and sub-rational beings of all kinds follow it by instinct; higher beings attain to consciousness of it, and are free to abandon it, but only to their doom. This doctrine, in one version or another, has dominated European thought since Plato; it has appeared in many forms, and has generated many similes and allegories; at its centre is the vision of an impersonal Nature or Reason or cosmic purpose, or of a divine Creator whose power has endowed all things and creatures each with a specific function; these functions are elements in a single harmonious whole, and are intelligible in terms of it alone.

This was often expressed by images taken from architecture: of a great edifice of which each part fits uniquely in the total structure; or from the human body as an all-embracing organic whole; or from the life of society as a great hierarchy, with God as the *ens realissimum* at the summit of two parallel systems – the feudal order and the natural order – stretching downwards from Him, and reaching upwards to Him, obedient to His will. Or it is seen as the Great Chain of Being, the Platonic-Christian analogue of the world-tree Ygdrasil, which links time and space and all that they contain. Or it has been represented by an analogy drawn from music, as an orchestra in which each instrument or group of instruments has its own tune to play in the infinitely rich polyphonic score. When, after the seventeenth century, harmonic metaphors replaced polyphonic images, the instruments were no longer conceived as playing specific melodies, but as producing sounds which, although they might not be wholly intelligible to any given group of players (and might even sound discordant or superfluous if taken in isolation), yet contributed to the total pattern perceptible only from a loftier standpoint.

The idea of the world and of human society as a single intelligible structure is at the root of all the many various versions of natural law – the mathematical harmonies of the Pythagoreans, the logical ladder of Platonic Forms, the genetic-logical pattern of Aristotle, the divine *Logos* of the Stoics and the Christian churches and of their secularised offshoots. The advance of the natural sciences generated more empirically conceived versions of this image as well as anthropomorphic similes: of Dame Nature as an adjuster of conflicting tendencies (as in Hume or Adam Smith), of Mistress Nature as the teacher of the best way to happiness (as in the works of some French Encyclopedists), of Nature as embodied in the actual customs or habits of organised social wholes; biological, aesthetic, psychological similes have reflected the dominant ideas of an age.

This unifying monistic pattern is at the very heart of traditional rationalism, religious and atheistic, metaphysical and scientific, transcendental and naturalistic, that has been characteristic of western civilisation. It is this rock, upon which western beliefs and lives had been founded, that Machiavelli seems, in effect, to have split open. So great a reversal cannot, of course, be due to the acts of a single individual. It could scarcely have taken place in a stable social and moral order; many beside him, ancient sceptics, medieval nominalists and secularists, Renaissance humanists, doubtless supplied their share of the dynamite. The purpose of this essay is to suggest that it was Machiavelli who lit the fatal fuse.

If to ask what are the ends of life is to ask a real question, it must be capable of being correctly answered. To claim rationality in matters of conduct was to claim that correct and final solutions to such questions can in principle be found.

When such solutions were discussed in earlier periods, it was normally assumed that the perfect society could be conceived, at least in outline; for otherwise what standard could one use to condemn existing arrangements as imperfect? It might not be realisable here, below. Men were too ignorant or too weak or too vicious to create it. Or it was said (by some materialistic thinkers in the centuries following *The Prince*) that it was technical means that were lacking, that no one had yet discovered methods of overcoming the material obstacles to the golden age; that we were not technologically or educationally or morally sufficiently advanced. But it was never said that there was something incoherent in the very notion itself.

Plato and the Stoics, the Hebrew prophets and Christian medieval thinkers and the writers of Utopias from More onward had a vision of what it was that men fell short of; they claimed, as it were, to be able to measure the gap between the reality and the ideal. But if Machiavelli is right, this tradition — the central current of western thought — is fallacious. For if his position is valid then it is impossible to construct even the notion of such a perfect society, for there exist at least two sets of virtues – let us call them the Christian and the pagan – which are not merely in practice, but in principle incompatible.

If men practise Christian humility, they cannot also be inspired by the burning ambitions of the great classical founders of cultures and religions; if their gaze is centred upon the world beyond – if their ideas are infected by even lip-service to such an outlook – they will not be likely to give all that they have to an attempt to build a perfect city. If suffering and sacrifice and martyrdom are not always evil and inescapable necessities, but may be of supreme value in themselves, then the glorious victories over fortune which go to the bold, the impetuous and the young might neither be won nor thought worth winning. If spiritual goods alone are worth striving for, then of how much value is the study of *necessità* – of the laws that govern nature and human lives – by the manipulation of which men might accomplish unheard-of things in the arts and the sciences and the organisation of social lives?

To abandon the pursuit of secular goals may lead to disintegration and a new barbarism; but even if this is so, is it the worst that could happen? Whatever the differences between Plato and Aristotle, or of either of these thinkers from the Sophists or Epicureans or the other Greek schools of the fourth and later centuries, they and their disciples, the European rationalists and empiricists of the modern age, were agreed that the study of reality by minds undeluded by appearances could reveal the correct ends to be pursued by men – that which would make men free and happy, strong and rational.

Some thought that there was a single end for all men in all circumstances, or different ends for men of different kinds or in dissimilar historical environments. Objectivists and universalists were opposed by relativists and subjectivists, metaphysicians by empiricists, theists by atheists. There was profound disagreement about moral issues; but what none of these thinkers, not even the sceptics, had suggested was that there might exist ends – ends in themselves in terms of which alone everything else was justified – which were equally ultimate, but incompatible with one another, that there might exist no single universal overarching standard that would enable a man to choose rationally between them.

This was indeed a profoundly upsetting conclusion. It entailed that if men wished to live and act consistently, and understand what goals they were pursuing, they were obliged to examine their moral values. What if they found that they were compelled to make a choice between two incommensurable systems, to choose as they did without the aid of an infallible measuring rod which certified one form of life as being superior to all others and could be used to demonstrate this to the satisfaction of all rational men? Was it, perhaps, this awful truth, implicit in Machiavelli's exposition, that has upset the moral consciousness of men, and has haunted their minds so permanently and obsessively ever since?

Machiavelli did not himself propound it. There was no problem and no agony for him; he shows no trace of scepticism or relativism; he chose his side, and took little interest in the values that this choice ignored or flouted. The conflict between his scale of values and that of conventional morality clearly did not (*pace* Croce and the other defenders of the 'anguished humanist' interpretation) seem to worry Machiavelli himself. It upset only those who came after him, and were not prepared, on the one hand, to abandon their own moral values (Christian or humanist) together with the entire way of thought and action of which these were a part; nor, on the other hand, to deny the validity of, at any rate, much of Machiavelli's analysis of the political facts, and the (largely pagan) values and outlook that went with it, embodied in the social structure which he painted so brilliantly and convincingly.

Whenever a thinker, however distant from us in time or culture, still stirs passion, enthusiasm or indignation, or any kind of intense debate, it is generally the case that he has propounded a thesis which upsets some deeply established *idée reçue*, a thesis which those who wish to cling to the old conviction nevertheless find it hard or impossible to dismiss or refute. This is the case with Plato, Hobbes, Rousseau, Marx.

I should like to suggest that it is Machiavelli's juxtaposition of the two outlooks – the two incompatible moral worlds, as it were – in the minds of his readers, and the collision and acute moral discomfort which follow, that, over the years, has been responsible for the desperate efforts to interpret his doctrines away, to represent him as a cynical and therefore ultimately shallow defender of power politics, or as a diabolist, or as a patriot prescribing for particularly desperate situations which seldom arise, or as a mere time-server, or as an embittered political failure, or as a mere mouthpiece of truths we have always known but did not like to utter, or again as the enlightened translator of universally accepted ancient social principles into empirical terms, or as a crypto-republican satirist (a descendant of Juvenal, a forerunner of Orwell); or as a cold scientist, a mere political technologist free from moral implications; or as a typical Renaissance publicist practising a now obsolete genre; or in any of the numerous other roles that have been and are still being cast for him.

Machiavelli may have possessed some, at any rate, of these attributes, but concentration on one or other of them as constituting his essential, 'true' character, seems to me to stem from reluctance to face, still more discuss, the uncomfortable truth which Machiavelli had, unintentionally, almost casually, uncovered; namely, that not all ultimate values are necessarily compatible with one another – that there might be a conceptual (what used to be called 'philosophical') and not merely a material obstacle to the notion of the single ultimate solution which, if it were only realised, would establish the perfect society.

III

Yet if no such solution can, even in principle, be formulated, then all political and, indeed, moral problems are thereby transformed. This is not a division of politics from ethics. It is the uncovering of the possibility of more than one system of values, with no criterion common to the systems whereby a rational choice can be made between them. This is not the rejection of Christianity for paganism (although Machiavelli clearly preferred the latter), nor of paganism for Christianity (which, at least in its historical form, he thought incompatible with the basic needs of normal men), but the setting of them side by side, with the implicit invitation to men to choose either a good, virtuous, private life, or a good, successful, social existence, but not both.

What has been shown by Machiavelli, who is often (like Nietzsche) congratulated for tearing off hypocritical masks, brutally revealing the truth, and so on, is not that men profess one thing and do another (although no doubt he shows this too), but that when they assume that the two ideals are compatible, or perhaps are even one and the same ideal, and do not allow this assumption to be questioned, they are guilty of bad faith (as the existentialists call it, or of 'false consciousness', to use a Marxist formula), which their actual behaviour exhibits. Machiavelli calls the bluff not just of official morality – the hypocrisies of ordinary life – but of one of the foundations of the central western philosophical tradition, the belief in the ultimate compatibility of all genuine values. His own withers are unwrung. He has made his choice. He seems wholly unworried by, indeed scarcely aware of, parting company with traditional western morality.

But the question that his writings have dramatised, if not for himself, then for others in the centuries that followed, is this: what reason have we for supposing that justice and mercy, humility and *virtù*, happiness and knowledge, glory and liberty, magnificence and sanctity, will always coincide, or indeed be compatible at all? Poetic justice is, after all, so called not because it does, but because it does not, as a rule, occur in the prose of ordinary life, where, *ex hypothesi*, a very different kind of justice operates: 'a state and a people are governed in a different way from an individual'. Hence what talk can there be of indestructible rights, either in the medieval or the liberal sense? The wise man must eliminate fantasies from his own head, and should seek to dispel them from the heads of others; or, if they are too resistant, he should at least, as Pareto or Dostoevsky's Grand Inquisitor recommended, exploit them as a means to a viable society.

'The march of world history stands outside virtue, vice and justice,' said Hegel. If for 'the march of history' you substitute 'a well governed *patria*', and interpret Hegel's notion of virtue as it is understood by Christians or ordinary men, then Machiavelli is one of the earliest proponents of this doctrine. Like all great innovators, he is not without ancestry. But the names of Palmieri and Pontano, and even of Carneades and Sextus Empiricus, have left little mark on European thought.

Croce has rightly insisted that Machiavelli is not detached or cynical or irresponsible. His patriotism, his republicanism, his commitment, are not in doubt. He suffered for his convictions. He thought continually about Florence and Italy, and of how to save them. Yet it is not his character, nor his plays, his poetry, his histories, his diplomatic or political activities, that have gained him his unique fame.[1] Nor can

---

[1] The moral of his best comedy, *Mandragola*, seems to me close to that of the political tracts: that the ethical doctrines professed by the characters are wholly at variance with what they do to attain their various ends: virtually every one of them in the end obtains what he wants; if Callimaco had resisted temptation, or the lady he seduces had been smitten with remorse, or Fra Timoteo attempted to practise the maxims of the Fathers and the Schoolmen with which he liberally seasons his speeches, this could not have occurred. But all turns out for the best, though not from the point of view of accepted morality. If the play castigates hypocrisy and stupidity, the standpoint is not that of virtue but of candid hedonism. The notion that Callimaco is a kind of prince in private life, successful in creating and maintaining his own world by the correct use of guile and fraud, the exercise of *virtù*, a bold challenge to *fortuna*, and so on, seems plausible. For this see Henry Paolucci, Introduction to *Mandragola* (New York, 1957).

this be due only to his psychological or sociological imagination. His psychology is often excessively primitive. He scarcely seems to allow for the bare possibility of sustained and genuine altruism; he refuses to consider the motives of men who are prepared to fight against enormous odds, who ignore *necessità* and are prepared to lose their lives in a hopeless cause.

His distrust of unworldly attitudes, absolute principles divorced from empirical observation, is fanatically strong – almost romantic in its violence; the vision of the great prince playing upon human beings like an instrument intoxicates him. He assumes that different societies must always be at war with each other, since they have differing purposes. He sees history as an endless process of cut-throat competition, in which the only goal that rational men can have is to succeed in the eyes of their contemporaries and of posterity. He is good at bringing fantasies down to earth, but he assumes, as Mill was to complain about Bentham, that this is enough. He allows too little to the ideal impulses of men. He has no historical sense and little sense of economics. He has no inkling of the technological progress which is about to transform political and social life, and in particular the art of war. He does not understand how either individuals, communities or cultures develop and transform themselves. Like Hobbes, he assumes that the argument or motive for self-preservation automatically outweighs all others.

He tells men above all not to be fools: to follow a principle when this may involve you in ruin is absurd, at least if judged by worldly standards; other standards he mentions respectfully, but takes no interest in them: those who adopt them are not likely to create anything that will perpetuate their name. His Romans are no more real than the stylised figures in his brilliant comedies. His human beings have so little inner life or capacity for cooperation or social solidarity that, as in the case of Hobbes's not dissimilar creatures, it is difficult to see how they could develop enough reciprocal confidence to create a lasting social whole, even under the perpetual shadow of carefully regulated violence.

Few would deny that Machiavelli's writings, more particularly *The Prince*, have scandalised mankind more deeply and continuously than any other political treatise. The reason for this, let me say again, is not the discovery that politics is the play of power – that political relationships between and within independent communities involve the use of force and fraud, and are unrelated to the principles professed by the players. That knowledge is as old as conscious thought about politics – certainly as old as Thucydides and Plato. Nor is it merely caused by the examples that he offers of success in acquiring or holding power – the descriptions of the massacre at Sinigaglia or the behaviour of Agathocles or Oliverotto da Fermo are no more or less horrifying than similar stories in Tacitus or Guicciardini. The proposition that crime can pay is nothing new in western historiography.

Nor is it merely his recommendation of ruthless measures that so upsets his readers: Aristotle had long ago allowed that exceptional situations might arise, that principles and rules could not be rigidly applied to all situations; the advice to rulers in the *Politics* is tough-minded enough; Cicero is aware that critical situations demand exceptional measures – *ratio publicae utilitatis, ratio status*, were familiar in the thought of the Middle Ages. 'Necessity knows no law' is a Thomist sentiment: Pierre d'Auvergne says much the same. Harrington said this in the following century, and Hume applauded him.

These opinions were not thought original by these, or perhaps any, thinkers. Machiavelli did not originate, nor did he make much use of, the notion of *raison d'état*. He stressed will, boldness, address, at the expense of the rules laid down by calm *ragione*, to which his colleagues in the *Pratiche Fiorentine*, and perhaps the Oricellari Gardens, may have appealed. So did Leon Battista Alberti when he declared that *fortuna* crushes only the weak and propertyless; so did contemporary poets; so, too, in his own fashion, did Pico della Mirandola in his great apostrophe to the powers of man, who, unlike the angels, can transform himself into any shape – the ardent image which lies at the heart of European humanism in the north as well as the Mediterranean.

Far more original, as has often been noted, is Machiavelli's divorce of political behaviour as a field of study from the theological world-picture in terms of which this topic is discussed before him (even by Marsilio) and after him. Yet it is not his secularism, however audacious in his own day, that could have disturbed the contemporaries of Voltaire or Bentham or their successors. What shocked them is something different.

Machiavelli's cardinal achievement is, let me repeat, his uncovering of an insoluble dilemma, the planting of a permanent question mark in the path of posterity. It stems from his *de facto* recognition that ends equally ultimate, equally sacred, may contradict each other, that entire systems of value may come into collision without possibility of rational arbitration, and that not merely in exceptional circumstances, as a result of abnormality or accident or error – the clash of Antigone and Creon or in the story of Tristan – but (this was surely new) as part of the normal human situation.

For those who look on such collisions as rare, exceptional and disastrous, the choice to be made is necessarily an agonising experience for which, as a rational being, one cannot prepare (since no rules apply). But for Machiavelli, at least of *The Prince*, the *Discourses*, *Mandragola*, there is no agony. One chooses as one chooses because one knows what one wants, and is ready to pay the price. One chooses classical civilisation rather than the Theban desert, Rome and not Jerusalem, whatever the priests may say, because such is one's nature, and – he is no existentialist or romantic individualist *avant la parole* – because it is that of men in general, at all times, everywhere. If others prefer solitude or martyrdom, he shrugs his shoulders. Such men are not for him. He has nothing to say to them, nothing to argue with them about. All that matters to him and those who agree with him is that such men be not allowed to meddle with politics or education or any of the cardinal factors in human life; their outlook unfits them for such tasks.

I do not mean that Machiavelli explicitly asserts that there is a pluralism or even a dualism of values between which conscious choices must be made. But this follows from the contrasts he draws between the conduct he admires and that which he condemns. He seems to take for granted the obvious superiority of classical civic virtue and brushes aside Christian values, as well as conventional morality, with a disparaging or patronising sentence or two, or smooth words about the misinterpretation of Christianity.[1] This worries or infuriates those who

---

[1] e.g. in the passages from the *Discourses* cited above, or when he says, 'I believe the greatest good to be done and the most pleasing to God is that which one does to one's native city.' I must thank Myron Gilmore for this reference to *A Discourse on Remodelling the Government of Florence* (Gilbert, op. cit. (p. 33, note 4 above), vol. 1, pp. 113–14). This sentiment is by no means unique in Machiavelli's works: but, leaving aside his wish to flatter Leo X, or the liability of all authors to fall into the clichés of their own time, are we to suppose that Machiavelli means us to think that when Philip of Macedon transplanted populations in a manner that (unavoidable as it is said to have been) caused even Machiavelli a qualm, what Philip did, provided it was good for Macedon, was pleasing to God and, *per contra*, that Giovanpaolo Baglioni's failure to kill the Pope and the Curia was displeasing to Him? Such a notion of the Deity is, to say the least, remote from that of the New Testament. Are the needs of the *patria* automatically identical with the will of the Almighty? Are those who permit themselves to doubt this in danger of

disagree with him the more because it goes against their convictions without seeming to be aware of doing so – and recommends wicked courses as obviously the most sensible, something that only fools or visionaries will reject.

If what Machiavelli believed is true, this undermines one major assumption of western thought: namely that somewhere in the past or the future, in this world or the next, in the church or the laboratory, in the speculations of the metaphysician or the findings of the social scientist, or in the uncorrupted heart of the simple good man, there is to be found the final solution of the question of how men should live. If this is false (and if more than one equally valid answer to the question can be returned, then it is false) the idea of the sole true, objective, universal human ideal crumbles. The very search for it becomes not merely Utopian in practice, but conceptually incoherent.

One can surely see how this might seem unfaceable to men – believers or atheists, empiricists or apriorists – brought up on the opposite assumption. Nothing could well be more upsetting to those brought up in a monistic religious or, at any rate, moral, social or political system, than a breach in it. This is the dagger of which Meinecke speaks, with which Machiavelli inflicted the wound that has never healed; even though Felix Gilbert is right in thinking that he did not bear the scars of it himself. For he remained a monist, albeit a pagan one.

Machiavelli was doubtless guilty of much confusion and exaggeration. He confused the proposition that ultimate ideals may be incompatible with the very different proposition that the more conventional human ideals – founded on ideas of natural law, brotherly love, and

---

heresy? Machiavelli may at times have been represented as too Machiavellian; but to suppose that he believed that the claims of God and of Caesar were perfectly reconcilable reduces his central thesis to absurdity. Yet of course this does not prove that he lacked all Christian sentiment: the *Esortazione alla penitenza* composed in the last year of his life (if it is genuine and not a later forgery) may well be wholly sincere, as Ridolfi and Alderisio believe; Capponi may have exaggerated the extent to which he 'drove religion from his heart', even though 'it was not wholly extinct in his thought'. The point is that there is scarcely any trace of such *états d'âme* in his political writings, with which alone we are concerned. There is an interesting discussion of this by Giuseppe Prezzolini in his already cited article (p. 41, note 1 above), in which this attitude is traced to Augustine, and Croce's thesis is, by implication, controverted.

human goodness – were unrealisable and that those who acted on the opposite assumption were fools, and at times dangerous ones; and he attributed this dubious proposition to antiquity, and believed that it was verified by history. The first of these assertions strikes at the root of all doctrines which believe in the possibility of attaining, or at least formulating, final solutions; the second is empirical, commonplace, and not self-evident. The two propositions are not, in any case, identical or logically connected.

Moreover he exaggerated wildly : the idealised types of the Perilean Greek or the Roman of the old Republic may be irreconcilable with the ideal citizen of a Christian commonwealth (supposing such were conceivable), but in practice – above all in history, to which our author went for illustrations if not for evidence – pure types seldom obtain: mixtures and compounds and compromises and forms of communal life that do not fit into easy classifications, but which neither Christians, nor liberal humanists, nor Machiavelli would be compelled by their beliefs to reject, can be conceived without too much intellectual difficulty. Still, to attack and inflict lasting damage on a central assumption of an entire civilisation is an achievement of the first order.

Machiavelli does not affirm this dualism. He merely takes for granted the superiority of Roman *antiqua virtus* (which may be maddening to those who do not) over the Christian life as taught by the church. He utters a few casual words about what Christianity might have become, but does not expect it to change its actual character. There he leaves the matter. Anyone who believes in Christian morality, and regards the Christian commonwealth as its embodiment, but at the same time largely accepts the validity of Machiavelli's political and psychological analysis and does not reject the secular heritage of Rome – a man in this predicament is faced with a dilemma which, if Machiavelli is right, is not merely unsolved but insoluble. This is the Gordian knot which, according to Vanini and Leibniz, the author of *The Prince* had tied – a knot which can be cut but not undone.[1] Hence the efforts to dilute his doctrines, or interpret them in such a way as to remove their sting.

After Machiavelli, doubt is liable to infect all monistic constructions. The sense of certainty that there is somewhere a hidden treasure – the final solution to our ills – and that some path must lead to it (for,

[1] Quoted by Prezzolini, op. cit. (p. 25, note 2 above), English version, pp. 222–3.

in principle, it must be discoverable); or else, to alter the image, the conviction that the fragments constituted by our beliefs and habits are all pieces of a jigsaw puzzle, which (since there is an *a priori* guarantee for this) can, in principle, be solved, so that it is only because of lack of skill or stupidity or bad fortune that we have not so far succeeded in discovering the solution, whereby all interests will be brought into harmony – this fundamental belief of western political thought has been severely shaken. Surely in an age that looks for certainties, this is sufficient to account for the unending efforts, more numerous today than ever, to explain *The Prince* and the *Discourses*, or to explain them away?

This is the negative implication. There is also one that is positive, and might have surprised and perhaps displeased Machiavelli. So long as only one ideal is the true goal, it will always seem to men that no means can be too difficult, no price too high, to do whatever is required to realise the ultimate goal. Such certainty is one of the great justifications of fanaticism, compulsion, persecution. But if not all values are compatible with one another, and choices must be made for no better reason than that each value is what it is, and we choose it for what it is, and not because it can be shown on some single scale to be higher than another; if we choose forms of life because we believe in them, because we take them for granted, or, upon examination, find that we are morally unprepared to live in any other way (although others choose differently); if rationality and calculation can be applied only to means or subordinate ends, but never to ultimate ends; then a picture emerges different from that constructed round the ancient principle that there is only one good for men.

If there is only one solution to the puzzle, then the only problems are firstly how to find it, then how to realise it, and finally how to convert others to the solution by persuasion or by force. But if this is not so (Machiavelli contrasts two ways of life, but there could be, and, save for fanatical monists, there obviously are, more than two), then the path is open to empiricism, pluralism, toleration, compromise. Toleration is historically the product of the realisation of the irreconcilability of equally dogmatic faiths, and the practical improbability of complete victory of one over the other. Those who wished to survive realised that they had to tolerate error. They gradually came to see merits in diversity, and so became sceptical about definitive solutions in human affairs.

But it is one thing to accept something in practice, another to justify it rationally. Machiavelli's 'scandalous' writings begin the latter process. This was a major turning point, and its intellectual consequences, wholly unintended by its originator, were, by a fortunate irony of history (which some call its dialectic), the bases of the very liberalism that Machiavelli would surely have condemned as feeble and characterless, lacking in single-minded pursuit of power, in splendour, in organisation, in *virtù*, in power to discipline unruly men against huge odds into one energetic whole. Yet he is, in spite of himself, one of the makers of pluralism, and of its – to him – perilous acceptance of toleration.

By breaking the original unity he helped to cause men to become aware of the necessity of having to make agonising choices between incompatible alternatives in public and in private life (for the two could not, it became obvious, be genuinely kept distinct). His achievement is of the first order, if only because the dilemma has never given men peace since it came to light (it remains unsolved, but we have learnt to live with it). Men had, no doubt, in practice, often enough experienced the conflict which Machiavelli made explicit. He converted its expression from a paradox into something approaching a commonplace.

The sword of which Meinecke spoke has not lost its edge: the wound has not healed. To know the worst is not always to be liberated from its consequences; nevertheless it is preferable to ignorance. It is this painful truth that Machiavelli forced on our attention, not by formulating it explicitly, but perhaps the more effectively by relegating much uncriticised traditional morality to the realm of Utopia. This is what, at any rate, I should like to suggest. Where more than twenty interpretations hold the field, the addition of one more cannot be deemed an impertinence. At worst it will be no more than yet another attempt to solve the problem, now more than four centuries old, of which Croce at the end of his long life spoke as 'Una questione che forse non si chiuderà mai : la questione del Machiavelli'.[1]

---

[1] *Quaderni della 'Critica'* 5 No 14 (July 1949), 1–9.

The Divorce between the Sciences
and the Humanities

I

My subject is the relation of the natural sciences to the humanities: more particularly, a growing tension between them; and especially the moment when, it seems to me, the great divorce between them, which had been brewing for some time, became clear for all who had eyes to see. It was not a divorce between 'two cultures': there have been many cultures in the history of mankind, and their variety has little or nothing to do with the differences between the natural sciences and the humanities. I have tried but altogether failed to grasp what is meant by describing these two great fields of human inquiry as cultures; but they do seem to have been concerned with somewhat different issues, and those who have worked and are working in them have pursued different aims and methods – a fact which, for better or for worse, became explicit in the eighteenth century.

I begin with a tradition in which many eminent scientists today still stand: the tradition of those who believe that it is possible to make steady progress in the entire sphere of human knowledge; that methods and goals are, or should be, ultimately identical throughout this sphere; that the path to progress has been, as often as not – or perhaps a good deal more often – blocked by ignorance, fantasy, prejudice, superstition and other forms of unreason; that we have in our day reached a stage when the achievements of the natural sciences are such that it is possible to derive their structure from a single integrated set of clear principles or rules which, if correctly applied, make possible indefinite further progress in the unravelling of the mysteries of nature.

This approach is in line with a central tradition in western thought which extends back at least as far as Plato. It appears to me to rest on at least three basic assumptions: (a) that every genuine question has one true answer and one only: all the others being false. Unless this is so, the question cannot be a real question – there is a confusion in it somewhere. This position, which has been made explicit by modern empiricist philosophers, is entailed no less firmly by the views of their theological and metaphysical predecessors against whom they have been engaged in long and uncompromising warfare. (*b*) The method which leads to correct solutions to all genuine problems is rational in character; and is, in essence, if not in detailed application, identical in all fields. (*c*) These solutions, whether or not they are discovered, are true universally, eternally and immutably: true for all times, places and men: as in the old definition of natural law, they are *quod semper, quod ubique, quod ab omnibus.*

Opinions within this tradition have, of course, differed about where the answers were to be sought: some thought they could only be discovered by specialists trained in, let us say, Plato's dialectical method, or Aristotle's more empirical types of investigation; or in the methods of various schools of sophists, or of the thinkers who trace their descent from Socrates. Others held that such truths were more accessible to men of pure and innocent soul, whose understanding had not been corrupted by philosophic subtleties or the sophistication of civilisation or destructive social institutions, as, for example, Rousseau and Tolstoy at times maintained. There were those, especially in the seventeenth century, who believed that the only true path was that of systems based on rational insight (of which mathematical reasoning offered the perfect example), which yielded *a priori* truths; others put their faith in hypotheses confirmed or falsified by controlled observation and experiment; still others preferred to rely on what seemed to them plain common sense – *le bon sens* – reinforced by careful observation, experiment, scientific method, but not replaceable by the sciences; and men have pointed to other roads to truth. What is common to all thinkers of this type is the belief that there is only one true method or combination of methods: and that what cannot be answered by it, cannot be answered at all. The implication of this position is that the world is a single system which can be described and explained by the use of rational methods; with the practical corollary that if man's life is to be organised at all, and not left to chaos and the play of uncontrolled nature and chance, then it can be organised only in the light of such principles and laws.

It is not surprising that this view was most strongly held and most influential in the hour of the greatest triumph of the natural sciences – surely a major, if not the major, achievement of the human mind: and especially, therefore, in the seventeenth century in western

Europe. From Descartes and Bacon and the followers of Galileo and Newton, from Voltaire and the Encyclopedists to Saint-Simon and Comte and Buckle, and, in our own century, H. G. Wells and Bernal and Skinner and the Viennese positivists, with their ideal of a unified system of all the sciences, natural and humane, this has been the programme of the modern Enlightenment; and it has played a decisive role in the social, legal and technological organisation of our world. This was perhaps bound sooner or later to provoke a reaction from those who felt that constructions of reason and science, of a single all-embracing system, whether it claimed to explain the nature of things, or to go further and dictate, in the light of this, what one should do and be and believe, were in some way constricting – an obstacle to their own vision of the world, chains on their imagination or feeling or will, a barrier to spiritual or political liberty.

This is not the first occasion on which this phenomenon occurred: the domination of the philosophical schools of Athens in the Hellenistic period was attended by a noticeable increase in mystery cults and other forms of occultism and emotionalism in which non-rational elements in the human spirit sought an outlet. There was the great Christian revolt against the great organised legal systems, whether of the Jews or the Romans; there were medieval antinomian rebellions against the scholastic establishment and the authority of the church – movements of this kind from the Cathars to the anabaptists are evidence enough of this; the Reformation was preceded and followed by the rise of powerful mystical and irrationalist currents. I will not dwell on more recent manifestions of this – in the German *Sturm und Drang*, in the romanticism of the early nineteenth century, in Carlyle and Kierkegaard and Nietzsche and the vast spectrum of modern irrationalism both on the right and on the left.

It is not, however, with this that I intend to deal, but with the critical attack upon the total claim of the new scientific method to dominate the entire field of human knowledge, whether in its metaphysical – *a priori* – or empirical-probabilistic forms. This attack, whether its causes were psychological or social (and I am inclined to think that they were, at least in part, due to a reaction on the part of humanists, especially the inward-looking, anti-materialistic Christians among them, against the all-conquering advance of the physical sciences), was itself based on rational argument, and in due course led to the great divorce between the natural sciences and the humanities – *Naturwissenschaft* and *Geisteswissenschaft* – a divorce the validity of which has been challenged ever since and remains a central and highly controversial issue to this day.

As everyone knows, the great triumphs of natural science in the seventeenth century gave the proponents of the scientific method immense prestige. The great liberators of the age were Descartes and Bacon, who carried opposition to the authority of tradition, faith, dogma or prescription into every realm of knowledge and opinion, armed with weapons used during the Renaissance and, indeed, earlier. Although there was much cautious avoidance of open defiance of Christian belief, the general thrust of the new movement was to bring everything before the bar of reason: the cruder forgeries and misinterpretations of texts, on which lawyers and clerics had rested their claims, had been exposed by humanists in Italy and Protestant reformers in France; appeals to the authority of the Bible, or Aristotle, or Roman law, had met with a good deal of acutely argued resistance based both on learning and on critical methods. Descartes made an epoch with his attempt to systematise these methods – notably in his *Discourse on Method* and its application in his *Meditations* – his two most popular and influential philosophical treatises. Spinoza's *Treatise on the Improvement of the Mind*, his quasi-geometrical method in the *Ethics* and the severely rationalist assumptions and rigorous logic in his political works and his criticisms of the Old Testament, had carried the war further into the enemy's camp. Bacon and Spinoza, in their different ways, sought to remove obstacles to clear, rational thinking. Bacon exposed what he considered the chief sources of delusion: 'idols' of 'the tribe', 'the den', 'the market-place' and 'the theatre' – effects, in his view, of the uncritical acceptance of the evidence of the senses, of one's own predilections, of misunderstanding of words, of confusions bred by the speculative fantasies of philosophers, and the like. Spinoza stressed the degree to which emotions clouded reason, and led to groundless fears and hatreds which led to destructive practice; from Valla to Locke and Berkeley there were frequent warnings and examples of fallacies and confusions due to the misuse of language.

The general, if not the universal, tendency of the new philosophy was to declare that if the human mind can be cleared of dogma, prejudice and cant, of the organised obscurities and Aristotelian patter of the schoolmen, then nature will at last be seen in the full symmetry and harmony of its elements, which can be described, analysed and represented by a logically appropriate language – the language of the mathematical and physical sciences. Leibniz seems to have believed not only in the possibility of constructing a logically perfect language, which would reflect the structure of reality, but in something not unlike a general science of discovery. His views spread far beyond philosophical or scientific circles – indeed, theoretical knowledge was still conceived as one undivided realm; the frontiers between philosophy, science, criticism, theology, were not sharply drawn. There were invasions and counter-invasions; grammar, rhetoric, jurisprudence, philosophy, made forays into the fields of historical learning and natural knowledge, and were attacked by them in turn. The new rationalism spread into the creative arts. Just as the Royal Society in England formally set itself against the use of metaphor and other forms of rhetorical speech, and demanded language that was plain and literal and precise, so there was in France at this time a corresponding avoidance of metaphor, embellishment and highly coloured expression in, for example, the plays of Racine or Molière, in the verse of La Fontaine and Boileau, writers who dominated the European scene; and because such luxuriance was held to flourish in Italy, Italian literature was duly denounced in France for the impurity of its style. The new method sought to eliminate everything that could not be justified by the systematic use of rational methods, above all the fictions of the metaphysicians, the mystics, the poets; what were myth and legend but falsehoods with which primitive and barbarous societies were gulled during their early, helpless childhood? At best, they were fanciful or distorted accounts of real events or persons. Even the Catholic church was influenced by the prevailing scientific temper, and the great archival labours of the Bollandists and Maurists were conducted in a semi-scientific spirit.[1]

It was natural enough that history was one of the earliest victims of what might be called the positivist character of the new scientific movement. Scepticism about historical veracity was no new thing: ignorance and fantasy, as well as malicious invention, had been attributed to Herodotus by Plutarch; and these charges against narrative history had been repeated at intervals by those who preferred certainty to conjecture. The sixteenth century in particular, perhaps as a result of the mobilisation of history in the religious wars by the various factions, saw a rise of scepticism and doubt: Cornelius Agrippa, in 1531,

[1] M. H. Fisch has correctly pointed out that the dissolution of monasteries had released a mass of documentary evidence which had not hitherto been available, and this contributed to the fact that the church, in repelling attacks on her historical claims, had recourse to weapons of historical research.

dwells on the carelessness and contradictions of historians, and their shameless inventions to cover up their ignorance or fill gaps in knowledge where there is no available evidence; on the absurdity of idealising the characters of the main actors in the story; he speaks of the distortion of facts as being due to the historians' passions – wishes, hatreds and fears, desire to please a patron, patriotic motives, national pride – Plutarch glorified the Greeks in comparison with the Romans, and in his own day polemical writers extolled the virtues of Gauls over Franks, and vice versa. How can truth emerge in these conditions? In the same vein Patrizzi, at the turn of the century, declares that all history ultimately rests on eye-witness evidence: and argues that those who are present are likely to be involved in the issues, and are therefore liable to be partisan; while those who can afford to be objective because they are neutral and uninvolved are unlikely to see the evidence jealously preserved by the partisans, and have to depend upon the biased accounts of the interested parties.

Such Pyrrhonism grows with the century: it is characteristic of Montaigne, Charron, La Mothe le Vayer, and of course, later in the century, in a more extreme form, of Pierre Bayle, to take but a few examples. So long as history is regarded as a school of virtue, the purpose of which is to celebrate the good and expose the wicked, to show the unaltering character of human nature at all times, everywhere, to be simply moral and political philosophy teaching by examples, it may not matter greatly whether such history is accurate or not. But once a desire for truth for its own sake asserts itself, or something more novel is born, the desire to create an advancing science – to accumulate knowledge, to know more than our predecessors and to be aware of this – this leads to the realisation that this can be achieved only if the reputable practitioners in the field recognise the validity of the same principles and methods and can test each other's conclusions, as has been (and is) the case in physics or mathematics or astronomy and in all the new sciences. It is this new outlook that made the claims of history to be a province of knowledge seem so precarious.

Much of the most formidable attack came from Descartes. His views are well known: true science rests on axiomatic premises, from which, by the use of rational rules, irrefutable conclusions can be drawn: this is how we proceed in geometry, in algebra, in physics. Where are the axioms, the transformation rules, the inescapable conclusions, in historical writing? The progress of true knowledge is the discovery of eternal, unalterable, universal truths: every generation of seekers after truth stands on the shoulders of its predecessors and begins where these others left off, and adds to the growing sum of human knowledge. This is plainly not the case in historical writing, or indeed in the field of the humanities in general. Where, in this province, is the single, ever-mounting edifice of science? A schoolboy today knows more geometry than Pythagoras : what do the greatest classical scholars of our time know about ancient Rome that was not known to Cicero's servant girl? What have they added to her store? What, then, is the use of all these learned labours? Descartes implies that he does not wish to prevent men from indulging in this pastime – they may find it agreeable enough to while away their leisure in these ways – it is no worse, he says, than learning some quaint dialect, say, Swiss or bas-Breton; but it is not an occupation for anyone seriously concerned with increasing knowledge. Malebranche dismisses history as gossip; this is echoed by other Cartesians; even Leibniz, who composed a sizeable historical work himself, gives a conventional defence of history as a means of satisfying curiosity about origins of families or states, and as a school of morals. Its inferiority to mathematics, and philosophy founded on the mathematical and natural sciences and the other discoveries of pure reason, must be obvious to all thinking men.

These attitudes did not, of course, kill historical studies. Methods of scholarship had advanced greatly since the middle of the fifteenth century, especially by the use made of antiquities. Monuments, legal documents, manuscripts, coins, medals, works of art, literature, buildings, inscriptions, popular ballads, legends, could be employed as aids to, and sometimes even substitutes for, unreliable narrative history. The great jurists of the sixteenth century, Budé, Alciati, Cujas, Dumoulin, Hotman, Baudouin and their disciples, and in the following century Coke and Matthew Hale in England, Vranck in the Low Countries, de Gregorio in Italy and Sparre in Sweden, performed major labours of reconstructing legal texts, both Roman and medieval. The school of universal historians in France – Pasquier, Le Roy, Le Caron, Vignier, La Popelinière, and, indeed, the polymath Bodin – originated at least the conception of cultural history;[1] and were fol-

---

[1] Phrases like 'les saisons et mutations de moeurs d'un peuple', or 'la complexion et humour' of a nation, or 'façons de vivre', or 'forme de vivre', 'la police' or 'les motifs, les opinions et les pensées des hommes', 'le génie du siècle, des opinions, des moeurs, des idées dominantes', 'des passions qui conduisaient les hommes' were very common throughout the sixteenth and seventeenth centuries.

lowed in the seventeenth century by writers like the Abbé de Saint Réal, Dufresnoy, Charles Sorel, Père Gabriel Daniel, and, of course, Boulainvilliers and Fénelon. These early outlines of cultural history, and in particular the growing awareness of the differences rather than the similarities between different societies, ages, civilisations, were a novel development, which, in due course, revolutionised historical notions. Nevertheless, their proponents showed a greater propensity for denouncing useless erudition, and for making up programmes of what historians should do, than for indicating precise methods of performing these tasks or, indeed, performing them. Much of this was meta-history, or theories of history, rather than concrete historical writing. Moreover, the scientific model (or 'paradigm') which dominated the century, with its strong implication that only that which was quantifiable, or at any rate measurable – that to which in principle mathematical methods were applicable – was real, strongly reinforced the old conviction that to every question there was only one true answer, universal, eternal, unchangeable; it was, or appeared to be, so in mathematics, physics, mechanics and astronomy, and soon would be in chemistry and botany and zoology and other natural sciences; with the corollary that the most reliable criterion of objective truth was logical demonstration, or measurement, or at least approximations to this.

Spinoza's political theory is a good example of this approach: he supposes that the rational answer to the question of what is the best government for men is in principle discoverable by anyone, anywhere, in any circumstances. If men have not discovered these timeless solutions before, this must be due to weakness, or the clouding of reason by emotion, or perhaps bad luck: the truths of which he supposed himself to be giving a rational demonstration could presumably have been discovered and applied by human reason at any time, so that mankind might have been spared many evils. Hobbes, an empiricist, but equally dominated by a scientific model, presupposes this also. The notion of time, change, historical development, does not impinge upon these views. Furthermore, such truths, when discovered, must add to human welfare. Consequently the motive for the search is not curiosity, or desire to know the truth as such, so much as utilitarian – the promotion of a better life on earth by making man more rational and therefore wiser, more just, virtuous and happy. The ends of man are given: given by God or nature. Reason, freed from its trammels, will discover what they are: all that is necessary is to find the right means for their attainment.

This is the ideal from Francis Bacon to H. G. Wells and Julian Huxley and many of those who, in our day, believe in moral and political arrangements based on a scientific theory of sociology and psychology. The most famous figure in this entire movement, not in that of science itself, but of the application of its discoveries to the lives of men – certainly its most gifted propagandist – was Voltaire. Its earliest and strongest opponent was the Neapolitan philosopher Giambattista Vico. The contrast between their views may serve to throw light upon the radical difference of attitudes which brought about a crucial parting of the ways.

II

Voltaire is the central figure of the Enlightenment, because he accepted its basic principles and used all his incomparable wit and energy and literary skill and brilliant malice to propagate these principles and spread havoc in the enemy's camp. Ridicule kills more surely than savage indignation: and Voltaire probably did more for the triumph of civilised values than any writer who ever lived. What were these principles? Let me repeat the formula once more: there are eternal, timeless truths, identical in all the spheres of human activity – moral and political, social and economic, scientific and artistic; and there is only one way of recognising them: by means of reason, which Voltaire interpreted not as the deductive method of logic or mathematics, which was too abstract and unrelated to the facts and needs of daily life, but as *le bon sens*, the good sense which, while it may not lead to absolute certainty, attains to a degree of verisimilitude or probability quite sufficient for human affairs, for public and private life. Not many men are fully armed with this excellent faculty, for the majority appear to be incurably stupid; but those few who do possess it are responsible for the finest hours of mankind. All that is of value in the past are these fine hours: from them alone we can learn how to make men good, that is, sane, rational, tolerant, or, at any rate, less brutish and stupid and cruel; how to enact laws and governments which will promote justice, beauty, freedom and happiness and diminish brutality, fanaticism, oppression, with which the greater part of human history is filled.

The task of modern historians is therefore plain: to describe and celebrate these moments of high culture and contrast them with the surrounding darkness – the barbarous ages of faith, fanaticism and stupid and cruel acts. In order to do this historians must give more attention than the ancients to 'customs, laws, manners, commerce, finance, agriculture, population': and also trade, industry, colonisation and the development of taste. This is far more important than accounts of wars, treaties, political institutions, conquerors, dynastic tables, public affairs, to which historians have attached far too much significance hitherto. Madame du Chatelet, Voltaire tells us, said to him : 'What is the point for a Frenchwoman like me . . . of knowing that in Sweden Egil succeeded King Haquin; or that Ottoman was the son of Ortugul?' She was perfectly right : the purpose of the work which he wrote ostensibly for the illumination of this lady (the famous *Essai sur les moeurs*) is, therefore, not 'to know in which year one prince who doesn't deserve to be remembered succeeded another barbarian prince of some uncouth nation'. 'I wish to show how human societies came into existence, how domestic life was lived, what arts were cultivated, rather than tell once again the old story of disasters and misfortunes . . . those familiar examples of human malice and depravity.' He intends to recount the achievement of 'the human spirit in the most enlightened of ages', for only that is worthy of mention which is worthy of posterity.

History is an arid desert with few oases. There are only four great ages in the west in which human beings rose to their full stature and created civilisations of which they can be proud : the age of Alexander, in which he includes the classical age of Athens ; the age of Augustus, in which he includes the Roman Republic and the Empire at their best ; Florence during the Renaissance ; and the age of Louis XIV in France. Voltaire assumes throughout that these are élitist civilisations, imposed by enlightened oligarchies on the masses, for the latter lack reason and courage, want only to be amused and deceived, and so are naturally prey to religion, that is, for him, to abominable superstitions. 'Only governments can . . . raise or lower the level of nations.'

The basic assumption is, of course, that the goals pursued in these four great cultures are ultimately the same : truth, light, are the same everywhere, it is only error that has myriad forms. Moreover, it is absurd to confine inquiry to Europe and that portion of the near east whence sprang little but the cruelties, fanaticism and nonsensical beliefs of the Jews and the Christians who, whatever Bossuet may seek to demonstrate, were and remain enemies of truth and progress and toleration. It is absurd to ignore the great and peaceful kingdom of

China, governed by enlightened Mandarins, or India, or Chaldaea and other parts of the world which only the absurd vanity of Christian Europe excludes from the orbit of history. The purpose of history is to impart instructive truths, not to satisfy idle curiosity, and this can only be done by studying the peaks of human achievement, not the valleys. The historian should not peddle fables, like Herodotus, who is like an old woman telling stories to children, but teach us our duties without seeming to do so, by painting for posterity not the acts of a single man but the progress of the human spirit in the most enlightened ages. 'If you have no more to tell us than that one barbarian succeeded another barbarian on the banks of the Oxus or the Ixartes, what use are you to the public?' Why should we be interested in the fact that 'Quancum succeeded Kincum, and Kicum succeeded Quancum'? We do not wish to know about the life of Louis the Fat, or Louis the Obstinate, or even the barbarous Shakespeare and the tedious Milton: but about the achievements of Galileo, Newton, Tasso, Addison; who wants to know about Shalmaneser of Mardokempad? Historians must not clutter the minds of their readers with accounts of religious wars or other stupidities that degrade mankind, unless it be to show them how low human beings can sink: accounts of Philip II of Spain, or Christian of Denmark, are cautionary tales to warn mankind of the dangers of tyranny; or if, like Voltaire himself, one does write a lively and entertaining biography of Charles XII of Sweden, it is for the sole end of pointing out to men the dangers of a life of reckless adventure. What *is* worth knowing is why the Emperor Charles V did not profit more by his capture of King Francis I of France; or what the value of sound finance was to Elizabeth of England, or Henry IV or Louis XIV in France, or the importance of the *dirigiste* policy of Colbert compared with that of Sully. As for horrors, they too are to be detailed if we are to avoid another St Bartholomew's Eve or another Cromwell.

The task of the historian, he says again and again, is to recount the achievements of those regrettably rare periods when the arts and sciences flourished and nature was made to yield the necessities, comforts and pleasures of man. Meinecke rightly described Voltaire as 'the banker of the Enlightenment', the keeper of its achievements, a kind of scorer in the contest of light against darkness, reason and civilisation against barbarism and religion, Athens and the Rome of the virtuous Caesars against Jerusalem and the Rome of the Popes, Julian the Apostate versus Gregory of Nazianzus. But how are we to tell what actually happened in the past? Has not Pierre Bayle thrown terrible doubts on the authenticity of particular reports of facts, and shown how unreliable and contradictory historical evidence can be? This may be so, but it is not particular facts that matter, according to Voltaire, so much as the general character of an age or a culture. The acts of single men are of small importance, and individual character is too difficult to elucidate : when we can scarcely tell even what the true character of Mazarin was like, how can we possibly do this for the ancients? 'Soul, character, dominant motives, all that sort of thing is an impenetrable chaos which can never be firmly grasped. Whoever, after centuries, would disentangle this chaos simply creates more.'

How, then, are we to recover the past? By the light of natural reason – *le bon sens*. 'Anything not in keeping with natural science, with reason, with the nature [*trempe*] of the human heart is false' – why bother with the ravings of savages and the inventions of knaves? We know that monuments are 'historical lies' and 'that there is not a single temple or college of priests, not a single feast in the church, that does not originate in some stupidity'. The human heart is the same everywhere; and good sense is enough to detect the truth.

Le bon sens served Voltaire well : it enabled him to discredit much clerical propaganda and a good many naïve and pedantic absurdities. But it also told him that the empires of Babylon and Assyria could not possibly have coexisted next door to each other in so confined a space ; that accounts of temple prostitutes were obvious nonsense; that Cyrus and Croesus were fictional beings; that Themistocles could not possibly have died of drinking ox blood; that Belus and Ninus could not have been Babylonian kings, for '-us' is not a Babylonian ending; that Xerxes did not flog the Hellespont. The Flood is an absurd fable : as for the shells found on tops of mountains, these may well have dropped from the hats of pilgrims. On the other hand, he found no difficulty at all in accepting the reality of satyrs, fauns, the Minotaur, Zeus, Theseus, Hercules, or the journey of Bacchus to India, and he happily accepted a forged Indian classic, the *Ezour-Veidam*. Yet Voltaire undoubtedly expanded the area of proper historical interest beyond politics, wars, great men, by insisting on 'the need to describe how men travelled, lived, slept, dressed, wrote', their social and economic and artistic activities. Jacques Coeur was more important than Joan of Arc. He complains that Pufendorf, who has had access to the state archives of Sweden, has told us nothing about the natural resources of that country, the causes of its poverty, what part it played in the

Gothic invasions of the Roman Empire; these are novel and important demands. Voltaire denounced Europocentrism; he sketched the need for social, economic, cultural history, which, even though he did not himself realise his programme (his own histories are marvellously readable but largely anecdotal in character – there is no real attempt at synthesis), stimulated the interest of his successors in a wider field. At the same time he devalued the historical nature of history, for his interests are moral, aesthetic, social: as a *philosophe* he is part moralist, part tourist and *feuilletoniste*, and wholly a journalist, albeit of incomparable genius. He does not recognise, even as a cultural historian – or cataloguer – the multiplicity and relativity of values at different times and places, or the genetic dimension in history: the notion of change and growth is largely alien to him. For Voltaire there are only bright ages and dark, and the dark are due to the crimes, follies and misfortunes of men. In this respect he is a good deal less historical than some of his predecessors in the Renaissance. He looks on history, in a loose fashion, as an accumulation of facts, casually connected, the purpose of which is to show men under what conditions those central purposes which nature has implanted in the heart of every man can best be realised: who are the enemies of progress, and how they are to be routed. Thereby Voltaire probably did more than anyone else to determine the entire direction of the Enlightenment: Hume and Gibbon are possessed by the same spirit.

Not until the reaction against the classification of all human experience in terms of absolute and timeless values – a reaction which first began in Switzerland and England among critics and historians of Greek and Hebrew literature, and, penetrating to Germany, created the great intellectual revolution of which Herder was the most influential apostle – did history, as we understand it today, come into its own. Nevertheless, it is to Voltaire, Fontenelle and Montesquieu (who, contrary to the accepted view of him, was no less convinced of the absolute and timeless nature of ultimate human ends, however much means and methods might vary from clime to clime) that we owe the more scientific branches of later historical writing: economic history, the history of science and technology, historical sociology, demography, all the provinces of the knowledge of the past which owe their existence to statistical and other quantitative techniques. But the history of civilisation which Voltaire supposed himself to be initiating was in the end created by the Germans, who looked on him as the arch-enemy of all that they held dear.

Yet even before the Counter-Enlightenment of the Swiss and the English and the Germans, a new conception of the study of history came into being. It was anti-Voltairean in character, and its author was an obscure Neapolitan whom Voltaire had almost certainly never heard of: and if he had, would have treated with disdain.

III

Giambattista Vico was born in Naples in 1668 and lived there or in its environs until his death in 1744. Throughout his long life he was little known, the very exemplar of a lonely thinker. He was educated by priests, worked for some years as a private tutor, became a minor professor of rhetoric at the University of Naples, and after many years of composing inscriptions, Latin eulogies and laudatory biographies for the rich and the great in order to supplement his meagre income, was rewarded in the last years of his life by being appointed official historiographer to the Austrian Viceroy of Naples.

He was steeped in the literature of humanism, in the classical authors and antiquities, and especially in Roman law. His mind was not analytical or scientific but literary and intuitive. Naples under Spanish and Austrian rulers was not in the vanguard of the new scientific movement; although experimental scientists were at work there, so were the church and the Inquisition. If anything, the Kingdom of the Two Sicilies was something of a backwater, and Vico, by inclination a religious humanist with a rich historical imagination, was not in sympathy with the great scientific materialist movement that was determined to sweep away the last relics of the scholastic metaphysics. Nevertheless, in his youth, he fell under the sway of the new currents of thought: he read Lucretius, and the Epicurean conception of gradual human development from primitive, semi-bestial beginnings remained with him, despite his Christian faith, all his life. Influenced by the all-powerful Cartesian movement, he began by believing mathematics to be the queen of the sciences. But evidently something in him rebelled against this. In 1709, at the age of forty, in an inaugural lecture, with which professors in the University of Naples were obliged to start each academic year, he published a passionate defence of humanist education: men's minds (*ingenia*) were shaped by the language – the words and the images – which they inherited, no less than their minds, in turn, shaped their modes of

93

expression; the search after a plain, neutral style, like the attempt to train the young exclusively in the dry light of the Cartesian analytic method, tended to rob them of imaginative power. Vico defended the rich, traditional Italian 'rhetoric', inherited from the great humanists of the Renaissance, against the austere and deflationary style of the French rationalist science-influenced modernists.

Evidently he continued to brood on the two contrasted methods, for in the following year he arrived at a truly startling conclusion: mathematics was indeed, as had always been claimed for it, a discipline which led to wholly clear, irrefutable propositions of universal validity. But this was so not because the language of mathematics was a reflection of the basic and unalterable structure of reality, as thinkers since the days of Plato or even Pythagoras had maintained: it was so because mathematics was not a reflection of anything. Mathematics was not a discovery but a human invention: starting from definitions and axioms of their own choosing, mathematicians could, by means of rules of which they or other men were authors, arrive at conclusions that did indeed logically follow, because the man-made rules, definitions and axioms saw to it that they did so. Mathematics was a kind of game (although Vico did not call it that), in which the counters and the rules were man-made; the moves and their implications were indeed certain, but at the cost of describing nothing – a play of abstractions controlled by their creators. Once this system was applied to the natural world – for instance, as in physics or mechanics – it yielded important truths, but inasmuch as nature had not been invented by men, and had its own characteristics and could not, like symbols, be freely manipulated, the conclusions became less clear, no longer wholly knowable. Mathematics was not a system of laws which governed reality, but a system of rules, in terms of which it was useful to generalise about, analyse and predict, the behaviour of things in space.

Here Vico made use of an ancient scholastic proposition at least as old as St Augustine: that one could know fully only what one had oneself made. A man could understand fully his own intellectual or poetical construction, a work of art or a plan, because he had himself made it, and it was therefore transparent to him: everything in it had been created by his intellect and his imagination. Indeed, Hobbes had asserted as much in the case of political constitutions. But the world – nature – had not been made by men: therefore only God, who had made it, could know it through and through. Mathematics seemed so marvellous an achievement precisely because it was wholly man's own work – the nearest to divine creation that man could attain to. And there were those in the Renaissance who spoke of art, too, in this fashion, and said that the artist was a creator, *quasi deus*, of an imaginary world created alongside the real world, and the artist, the god who had created it, knew it through and through. But about the world of external nature there was something opaque: men could describe it, could tell how it behaved in different situations and relationships, could offer hypotheses about the behaviour of its constituents – physical bodies and the like; but they could not tell why – for what reason – it was as it was, and behaved as it did: only he who made it, namely God, knew that – men had only an outside view, as it were, of what went on on the stage of nature. Men could know 'from the inside' only what they had made themselves and nothing else. The greater the man-made element in any object of knowledge, the more transparent to human vision it will be; the greater the ingredient of external nature, the more opaque and impenetrable to human understanding. There was an impassable gulf between the man-made and the natural: the constructed and the given. All provinces of knowledge could be classified along this scale of relative intelligibility.

Ten years later Vico took a radical step: there existed a field of knowledge besides that of the most obviously man-made constructions – works of art, or political schemes, or legal systems, and indeed, all rule-determined disciplines – which men could know from within: human history; for it, too, was made by men. Human history did not consist merely of things and events and their compresences and sequences (including those of human organisms viewed as natural objects) as the external world did; it was the story of human activities, of what men did and thought and suffered, of what they strove for, aimed at, accepted, rejected, conceived, imagined, of what their feelings were directed at. It was concerned, therefore, with motives, purposes, hopes, fears, loves and hatreds, jealousies, ambitions, outlooks and visions of reality; with the ways of seeing, and ways of acting and creating, of individuals and groups. These activities we knew directly, because we were involved in them as actors, not spectators. There was a sense, therefore, in which we knew more about ourselves than we knew about the external world; when we studied, let us say, Roman law, or Roman institutions, we were not contemplating objects in nature, of whose purposes, or whether they had any, we could know nothing. We had to ask ourselves what these Romans were at, what they strove to do, how they lived and thought, what kind of relationships with other men they were anxious to promote or frustrate. We could not ask this about natural objects: it was idle to ask what cows or trees or stones, or molecules or cells, were *at*: we had no reason to suppose that they pursued purposes; or if they did, we could not know what they were; since we had not made them, we could have no Godlike 'inside' view of what ends, if any, they pursued or had been created to fulfil. There was, therefore, a clear sense in which our knowledge was superior, at least in kind, about intentional behaviour – that is, action – to our knowledge of the movement or position of bodies in space, the field of the magnificent triumphs of seventeenth-century science. What was opaque to us when we contemplated the external world was, if not wholly transparent, yet surely far more so when we contemplated ourselves. It was therefore a perverse kind of self-denial to apply the rules and laws of physics or of the other natural sciences to the world of mind and will and feeling; for by doing this we would be gratuitously debarring ourselves from much that we could know.

If anthropomorphism was falsely to endow the inanimate world with human minds and wills, there was presumably a world which it was proper to endow with precisely these attributes, namely, the world of man. Consequently, a natural science of men treated as purely natural entities, on a par with rivers and plants and stones, rested on a cardinal error. With regard to ourselves we were privileged observers with an 'inside' view: to ignore it in favour of the ideal of a unified science of all there is, a single, universal method of investigation, was to insist on wilful ignorance in the name of a materialist dogma of what could alone be known. We know what is meant by action, purpose, effort to achieve something or to understand something – we know these things through direct consciousness of them. We possess self-awareness. Can we also tell what others are at? Vico never directly tells us how this is achieved, but seems to take it for granted that solipsism needs no refutation; and, moreover, that we communicate with others because we can and do grasp in some direct fashion, less or more successfully, the purpose and meaning of their words, their gestures, their signs and symbols; for if there were no communication, there would be no language, no society, no humanity. But even if this applies to the present and the living, does it also apply to the past? Can we grasp the acts, the thoughts, the attitudes, the beliefs, explicit and implicit, the worlds of thought and feeling of societies dead and gone?If so, how is this achieved? Vico's answer to this problem is perhaps the boldest and most original of his ideas.

He declared that there were three great doors that lead into the past: language; myths; and rites, that is, institutional behaviour. We speak of metaphorical ways of expression. The aesthetic theorists of his day (Vico tells us) regard this simply as so much embellishment, a heightened form of speech used by poets as a deliberate device to give us pleasure or move us in particular ways, or ingenious ways of conveying important truths.[1] This rests on the assumption that what is expressed metaphorically could, at least in principle, be as well expressed in plain, literal prose, although this might be tedious and not give us the pleasure caused by poetic speech. But, Vico maintains, if you read primitive utterances (Latin and Greek antiquities, which he knew best, provide him with the majority of his examples) you will soon realise that what we call metaphorical speech is the natural mode of expression of these early men. When we say that our blood is boiling, this may for us be a conventional metaphor for anger, but for primitive man anger literally resembled the sensation of blood boiling within him; when we speak of the teeth of ploughs, or the mouths of rivers, or the lips of vases, these are dead metaphors or, at best, deliberate artifice intended to produce a certain effect upon the listener or reader. But to our remote ancestors ploughs actually appeared to have teeth, rivers, which for them were semi-animate, had mouths: land was endowed with necks and tongues, metals and minerals with veins, the earth had bowels, oaks had hearts, skies

[1] So Fontenelle, whose influence was inferior only to Voltaire's, identifies progress in the arts (as in everything else) with increase in order, clarity, precision, netteté, whose purest expression is geometry – the Cartesian method which cannot but improve whatever it touches, in every province of knowledge and creation. Mythology for him, as for Voltaire, is the product of savagery and ignorance. He is suspicious of all metaphor, but especially of images fabuleuses, which spring from a 'totally false and ridiculous' conception of things – their use can only help to disseminate error. Poets in primitive times employed mythological language ornamentally, but also as a stratagem to represent themselves as directly inspired by the gods; modern writers should at least use images spirituelles – personified abstractions – about, say, time, space, deity, which speak to reason, not to irrational feeling. The intellectual power, courage, humanity and unswerving pursuit of truth with which the lumières of the age fought against nonsense and obscurantism in theory and barbarous cruelties in practice need not blind us to the vices of their virtues, which have exacted their own terrible price.

smiled and frowned, winds raged, the whole of nature was alive and active. Gradually, as human experience changed, this, once natural, speech, which Vico calls poetical, lingered on as turns of phrase in common speech whose origins had been forgotten or at least were no longer felt, or as conventions and ornament used by sophisticated versifiers. Forms of speech express specific kinds of vision; there is no universal, 'literal' speech which denotes a timeless reality. Before 'poetical' language, men used hieroglyphs and ideograms which convey a vision of the world very different from our own – Vico declares that men sang before they spoke, spoke in verse before they spoke in prose, as is made plain by the study of the kinds of signs and symbols that they used, and the types of use they made of them.

The task before those who wish to grasp what kinds of lives have in the past been led in societies different from their own is to understand their worlds: that is, to conceive what kind of vision of the world men who used a particular kind of language must have had for this type of language to be a natural expression of it. The difficulty of this task is brought home most forcibly by the mythological language which Vico cites. The Roman poet says 'Jovis omnia plena.' What does this mean? Jove – Jupiter – is to us the father of the gods, a bearded thunderer, but the word also means sky or air. How can 'everything' be 'full' of a bearded thunderer, or the father of the gods? Yet this, evidently, is how men spoke. We must therefore ask ourselves what the world must have been like for those to whom such use of language, which is almost meaningless to us, made sense. What could be meant by speaking of Cybele as an enormous woman, and also, at the same time, as the whole of the earth, of Neptune as a bearded marine deity wielding a trident, and also as all the seas and oceans of the world? Thus Heracles is a demigod who slew the Hydra, but is at the same time the Athenian and Spartan and Argive and Theban Heracles; he is many and also one; Ceres is a female deity but also all the corn in the world.

It is a very strange world that we must try, as it were, to transpose ourselves into, and Vico warns us that it is only with the most agonising effort that we can even attempt to enter the mentality of the primitive savages of whose vision of reality these myths and legends are records. Yet it can, to some degree, be achieved, for we possess a faculty that he calls *fantasia* – imagination – with which it is possible to 'enter' minds very different from our own.

How is this done? The nearest we can come to grasping Vico's thought is his parallel between the growth of a species and the growth of the individual: just as we are able to recollect the experiences of childhood (and in our day psychoanalysis has probed further than this), so it must be possible to recapture to some degree the early collective experience of our race, even though this may require terrible effort. This is based on the parallel of the macrocosm to the individual microcosm – phylogenesis resembling ontogenesis, an idea which dates back at least to the Renaissance. There is an analogy between the growth of an individual and that of a people. If I can recollect what it was to have been a child, I shall have some inkling of what it was to have belonged to a primitive culture. Judging others by analogy with what I am now will not do: if animism is the false attribution of human characteristics to natural objects, a similar fallacy is involved in attributing to primitives our own sophisticated notions; memory, not analogy, seems closer to the required faculty of imaginative understanding – *fantasia* – whereby we reconstruct the human past.[1]

The categories of experience of different generations of men differ; but they proceed in a fixed order which Vico thinks he can reconstruct by asking the right questions of the evidence before us. We must ask what kind of experience is presupposed by, renders intelligible, a particular use of symbols (that is, language), what particular vision is embodied in myths, in religious rites, in inscriptions, in the monuments of the past. The answers will enable us to trace human growth and development, to visualise, 'enter into' the minds of men creating their world by effort, by work, by struggle. Each phase of this process conveys, indeed communicates, its experience in its own characteristic forms – in hieroglyphs, in primitive song, in myths and legends, in dances and laws, in ceremonial and elaborate religious rites, which to Voltaire or Holbach or d'Alembert were merely obsolete relics of a barbarous past or a mass of obscurantist hocus-pocus. The development of social consciousness and activity is traceable (Vico maintains) also in the evolution of etymology and syntax, which reflects successive phases of social life, and develops *pari passu* with them. Poetry is not conscious embellishment invented by sophisticated writers, nor is it secret wisdom in mnemonic form – it is a direct form of self-expression of our remote ancestors, collective and communal; Homer is the

[1] This is a contrast which Leon Pompa has stressed both in writing and in conversation with the author. I am inclined to think that his interpretation comes closest to Vico's thought, and that I did not pay sufficient attention to this issue in my previous discussions of the subject.

voice not of an individual poet but of the entire Greek people. This notion, in this specific formulation of it, was destined to have a rich flowering in the theories of Winckelmann and Herder, who, when they first developed their ideas, had not, so far as one can tell, so much as heard of Vico.

As for the unaltering character of basic human nature – the central concept of the western tradition from the Greeks to Aquinas, from the Renaissance to Grotius, Spinoza, Locke – this could not be so, for man's creations – language, myth, ritual – tell a different story. The first men were savage brutes, cave-dwellers who used 'mute' signs – gestures and then hieroglyphs. The first peal of thunder filled them with terror. Awe – a sense of a power greater than themselves brooding over them – awakened in them. They gathered together for self-protection; there follows the 'age of the gods' or *patres*, stern heads of primitive human tribes. Outside their fortifications there is no security : men attacked by other men stronger than themselves seek protection and are given it by the 'fathers' at the price of becoming slaves or clients. This marks the 'heroic' age of oligarchies, of harsh and avaricious masters, users of 'poetic' speech, ruling over slaves and serfs. There comes a moment when these last revolt, extort concessions, particularly with regard to marriage and burial rites, which are the oldest forms of human institution. They cause their new rites to be recorded – this constitutes the earliest form of law. This, in turn, generates prose, which leads to argument and rhetoric, and so to questioning, to philosophy, scepticism, egalitarian democracy, and, in the end, the subversion of the simple piety, solidarity and deference to authority of primitive societies, to their atomisation and disintegration, to destructive egoism and alienation,[1] and ultimate collapse, unless some Augustus restores authority and order, or an earlier, more primitive and vigorous tribe, with still unexhausted energies and firm discipline, falls upon it and subjugates it ; if this does not happen, there is a total breakdown. The primitive life in caves begins again, and so

[1] The passage in Vico's *New Science* describing the end of a decadent civilisation is worth quoting : ' . . . no matter how great the throng and press of their bodies, [men] live like wild beasts in a deep solitude of spirit and will, scarcely any two being able to agree since each follows his own pleasure or caprice'. *The New Science of Giambattista Vico*, trans. Thomas Goddard Bergin and Max Harold Fisch, revised ed. (New York, 1968), paragraph 1106. All subsequent quotations from the *New Science* are from this translation, and all subsequent references are to its paragraphs, thus: *N.S.* 1106.

the entire cycle repeats itself once more, *corsi e ricorsi*, from the barbarism of savage life to the second barbarism of decay.

There is no progress from the imperfect towards perfection, for the very notion of perfection entails an absolute criterion of value; there is only intelligible change. The stages are not mechanically caused each by its predecessor, but can be seen to flow from the new needs created by the satisfaction of the old ones in the unceasing self-creation and self-transformation of perpetually active men. In this process, war between the classes, in Vico's schema, plays a central role. Here again, Vico draws heavily on mythology. Voltaire tells us that myths are 'the ravings of savages and the inventions of knaves', or at best harmless fancies conjured up by poets to charm their readers. For Vico they are, as often as not, far-reaching images of past social conflicts out of which many diverse cultures grew. He is an ingenious and imaginative historical materialist: Cadmus, Ariadne, Pegasus, Apollo, Mars, Heracles, all symbolise various turning points in the history of social change.[1] What to the rational thought of a later age

[1] For instance, the story of Theseus and Ariadne is concerned with early seafaring life: the Minotaur represents the pirates who abduct Athenians in ships, for the bull is a characteristic ancient emblem on a ship's prow, and piracy was held in high honour by both the Greeks and the ancient Germans. Ariadne is the art of seafaring, the thread is a symbol of navigation, and the labyrinth is the Aegean Sea. Alternatively, the Minotaur is a half-cast child, a foreigner come to Crete – an early emblem of racial conflict. Cadmus is primitive man, and his slaying of the serpent is the clearing of the vast forest. He sows the serpent's teeth in the ground – the teeth are the teeth of a plough, the stones he casts about him are the clods of earth which the oligarchy of heroes retain against the land-hungry serfs; the furrows are the orders of feudal society; the armed men who spring up from the teeth are heroes, but they fight, not each other, as the myth relates (here Vico decides to 'correct' the evidence), but the robbers and vagabonds who threaten the lives of the settled farmers. The wounding of Mars by Minerva is the defeat of the plebeians by the patricians. In the case of Pegasus, wings represent the sky, the sky represents the birds, flight yields the all-important auspices. Wings plus a horse is equivalent to horse-riding nobles with the right of taking auspices, and therefore authority over the people, and soon such myths represent powers, institutions, and often embody radical changes in the social order; mythological creatures like Draco – a serpent found in China and Egypt too – or Heracles, or Aeneas (whose descent to Avernus is, of course, a symbol of sowing), are not for Vico historical persons, but, like Pythagoras and Solon, are viewed by him as mere symbols of political structures, and not to be fitted into any chronological framework.

seemed bizarre combinations of attributes – Cybele, who is both a woman and the earth, horses with wings, centaurs, dryads and the like – are in reality efforts by our ancestors to combine certain functions, or ideas, in a single concrete image. Vico calls such entities 'impossible universals', images compounded of incompatible characteristics, for which their descendants, who think in concepts and not in sensuous terms, have substituted an abstract phraseology. The transformation of the denotations of particular words and their modifications can also, for Vico, open windows on to the evolution of social structures. This is because language tells us 'the histories of the institutions signified by the words'. Thus the career of the word 'lex' tells us that life in 'the great forest of the earth' was followed by life in huts, and after that villages, cities, academies.[1]

Vico's particular attributions are at times wholly implausible or wild. But this matters less than the fact that he conceived the idea of applying to the accumulated antiquities of the human race a species of Kant's transcendental method, that is, an attempt to conceive what the experience of a particular society must have been like for this or that myth, or mode of worship, or language, or building, to be their characteristic expression. This opened new doors. It discredited the idea of some static spiritual kernel of timeless and unchanging 'human nature'. It reinforced the old Epicurean-Lucretian notion of a process

---

[1] *N.S.* 239–40. This is a good example of Vico's freely roaming historical imagination: he groups together 'lex' (acorn), 'ilex', 'aquilex', 'legumen' and 'legere' as typical 'sylvan' words, plainly drawn from life in the forest, which then came to mean quite different activities and objects. At first, 'lex' 'must have meant a collection of acorns'. 'Ilex' is 'oak', 'for the oak produces the acorns by which the swine are drawn together' (so, too, 'aquilex' means 'collector of waters'). '*Lex* was next a collection of vegetables, from which the latter were called *legumina*. Later on, at a time when vulgar letters had not yet been invented for writing down the laws, *lex* by a necessity of civil nature must have meant a collection of citizens, or the public parliament; so that the presence of the people was the *lex*, or 'law', that solemnised the wills that were made *calatis comitiis*, in the presence of the assembled *comitia*. Finally, collecting letters, and making, as it were, a sheaf of them for each word, was called *legere*, reading.' This is a characteristically fanciful piece of genetic sociological philology; yet in due course this socio-linguistic approach led to rich and important branches of the humanities in the form of historical jurisprudence, social anthropology, comparative religion and the like, particularly in their relations with the genetic and historical aspects of linguistic theory.

of slow growth from savage beginnings. There is no timeless, unalterable concept of justice or property or freedom or rights – these values alter as the social structure of which they are a part alters, and the objects created by mind and imagination in which these values are embodied alter from phase to phase. All talk of the matchless wisdom of the ancients is therefore a ludicrous fantasy: the ancients were frightening savages, *grossi bestioni*, roaming the great forest of the earth, creatures remote from us. There is no omnipresent natural law: the lists of absolute principles spelt out by the Stoics or Isidore of Seville or Thomas Aquinas or Grotius were neither explicitly present in the minds, nor implicit in the acts, of the barbarous early fathers, even of the Homeric heroes. The rational egoists of Hobbes, Locke or Spinoza are arbitrary and unhistorical; if men had been as they are depicted by these thinkers, their history becomes unintelligible.

Each stage of civilisation generates its own art, its own form of sensibility and imagination. Later forms are neither better nor worse than earlier, but simply different, to be judged each as the expression of its own particular culture. How can early men, whose signs were 'mute', who 'spoke with their bodies', who sang before they spoke (as, Vico adds, stammerers still do), be judged by the criteria of our own sophisticated culture? At a time when the great French arbiters of taste believed in an absolute standard of artistic excellence and knew that the verse of Racine and Corneille (or, indeed, Voltaire) was superior to anything by the shapeless Shakespeare or the unreadable Milton, or, before them, the bizarre Dante, and perhaps the works of the ancients too, Vico maintained that the Homeric poems were a sublime expression of a society dominated by the ambition, avarice and cruelty of its ruling class; for only a society of this kind could have produced this vision of life. Later ages may have perfected other aids to existence, but they cannot create the *Iliad*, which embodies the modes of thought and expression and emotion of one particular kind of way of life; these men literally saw what we do not see.

The new history is to be the account of the succession and variety of men's experience and activity, of their continuous self-transformation from one culture to another. This leads to a bold relativism, and kills, among other things, the notion of progress in the arts, whereby later cultures are necessarily improvements on, or retrogressions from, earlier ages, each measured by its distance from some fixed, immutable ideal, in terms of which all beauty, knowledge, virtue, must be judged. The famous quarrel between the ancients and the moderns can have no sense for Vico: every artistic tradition is intelligible only to those who grasp its own rules, the conventions that are internal to it, an 'organic' part of its own changing pattern of the categories of thought and feeling. The notion of anachronism, even if others had some inkling of it, is rendered central by him. Vico tells us that Polybius once said that it was a misfortune for mankind that it was priests and not philosophers who had presided over its birth; how much error and cruelty would have been spared it but for these mendacious charlatans.[1] Lucretius passionately reiterated this charge. To those who live after Vico, it is as if one were to suggest that Shakespeare could have written his plays at the court of Genghis Khan, or Mozart composed in ancient Sparta. Vico goes far beyond Bodin and Montaigne and Montesquieu:[2] they (and Voltaire) may have believed in different social *esprits*, but not in successive stages of historical evolution, each phase of which has its own modes of vision, forms of expression, whether one calls them art or science or religion. The idea

---

[1] This is in fact based on a misreading of Polybius' text, but it furnished Vico with an occasion for his historicist thesis: and even though Polybius did not commit this fallacy, it forms a strand in the tradition of the Enlightenment against which Vico rebelled.

[2] The difference of the earlier and later attitudes is brought out by the interest in myths and fables on the part of, say, Bodin and Bacon and even Montesquieu on the one hand, and Vico on the other. The former thinkers do not think of myths and fables as inventions of lying priests or merely results of 'human weakness' (to use Voltaire's phrase), but they look to antiquities of this kind for information about the *moeurs* and *façons de vivre* in early or remote societies for the express purpose of discovering whether there are historical lessons to be learned with relevance to their own times and circumstances. Even though temperamentally they may have been intensely curious about other societies, and collected these facts for their own sakes, the ostensible motive was certainly utilitarian – they wished to improve human life. Vico looks at myths as evidence of the different categories in which experience was organised – spectacles, unfamiliar to us, through which early man and remote peoples looked at the world in which they lived: the purpose is to understand whence we come, how we came to be where we are, how much or how little of the past we still carry with us. His approach is genetic, for it is only through its genesis, reconstructed by *fantasia*, guided by rules which he thinks he has discovered, that anything can be truly understood: not by some intuition of timeless essences, or empirical description or analysis of an object's present state. This marks a genuine turning-point in the conception of history and society.

of the cumulative growth of knowledge, a single corpus governed by single, universal criteria, so that what one generation of scientists has established, another generation need not repeat, does not fit this pattern at all. This marks the great break between the notion of positive knowledge and that of understanding.

Vico does not deny the utility of the latest scientific techniques in establishing facts. He claims no intuitive or metaphysical faculty which can dispense with empirical investigation. Tests for the authenticity of documents and other evidence, for dating, for chronological order, for establishing who did or suffered what and when and where, whether we are dealing with individuals or classes or societies, for establishing bare facts, the newly established scientific methods of investigation, may well be indispensable. The same applies to the investigation of impersonal factors – geographical or environmental or social – to the study of natural resources, fauna, flora, social structure, colonisation, commerce, finance; here we must use the methods of science, which establish the kind of probability of which Bodin and Voltaire spoke, and every historian who uses sociological and statistical methods has done ever since. With all this Vico has no quarrel. What, then, is novel in his conception of history, over which he tells us he spent twenty years of continuous labour?

It is, I think, this: that to understand history is to understand what men made of the world in which they found themselves, what they demanded of it, what their felt needs, aims, ideals were; he seeks to discover their vision of it, he asks what wants, what questions, what aspirations determined a society's view of reality; and he thinks that he has created a new method which will reveal to him the categories in terms of which men thought and acted and changed themselves and their worlds. This kind of knowledge is not knowledge of facts or of logical truths, provided by observation or the sciences or deductive reasoning; nor is it knowledge of how to do things; nor the knowledge provided by faith, based on divine revelation, in which Vico professed belief. It is more like the knowledge we claim of a friend, of his character, of his ways of thought or action, the intuitive sense of the nuances of personality or feeling or ideas which Montaigne describes so well, and which Montesquieu took into account.

To do this, one must possess imaginative power of a high degree, such as artists, and, in particular, novelists require. And even this will not get us far in grasping ways of life too remote from us and unlike our own. Yet even then we need not totally despair, for what we are seeking to understand is men – human beings endowed, as we are, with minds and purposes and inner lives – their works cannot be wholly unintelligible to us, unlike the impenetrable content of non-human nature. Without this power of what he describes as 'entering into' minds and situations the past will remain a dead collection of objects in a museum for us.

This sort of knowledge, not thought of in Descartes' philosophy, is based on the fact that we do know what men are, what action is, what it is to have intentions, motives, to seek to understand and interpret, in order to make oneself at home in the non-human world, what Hegel called *bey sich selbst seyn*. The most famous passage in the *New Science* expresses this central insight most vividly:

> ...in the night of thick darkness enveloping the earliest antiquity, so remote from ourselves, there shines the eternal and never failing light of a truth beyond all question: that the world of civil society has certainly been made by men, and that its principles are therefore to be found within the modifications of our own human mind. Whoever reflects on this cannot but marvel that the philosophers should have bent all their energies to the study of the world of nature, which, since God made it, He alone knows; and that they should have neglected the study of the world of nations, or civil world, which, since men had made it, men could come to know.[1]

Men have made their civil world – that is, their civilisation and institutions – but, as Marx was later to point out, not out of 'whole cloth', not out of infinitely malleable material; the external world, men's own physical and psychical constitution, play their part. This does not concern Vico: he is interested only in the human contribution: and when he speaks of the unintended consequences of men's actions, which they have not deliberately 'made', he attributes them to Providence, which guides men for their ultimate benefit in its own inscrutable way. That too, then, like nature, is outside man's conscious control. But what he means is that what one generation of men has experienced and done and embodied in their works, another generation can grasp, although, it may be, with difficulty and imperfectly. For this one must possess a developed *fantasia* – Vico's term for imaginative insight, which he accuses the French theorists of undervaluing. This is the capacity for conceiving more than one way of categorising reality, like the ability to understand what it is to be an

[1] *N.S.* 331.

artist, a revolutionary, a traitor, to know what it is to be poor, to wield authority, to be a child, a prisoner, a barbarian. Without some ability to get into the skin of others, the human condition, history, what characterises one period or culture as against others, cannot be understood. The successive patterns of civilisation differ from other temporal processes – say, geological – by the fact that it is men – ourselves – who play a crucial part in creating them. This lies at the heart of the art or science of attribution : to tell what goes with one form of life and not with another cannot be achieved solely by inductive methods.

Let me give an example of Vico's method : he is arguing that the story that the Romans borrowed the Twelve Tables (the original Roman code of laws) from the Athens of Solon's day cannot be true ; for it is not possible for such barbarians as the Romans must have been in Solon's time to have known where Athens was, or that it possessed a code that might be of value to them. Moreover, even on the improbable assumption that these early Romans knew that there was a more civilised or better organised society to the south-east of them (even though the barbarous tribes of early Rome could scarcely have entertained, however inchoately, such notions as civilisation or a city state), they could not have translated Attic words into idiomatic Latin without a trace of Greek influence on it, or used, for example, such a word as *auctoritas*, for which no Greek equivalent existed.

This kind of argument rests not on an accumulation of empirical evidence about human behaviour in many times and places upon which sociological generalisations can be made to rest. Such notions as advanced culture, and what distinguishes it from barbarism, are for Vico not static concepts, but describe stages in the growth of self-awareness in individuals and societies, differences between the concepts and categories in use at one stage of growth from those that shape another, and the genesis of one from another, to understand which ultimately stems from understanding what childhood and maturity are. In the early fifteenth century, the Italian humanist Bruni had declared that whatever was said in Greek could equally well be said in Latin too. This is precisely what Vico denies, as the example of *auctoritas* shows. There is no immutable structure of experience, to reflect which a perfect language could be invented, and into which imperfect approximations to such a language could be transposed. The language of so-called primitives is not an imperfect rendering of what later generations will express more accurately : it embodies its own unique vision of the world, which can be grasped, but not translated totally into the language of another culture. One culture is not a less perfect version of another: winter is not a rudimentary spring; summer is not an undeveloped autumn.

The worlds of Homer, or the Bible, or the Kalevala, cannot be understood at all if they are judged in terms of the absolute criteria of Voltaire or Helvétius or Buckle, and given marks according to their distance from the highest reaches of human civilisation, as exemplified in Voltaire's *Musée imaginaire*, where the four great ages of man hang side by side as aspects of the single, selfsame peak of human attainment. To say this is a truism which I may be thought to have laboured far too long: it was not a truism in the early eighteenth century. The very notion that the task of historians was not merely to establish facts and give causal explanations for them, but to examine what a situation meant to those involved in it, what their outlook was, by what rules they were guided, what 'absolute presuppositions' (as Collingwood called them) were entailed in what they (but not other societies, other cultures) said or did – all that is certainly novel and profoundly foreign to the thought of the *philosophes* and scientists of Paris. It coloured the thoughts of those who first reacted against the French Enlightenment, critics and historians of national literatures, in Switzerland, in England, in Germany – Bodmer and Breitinger and von Muralt, Hebrew scholars like Lowth, and the Homeric critics like Blackwell, social and cultural thinkers like Young and Adam Ferguson, Hamann and Möser and Herder. After them came the great generation of classical scholars, Wolf and Niebuhr and Boeckh, who transformed the study of the ancient world, and whose work had a decisive influence on Burckhardt and Dilthey and their successors in the twentieth century. From these origins came comparative philology and comparative anthropology, comparative jurisprudence and religion and literature, comparative histories of art and civilisation and ideas – the fields in which not merely knowledge of facts and events, but understanding – what Herder was the first to call *Einfühlung*, empathy – is required.

The use of informed imagination about, and insight into, systems of value, conceptions of life of entire societies, is not required in mathematics or physics, geology or zoology, or – though some would deny this – in economic history or even sociology if it is conceived and practised as a strictly natural science. This statement is intentionally extreme, intended to emphasise the gap that opened between natural science and the humanities as the result of a new attitude to the human past. No doubt in practice there is a great overlap between impersonal history as it is conceived by, say, Condorcet or Buckle or Marx, who believed that human society could be studied by a human science in principle analogous to that which tells us about the behaviour of 'bees or beavers' (to use Condorcet's analogy), contrasted with the history of what men believed in and lived by, the life of the spirit, blindness to which Coleridge and Carlyle imputed to the utilitarians, and Acton to Buckle (in his famous attack upon him), and Croce to the positivists. Vico began this schism: after that there was a parting of the ways. The specific and unique versus the repetitive and the universal, the concrete versus the abstract, perpetual movement versus rest, the inner versus the outer, quality versus quantity, culture-bound versus timeless principles, mental strife and self-transformation as a permanent condition of man versus the possibility (and desirability) of peace, order, final harmony and the satisfaction of all rational human wishes – these are some of the aspects of the contrast.[1]

These conceptions of their subject-matter and method, which are by now taken for granted by historians of literature, of ideas, of art, of law, and by historians of science too, and most of all by historians and sociologists of culture influenced by this tradition, are not as a

[1] Erich Auerbach seems to me to have put this with eloquence and precision: 'When people realise that epochs and societies are not to be judged in terms of a pattern concept of what is desirable absolutely speaking but rather in every case in terms of their own premises; when people reckon among such premises not only natural factors like climate and soil but also the intellectual and historical factors; when, in other words, they come to develop a sense of historical dynamics, of the incomparability of historical phenomena . . . so that each epoch appears as a whole whose character is reflected in each of its manifestations; when, finally, they accept the conviction that the meaning of events cannot be grasped in abstract and general forms of cognition and that the material needed to understand it must not be sought exclusively in the upper strata of society and in major political events but also in art, economy, material and intellectual culture, in the depths of the workaday world and its men and women, because it is only there that one can grasp what is unique, what is animated by inner forces, and what, in both a more concrete and a more profound sense, is universally valid . . .'. I know of no better formulation of the difference between history as science and history as a form of self-knowledge incapable of ever becoming fully organised, and to be achieved – as Vico warned us – only by 'unbelievable effort'. *Mimesis* (Princeton, 1968), pp. 443–4.

rule, and do not need to be, consciously present to the minds of natural scientists themselves. Yet, before the eighteenth century, there was, so far as I know, no sense of this contrast. Distinctions between the vast realm of philosophy – natural and metaphysical – theology, history, rhetoric, jurisprudence, were not too sharply drawn; there were disputes about method in the Renaissance, but the great cleavage between the provinces of natural science and the humanities was, for the first time, made, or at least revealed, for better or for worse, by Giambattista Vico. Thereby he started a great debate of which the end is not in sight.

Where did his central insight originate? Did the idea of what a culture is, and what it is to understand it in its unity and variety, and its likeness, but, above all, its unlikeness to other cultures, which undermines the doctrine of the identity of civilisation and scientific progress conceived as the cumulative growth of knowledge – did this spring fully armed like Pallas Athene out of his head? Who, before 1725, had had such thoughts? How did they percolate – if, indeed, they ever did – to Hamann and Herder in Germany, some of whose ideas are strikingly similar? These are problems on which, even now, not enough research has been done by historians of ideas. Yet fascinating as they are, their solution seems to me to be less important than the central discoveries themselves; most of all, the notion that the only way of achieving any degree of self-understanding is by systematically retracing our steps, historically, psychologically and, above all, anthropologically, through the stages of social growth that follow empirically discoverable patterns, or, if that is too absolute a term, trends or tendencies with whose workings we are acquainted in our own mental life, but moving to no single, universal goal; each a world on its own, yet having enough in common with its successors, with whom it forms a continuous line of recognisably human experience, not to be unintelligible to their inhabitants. Only in this fashion, if Vico is right, can we hope to understand the unity of human history – the links that connect our own 'magnificent age' to our 'squalid' beginnings in the 'great forest of the earth'.

Vico's Concept of Knowledge

Vico's fundamental distinction, as everyone with the least acquaintance with his writings knows, is between *verum* and *certum*. *Verum* is *a priori* truth, and is attained in, for example, mathematical reasoning, where every step is rigorously demonstrated. Such *a priori* knowledge can extend only to what the knower himself has created. It is true of mathematical knowledge precisely because men themselves have made mathematics. It is not, as Descartes supposed, discovery of an objective structure, the eternal and most general characteristics of the real world, but rather invention: invention of a symbolic system which men can logically guarantee only because men have made it themselves, irrefutable only because it is a figment of man's own creative intellect: 'geometrica demonstramus, quia facimus; si physica demonstrare possemus, faceremus'.[1] 'The criterion and rule of truth is to have made it,' Vico said a year later, in 1710.[2] *Faceremus*: but this is not possible: men cannot make the physical world: 'physica a caussis probare non possumus, quia elementa rerum naturalium extra nos sunt'.[3] Only God can know these *elementa*, because he has made them all. This includes the Zenonian 'metaphysical points',[4] of which the attribute is *conatus*, the *conatus* which with *motus* makes the world go round, whereby 'flamma ardet, planta adolescit, bestia per prata lascivit',[5] and so on. None of this is wholly transparent to us, for we

[1] 'We demonstrate geometry because we make it; if we could demonstrate the propositions of physics, we should be making it.' *De nostri temporis studiorum ratione* (1709), chapter 4. *Opere*, ed. Roberto Parenti (Naples, 1972) (hereafter *Opere*), vol. 1, p. 83.

[2] *De antiquissima italorum sapientia*, chapter 1, section 2. *Opere*, vol. 1, p. 194.

[3] 'We cannot demonstrate physics from its causes, because the elements which compose nature are outside us.' ibid., chapter 3. *Opere*, vol. 1, p. 203.

[4] ibid., chapter 4, section 2 ('De punctis metaphysicis et conatibus'). *Opere*, vol. 1, p. 205.

[5] 'The flame burns, the plant grows, the beast frolics in the fields.' ibid., section 6. *Opere*, vol. 1, p. 224.

did not make it; and, since this is not *factum* by us, it is not *verum* for us. So much is clear. There is no assumption of continuity between, on the one hand, natural forces of this kind and human activity, intellectual or imaginative, on the other. Other thinkers – Herder, Schelling, the *Naturphilosophen*, and the romantics – believed in such continuity, and perhaps they counted earlier thinkers among their ancestors – Renaissance scientists and mystics and a tradition which stretches back to the Greeks and forward to modern theologians and metaphysicians. But this is not what Vico believed. He did not identify, but on the contrary sharply distinguished, natural processes, which are more or less impenetrable, and human volitions, thoughts, images, forms of expression, which we 'create' ourselves. We do not know the natural processes *per caussas*, for we do not enter their workings. Hence, for us they are not a form of *verum* but of *certum*; of them we have not a (Platonic) *scienza* but only *coscienza*. This is Vico's dualism: it cuts across the metaphysical map in a different direction from that of Descartes, but it is no less sharply dualistic, with its obvious debt to Plato and to the Christian separation of spirit from matter.

What else, besides mathematics, falls on the *scienza-verum* side of the great division? That which earlier Renaissance thinkers – Manetti, Pico, Campanella – had spoken of, all that we had wrought ourselves: houses, towns, cities, pictures, sculptures, arts and sciences, languages, literatures, all are ours, said Manetti in 1452;[1] and Pico, Bouelles and Ficino had spoken of man's autonomy. Vico echoes this, 'Tandem deus naturae artifex: animus artium, fas sit dicere, deus.'[2] This is Vico's position in, say, 1709–10, the period of *De nostri* and *De antiquissima*. He has broken the spell of Cartesianism from which he had begun. Descartes is severely taken to task for recommending application of the geometric method to regions for which it is unsuitable, for example, poetry and rhetoric. The narrowing educational influence of the Cartesian insistence on the deductive method as the sole path to knowledge is condemned; it is denounced as a kind of

---

[1] Gianozzo Manetti, *De dignitate et excellentia hominis*, quoted by Giovanni Gentile, 'Il concetto dell'uomo nel rinascimento', *Giornale storico della letteratura italiana* 67 (1916), 17–75, repr. in his *Giordano Bruno e il pensiero del rinascimento* (Florence, 1920). The passage here paraphrased is on pp. 66–7 (175–6).

[2] 'While God is the maker of nature, the spirit [of man] is, if one may put it so, the god of the arts.' *Le orazioni inaugurali, Il de Italorum sapientia e le polemiche*, ed. Giovanni Gentile and Fausto Nicolini (Bari, 1914), p. 8.

pedagogic despotism which suppresses various other faculties and methods of mental development, especially the imagination. Nicolini is surely right in stressing that Vico was particularly opposed to Descartes' *Discours de la méthode*, with its fanatical monism and especially its contempt for scholarship and humane studies. But at this stage mathematics is still described by Vico as being 'like a divine science, since in it the true and the made coincide'.[1] There are two types of knowledge: *scienza*, knowledge *per caussas*, which can give complete truth, truth one can have only of what one has made – for example, of logical, mathematical, poetical creations; and *coscienza*, the knowledge of the 'outside' observer of the external world – nature, men, things, *motus*, *conatus*, and so on. Here Vico is undoubtedly influenced by Bacon and Hobbes, by experimentalism, the possibility of understanding processes and objects that we can to some degree reproduce artificially in the laboratory, and perhaps also by the Neapolitan empiricists of the seventeenth century. All this is novel enough. But his boldest contribution, the concept of 'philology', anthropological historicism, the notion that there can be a science of mind which is the history of its development, the realisation that ideas evolve, that knowledge is not a static network of eternal, universal, clear truths, either Platonic or Cartesian, but a social process, that this process is traceable through (indeed, is in a sense identical with) the evolution of symbols – words, gestures, pictures, and their altering patterns, functions, structures and uses – this transforming vision, one of the greatest discoveries in the history of thought, was still in the future. Descartes in a notorious passage in *La Recherche de la vérité* observed that a man 'needs Greek and Latin no more than Swiss or bas-Breton; to know the history of the Roman Empire no more than of the smallest country in Europe',[2] or in the *Discours* complained about the idle exaggerations of historians as a mere loading of the mind with superfluous information. On this Vico as yet had nothing to say. In 1709 he still accepts Descartes' gibe that all that classical scholars can at most hope to discover is what was known to 'Cicero's servant girl'. History is not rated higher than physics: the study of *certum – conscientia* – is entitled indeed to a province of its own, which *scientia* or geometric method must not invade, but it is an inferior discipline.

[1] op. cit. (p. 111, note 2 above), chapter 1, section 2. *Opere*, vol. 1, p. 194. Cf. also *N.S.* (see p. 100, note 1 above) 349.

[2] *Oeuvres de Descartes*, ed. Charles Adam and Paul Tannery (Paris, 1897–1913), vol. 10 (1908), p. 503.

No doubt Vico had been deeply impressed by Lucretius and his account of the bestial beginnings of men; by Bacon's stress on the part played by myth and imagination in human progress (as expounded in *De augmentis*, that 'golden book');[1] by Hobbes, not only on account of his doctrine of experiment as an imitation of – and thereby a means of insight into – nature, but also by his view that 'civil philosophy', that is, political science, is demonstrative, and belongs to the realm of *verum*, because 'we make the commonwealth ourselves',[2] not historically, but as a rational, deliberate pattern, an intellectual artefact. And Tacitus delighted him with his sharp insights into individual character in action, as he delighted Machiavelli. But none of this coalesced, none of it would have come to life in the new synthesis, the new conception of philosophy as the consciousness of the cumulative experience of entire societies, without the central principle which is Vico's ultimate claim to immortality: the principle according to which man can understand himself because, and in the process, of understanding his past – because he is able to reconstruct imaginatively (in Aristotle's phrase) what he did and what he suffered, his hopes, wishes, fears, efforts, his acts and his works, both his own and those of his fellows. With their experience his own is interwoven, his own and his (and their) ancestors', whose monuments, customs, laws, but above all words, still speak to him; indeed, if they did not, and if he did not understand them, he would not understand his fellows' or his own symbols, he would not be able to communicate or think or conceive purposes, to form societies or become fully human.

Enough has been written on Vico's historicism, on his idea of a culture (a notion of which, if he was not its original begetter, he was the first to grasp the full importance for historians and philosophers alike), to make it unnecessary to stress its salient characteristics. Nor would this be an easy task: Vico had not (as Heine once observed of Berlioz) enough talent for his genius. Too many new ideas are struggling for simultaneous expression. Vico is trying to say too much, and his notions are often mere sketches, inchoate, ill-formed; he cannot keep a cool head in the storm of inspiration; he is at times carried away by the flood of disorganised ideas, and differs greatly in this respect from such great intellectual organisers and architects as Descartes

[1] op. cit. (p. 111, note 1 above). *Opere*, vol. 1, p. 75.

[2] Epistle Dedicatory to 'Six Lessons to the Savilian Professors of the Mathematics', *The English Works of Thomas Hobbes*, ed. Sir William Molesworth, vol. 7 (London, 1845), p. 184.

or Leibniz or Kant or even Hegel. Vico's exposition often attains to rhapsodic, at times volcanic, power; but this does not make for coherent exposition. There are, as his critics have not been slow to point out, many obscurities and contradictions in his tumultuous writing.

In what sense, we may well ask, do men 'make' their history?[1] Conscious effort, deliberate attempts to explain the world to oneself, to discover oneself in it, to obtain from it what one needs and wants, to adapt means to ends, to express one's vision or describe what one sees or feels or thinks, individually or collectively – understanding, communication, creation – all these could be described as kinds of doing and making. But this omits too much: unconscious and irrational 'drives', which even the most developed and trained psychological methods cannot guarantee to lay bare; the unintended and unforeseen consequences of our acts, which we cannot be said to have 'made' if making entails intention; the play of accident; the entire natural world by interaction with which we live and function, which remains opaque inasmuch as it is not, *ex hypothesi*, the work of our hands or mind; since we do not 'make' this, how can anything it possesses be grasped as *verum*? How can there be a *scienza* of such an amalgam? Furthermore, what is the relationship of the altering categories and the forms of symbolism which embody them – the procession (the fact that it is cyclical is not relevant here) from the dark caves of the *grossi bestioni* to the divine, the mythopoeic, and the heroic, poetic, metaphor-creating cultures, and from them to the humane, prose-using democracies – the relation of these changing forms of vision to creation, to the eternal laws, the *storia ideale eterna*, and the principles of the 'civil theology' to which all cultures are subject? Since not we but God made the everlasting laws of the *corsi e ricorsi*, how can *we* know them? What kind of *a priori* intuitions are being claimed? And is the Renaissance parallel between the microcosm and macrocosm self-evidently valid? Is it really so obvious that phylogenesis – the history of the tribe – can be deduced from ontogenesis, from our individual recollections of our own mental and emotional growth? What guarantees this *a priori* historical phenomenology? By what faculty do we divine it? And what is the role of Providence in the *storia ideale*? If men make their history, does Providence 'make' them create it as they do? If Providence turns men's

[1] Bruce Mazlish has formulated some of these difficulties in his interesting essay on Vico, in *The Riddle of History: The Great Speculators from Vico to Freud* (New York, 1966).

bestial lusts, terrors, vices, into means for social and moral order, security, happiness, rational organisation, what part is played in all this by men's own motives, purposes, choices? In what sense are men free, as Vico maintained? And, whatever the answer to this ancient theological puzzle, how do we know that it is indeed a providence that shapes our lives? What, if any, is the relation of Vico's undoubted Christian faith, his Catholic orthodoxy, to his anthropological, linguistic, historical naturalism, or of his teleology to his belief that to each order of culture belong its own peculiar modes of consciousness, not necessarily superior or inferior to its predecessors or successors? I do not know if answers can be found to such questions, which historians of ideas have not settled; perhaps Vico himself has not left us sufficient means for solving them; they arose again with the German philosophers of history and, in new guises, remain to plague us to this day. Be that as it may, the claim for Vico that I wish to make is more circumscribed. It is this: that he uncovered a species of knowing not previously clearly discriminated, the embryo that later grew into the ambitious and luxuriant plant of German historicist *Verstehen* – empathetic insight, intuitive sympathy, historical *Einfühlung*, and the like. It was, nevertheless, even in its original, simple form, a discovery of the first order.

To apply the old medieval maxim that one can fully know only what one has made to such provinces as mathematics, mythology, symbolism, language, is evidence enough of philosophical insight, a revolutionary step on which the cultural anthropology and the philosophical implications of the new linguistic theories of our own time have cast a new and extraordinary light. But Vico did more than this. He uncovered a sense of knowing which is basic to all humane studies: the sense in which I know what it is to be poor, to fight for a cause, to belong to a nation, to join or abandon a church or a party, to feel nostalgia, terror, the omnipresence of a god, to understand a gesture, a work of art, a joke, a man's character, that one is transformed or lying to oneself. How does one know these things? In the first place, no doubt, by personal experience; in the second place because the experience of others is sufficiently woven into one's own to be seized quasi-directly, as part of constant intimate communication; and in the third place by the working (sometimes by a conscious effort) of the imagination. If a man claims to know what it is like to lose one's religious faith – in what way it transforms the shape of one's world – his claim may or may not be valid; he may be lying or deluding himself, or misidentifying his experience. But the sense in which he claims to know this is quite different from that in which I know that this tree is taller than that, or that Caesar was assassinated on the Ides of March, or that seventeen is a prime number, or that 'vermilion' cannot be defined, or that the king in chess can move only one square at a time. In other words, it is not a form of 'knowing that'. Nor is it like knowing how to ride a bicycle or to win a battle, or what to do in case of fire, or knowing a man's name, or a poem by heart. That is to say, it is not a form of 'knowing how' (in Gilbert Ryle's sense). What then is it like?

It is a species of its own. It is a knowing founded on memory or imagination. It is not analysable except in terms of itself, nor can it be identified save by examples, such as those adduced above. This is the sort of knowing which participants in an activity claim to possess as against mere observers: the knowledge of the actors, as against that of the audience, of the 'inside' story as opposed to that obtained from some 'outside' vantage point; knowledge by 'direct acquaintance' with my 'inner' states or by sympathetic insight into those of others, which may be obtained by a high degree of imaginative power; the knowledge that is involved when a work of the imagination or of social diagnosis or a work of criticism or scholarship or history is described not as correct or incorrect, skilful or inept, a success or a failure, but as profound or shallow, realistic or unrealistic, perceptive or stupid, alive or dead. What this capacity is, the part that it plays in the understanding of the simplest communication addressed by one sentient creature to another, and *a fortiori* in the creation of adequate vehicles of expression, of criticism, above all in the recovery of the past not as a collection of factual beads strung on a chronicler's string (or of 'ideas', arguments, works of art, similarly treated by the taxonomists and antiquaries of the humanities), but as a possible world, a society which could have had such characteristics whether it had precisely these or not – the nature of this kind of knowing is Vico's central topic. The past can be seen through the eyes – the categories and ways of thinking, feeling, imagining – of at any rate possible inhabitants of possible worlds, of associations of men brought to life by what, for want of a better phrase, we call imaginative insight. There must exist a capacity for conceiving (or at least a claim to be able to conceive) what 'it must have been like' to think, feel, act, in Homeric Greece, in the Rome of the Twelve Tables, in Phoenician colonies given to human sacrifice, or in cultures less remote or exotic but still requiring suspension of the most deeplying assumptions of the inquirer's own civilisation. It cannot be otherwise if one is to begin to achieve any understanding of the 'inner' structure of something outside one's immediate range of vision, whether it is real or a dream. This remains true, whatever view one takes of the great controversy about the methods of the natural sciences as against those of the humane studies.

The identification of this sense of 'knowing', which is neither deductive nor inductive (nor hypothetico-deductive), neither founded on the direct perception of the external world nor a fantasy which lays no claim to truth or coherence, is Vico's achievement. His programme for the 'new' approach to the human sciences is founded upon it. His claim may be extravagant; to call something knowledge which is so obviously fallible and needs empirical research to justify its findings may be an error. But he did uncover a mode of perception, something entailed in the notion of understanding words, persons, outlooks, cultures, the past.

When did he conceive this? When did he move from criticism of the unhistorical, indeed anti-historical, approach of Descartes, and of Grotius and Selden (whom he had admired so deeply), to his new conception of historical method? Perhaps not much before 1720, when in the De uno[1] (that is, the first part of the Diritto universale) the first bold application of the verum–factum principle to human history is made, an application which later will be fully formulated in the celebrated passage of the last edition of the Scienza nuova,[2] which is dedicated to the effort to show how the findings of 'philology' can at last be united with 'philosophy' – the eternal principles revealed through reason planted in us by God and developed with the help of his providence, the path from certum to verum, to the pure Platonic vision from which Vico all his life drew inspiration. Yet the rudiments of this thought already appear in 1710, in the second chapter of the De antiquissima, where we are told that 'Historici utiles, non qui facta crassius et genericas caussas narrant, sed qui ultimas factorum circumstantias persequuntur, et caussarum peculiares reserant.'[3] This undoubtedly reflects the influence of Bacon, but the emphasis on the

---

[1] De uno universi iuris principio et fine uno (Naples, 1720).

[2] Published in Naples in 1744. The passage in question is N.S. 331, quoted on p. 106 above.

[3] 'The useful historians are not those who give general descriptions of facts and explain them by reference to general conditions, but those who go into the greatest detail and reveal the particular cause of each event.' Opere, vol. 1, p. 200.

concrete and the unique in the writing of history is a presage of what is to come ten years later. Leibniz also tried to formulate a doctrine of *a priori* definitions of individual entities by purely rational-logical methods, a path which, unlike Vico's, proved to be philosophically sterile.

No one understood the full originality of Vico in his lifetime or for nearly a century after his death, not even those few who actually read him: neither his fervent Neapolitan and Venetian admirers in the eighteenth century nor the famous men who commented on him later so superficially — Goethe and Jacobi, Galiani and Chastellux, Hamann and Herder (who arrived at similar ideas themselves), Joseph de Maistre and Ballanche; no one before Michelet seems to have had an inkling that Vico had opened a window to a new realm of thought, still less that those who made the effort to unravel the terrible tangles of his immensely suggestive but often dark ideas would never again be able to return to their beginnings — to the blissful simplicity and symmetry of Descartes or Spinoza, Hume or Russell (or even Kant), still less to that of the positivist historians and historical theorists; not, at any rate, without an acute and constant sense of the defectiveness of their conceptions of the mind and its powers, and consequently of what men are and how they come to be what they are. Not until the days of Dilthey and Max Weber did the full novelty of the implications for the philosophy of mind and epistemology of Vico's theses about the imaginative resurrection of the past begin to dawn upon some of those who, in their turn, resurrected him.

Vico and the Ideal of the Enlightenment

M Y topic – the relationship of Vico's views to the notion of a perfect society – is not an issue central to Vico himself. He does not directly treat it, so far as I know, in any of his published works. But I hope to show that his central thesis is relevant to this idea – one of the most persistent in the history of human thought – and indeed incompatible with it. It is one of the marks of writers of genius that what they say may, at times, touch a central nerve in the minds or feelings of men who belong to other times, cultures or outlooks, and set up trains of thought and entail consequences which did not, or could not, occur to such writers, still less occupy their minds. This seems to me to be the case with regard to Vico's celebration of the power and beauty of primitive poetry, and the implications of this for the idea of progress in the arts, or culture, or the concept of an ideal society against which the imperfections of real societies can be assessed.

The concept of the perfect society is one of the oldest and most deeply pervasive elements in western thought, wherever, indeed, the classical or Judaeo-Christian traditions are dominant. It has taken many forms – a Golden Age, a Garden of Eden in which men were innocent, happy, virtuous, peaceful, free, where everything was harmonious, and neither vice nor error nor violence nor misery was so much as thought of; where nature was bounteous and nothing was lacking, there was no conflict, and not even the passage of time affected the full, permanent and complete satisfaction of all the needs, physical, mental and spiritual, of the blessed dwellers in these regions. Then a catastrophe occurred that put an end to this condition; there are many variants of this – the flood, man's first disobedience, original sin, the crime of Prometheus, the discovery of agriculture and metallurgy, primitive accumulation, and the like. Alternatively, the Golden Age was placed not in the beginning but at the end: in the millennial rule of the saints which will precede the Second Coming; or in life beyond the grave, in the Isles of the Blest, in Valhalla; or in the paradise of the three monotheistic religions; Homer finds a semblance of earthly paradise on the isle of the Phaeacians, or among the blameless Ethiopians whom Zeus loved to visit. When the hold of myth and institutional religion weakened, secular, no longer wholly flawless, more human Utopias began to succeed these – from the ideal communities of Plato, Crates, Zeno, Euhemerus, to Iambulus' Islands of the Sun, Plutarch's idealised Sparta, Atlantis, and the like.

Whatever the origins of such visions, the conception itself rests on the conviction that there exist true, immutable, universal, timeless, objective values, valid for all men, everywhere, at all times; that these values are at least in principle realisable, whether or not human beings are, or have been, or ever will be, capable of realising them on earth; that these values form a coherent system, a harmony which, conceived in social terms, constitutes the perfect state of society: that indeed, unless such perfection is at least conceivable, it is difficult or impossible to give sense to descriptions of existing states of affairs as imperfect; for the miseries, vices, and all the other shortcomings of existing human arrangements – cruelty, injustice, disease, scarcities, mental and physical torments, everything, indeed, that afflicts men – must be seen as so many fallings-short of the ideal or optimal state of affairs. How this optimum is to be attained is another question. But whether the answer is to be found in sacred texts, the visions of inspired prophets, institutionalised religion, metaphysical insights, or in more historically rooted social ideals, or the constellations of the simple human values of beings uncorrupted by destructive civilisation, there is a common assumption which underlies all these conflicting doctrines: namely, that a perfect society is conceivable, whether it is an object of prayer and hope, a mere vision of unrealised and unrealisable human potentialities, a nostalgic sighing after a real or imaginary past, the final goal toward which history is inexorably marching, or a practical programme which enough ability, energy and moral clarity could in principle realise.

The neoclassicism of the Renaissance gave birth to a great revival of such visions of perfection. More and Patrizzi, Doni and Campanella, Christian Utopians of the early seventeenth century, Francis Bacon, Harrington, Winstanley, Foigny, Fénelon, Swift, Defoe, mark only the beginning of such visions of society, which continued until comparatively recent times, when for reasons that will be familiar to everyone, they suffered a considerable slump. The late seventeenth and early eighteenth centuries were singularly rich in such romances, fed by fanciful accounts of the peace and harmony of primitive societies in America or elsewhere. All this is familiar enough. The principal point I wish to make is that not the least original of Vico's attributes is that in this instance, too, he took an independent line of his own and sailed his boat against the stream.

It might be said that since he felt himself to be a pious Christian, the temptation to construct a secular Utopia was, in his case, not too strong: man cannot attain to perfection on this earth, the Kingdom of God is not of this world; man is weak and sinful, the attempt even to imagine a perfect kingdom on earth implies a denial of the irremediable finiteness of man and his works, even of the works of his mind and imagination. Yet Campanella was a monk and a Christian, whatever the Inquisition may have thought; so, indubitably, were Sir Thomas More, who died for his faith, and Samuel Gott, and Archbishop Fénelon, and the authors of *Antagil* and *Christianopolis*, and many others – but this did not seem to deter them from designing earthly Utopias. Nor is there any emphasis in Vico's work on human impotence and wickedness; if anything, he stresses the opposite – man's magnificent creative capacities, which make him the instrument of Providence in transforming his social and cultural life. Nor is this all: there is the curious paradox of a faithful son of the Catholic church who nevertheless advocates a cyclical theory of history, which seems to leave no room for the radical transformation of history, once and for all, by the incarnation and the resurrection of Christ, nor for the movement of history toward the single far-off divine event by which it is completed and transcended. To reconcile Vico's belief in *corsi* and *ricorsi* with Christian revelation has been (or should have been) a standing crux to his interpreters – greater, if anything, than the difficulty of fitting Plato's cyclical theory of successive social orders with his apparent belief in, at any rate, the theoretical possibility of an ideal state. Whatever the explanation in Plato's case, for Vico there can surely be no avenue to total fulfilment on earth: if no social structure can last, if collapse into the 'barbarism of reflection'[1] is inevitable before the new beginning, in the endless repetitive spiral of cultural development, the notion of a perfect society, which implies an unchanging, static order, seems automatically excluded. That, indeed, is perhaps why, for example, Polybius, who believes in cycles, offers no Utopia. Nor does Machiavelli, who holds a similar view and predicts that even his neo-Roman state, which he regards as feasible and not Utopian, will not last. It is this doctrine, rather than the mounting

[1] *N.S.* (see p. 100, note 1 above) 1106.

empiricism of Vico's age, that seems to me to be a decisive anti-Utopian influence. For even if, like Bodin or Montesquieu, one pays due attention to the variety of human lives caused by differences in natural environment, climate and so on, one can still suppose that every type of society is free to strive for, and certainly to conceive of, its own individual path to perfection. Moreover, Bodin and Montesquieu, while they maintain that the means open to dissimilar societies may differ, seem to have no doubt about the universality, objectivity, immutability of ultimate values – peace, justice, happiness, rational organisation, and, in Montesquieu's case, individual freedom to do what is right and avoid what is wrong. With Vico, matters are somewhat different. Let me try to explain why I believe this to be the case.

Vico is not essentially a relativist, though he has sometimes been called that. The world of primitive savages is utterly different from our own glorious age, but by means of an agonising effort it is possible to enter the minds of those *grossi bestioni*, see or attempt to see the world with their eyes, and understand their *Weltanschauung*, their values, their motives, aims, categories, concepts. For Vico, to understand them and their world is to see their point, to grasp the way in which they necessarily belong to, and indeed express, a particular stage of social development, a stage which is the origin of our own condition, a phase of the creative process, to understand which is the only way to understand ourselves. Each epoch in Vico's *storia ideale eterna*[1] is related by a species of social causation to both its predecessor and its successor in the great chain the links of which are connected in an unalterable, cyclical order. But whereas for those metaphysical thinkers who believe in progress nothing that is of permanent value need be lost irretrievably, for in some form it is preserved in the next higher stage; and whereas for those who contemplate the perfect society all ultimate values can be combined, like the pieces of a jigsaw puzzle, in the single, final solution, for Vico this cannot be so. For change – unavoidable change – rules all man's history, not determined by mechanical causes, as he thinks it is for the Stoics or Spinoza, nor due to chance, as it is for Epicurus and his modern followers. For it follows a divinely determined pattern of its own. But in the course of this process gains in one respect necessarily entail losses in another, losses which cannot be made good if the new values, which are part of the unalterable historical process, are, as indeed they must be, realised,

[1] *N.S.* 349 etc.

each in its due season. If this is so, then some valuable forms of experience are doomed to disappearance, not always to be replaced by something necessarily more valuable than themselves. And this means that it must always be the case that some values are not compatible, historically compatible, with others, so that the notion of an order in which all true values are simultaneously present and harmonious with each other is ruled out, not on the ground of unrealisability due to human weakness or ignorance or other shortcomings (the overcoming of which could be at least imagined), but owing to the nature of reality itself. This means that the idea of perfection is ruled out not so much for empirical reasons but because it is conceptually incoherent, not compatible with what we see history necessarily to be.

THE DISCOVERY OF THE TRUE HOMER

Let me give the most vivid example of this in Vico's *New Science*. In the second book, called 'Poetic Wisdom', Vico declares that

> the first men of the gentile nations, children of nascent mankind, created things according to their own ideas . . . by virtue of a wholly corporeal imagination. And because it was quite corporeal, they did it with marvellous sublimity; and sublimity such and so great that it excessively perturbed the very persons who by imagining did the creating, for which they were called 'poets', which is Greek for 'creators'.[1]

And again: 'The most sublime labour of poetry is to give sense and passion to insensate things', as children talk in play to inanimate things as if they were living persons.[2] For 'in the world's childhood men were by nature sublime poets'.[3] And again: 'Imagination is more robust in proportion as reasoning power is weak.'[4] Because men's senses were stronger when men were more brutish, since Providence gave these to them for physical self-protection, and grew less so in the age of reflection – reflection which took the place of instinct – 'the heroic descriptions, as we have them in Homer, are so luminously and splendidly

---

[1] He goes on to say that one of the labours of 'great poetry' is 'to invent sublime fables suited to the popular understanding'. He then [mis]quotes Tacitus' 'fingebant simul credebantque' – 'they no sooner imagined than they believed' (*Annals*, book 6). *N.S.* 376. Subsequent references to the *New Science* in this essay are given by paragraph number alone.

[2] 186.   [3] 187.   [4] 185.

clear that all later poets have been unable to imitate them, to say nothing of equalling them'.[1] Yet the heroes of the age (toward the end of which Homer lived) are described by Vico as being 'boorish, crude, harsh, wild, proud, difficult, and obstinate'.[2]

Vico has no illusions about either the age of the gods or that of the heroes. He speaks of the practice of human sacrifice – by Phoenicians, Carthaginians, Gauls, Germans, American Indians, Scythians, in the golden age of Latium (Plautus's *Saturni hostiae*) – and remarks: 'Such a mild, benign, sober, decent, and well-behaved time it was!'[3] Such is man in 'the innocence of the golden age'.[4] He does not doubt that it was this religious-Cyclopean authority,[5] based on terror, that was needed to create the first disciplined savage human societies.[6]

Then came the heroes. The central figure of the heroic age is Achilles, the Achilles 'who referred every right to the tip of his spear'.[7] 'This is the hero that Homer sings of to the Greek peoples as an example of heroic virtue and to whom he gives the fixed epithet "blameless"!'[8] Vico compares this to the barbarian times of the *ricorso* (the age of medieval Christian chivalry) and 'the vindictive satisfactions of the knights-errant of whom the romancers sing'.[9] Such heroes are Brutus, who killed his sons; Scaevola, who burnt his hand; Manlius, who killed his children; Curtius, the Decii, Fabricius and the rest – 'what did any of them do for the poor and unhappy Roman plebs?'[10] What they did, Vico tells us, was to ruin, rob, imprison, whip them. Anyone who tried to help the plebs – Manlius Capitolinus, or King Agis in Sparta – was declared a traitor and killed. In these societies, according to Vico, there is no virtue, justice, mercy, but avarice, arrogance, inequality, cruelty. This is the heroic age, the age to which Homer belonged and which he celebrated. Heroic ages are times of cruel laws, 'supreme arrogance', 'intolerable pride, profound avarice and pitiless cruelty':[11] 'the haughty, avaricious, and cruel practices of the nobles toward the plebeians, which we see clearly portrayed in Roman history'.[12]

In the third book of the *New Science*, called 'The Discovery of the True Homer', Vico notes that 'Scaliger is indignant at finding almost all [Homer's] comparisons to be taken from beasts and other savage things',[13] but this is part of his poetic genius:

[1] 707.	[2] 708.	[3] 517.	[4] 518.
[5] 523.	[6] 518.	[7] 923.	[8] 667.
[9] ibid.	[10] 668.	[11] 38.	[12] 272.
[13] 785.			

to attain such success in them – for his comparisons are incomparable – is certainly not characteristic of a mind chastened and civilised by any sort of philosophy. Nor could the truculent and savage style in which he describes so many, such varied, and such bloody battles, so many and such extravagantly cruel kinds of butchery as make up all the sublimity of the *Iliad* in particular, have originated in a mind touched and humanised by any philosophy.[1]

Yet this barbarian poet made it difficult, according to Horace, to invent any new characters after him.[2] This is so because, Vico declares, 'Homer, who preceded philosophy and the poetic and critical arts, was yet the most sublime of all the sublime poets', so that 'after the invention of philosophies and of the arts of poetry and criticism there was no poet who could come within a long distance of competing with him'.[3] The sentiments and the 'modes of speech' and the actions of such 'sublime natures' can be 'wild, crude, and terrible', and this can be produced only in a heroic age – at the end of one of which the Homeric poems were created; later this is no longer possible.[4]

According to Vico, this is so because this kind of sublimity 'is inseparable from popularity'.[5] Homer's poetic characters are 'imaginative universals' to which all the attributes of a genus are attributed. They are generic types (not altogether dissimilar to Weber's ideal types), so that to these men Achilles *is* heroic valour, quick temper, pride, honour, and liability to anger and violence, right as might; Ulysses *is* heroic wisdom – 'wariness, patience, dissimulation, duplicity, deceit'.[6] Once true concepts – abstract universals – are created by the civilised reason and not the imagination of an entire society, this kind of sublimity comes to an end. This is so because, before writing is invented, men possess 'vivid sensation', 'strong imagination', 'sharp wit', 'robust memory', which they later lose.[7]

Homer is 'the father and prince of all sublime poets'.[8] He is 'celestially sublime', possesses a 'burning imagination'.[9] 'The frightfulness of the Homeric battles and deaths gives to the *Iliad* all its marvellousness.'[10] This could not have sprung from 'a calm, cultivated, and gentle philosopher'.[11] This is what makes Homer the greatest of poets for Vico. It is this that makes him a master of 'wild and savage com-

[1] 785. [2] 806. [3] 807. [4] 808.
[5] 809. [6] ibid. [7] 819. [8] 823.
[9] 825. [10] 827. [11] 828.

parisons',[1] or 'cruel and fearful descriptions of battles and deaths'[2] and 'sentences filled with sublime passions',[3] with 'expressiveness and splendour'[4] of style impossible in the ages of philosophy, criticism, poetry as a civilised art, which came later.[5]

Vico's central point is that poetic feeling, which 'must plunge deep into particulars',[6] cannot exist when men think in concepts: inspired singers, of whom Homer is the greatest, cannot coexist with philosophers. Whatever these later, milder, more rational times – the age of men – may create, namely, the arts and sciences of elaborate civilisations, they cannot give us within the same 'cycle' 'burning imagination' or celestial sublimity.[7] This has vanished. We can realise the splendour of this primitive poetry only by understanding the 'wild, crude, and terrible'[8] world from which it springs; we can do this only if we abandon the idea of the artistic superiority of our own 'magnificent times'.[9]

All this was composed at a time when one of the dominant aesthetic theories was still that of timeless and objective criteria of excellence in the arts, in morality, in every other normative sphere. Some critics believed in steady progress in the arts, based on growth in rationality and the gradual elimination of the savage world of myth and fable and primitive, unbridled imagination, the dark and brutal age which we have left behind us. There were also those who believed that classical poetry, and especially Roman, was superior to that of the moderns. In both cases, it was assumed without much question that there existed a single, timeless standard of judgement whereby some thought that they could demonstrate the superiority of, say, Racine or Addison to Milton or Shakespeare or Homer, while others believed that they could demonstrate that Sophocles or Virgil were greater poets than any poet of a later age. A corollary of this was that the quality, the degree of excellence, of an art was part and parcel of the general quality of an age and its culture. For Voltaire or Fontenelle, the art or poetry of classical Athens or Rome, or Renaissance Florence, or France under Louis XIV, were magnificent, inasmuch as they were produced by and for enlightened men like themselves, in contrast with the ages of ignorance, fanaticism, barbarism, persecution, the art of which was as degraded as the societies in which a few savage captains quarrelled

[1] 893. [2] 894. [3] 895. [4] 896.
[5] 897. [6] 821. [7] 825. [8] 808.
[9] 123.

with a handful of fanatical bishops for control over a collection of idiotic serfs (to use Voltaire's summary of early medieval Europe).

Vico's position was radically different from this and a harbinger of things to come. He does not deny the cruelty, avarice, arrogance, inhumanity of the master class of the 'heroic' ages. But a certain kind of sublime art can spring only from such soil. Clearly, an age in which there is a recognised standard of justice for all men, in which human sacrifice is not practised and rational methods of uncovering the facts of the past have superseded myth and legend, is in certain obvious respects superior to a culture in which Agamemnon causes his daughter to be slaughtered as an offering to the goddess, or men see the sky as a huge, animate body whose anger is expressed in thunder and lightning. But the increase in humanity and knowledge (which means the peak of a cycle) is inevitably accompanied by a loss of primitive vigour, directness, imaginative force, beyond any made possible by the development of the critical intellect. Each succeeding age develops its own unique mode of expression, which is repeated, with perhaps some variation, at the corresponding stage of each successive cycle of the 'ideal eternal history'. There is no need to compare and grade on some single scale of merit each cultural phase and its creations and forms of life and action; indeed, it is not possible to do so, for they are evidently incommensurable. Nevertheless, the children of one culture can attain to an understanding of the life and activity – the thought, behaviour, art, religion, the entire vision of life – of another culture, of what our ancestors could create while we cannot, because they were what they were, and we are what we are, occupying, as we do, different segments of the same cycle.

This is not relativism, for we are able not merely to record but to understand the outlooks of other societies, however imperfectly, without assimilating them to our own; nor is it the old absolutism whereby we can pronounce their works to be superior or inferior to each other, or to our own, by the use of some unaltering criterion valid for all men, everywhere, at all times. But if this is so, then the very notion of a harmonious synthesis in one perfect whole of all that is best is not so much attainable or unattainable (even in principle) as unintelligible. The unparalleled power of the imagination in the early ages cannot, conceptually cannot, be combined with a developed critical capacity, philosophical or scientific knowledge, depth of intellectual analysis. It is absurd to ask whether Aeschylus' *Agamemnon* is a better or worse play than *King Lear*. When Shaw said 'There is nothing in the Bible greater in inspiration than Beethoven's Ninth Symphony',[1] he uttered (if Vico is right) a proposition which was neither true nor false but one that, on examination, turns out to be senseless.

To a disciple of Vico, the ideal of some of the thinkers of the Enlightenment, the notion of even the abstract possibility of a perfect society, is necessarily an attempt to weld together incompatible attributes – characteristics, ideals, gifts, properties, values that belong to different patterns of thought, action, life, and therefore cannot be detached and sewn together into one garment. For a Vichian this notion must be literally absurd: absurd because there is a conceptual clash between, let us say, what gives splendour to Achilles and what causes Socrates or Michelangelo or Spinoza or Mozart or the Buddha to be admired; and since this applies to the respective cultures, in the context of which alone men's achievements can be understood and judged, this fact alone makes this particular dream of the Enlightenment incoherent. The scepticism or pessimism of a good many thinkers of the Enlightenment – Voltaire, Hume, Gibbon, Grimm, Rousseau – about the possibility of realising this condition is beside the point. The point is that even they were animated by a conception of ideal possibilities, however unattainable in practice. In this, at least, they seem to be at one with the more optimistic Turgot and Condorcet. After Vico, the conflict of monism and pluralism, timeless values and historicism, was bound sooner or later to become a central issue. If Vico had done no more than raise it, indirectly yet at its profoundest level, in his seminal chapter on 'The Discovery of the True Homer', this alone should have been sufficient to reveal the power and originality of his thought.

---

[1] 'The Bible', in 'Parents and Children' (preface to *Misalliance*), *The Works of Bernard Shaw* (London, 1930–8), vol. 13 (1930), p. 99.

Montesquieu

I

JEREMY BENTHAM, in one of the lyrical moments which are more frequent in his writings than is commonly supposed, writing half a century after the death of Montesquieu, exclaimed: 'Locke – dry, cold, languid, wearisome, will live for ever. Montesquieu – rapid, brilliant, glorious, enchanting, will not outlive his century.'[1] And, adding the name of Descartes to that of Montesquieu, he condemned both to oblivion on the ground that, interesting as their views may once have been, they contained a greater number of false propositions than true. These great systems must be accorded due tribute, and, after that, decent burial. For they have played out their part. The errors of which they are largely compounded must be rooted out, and not again allowed to haunt the minds of men.

This judgement, with its characteristically quantitative assessment of merit, has itself been long forgotten. But it may have seemed not unreasonable in the nineteenth century, particularly towards the end of it, when much that Montesquieu stood for appeared to have been peacefully absorbed in the outlook and institutions of civilised nations. Montesquieu advocated constitutionalism, the preservation of civil liberties, the abolition of slavery, gradualism, moderation, peace, internationalism, social and economic progress with due respect to national and local tradition. He believed in justice and the rule of law; defended freedom of opinion and association; detested all forms of extremism and fanaticism; put his faith in the balance of power and the division of authority as a weapon against despotic rule by individuals or groups or majorities; and approved of social equality, but not to the point at which it threatened individual liberty; and of liberty, but not to the point where it threatened to disrupt orderly government. A century after his death most of these ideals were, at least in theory, shared by the civilised governments and peoples of Europe. There were, it is

[1] *The Works of Jeremy Bentham*, ed. John Bowring (Edinburgh, 1843), vol. 10, p. 143.

true, despotic systems in the Russian Empire and in Asia, clericalism in Spain, intermittent chaos and corruption in Latin America, barbarism in Africa, a disquieting growth of nationalism and imperialism in Europe. But the essentials of Montesquieu's teaching formed the heart of the liberal creed everywhere; his doctrines had been well understood; it did not seem that he had anything new to tell the twentieth century. Time had made patent his errors. His knowledge of history, geography, ethnology, had lagged behind even his own times. His most famous doctrine, that of the separation of powers, an enthusiastic but mistaken tribute to the system that he had so falsely imagined to prevail in England, only to mislead Blackstone and De Lolme in their turn, had proved impracticable in France during the great Revolution, and had been much too faithfully adopted in the United States, with results not altogether fortunate. The conservative aspects of his teaching – the emphasis on the value of slow, 'organic' evolution as against precipitate reform; on the unique character of different civilisations, and traditional ways of life, and the undesirability of applying the same uniform methods to them all; on the virtues of hereditary aristocracies and inherited skills and professions, and on the vices of mechanical equality – all these had surely been better and more eloquently stated by Burke, and integrated into a great synoptic metaphysical vision by Hegel and his followers. As for the liberal aspects of his teaching – his defence of individual liberty, the integrity and independence of the administration of justice, and civilised and humane relations between nations and individuals alike – these had long degenerated into commonplaces of liberal eloquence which begin with Tocqueville and Mill and rise to a pathetic height with Jaurès and President Wilson. Finally there was the most original achievement of all – the adumbration of the sciences of sociology and anthropology, founded upon the comparative study of human institutions everywhere, and of their physical and psychological causes and conditions. This, in the hands of the great French positivist school, as well as their English and German rivals and disciples, had become a flourishing, highly specialised *métier* the practitioners of which looked back upon this eminent precursor with respect and curiosity, but no more. For his science was a mere collection of epigrams and maxims: his errors of fact were too numerous, his social history a string of anecdotes, his generalisations too unreliable, his concepts too metaphysical, and the whole of his work, suggestive though it might be in parts, and an acknowledged masterpiece of literature, was unsystematic, inconsistent, and in places regrettably frivolous. He was an honoured ancestor, a frozen Augustan figure in a Roman toga, and no more. Whereas his immediate successors, Rousseau, Kant, Hume, Bentham, had said things still capable of agitating men's minds, and causing hot dissension, Montesquieu was chiefly remembered as a writer of great charm, an observant, civilised, sceptical *grand seigneur*, the author of a work once greeted as epoch-making, and vastly influential in its own day, but, a century after its appearance, looked on as a huge fossil in the stream of thought, a monument to an age dead and gone. This was certainly the view of Comte and Buckle, Herbert Spencer and Durkheim, themselves half forgotten now, and scarcely anyone in those days troubled to deny or to doubt it. However just this view may have seemed in its own time, it is not, I think, so plausible in ours. On the contrary I should like to argue that Montesquieu's views have far more relevance to our own situation than those of his nineteenth-century successors. It is their views rather than his that seem obsolete in the bleak light of today.

II

Let me begin with some well-known facts: Charles-Louis de Secondat, Baron de la Brède, was born in the Castle of La Brède, near Bordeaux, on 18 January 1689. His father was a magistrate, his mother a pious lady. A beggar who happened to be passing by the castle was given him as a godfather so that he might all his life remember that the poor were his brothers. He was brought up by peasants and taught by priests, and in his youth dabbled in the natural sciences, biological rather than physical. At the age of thirty-two he made his literary début with the *Lettres persanes*, which was received as an audacious, beautifully written, and entertaining satire on French society and the church of Rome, perhaps bolder than, but not in essence very different from, the fashionable sceptical literature of the time, of which a flood had been released by the death of Louis XIV. He had the routine career of an eminent provincial official, who was also a man of letters. He inherited from his uncle the title of Montesquieu and the office of Président à Mortier of the court of Bordeaux, was duly elected to the Bordeaux Academy and later to the *Académie française*, settled down to life on his estate and his judicial functions, paid occasional visits to Paris intellectual *salons*, and towards the fortieth year of his life began the work which some twenty years later was to give him world fame. He died in Paris seven years after completing it, universally admired and mourned.

It is clear that he thought that he had made a stupendous discovery. He tells us that after a long and painful period of intellectual wandering, during which the light appeared to him intermittently, only to be lost again in the darkness, he suddenly perceived a central principle which made all things clear, and which made the chaos of hitherto unrelated facts appear as a lucid and rational order.[1] He speaks of this moment of illumination like others who had had a transforming experience. Descartes and Vico, Hume, Gibbon and Rousseau have spoken in similar terms of the crises which had changed their vision of life.

What was it that moved this very sober and sceptical man so deeply? He lived at a time when the world appeared to rationalist thinkers to be divided into two realms: on the one hand that of nature, the laws and principles of which had at last been discovered, so that the movements of every particle in space could at last be explained in terms of a few simple laws and rules of deduction; and on the other, that of human habits and institutions, where everything still seemed uncharted and unchartable. The human scene presented itself as a field for the play of blind chance and irrational forces, good and bad fortune, the whims of despots, adventurers, and popular passions, which left the way open to metaphysical and theological explanations unsupported by anything worthy of the name of evidence, conducted by methods the opposite of rational, the happy hunting-ground of bigots and charlatans and their dupes and slaves. This was the standard attitude of the anti-clerical opposition; and the writings of the rationalists of the time, stifled by the ecclesiastical censorship during the last years of Louis XIV, had been directed to exposing the scandal. It was not surprising that Descartes had dismissed history, and humane studies generally, as being of no interest to seekers after the truth: the subject-matter seemed incapable of yielding precise definitions, clear rules of evidence, axioms, from which true conclusions

---

[1] '... quand j'ai découvert mes principes, tout ce que je cherchois est venu à moi'. *De l'esprit des lois* (hereafter *E.L.*), preface. *Oeuvres complètes de Montesquieu*, ed. A. Masson, 3 vols (Paris, 1950–55), vol. 1 A, p. lxii. All subsequent references to Montesquieu's works are given in this edition, whose first volume is a facsimile of the 1758 edition in three volumes, here referred to as A, B, C.

could be deduced by unassailably valid means. Descartes spoke of history as a tissue of idle gossip and travellers' tales, suitable only for whiling away an idle hour. Vico had, indeed, claimed that he had found a thread in this seeming labyrinth, and could organise the scattered data by means of the new principles which he had brought to light. But he was an obscure, poverty-ridden Neapolitan recluse, and no one in France read him, or paid the slighest attention to him at this time. The story that Montesquieu had read the *Scienza nuova* seems to be pure legend. He speaks as if, for the first time in human history, he had uncovered the fundamental laws which govern the behaviour of human societies, much as natural scientists in the previous century had discovered the laws of the behaviour of inanimate matter. He speaks of the genesis of legal systems, but he obviously means something far wider : the entire institutional framework within which specific human societies live; not merely their systems of law, but the patterns, and the laws of the development, of their political, religious, moral and aesthetic behaviour. Once these are grasped, a science of man is possible. Henceforth a rational science of government can be constructed, and, what concerns him more closely, the behaviour of both governors and governed can be tested by it : a social technology can be elaborated, means can be fitted to ends in accordance with principles derived from experience and observation.

Montesquieu is a child of his age in attributing human misery largely to fear of the unknown, the unnerving and debilitating effect of ignorance and superstition, and the able exploitation of these by charlatans and power-seekers in all spheres. The crippling sense of the fortuitousness and precariousness of all that depends on human relationships can and must be dissipated once and for all. Just as discoveries in the realms of physics and biology have transformed such very different arts as architecture and medicine, so his great social discoveries should be able to transform the art of government in its widest sense, and create societies in which men control their own destinies, instead of remaining at the mercy of natural forces and their own vices and follies. To this end societies must be studied in the systematic way in which anatomists study human organisms, or zoologists and botanists determine the behaviour of animals and plants. In a celebrated passage Montesquieu stated the central conception on which his work was to be based : 'Men are governed by many things: climate, religion, law, the maxims of government, the examples of past things, customs, manners; and from the combination of such influences a general

spirit is produced.'[1] Societies are not fortuitous collections of heterogeneous elements, nor artificial constructions; they are forms of
natural development, and the laws which men obey should be adapted
to the character of this development. Human lives are subject to
various causes of which some are unalterable, while others can be
changed, but the process of change is always slow and, at times, very
difficult.

Each human society differs from every other. Hence laws

> should be so adapted to the people for which they are created, that it
> should be a great coincidence if the laws of one nation suit another
> ... They ought to be fitted to the *physical conditions* of a country, to
> its climate, whether cold, hot or temperate; to the nature of its soil,
> to its situation and extent, and to the way of life of its people whether
> it is agricultural or pastoral or that of hunters. They ought to be
> adapted to the degree of liberty which the constitution can bear, to
> the religion of the inhabitants, to their disposition, their wealth,
> their number, their commerce, and to their habits and manners.
> Finally they are connected with one another, with their source of
> origin, with the design of the lawgiver, and with the order of things
> in which they are established. They must be considered from all
> these points of view.
>
> This is what I propose to do in this work. I shall examine all
> these relationships which collectively form what may be called *the
> spirit of the laws*.[2]

These were to be the principles of the new sciences of sociology,
anthropology and social psychology; and one can understand why
Montesquieu was so profoundly excited by his discovery. Neither God
nor chance rules the world; Bossuet and the sceptics are equally mistaken. The behaviour of human beings, both individually and in the
aggregate, is in principle intelligible, if the facts are observed patiently
and intelligently, hypotheses formulated and verified, laws established,
with the same degree of genius and success – and why not? – as had
attended the great discoveries of physics, astronomy and chemistry,
and seemed likely soon to bring about similar triumphs in the realm of
biology, physiology and psychology. The success of physics seemed to
give reason for optimism: once appropriate social laws were discovered,
rational organisation would take the place of blind improvisation,

[1] *E.L.* xix 4: vol. I A, p. 412.
[2] ibid. i 3: vol. I A, pp. 8–9.

and men's wishes, within the limits of the uniformities of nature, could in principle all be made to come true. Never again was there so much confidence as in the eighteenth century; Helvétius and Condillac, Holbach and Condorcet, and, in a more qualified degree, Diderot and Turgot, Voltaire and d'Alembert, believed that they were living on the threshold of a new age, within sight of the ideal ending. The enemy was still strong, but the advance of science would inevitably render him progressively more ridiculous and impotent. Nothing could in the end stand in the path of scientific knowledge, and knowledge alone could make men happy and virtuous, wise and free. This victorious gospel travelled far beyond the confines of the French *salons*, it found a responsive echo in almost every country in Europe, and even in Russia. The darker the oppression, the brighter the future seemed. In England, admired as the freest and most enlightened society of the age, enthusiasm was more moderate, but here too the doctrine was viewed with much benevolence or sympathy. Of its American career there is scarcely need to speak. The materialist aspects of this teaching were attacked on moral grounds by Rousseau and Mably, and on religious grounds by a handful of Christian theologians, Catholic and Protestant, but scarcely any serious intellectual arguments were, until late in the century, advanced against it. Not since the Middle Ages had western European thought achieved such solidarity. High as the social optimism of the nineteenth century sometimes rose, it did not again mount to the peaks reached at the time of its birth, in the early years of Louis XV.

Montesquieu, who can, in some sense, be regarded as one of the fathers of the Enlightenment, did not altogether share in this mood. There is a sceptical note which runs through all his writing, and it upset the more serious and ardent reformers; some of his opinions on specific political and social questions irritated the Encyclopedists, and made them suspicious of his ideals. It was clear, for instance, that however warmly he may have approved the attacks of his young friend Helvétius on the injustice and the cruelty, the intolerance and the corruption, the ignorance and the stupidity of both church and state in France in his time, he had little sympathy with his more positive and revolutionary doctrines. Montesquieu's reasons for this, which critics in his own and in the nineteenth century were inclined to put down to his timidity and natural conservatism, have become a good deal clearer to us today.

By temperament Montesquieu is an empiricist who seeks to explain everything by naturalistic means wherever and whenever he can. He inherited certain metaphysical concepts, such as natural law and natural purpose, which enter into the thought of the majority of enlightened persons in his time, even when they profess to be wholly emancipated from them. Nevertheless, what he principally stressed was the fruit of observation. He observed curiously, minutely and insatiably, all his life. His accounts of his travels, his historical sketches, his scattered notes on a wide variety of topics, are detailed, vivid and penetrating. He was fascinated by what he saw and what he learnt, for its own sake, whether or not it offered evidence for a hypothesis or pointed a moral that he wished to emphasise. Hence the numberless digressions and asides with which his works abound, and which seem merely diverting to those who expect a systematic, logically constructed political treatise, and treat facts solely as material for generalisations and laws. Although ostensibly in search of such laws, Montesquieu loses himself in concrete detail. This alone is real for him: his vignettes of characters and situations are not stylised, neither caricatures nor idealisations in the manner of his century. His Persians, whether at home or abroad, are neither naïve savages nor monsters of malicious insight; Usbek and Rica are neither superior nor inferior to the Parisians whom they describe, but so dissimilar that what is obvious and normal in one culture seems perverse and ludicrous to another; each group of persons sets off the features of the other in high, often ironical, but never consciously exaggerated, relief. The same episodic method is used in *De l'esprit des lois*: the author delights too greatly in particular facts or events for what they are in themselves to press them too hard into the service of the hypotheses they are called in to support. Many efforts have been made to explain the order of the chapters of *De l'esprit des lois*, which on the face of it is a shapeless amalgam of disquisitions on various topics, in no apparent order. It would be ungenerous to disparage the devoted labours of so many scholars and commentators, yet one sometimes wonders if they are not all so much misdirected ingenuity. Montesquieu is not a systematic philosopher, not a deductive thinker, not a historian, not a scientist, and one of his great merits lies in the very fact that although he claims to be founding a new science in the spirit of Descartes, his practice is better than his professions, and he is, in fact, doing nothing of the kind, because he realises that the material will not allow of it. With the result that, while on the one hand he knows that investigation of social facts is indispensable to the task which he has set himself, he is at the same time dimly aware of the fact that to attempt to marshal the data into some pre-established pattern, whether metaphysical or inductive, is, in fact, an excessively artificial proceeding, repugnant to the nature of this particular topic, and will turn out, as later sociology has all too often proved to be, exceedingly sterile in results. Indeed, he virtually says as much : 'On ne s'est guère jamais trompé plus grossièrement que lorsqu'on a voulu réduire en système les sentiments des hommes, et, sans contredit, la plus mauvaise copie de l'homme est celle qui se trouve dans les livres, qui sont un amas de propositions générales, presque toujours fausses.'[1]

But if the sentiments of men cannot be reduced to general propositions, how is one to proceed? What does a new discovery consist in if it is not achieved by means of generalisations derived from the carefully amassed facts (according to methods recommended by, say, Auguste Comte or Herbert Spencer a century later) and applied to the particular cases that are of interest to the political scientist or the practical legislator or administrator? For all that Montesquieu speaks of Cartesian methods, he does not, fortunately for himself and posterity, apply them. What he does is rather to advance tentative principles and hypotheses; to defend them by adducing the never wholly conclusive evidence of observation, and employ them, and invite others to employ them, in the light of what he calls reason, i.e. their own best judgement, in the manner which the subject-matter itself seems to call for; not mechanically, nor by experimental methods which could, in principle, be taught to competent but uninspired practitioners, in the way in which, for example, chemical or physical methods can, to a large extent, be taught. Montesquieu's principles resemble maxims and aphorisms more than conclusions of careful inductions. So, for example, he makes no serious attempt to adduce evidence for a proposition as fundamental to his entire thesis as that man is by nature social, and that there is, therefore, no need for a Hobbesian hypothesis of social contract to explain why men gather in societies. He

[1] *Mes pensées* 30 (549): vol. 2, p. 9. In the Masson edition the *Pensées* are numbered in the order in which they appear in Montesquieu's manuscript notebooks; the number in brackets refers to the order adopted by M. H. Barckhausen in the first edition of the *Pensées*: *Pensées et fragments inédits de Montesquieu* (Bordeaux, 1899, 1901).

merely asserts, without much argument, that Hobbes's man in a state of nature, hostile, isolated and self-centred, is a myth; that the genesis of society needs no special explanation: for society is the result not of artificial measures to prevent mutual extermination, or of the deliberate search for security or power, but comes into being as a result of biological laws as naturally as do flocks of birds or herds of animals; so that wars and fears of wars, so far from being a motive for social cohesion as Hobbes had taught, only occur after societies have come into being, when a man, in combination with other men, feels strong enough to attack others out of a desire to dominate or destroy rival power-seekers, a desire which is itself necessarily social – capable of arising only in communal life. Moreover, he thinks[1] that human societies should not be looked at as collocations of isolable human atoms or artificial structures brought together by a deliberate plan, but are much more akin to biological organisms which have their own laws of behaviour, observable only to those who study societies as unities and not as artificial conglomerates. Each social organism will differ in certain respects from other similar organisms; and each must be studied separately, if only to determine the effect upon it of the various material and mental (what he calls moral) influences, which themselves will differ as the relevant geographical position, climate, size, internal organisation, stage of development and so on differ. Many mental properties, of course, men do have in common; they seek self-preservation and all that that entails; they seek social cohesion, they need to be governed; they seek for the satisfaction of various physical and mental cravings. But their differences are more important, for only in terms of them can the differences in development of different human societies, the differences of institutions and outlooks and of physical, moral and mental characteristics, be explained. Montesquieu abhors the concept of man in general, no less than do later thinkers like Burke or Herder, or the cultural anthropologists of our own time. Well might he have said with de Maistre: 'I have seen, in my life, Frenchmen, Italians, Russians . . . but as for *man*, I declare that I have never met him in my life',[2] and added that Nature was a lady not known to him. Something of the sort had certainly been said by Vico, but, as I said before, his work seems to have been totally unknown to Montesquieu. By the time it became celebrated, a century later, the original truths which Vico enunciated so boldly, but in

[1] See p. 134 above.
[2] *Considérations sur la France* (Lyon/Paris, 1866), p. 88.

language at times dark and confused, were already the common property of educated Europeans, largely as a result of the influence of Montesquieu himself and of his German and French disciples – Herder and the historical school in Germany, and later the new social historians, influenced by Saint-Simon, in France. These were bold and fruitful notions, but they rested on *aperçus* and unsystematic observation dominated by moral purpose, not on careful and exhaustive, morally neutral researches like those made by his contemporaries Buffon and Linnaeus.

Yet, systematic or not, it was a novel thing to say that human societies were in the first place made what they were by physical factors; but that as they developed they were modified more directly and profoundly by mental than by material causes. Like a botanist of human society, Montesquieu describes the ideal types of the organisms he classifies. The celebrated division of societies into monarchical, aristocratic, republican and despotic is his attempted improvement on Aristotle. As a classification it doubtless leaves much to be desired; its importance rests not on the degree to which the concepts which he employs yielded fertile methods of analysis or prediction, but in the fact that this type of classification – by idealised models, analogous to the perfect bodies of physics – was destined to have a remarkable career in the sociological and historical analyses of Herder and Saint-Simon, Hegel and Comte, Durkheim and Max Weber.

Montesquieu's concept of types is not empirical; it springs from the ancient doctrine of natural kinds; it is thoroughly metaphysical and Aristotelian. According to him each type of society possesses an inner structure, an inner dynamic principle or force, which makes it function as it does – and this 'inner' force differs from type to type. Whatever strengthens the 'inner' principle causes the organism to flourish, whatever impairs it causes it to decay. His catalogue of these forces is very famous; monarchy rests on the principle of honour, aristocracy on that of moderation, the republican regime on that of virtue (that is, public spirit, *civisme*, almost team spirit), and despotism on that of terror. Montesquieu conceives of social organisms in the manner of Aristotle as teleological – purposive – wholes, as entelechies. The model is biological, not chemical. The inner spring of these societies is conceived by him as that which causes them to fulfil themselves by moving towards an inner goal, in terms of which alone they can be understood. This is the notorious notion of 'inner' forces, the substitution of final for mechanical causes, which had been abandoned by the new science, and had been so brilliantly parodied by Molière in *Le Bourgeois Gentilhomme*. Nor does Montesquieu's appeal to history for support of his symmetrical schema carry any greater degree of conviction than the very similar efforts of Spengler and Arnold Toynbee to present their own ethical or theological systems in the guise of objective laws.

Montesquieu does not pretend to have founded his notion of the archetypes of society upon statistics derived from observation; it is not a hypothesis of a corrigible kind, founded upon empirical data. He attaches immense importance to it, for his entire philosophy of history is founded upon this central notion : individuals and states decay when they contravene the rules of their particular 'inner' constitution. Each state or human community has its own separate, individual, unique path of proper development, created in the first place by material causes, and the business of statesmen is to understand what this constitution is, and therefore what specific rules will alone preserve and strengthen it. These are the famous relations – the necessary rapports – which legal systems must fit if they are to perform their task, that is, render the human beings of a given society adequately healthy, happy, efficient, free and just, and provide them with other attributes the desirability of which is more or less taken for granted. The simile is, as so often in classical Greek philosophy, medical. The business of legislators and administrators, judges, and of everyone concerned with social issues in any form, is to preserve, maintain, improve the health of society. What does this health consist in? This is tantamount to asking what the ends of mankind are; and if the ends of different men or societies clash, how they should be reconciled; and whether, indeed, divergent interests can or should be reconciled at all. Montesquieu is only too well aware of the wide differences between the answers – the varieties of religious and philosophical systems which have sought to formulate the ultimate goal which men should, or in fact do, seek; or would seek if they were rational or knew what was right or true. He rejects out of hand the ends put forward by the Christian theologians of his time. Religion to him is a natural phenomenon like any other, brought about by natural causes that have led to Protestantism and toleration in the north of Europe, Catholicism and persecution in the south, Islam and a static fanaticism in the east, and so on. He sets himself to investigate these causes – hot and cold, wet and dry climates, fertile or sterile soils, distance from the sea, proximity to mountains – which create needs and with them institutions designed to satisfy them. How is one to evaluate human institutions, legislation, forms of life? It used to be said, both for him and against him, that he was content merely to observe and describe – the politically committed, whether in Montesquieu's day or ours, probably find so much detachment morally almost sinister, perhaps even danger-ous – but this is an illusion. Montesquieu's tone is moderate; his words were intended, as he once remarked,[1] to afford the reader the pleasure of watching grave and dignified theologians not thrown roughly on the ground, but sliding gently into the abyss. But he is concerned with moral issues no less deeply and directly than the more vehement controversialists of his time, and differs from them, not so much in his conception of the problems of behaviour as in his solutions and, of course, the tone and temper of the argument. He does not so much as discuss the single criterion of contemporary utilitarians. He remarks casually that men are made to preserve themselves[2] or that 'Happiness and unhappiness consist in a certain disposition, favourable or unfavourable, of the organs'[3] or that 'interest is the greatest mon-arch on earth'.[4] But these are the typical maxims of almost any eighteenth-century moralist. Nowhere does he say or imply that happiness, or the satisfaction of certain specified wants, is the sole end, or that the pursuit of it, in however perverted and ignorant a form, is the sole motive of human behaviour. The true answers to these ques-tions, which agitated the eighteenth century so deeply, seemed to Montesquieu so obvious that he scarcely troubled to formulate them save by implication. Different societies clearly seek different ends; they seek them because they seek them, because their 'inner' principles so respond to their environments. To the degree to which men resemble each other and live in similar conditions, their ends, too, will be similar. To the degree to which they differ from one another – and this in-terests him more than their similarities – their ends will differ accord-ingly. He simply cannot see a problem where others have perceived one. A physician does not, after all, usually ask himself what pre-cisely it is that good health consists in, and why; he takes it for granted, and calls himself a physician because he knows a healthy and normal organism from one which is sick or abnormal, and knows, moreover, that what is good for one type of organism may be fatal to

---

[1] See the letter to Madame du Deffand, 13 September 1754: vol. 3, p. 1515.
[2] e.g. *Lettres persanes* 143: vol. 1 C, p. 298.
[3] *Mes pensées* 30 (549): vol. 2, p. 8.
[4] *Lettres persanes* 106: vol. 1 C, p. 212.

another, and that what is needed in one climate is unnecessary or dangerous in another. Similarly Montesquieu assumed that the idea of political and moral health is too familiar to need analysis, that when it is present this is quite patent, and that to be rational is to recognise it for what it is, to know the symptoms, to know how to cure the relevant diseases and how to maintain the organism. No doubt great imaginative insight is needed to grasp the needs and habits of organisms very different from one's own. One of the salient characteristics of the *Lettres persanes* is that Montesquieu's travelling Persians are made to look at French and European institutions and habits with a singularly fresh eye, so that what is regarded as obvious and natural in Paris or Rome seems to them as odd or ridiculous or mad as do Persian customs, with equally great or little reason, to correspondingly prejudiced European travellers. This is Montesquieu's notorious relativism, the belief that there is no single set of values suitable for all men everywhere, no single solution to social or political problems in all countries. In virtue of it he has been regarded as a moral sceptic, a subjectivist, uncertain of what is right, unable to provide an objective standard for moral or political behaviour. But this is a misconception of his views. Montesquieu believed in what might be called social hygiene in the largest possible sense. He did not think that great disagreement occurred or could occur among men, provided that they were sufficiently rational and dispassionate, about what constitutes progress, or social solidarity, or weakness, or decadence in a society. In the course of his work on the greatness and decline of the Romans, he points out that what caused Rome to decay was the fact that it sinned against the central 'principle' of the Roman Republic. For republics can be healthy only if they are of a certain size, and their citizens can obtain proper satisfaction for their physical and spiritual wants only so long as certain institutions peculiar to republics are kept in a state of sound repair. Hence what ruined Rome was excess – imperialist over-expansion – and the supersession of 'republican virtue' by personal despotism directly resulting from this sin against the 'inner' principle of the republican structure. In saying this he may have wondered how far his explanation would prove acceptable, but he did not begin to imagine that anyone could question the values involved – for example that the Roman Empire did decline in the third or fourth or fifth centuries, or that it was better – more worthwhile – to be Cicero than to be Heliogabalus, although, of course, Heliogabalus may have enjoyed himself rather more.

Montesquieu conceived that his own original contribution to the subject was to explain the 'organic' causes of the rise or decline of states or societies, and that his particular achievement was to demonstrate the impossibility of universal solutions, to explain that what was good for some people in some situations was not necessarily equally good for others in different conditions, not only because of differences of means, but also of ends; that one society was not necessarily superior to another merely because it differed in its needs or the ways in which it set about solving them. It does not seem to have occurred to him that differences of ultimate values themselves might be questioned by equally civilised men, that two equally rational human beings endowed with knowledge and imagination – above all sufficient historical or anthropological sympathy to conceive of conditions very different from their own – could quarrel about ends, and dismiss each other's moral notions as objectively and demonstrably false or wicked. Rationality to him was not merely knowledge of how to adapt means to ends, or an adequate grasp of historical causation – in particular of the ways in which social structures grew, cohered, decayed – but lay in understanding the entire field of the interplay between nature and men; in understanding which desires and activities were self-destructive and suicidal and which were not; in understanding the vast variety of ends pursued by men in a vast variety of conditions; furthermore, in finding out how, if these ends collided with each other, they could at times be reconciled; or, if not wholly reconciled, whether a compromise between them could or could not be obtained. Some of these ends were doubtless more universal, or deeper in the nature of those who pursued them, than others. This was a matter of observation, factual study. There were no ultimate and universal standards beyond those which different societies in fact employed in different circumstances. Consequently there was no sense in seeking a single objective criterion or criteria in terms of which these ends themselves could be judged and approved or condemned. He did not, like Hume, say that only that was good or right which men approved, for he did not pay much attention to sentiment. Moral and political values for him revealed themselves in behaviour rather than in articulated thought or feeling; if they fitted the circumstances – if they suited the instincts of a given society, and were not self-destructive – they were not to be criticised. 'The names of good, beautiful, noble, great, perfect, are attributes of objects relative to the beings who contemplate them. Keep this principle in your head. It is the sponge which wipes away almost all prejudices.'[1]

Where no notion of objective ends exists, subjectivism, which is its correlative, means little. Nor is this attitude sceptical or morally indifferent; and if it be said that it belongs to a man not principally interested in moral problems, or to one who does not probe too deeply into the goals and principles for which men are prepared to give their lives, there is little that can be said in reply. Montesquieu's position is very similar to that of Aristotle in this matter; and is, perhaps, more sympathetic to civil servants or lawyers than to followers of Pascal or Dostoevsky.

There are few things more disliked by those who wish to improve the world than dispassionate description of the facts, and Helvétius and his friends earnestly tried to dissuade Montesquieu from publishing his book on the spirit of the laws, on the ground that it could only do his reputation harm. It seemed to them to waste time on meticulous descriptions of too many forms of human error and aberration, almost as if the author placed some value on them merely because they existed. Helvétius declared that only two types of government were known to him: the good, which had not come into being yet, and the bad, namely that which transferred the money of the poor into the pockets of the rich; '. . . true political science is the science not of *what is*, but of *what ought to be*,'[2] said the Abbé Sieyès towards the end of the eighteenth century, but he might just as well have said it fifty years earlier, for this is the view of almost all the rational thinkers of the great century. The proper concern of an intelligent man was with science; and science meant not mere description and systematisation, but practical rules designed to change things for the better by the most rapid and direct means. To this Montesquieu was conspicuously not sympathetic. He disliked and distrusted speed and violence. He poured

---

[1] Quoted by A. J. Grant, in 'Montesquieu', in F. J. C. Hearnshaw (ed.), *The Social and Political Ideas of Some Great French Thinkers of the Age of Reason* (London, 1930), p. 120. I have not been able to find the original source of this translation, though it is not dissimilar to a passage in the *Essai sur le goût* written for the *Encyclopédie* in 1757, published with modifications in Montesquieu's *Oeuvres posthumes*, 1783. Masson (see p. 133, note 1 above), vol. 1 C, pp. 611–12.

[2] In a manuscript of 1772 entitled 'Économie politique', cited by C. A. de Sainte-Beuve, *Causeries du lundi*, 2nd ed. (Paris, 1852–62), vol. 5 (1853), p. 153.

cold water on hopes of swift reform; he appeared to attach value to institutions merely because they existed; he distributed value judgements all too sparingly; he was evidently more interested in understanding than in action. Spinoza, it is true, had advocated some such attitude: but this was, in the eighteenth century, the least admired aspect of his war against the enemies of progress. Moreover, had not Montesquieu himself attacked Spinoza for his determinism and for wishing to suppress the passions without which men cannot act? But Montesquieu had omitted to add that the acts must be good and not bad; he seemed to show more interest in classifying types of activity than in their conduciveness to happiness. 'Of happiness, he says nothing',[1] said Bentham indignantly, echoing Helvétius; and the Neapolitan lawyer Filangieri accused him of having 'reasoned rather on what *has been* done than on what *ought* to be done'.[2] Montesquieu bore this type of criticism patiently, but one cannot help feeling that what the Encyclopedists had against him was not his addiction to the description of the truth for its own sake – which the best among them could not themselves resist – but the implications of his apparently neutral attitude. They felt that he was altogether too anxious to emphasise that durable and beneficial social structures were seldom simple, that large areas of political behaviour always remained very complex and obscure, that a radical change of one part of it might easily lead to unpredictable effects in others, and that the end might be worse than the beginning. They felt that his perpetual harping on the need to go along the grain, to act slowly and circumspectly, was meant to sabotage their ardent programmes, that his reminder that 'La nature agit toujours avec lenteur'[3] and the famous definition of the 'most perfect' government as 'celui qui conduit les hommes de la manière qui convient le plus à leur penchant et à leur inclination'[4] were altogether too

[1] op. cit. (p. 130, note 1 above), vol. 9, p. 123.

[2] Gaetano Filangieri, *La scienza della legislazione* (1784), in *La scienza della legislazione di Gaetano Filangieri con giunta degli opuscoli scelti*, vol. 1 (Milan, 1822), p. 12, trans. William Kendall in *The Science of Legislation, Translated from the Italian of the Chevalier Filangieri* (London/Exeter, 1792), p. 11. This is the same as Rousseau's reproach in *Émile*, book 5: 'il faut savoir ce qui doit être pour bien juger de ce qui est'. See Rousseau's *Oeuvres complètes*, ed. Bernard Gagnebin, Marcel Raymond and others (Paris, 1959–), vol. 4 (1969), pp. 836–7.

[3] *Lettres persanes* 114: vol. 1 C, p. 227.

[4] ibid. 80: vol. 1 C, p. 164.

lukewarm. Still, even this would have passed, if he had not also said that if reforms were really unavoidable, one should touch laws 'only with a trembling hand',[1] and, worse still, 'the troubles, expenses . . . even dangers of justice are the price which every citizen pays for his liberty'.[2] Bentham again explodes: 'the screen made out of the panegyric on *delay* and *forms*, I have seen it in use these five and fifty years: the name of the manufactory is visible on it. *Esprit des loix* the manufactory: *Montesquieu* and Co. the name of the firm: a more convenient or fashionable article was never made.'[3] No doubt the abuses which infuriated Bentham at the turn of the century were very different from those which Montesquieu detested in France in its early years. But there is also a genuine difference of outlook. Montesquieu cannot forget that simplicity, energy, speed, are the attributes of despotism, and go ill with individual liberty, which needs a looser social texture, a slower tempo.

If one must destroy, one should at least hesitate, feel qualms. The more radical reformers, naturally enough, distrusted this, and suspected Montesquieu of reactionary tendencies wrapped in the outer covering of scientific curiosity and enlightened opinions. Nor were they altogether mistaken.[4] For he was certainly opposed to revolution: Catherine the Great, and, following her, a school of conservative Russian thinkers, could (and did) cite his views in defence of the proposition that Russia had 'organic' need of autocracy; and his naturalism undoubtedly contained deep layers of inherited metaphysical belief. Yet this reactionary attacked slavery as no one had before him; saw nothing wicked or unnatural in suicide, divorce, incest; and looked on religion purely as a social institution.

'. . . when Montezuma insisted that the religion of the Spaniards was good for their country and the Mexican for his own, what he said was not absurd'.[5] This attitude was calculated to – and did – irritate both sides in the great controversy of his age. The theologians of the Sorbonne naturally condemned it. Montesquieu was denounced fiercely by the Jansenists, his books were put on the Index. But the party of Enlightenment, Voltaire and the Encyclopedists, were scarcely

---

[1] *Lettres persanes* 129: vol. 1 C, p. 257.

[2] *E.L.* vi 2: vol. 1 A, p. 100.

[3] op. cit. (p. 130, note 1 above), vol. 8, p. 481.

[4] Rousseau's criticism of Grotius in *Du contrat social* (book 1, chapters 2–4) is not unlike Bentham's attack on Montesquieu.

[5] *E.L.* xxiv 24: vol. 1 B, p. 103.

less indignant. For if this view was true it followed that scientific investigation was not capable of demonstrating that some moral purposes were correct and others not; that some or all religions were tissues of falsehood, and deleterious for this reason alone. In fact the whole system of values upon which the Enlightenment rested began to crumble if the very possibility of a single universal method for obtaining true answers to moral and metaphysical questions, true for all men, at all times, everywhere, *quod ubique, quod semper, quod ab omnibus*, was doubted or denied. Indeed, the very tone of Montesquieu, the whole tenor of his work was somehow felt to be subversive of the principles of the new age.[1] He was, it is true, an ally on such issues as the credibility of religious revelation, the authority of the church, the nature of royal authority, the irrationality of autocratic rule; he detested arbitrary oppression, the suppression of freedom of thought or speech, the benighted economic policies of the royal regime. He believed in knowledge, science, toleration. He hated armies, conquests, tyrants, priests. But there the agreement with the opposition virtually ended. He plainly did not believe in universal solutions, indeed in no simple or final solutions at all. It is true that he did not believe that man was in a state of original sin; but neither did he believe that he was infinitely perfectible. He believed that man was not impotent, only weak, that he could be made stronger, yet only with the greatest difficulty, and even then not very strong. He did not believe that ideal solutions could ever be realised, only approximations to them. He distrusted simplicity, and disbelieved in the permanence of any institution, any moral rule, save justice alone. He believed that only reason could solve human problems, but that by itself it could not effect much. He did not, like Hume, think reason to be necessarily the slave of the passions, only feebler than them, and maintained that since reason was weak and the passions strong, and, in any case, indestructible, they should be not fought but harnessed, and conditions created to direct them into desired channels – a doctrine later adopted by Saint-Simon, Comte and Pareto. '. . . out of the crooked timber of humanity no straight thing can ever be made' said Immanuel Kant,[2]

---

[1] Plato denounced a very similar attitude, which he attributed to the Sophists, and for much the same reasons.

[2] '. . . aus so krummem Holze, als woraus der Mensch gemacht ist, kann nichts ganz Gerades gezimmert werden'. 'Idee zu einer allgemeinen Geschichte in weltbürgerlicher Absicht', *Kant's gesammelte Schriften*, vol. 8 (Berlin, 1912), p. 23.

and this represents Montesquieu's view as against that of his friends, the optimistic planners of his day. Unlike them, he hates and fears all despots, even the most rational and enlightened, for he distrusts all central authority, all the great managers of society, all those who confidently and tidily arrange the destinies of others. He speaks with contempt and hostility of the *Décisionnaire universel* (a term he invented) who is never assailed by doubts, because societies organised by such persons, however well ordered and enlightened, are necessarily tyrannous. He believes passionately in the necessity for a minimum area of personal liberty for every citizen, whatever he may choose to do with it. He distrusts zeal, however benevolent, because it threatens to suffocate individuals ('virtue itself needs limits'),[1] and values personal liberty above all.

But there is a still graver charge against him : that he is not a wholehearted determinist. No one did more to draw attention to the many unnoticed ways in which material factors mould human character and institutions, or to indicate strategic points in the network of social relations (such as the connection of free trade and military security, or the influence of the growth of communications on despotic governments, or of the development of new weapons of unheard-of destructive force on international relations),[2] but he does not believe that this kind of explanation accounts for the whole of human behaviour. He believes that the laws which govern human conduct are not as allembracing as those which govern the behaviour of, say, inanimate matter in space. He believes in what he calls 'general causes' which create situations that render certain consequences no more than highly probable, that is to say, render certain – but only certain – possible courses of action impracticable. Accidents cause important consequences only because they operate in conjunction with explicable general causes : 'Had Caesar and Pompey thought as did Cato, others would have thought like Caesar and Pompey ; and the Republic, which was destined to perish, would have been drawn to the precipice by another hand.'[3] If Charles I of England had not administered a 'shock'

---

[1] *E.L.* xi 4 : vol. 1 A, p. 206.

[2] '. . . depuis l'invention de la poudre, il n'y a plus de place imprenable . . . Je tremble toujours qu'on ne parvienne à la fin à découvrir quelque secret qui fournisse une voie plus abrégée pour faire périr les hommes, détruire les peuples et les nations entières.' *Lettres persanes* 105 : vol. 1 C, pp. 208–9.

[3] *Considérations sur les causes de la grandeur des Romains et de leur décadence,* xi : vol. 1 C, p. 427.

to the form of life of his people in one way, he would, given the general situation, surely have done so in another;[1] and if Charles XII of Sweden had not been defeated at Poltava, he would have been defeated elsewhere[2] because a 'general cause' was in operation whereby the Swedish state and army were in such a condition that one lost battle could lose them the war. But this shows at most that certain possibilities could not have been realised, and that to assume that they were open is an unrealistic reading of history. But it does not follow that all alternatives are always closed, and only one path is causally necessitated.

Montesquieu's lapses from strict determinism were noted, with some distress, by Durkheim, when, as a young man, he began to investigate Montesquieu's claims to be the forerunner, if not the pioneer, of sociology.[3] Durkheim cannot understand why Montesquieu believed that the laws which govern human behaviour were less precisely statable, and less predictable in their effects, than those which governed the material world. When Montesquieu declares that material causes can to a large degree be counteracted by deliberate human action[4] – indeed, he congratulated Hume in 1749 on giving 'une beaucoup plus grand influence aux causes morales qu'aux causes physiques'[5] – Durkheim can scarcely conceal his indignation. If sociology is to be a science at all, it must surely regard human activities themselves as being neither more nor less subject to natural causes than the obstacles they are meant to overcome. He ends by accusing Montesquieu of gratuitously betraying the very science which he had been the first to conceive in a lucid and coherent manner. Durkheim was, of course, perfectly consistent, and if Montesquieu's claim to be the father of modern scientific sociology rested on strict application of the principles of Helvétius or Comte, it would, indeed, be gravely compromised. It is to the eternal credit of Montesquieu that he committed this very crime. He was guided by such actual facts as he had observed or believed to occur, and was not betrayed into arranging

---

[1] *De la politique*: vol. 3, p. 169.

[2] *E.L.* x 13: vol. 1 A, p. 195.

[3] *Quid Secundatus politicae scientiae instituendae contulerit* (Bordeaux, 1892), trans. as *Montesquieu's Contribution to the Rise of Social Science* in Émile Durkheim, *Montesquieu and Rousseau: Forerunners of Sociology* (Michigan, 1960).

[4] *E.L.* xiv 5, 6; xvi 12: vol. 1 A, pp. 312–13; 361.

[5] Letter to Hume, 19 May 1749: vol. 3, p. 123.

them in some symmetrical pattern whether they were susceptible to such arrangement or not. He observed some natural or historical regularities which seemed to him important, and these he faithfully reported. Equally, he tried to estimate the extent of the power of human action in certain types of situations. Some among these human actions he supposed that he could trace to natural causes; some, but not all. He declined to go beyond his evidence, to extrapolate mechanically, and to maintain that because some phenomena seemed determined by strict laws, all must be so. Men could bend things to their will, though not very much; they were weak, but Montaigne had greatly exaggerated their weakness and helplessness. Pascal had declared that uncritical acceptance of custom was the mystical cause of the authority of laws, and had implied that he who probed – and 'brought it back to its principle' – destroyed it, and Burke and de Maistre echoed this fervently. He who 'brings back' any phenomenon to its source, to its 'principle', said Montesquieu, strengthens it. Knowledge cannot possibly be a source of weakness: it is doubtless limited, and we must do the best we can; this may be little, but it is not nothing. The world is ruled by laws, but they do not account for everything. Montesquieu is displeased with Spinoza for saying that a man can be a great scoundrel and yet have committed no crime, because he is caused to act abominably by circumstances over which he has no control.[1] Natural causes are doubtless very powerful, but they can at times be counteracted by legislation and education; even the effects of the great sovereign 'whose empire is the first among all empires' – climate itself – can be modified and regulated by intensive moral education. One can modify and moderate ('régler', 'modérer', are the terms constantly used by Montesquieu) almost everything; one law can be checked by means of another, one power by another; the best constitution is that which is built like an elaborate mosaic of countervailing powers. The natural tendency of men is to gravitate downwards and not even to attempt the immensely difficult task of being rational or being free, of walking the narrow causeway between despotism and anarchy. Yet this can be achieved, but only by working deliberately and with difficulty towards an equilibrium. This equilibrium is always unstable. To preserve it needs enormous care and vigilance, and also the most accurate factual – that is, scientific – information obtainable. Ignorance, idleness, self-interest are potent enemies of human progress, but even more ruinous are bigots and desperadoes – monks who teach men to stunt

[1] *Mes pensées* 1266 (615): vol. 2, p. 343.

their natural faculties, great conquerors who exterminate men to gratify their personal ambitions, and worst of all, the great despotic organisers who buy the freedom of the state at the cost of enslaving their fellow citizens. The two worst citizens that France had ever had were Richelieu and Louvois; and, if he had dared, Montesquieu would have added Louis XIV.

Liberty is not total independence, nor is it licence. It is very hard to attain and preserve, but without it all things wither. No amount of efficiency of government, national glory, prosperity, social equality, can compensate for its loss. Monarchies are in particular danger of losing it, for they tend to end in despotism as rivers lose themselves in the ocean,[1] and despotism means the prevalence of fear, and where fear is universal and every citizen is in terror of someone, there is no security, no 'tranquillity of spirit',[2] and a disease is at work which in the end destroys the texture of normal social life. But what is liberty? Montesquieu says that it is not identical with being permitted to do whatever one may wish, for that would lead to anarchy, and so to the despotism inevitably called in to suppress it. To possess liberty is, in the famous formula, 'to be able to do what one ought to will, and not to be compelled to do what one ought not to will'.[3] But who shall tell us what we ought to will? The laws. Liberty is 'the right to do whatever the laws permit'.[4] But can there not be despotic laws? Yes, but in a rational society the laws will be founded upon justice. Justice is not definable as that which the laws happen to enjoin, nor that which the ruler wills simply because he wills it. To define justice in terms of actual laws is as absurd 'as if one were to say that before circles were actually drawn their radii were not all equal'.[5] Good laws embody the rules of justice, but these rules themselves are absolute and objective, independent of being formulated. What, then, is justice? It is 'a quality which belongs to men as much as existence';[6] it is 'un rapport de convenance, qui se trouve réellement entre deux choses: ce rapport est toujours le même, quelque être qui le considère, soit que ce soit dieu, soit que ce soit un ange, ou enfin que ce soit un homme'.[7] This fixed structure is none other than 'the necessary relations arising from the nature of things'[8] – the celebrated metaphysical definition of law with which *De l'esprit des lois* opens, and which

---

[1] *E.L.* viii 17: vol. 1 A, p. 167. [2] ibid. xi 6, p. 208.
[3] ibid. xi 3, p. 205. [4] ibid., p. 206.
[5] ibid. i 1, p. 3. [6] *Lettres persanes* 10: vol. 1 C, p. 26.
[7] ibid. 83, p. 169. [8] *E.L.* i 1: vol. 1 A, p. 1.

has puzzled and irritated modern commentators. 'La justice élève sa voix; mais elle a peine à se faire entendre dans le tumulte des passions.'[1] It is the voice of reality itself speaking: 'la justice est éternelle, et ne dépend point des conventions humaines' (nor, he could have added, on divine ones either); 'Et, quand elle en dépendroit, ce seroit une vérité terrible, qu'il faudroit se dérober à soi-même.'[2]

These formulations give one pause. Not that there is anything very new in them – the doctrine, even the cynical invitation to conceal the truth, is at least as old as Plato. Montesquieu's words, *mutatis mutandis*, could have occurred in many a medieval text; neither Hooker nor Grotius would have thought them in the least peculiar. Indeed, it is a piece of medieval theology translated into secular terms. Hume[3] accused Montesquieu of deriving this view of justice as an absolute objective relationship from Malebranche, and rightly considered it an unintelligible abstraction. It derives, of course, from a belief in natural law as conceived not merely by seventeenth-century jurists, but by eighteenth-century economists and social philosophers as well. The physiocratic doctrine of the coincidence of the true interests of all men is itself an application of the law of nature, an *a priori* system which can, indeed, be transgressed (though only to the cost of the transgressor) and which positive, man-made law is merely required to transcribe with literal accuracy. In this way the personal government of men, which, even in the hands of the wisest, retains some arbitrary element, will be replaced by the rule of law itself. It is not difficult to recognise in this the old theological natural order translated into economic or social terminology. Saint-Simon's formula about the government of men giving way to the administration of things, Marx's reiteration of it, Hegel's rational *Rechtsstaat* and all their progeny in modern legal and political theory, are rooted in the metaphysics of the natural order which, despite all efforts to restate it in empirical terms, retains indelible traces of its transcendental origin. But what is strange in the emergence of this time-honoured doctrine in *De l'esprit des lois* is its incompatibility with what is most original in Montesquieu's own great new discovery. His whole aim is to show that laws are not born in the void, that they are not the result of positive commands either of God or priest or king; that they are, like everything else in society, the expression of the changing moral habits, beliefs, general attitudes of a particular society, at a particular time, on

[1] *Lettres persanes* 83: vol. 1 C, p. 169.   [2] ibid., p. 170.
[3] *An Enquiry Concerning the Principles of Morals*, III ii 158, note.

a particular portion of the earth's surface, played upon by the physical and spiritual influences to which their place and period expose human beings. It is difficult to see how this doctrine, which is the foundation of the great German school of historical jurisprudence, of French post-revolutionary historiography, of the various modern sociological theories of law, can be reconciled with belief in universal, unvarying, everlasting rules, equally valid for all men in all places at all times – rules discovered by the faculty of reason as conceived by Descartes or Leibniz, that is, as a non-natural means of perceiving eternal verities – the very notion which it had been the great historic service of Montesquieu to overthrow. Indeed, Montesquieu goes further. If law is to be the expression of eternal justice, a 'necessity of nature' independent of men or times or places, it must be formulated so explicitly that the sole task of judges will be to apply it as rigorously and precisely as they can to the particular cases before them, and the sole task of administrators to translate it into action as fully and literally as possible. Montesquieu is exceedingly insistent upon this point; he wants to make the operations of the law as strict and automatic as possible. The entire tradition of judge-made law, of the use of legal fictions, of the interpretation of old statutes to fit new situations with due regard to their spirit and not their letter, with such understanding of the public interest as each generation may exercise according to its own lights, which are not necessarily those of other societies or other generations – this cardinal development, oddly omitted by this keen observer in his analysis of English institutions, seems deeply abhorrent to him. There must be no tampering with the letter of the law, no interpretation, no flexibility, no pragmatic adaptation. He seems to think that if a law ceases to be useful, and no longer fully embodies the principles of objective justice, it must be formally abrogated, and a new law specifically created by the legislative organ. This may lead to too much chopping and changing of laws, and a consequent weakening in respect for laws as such, as Hume duly pointed out. But on a strict interpretation of Montesquieu's doctrine of justice this is unavoidable. The social disadvantages must be ignored; for what is social utility before the eternal laws of nature?

The doctrine according to which positive law is itself to be tested by the criterion of strict conformity to some extra-legal set of principles – as revealed in sacred books, or in the utterances of privileged persons, or by a special faculty of rational intuition – is an abiding feature of legal theory in the west. It is in obvious conflict with the equally celebrated view which maintains that the law is only one among many aspects of social development, conditioned by the same sort of factors as social life in general, of which Hobbes's doctrine which Montesquieu rejects, that justice is whatever the laws ordain and nothing else, is merely an extreme, and indeed somewhat *outré*, version. There may, indeed, not exist a strictly logical contradiction between believing laws to be a function of social evolution, and belief in fixed standards of justice and the demand for explicit codification and rigorous application; for the standard may itself consist in some unvarying relationship between changing social factors, say the utilitarian principle of greatest happiness. But there is obviously a genuine disparity of attitude; and Montesquieu leaves us in no doubt that his notion of justice is not a natural function or relationship, but a transcendent eternal standard. The clash between the pragmatic theory of jurisprudence of, say, Holmes or Brandeis, and the older notion of the quasi-mechanical application of laws in the precise forms in which they are promulgated by the legislature, is a central issue that has divided jurists, especially in the United States, and has rightly been traced to profounder political, social, and indeed metaphysical differences. It is worth adding that Montesquieu's notion of absolute justice as the permanently valid standard for legislation is no less incompatible with the social interpretation of the law in the forms in which, for instance, Comtian positivists, or Marxists (with their theory of law as a superstructure dependent on a social and economic base), have understood it. Yet all these streams flow from Montesquieu: the contradiction is evidently present in his own thought.

Why did he fall into it? Perhaps it springs from his fear of despotism and arbitrariness, which took two different, not easily reconcilable directions. On the one hand he dwells over and over again on the fact that to each society belong the moral attitudes and habits and forms of life peculiar to it, that the mere passing of laws or issuing of regulations cannot by itself break these moral and social patterns, only obstruct them, and itself fail to be effective if it departs too far from the social laws which govern the evolution of the society in question. This is part of his great case against capricious interference, wanton oppression, and bullying by individual tyrants or despotic groups. Terror of this inspires the wish to preserve a hierarchical society, the desire to divide and balance, the distrust of all forms of zeal, the pleas for 'intermediary' powers, the defence of hereditary aristocracies and inherited professions, of local and provincial legislative and judicial bodies, of

survivals and relics of feudal institutions, of the neo-feudalism created
by selling offices to the new middle classes, of anomalies for their own
sake – all these being called upon to act as buffers between the perpetually encroaching central authority and the mass of the people
which it might otherwise mould much too freely and brutally to some
arbitrary pattern of its own. And, on the other hand, there is his passionate concern for legality, his insistence upon laws being written
down in clear words for all to see, which again is a means, and a
powerful one, designed always for the same overriding purpose – to
prevent the exercise of their own untrammelled wills by strong individuals (whether it be advocated by defenders of the royal power, like
the Abbé Dubos, or by believers in enlightened despotism, like
Voltaire), and to protect private persons from the power of rulers by
means of a guaranteed equality before explicitly formulated law.[1]

But whatever may be the psychological explanation of Montesquieu's attitude, the internal contradiction remains, and we find two
opposed lines of thought and practice, each claiming his authority.
The first is the pragmatic development of law, consciously amenable
to social change. Here again there is a parting of ways: it takes a conservative form in the writings of Burke and the German jurists, who
see the law as the expression of the deepest traditions and instincts
which have formed the character of a nation or a culture – bound up
with the 'organic' development of a community, not to be deflected
by the arbitrary *fiats* of rulers, or by 'artificial' reforms which are not
in harmony with its historical 'spirit'. In its other, radical, form, it has
been interpreted by social reformers and radicals as so many demands
that the law shall constantly respond to changing social needs and not
be tied to some obsolete principle valid only for some epoch dead and
gone. Both forms of evolutionary jurisprudence are equally incompatible with the Roman and Napoleonic tradition of codified law,
dedicated to the application of explicitly stated general principles, the
validity of which tends to be regarded as universal and eternal, independent of time and place and circumstance.

This internal conflict can also be discovered in Montesquieu's
typically eighteenth-century ambivalence in the use of words like
'reason' and 'nature'. Reason sometimes means intuitive perception
of general laws, in the sense in which Descartes and the rationalists

[1] It is almost as if he were convinced that the notion of absolute and eternal
standards of justice was a chimera, but feared that knowledge of this would
open the way to despotism and social instability (see p. 153, note 2 above).

had used this word, and at other times the (empirical) perception of what a given society needs for its 'sound' and healthy functioning in a given place and season. Nature is commonly gentle and slow, and achieves her ends by scarcely perceptible pressure; but she can also thunder and terrify: when, Montesquieu declares, I go too far, and consider the advantage of torture in a purely utilitarian spirit, what I hear is 'la voix de la nature qui crie contre moi'[1] and brings me back to my senses. At other times nature is not normative but simply the actual constitution of things and persons, the cause of the behaviour, needs, demands of men in specific circumstances, and in this sense constitutes the object of all the sciences. There is a kind of continuous dialectic in all Montesquieu's writings between absolute values which seem to correspond to the permanent interests of men as such, and those which depend upon time and place in a concrete situation.

IV

The contradiction remains unresolved. The only link between the two doctrines is their common libertarian purpose. What Montesquieu means by liberty is to be found not in his formal – and commonplace – definition of this concept as consisting in the right to do what the laws do not forbid, but in his exposition of other social and political ideas which throw light on his general scale of values. Montesquieu is, above all, not a thinker obsessed by some single principle, seeking to order and explain everything in terms of some central moral or metaphysical category in terms of which alone all truths must be formulated. He is not a monist but a pluralist, his virtuosity reaches its highest peak, he is most himself, when he tries to convey a culture or an outlook or a system of values different from his own and from that of the majority of his readers. A radical author said of him that he explained too well: that he seemed to justify everything.[2] And, indeed, so far is he from the vice prevalent in his day of grading all outlooks and cultures in terms of their distance from the enlightened standards of the eighteenth century, that he rendered himself suspect to both the obscurantists and the radicals of his time by too great a

[1] *E.L.* vi 17: vol. 1 A, p. 124.

[2] Letter to Saurin of 1747–8, included in Masson (see p. 133, note 1 above), vol. 3, pp. 1538–40. On the authorship of this letter, see R. Koebner, 'The Authenticity of the Letters on the *Esprit des lois* attributed to Helvétius', *Bulletin of the Institute of Historical Research* 24 (1951), 19–43.

tenderness for institutions different from those of the Christian west. The substitution of general principles for the faculty of sensing individual differences is, for him, the beginning of evil. His range of sympathies is genuinely very wide. He pleads convincingly for vastly different ways of life, each of which he represents as conditioned by its own physical environment, following its own intelligible path of development, and satisfying the needs of the human beings who lead them no less satisfactorily and fully than other cultures, at other times, in other lands and climates and geographical situations. This singular gift for identifying oneself imaginatively with a great variety of forms of life leads Montesquieu not merely to toleration (celebrated for it though he was) and to condoning abuses, but to a more positive attitude. He was one of the few thinkers of his age who had grasped one of the central characteristics of the moral history of mankind, that the ends pursued by men are many and various and often incompatible with one another, that this leads to unavoidable collisions between civilisations, to differences between the ideals of the same community at different times, and of different communities at the same time, and to conflicts within communities, classes, groups and within the individual consciousness. Furthermore he perceived that, given the vast variety of situations, and the extreme complexity and intricacy of individual cases, no single moral system, let alone a single moral or political goal, could provide the universal solution to all human problems, everywhere, at all times. To seek to impose such single systems, no matter how worthy and noble and widely believed, must always in the end lead to persecution and deprivation of liberty. Despotism is 'obvious, uniform throughout; passion alone is sufficient to establish it, and anyone can produce that'.[1] Only those societies are truly free which are in a state of 'agitation', unstable equilibrium; whose members are free to pursue – choose between – a variety of ends or goals. A state might itself be free, that is, independent of other states, but if it becomes frozen and suppresses opinion in the name of no matter how sacred a principle, its citizens are not free but enslaved. Montesquieu dislikes conflict; he prefers peace, conciliation, compromise. He is suspicious of all new creeds since they are usually the work of zealots and lead to strife. But once a creed has found a degree of acceptance, then, however foolish, it should be tolerated and not persecuted out of existence; for it is more important that people should be free to err than that they be coerced into holding correct opinions.

[1] *E.L.* v 14: vol. 1 A, p. 84.

Montesquieu was not a relativist about the truth. In common with most enlightened men of his period he believed that the objective truth in all realms was discoverable. But he believed even more deeply that societies which did not grant freedom of choice between ideals, with due precautions against open warfare between their adherents, would inevitably decay and perish.

This opposition to the enforcement of any orthodoxy, no matter what was at stake, no matter how lofty and deeply venerated might be the ideals of the orthodox, distinguishes Montesquieu from the theologians and the atheists, the idealistic radicals as well as the authoritarians of his time. It inaugurates the struggle within the camp of Enlightenment between democrats and liberals. They might unite against obscurantism and repression, clerical or secular, but the alliance is, at best, temporary. Despotism is no less despotic because it is self-inflicted or enthusiastic. Willing slaves are still slaves. This note is not heard again until Benjamin Constant and the liberal reaction against Jacobins and Legitimists alike. It is a point of view which, because it sets freedom above happiness, peace and virtue, is always suspect, always unpopular.

What emerges, and what seems of particular interest in the present day, is his very clear perception of the fact that no degree of knowledge, or of skill or of logical power, can produce automatic solutions of social problems, of a final and universal kind. The leaders of the French Enlightenment, the great popularisers of science, have rendered great service to mankind by the open war which they conducted against ignorance and obscurantism in every form, and in particular against brutality, stupidity, suppression of the truth, cynicism and disregard of human rights. Their fight for freedom and justice, even when they did not quite understand their own formulas, created a tradition to which a great many men owe their lives and liberties today. The majority of these same men, whose case for the prosecution was so unanswerable, also believed that as there was a science of the behaviour of things, so there could be a science of the behaviour of men; that anyone who had grasped the principles of this latter science could, by applying it, realise all the goals to which they were unitedly striving; that all these goals – truth, justice, happiness, freedom, knowledge, virtue, prosperity, physical and mental powers – were bound to one another 'by an indissoluble chain' as Condorcet had said,[1] or were at

[1] *Esquisse d'un tableau historique des progrès de l'esprit humain*, ed. O. H. Prior and Yvon Belaval (Paris, 1970), p. 228.

least compatible with one another; and that it was possible to bring them all into existence by transforming society in accordance with the infallible principles of the newly discovered scientific truth about social existence.

When the great French Revolution failed to make men happy and virtuous overnight, some of its adherents claimed either that the new principles had not been properly understood, or had been inefficiently applied, or that not these, but some other principles, were the true key to the solution of problems; that, for example, the purely political solution of the Jacobins had fatally oversimplified matters, and that social and economic causes should have been taken into greater consideration. When in 1848–9 these factors had been duly taken into account, and still the results had proved disappointing, the believers in a scientific solution declared that something else had been left out – say the war between the classes, or the Comtian principles of evolution, or some other essential factor. It is against the 'terrible simplifiers' of this type, whose intellectual lucidity and moral purity of heart seemed to make them all the readier to sacrifice mankind again and again in the name of vast abstractions upon altars served by imaginary sciences of human behaviour, that Montesquieu's cautious empiricism, his distrust of laws of universal application, and his acute sense of the limits of human powers, stand up so well. If there is a case for radical reforms, for rebellion and revolution, it is when the injustices of a regime are too intolerable, when 'nature cries out' against it; but such courses always involve risks, and can never be guaranteed, morally or materially, by infallible methods of calculating the social consequences. Human history is not susceptible to the simple laws which had so deeply hypnotised many noble thinkers, especially in France. 'La plupart des effets arrivent par des voies si singulières, ou dépendent de causes si imperceptibles et si éloignées qu'on ne peut guère les prévoir.'[1] And since this is so, all we can do is to try to frustrate as few human beings as possible, whatever their purposes. That government is best which accords best with men's 'penchant et leur inclination'.[2] In making laws one must, above all, have a sense, which only experience or history can sharpen, of what goes with what: for the rapports of laws with human nature and human institutions in their interplay with human consciousness are immensely complex, and these cannot

[1] *De la politique*: vol. 3, p. 166.
[2] *Lettres persanes* 80: vol. 1 C, p. 164 (cf. p. 146, note 4 above).

be computed by simple and tidy systems: timeless rules, rigidly imposed, will always end in blood.

Despite his archaic classifications of political institutions, his *a priori* conceptions of the inner principles of social growth and of absolute justice as an eternal relationship in nature, Montesquieu emerges as a far purer empiricist both with regard to means and with regard to ends than Holbach or Helvétius or even Bentham, not to speak of Rousseau or Marx. Conservatives, liberals, Fabian socialists have each derived their own conclusions from the tradition that he founded, and his undogmatic principles are only too relevant to our violent modern conflicts between rival ideologies. 'Montesquieu would have left nothing, perhaps, behind him', writes Maxime Leroy, 'save a state of mind, a sociological tendency, and the memory of his charming Persian fantasies . . . if he had not attached his name to the doctrine of the separation . . . of powers.'[1] Not much more, perhaps, than a dry sense of historical reality, as concrete as Burke's and free from his violent prejudices and romantic distortions; and an understanding of what men, or, at any rate, human societies, live by, unparalleled since Aristotle.

---

[1] *Histoire des idées sociales en France*, vol. 1: *De Montesquieu à Robespierre* (Paris, 1946), p. 110.

Hume and the Sources of German Anti-Rationalism

I

THE subject with which I intend to deal is central neither to Hume's thought, nor to his intellectual development, nor to his life, nor to the world in which he lived and wrote. I am concerned with the influence of certain ideas of Hume's on, or rather the use made of them by, a group of thinkers who, in most respects, utterly rejected all that Hume believed and stood for. The movement which they formed is, I think, best described as the German Counter-Enlightenment, which reached its height towards the end of the eighteenth century. Two, at least, of its leaders, Johann Georg Hamann and Friedrich Heinrich Jacobi, saw Hume as an out-and-out enemy, but, nevertheless, one with a difference: a man who, however little he may have intended it, supplied them with weapons, both offensive and defensive, against his close philosophical allies, the French Encyclopedists, whom above all others they wished to confute. Their use of some of Hume's writings, if he had conceived of its possibility, would almost certainly have astonished and, indeed, horrified their author; the moral and intellectual distance between him and these German irrationalists could scarcely have been greater. The history of ideas is not without its ironies.

It is a commonplace, which I do not need to labour, that the culture of the west in Hume's lifetime was largely dominated by the ideas of the French Enlightenment. Whatever the differences that divided the French *philosophes* and their disciples in other countries (and these differences were deeper and more numerous than is often supposed), there existed nevertheless a wide consensus: it rested on an acceptance of what was, in effect, a secular version of the old natural law doctrine according to which the nature of things possessed a permanent, unalterable structure, differences and changes in the world being subject to universal and immutable laws. These laws were discoverable in principle by the use of reason and controlled observation, of which the methods of the natural sciences constituted the most successful application. The most powerful instrument in the acquisition of knowledge was held to be mathematics. Whether this was due to the fact that the basic structure of reality was itself such that mathematics was an abstract representation, or symbolisation, of it, or, alternatively, whether mathematical methods were no more than the most reliable means of recording, predicting, and therefore controlling nature, whose real character remained inscrutable, was a less crucial issue than what followed from either assumption : namely, that the true path to knowledge was that of the natural sciences; that is to say, all statements with claims to truth must be public, communicable, testable – capable of verification or falsification by methods open to and accepted by any rational investigator. From this it followed that all other types of authority were to be rejected, and in particular such foundations of faith as sacred texts, divine revelation and the dogmatic pronouncements of its authorised interpreters, tradition, prescription, immemorial wisdom, private intuition and all other forms of non-rational or transcendent sources of putative knowledge. This principle was held to apply to both the human and the non-human world : to abstract disciplines, such as logic or mathematics, to the applied sciences which established the laws of the behaviour of inanimate bodies, plants, animals and human beings, and to the normative disciplines which revealed the true nature of ultimate human goals, and the correct rules of conduct, public and private, social and political, moral and aesthetic.

According to this doctrine, all genuine questions were in principle answerable : truth was one, error multiple; the true answers must of necessity be universal and immutable, that is, true everywhere, at all times, for all men, and discoverable by the appropriate use of reason, by relevant experience, observation and the methods of experiment, logic, calculation. A logically connected structure of rules, laws, generalisations, susceptible of demonstration or, at least in practice, of a high degree of confirmation (and, where required, of application appropriate to differing circumstances) could, at least in principle, be constructed, and could replace the chaotic amalgam of ignorance, laziness, guesswork, superstition, prejudice, dogma, fantasy, and, above all, what Helvétius called 'interested error', which enabled the cunning and the strong to dominate and exploit the stupid, ignorant and weak, and had throughout human history been largely responsible for the vices, follies and miseries of mankind. Only knowledge, that is, the growth of the sciences, could rescue mankind from these largely self-induced evils. Some believed that certainty in empirical matters was attainable, others that no more than high probability could be achieved; some were pessimistic about progress towards virtue or happiness, others were more sanguine. But the majority of the *philosophes* were agreed that if irrational passions could be controlled, and ignorance, prejudice, fear and greed diminished, an end could be made to the worst confusions in human thought and feeling, which led to blind fanaticism in thought and savage barbarism in practice.

This faith in the powers of reason and science was by no means universally held, even in the mid-eighteenth century in western Europe – at least not with equal confidence or fervour: it was regularly assailed by the insidious doubts of sceptics, by the hostility of the orthodox defenders of the authority of church and state, by the defenders of variety, individual and cultural, and of local and traditional values, as well as by the champions of the artistic imagination untrammelled by universal rules and regulations, who, by mid-century, had begun to attack the citadels of neo-classicism. Nevertheless, it would not, I believe, be inaccurate to say that the central tradition of the Enlightenment rested on the assumptions of which I have supplied so over-simplified and crude a summary. Despite pleas for historical understanding and the celebration of the beauty and strength of early epic poetry by such critics as von Muralt, Bodmer and Breitinger in Switzerland, Lowth, Blackwell and the Wartons, father and son, in England, and, most of all, by the founder of historicism, Giambattista Vico in Naples; despite the growing interest in the Bible as the national epic of the Jews, in Homer as the voice of the entire Greek people, in the sagas of the Norsemen and the Celts, in oriental literatures, in Shakespeare and Milton, in folk-song, myths, legends and, above all, diverse cultural traditions which could not be made to fit into the critical straitjackets provided by the Parisian arbiters of taste, this reaction remained largely confined to the province of literature and the arts; the central ideological edifice of the Enlightenment remained relatively unaffected.

The first formidable attack upon it, uncompromising, violent and fraught with lasting consequences, came from Germany. This is not the place in which to try to elaborate on the many factors which led to this German backlash against the French cultural domination of the western world. It was certainly not unconnected with the anti-rationalist currents in the Lutheran Reformation; nor with the relative – cultural as well as economic – deprivation of German-speaking populations in the hundred years that followed Luther's revolt, in contrast to the great cultural flowering of Italy, France, England, Spain and the Low Countries, which bred in the Germans a growing consciousness of their own provincialism, and with it a sense of inferiority, deepened by the disasters of the Thirty Years War. I am not a social historian. I am not qualified to speculate on either the roots or the effect of the inevitable rise of resentment and wounded self-esteem in German territories, particularly in relation to France, then in the full pride of its power, wealth and artistic achievement. Yet even to the eye of an amateur it seems obvious that this condition is not unconnected with the rise of pietism, one of the most introspective, austere and self-absorbed of all the inner currents of Lutheranism. The pietists, profoundly unpolitical in temper, contemptuous of the world and its varieties, sought direct communion of the individual soul with God. Liable to extremes of both emotion and self-discipline, they tended to be suspicious of hierarchy, ritual, learning and rational speculation – as against the living voice of the individual conscience with its absolute sense of moral and spiritual duty, infallible guide in the unending battle in and for the soul of sinful man between the word of God and the temptations of the world, the flesh and the devil. Pietism was particularly strong in East Prussia, where the attempt by Frederick the Great, in the middle years of the eighteenth century, to modernise that backward and semi-feudal province with the help of French-speaking officials was resented and resisted among the devout, conservative population. Much of this sentiment was probably at the root of the revulsion against the materialism, utilitarianism, ethical naturalism and atheism of the French *lumières* which one finds in such thinkers as Hamann, Lavater, Herder and, indeed, Kant himself. They and their disciples Jacobi, Fichte, Schelling, Baader, were in fact the philosophical wing of German cultural resistance movements – of the *Sturm und Drang*, of 'pre-romanticism' and, indeed, of romanticism itself.

Let me say something about the mysterious figure of Hamann, the Magus of the North, as Kant and others have called him, who was, perhaps, the most influential leader of this emotionally charged, basically religious opposition, a man described as the first émigré of the *Aufklärung*, the leader of the Vendée of the Enlightenment. Born in

1730 in Königsberg, he received, like his older friend and onetime patron, Kant, a strictly pietist upbringing. In the 1750s and 60s he was looked upon as a promising young publicist in the service of the German *Aufklärung*. He first made his name with a translation of a French treatise on commerce, accompanied by a disquisition of his own on the effects of trade and the social value of merchants. He admired Lessing, was taken up by Moses Mendelssohn, Nicolai and the other leaders of liberal German culture in Berlin; Kant and his friends had high hopes of their young protégé. However, during a brief sojourn in London in 1757–8, Hamann went through a spiritual crisis, returned to the pietist faith of his early years, and came back to Königsberg a convinced opponent of the Enlightenment. During the rest of his life – he died in 1788 – he published a series of violent attacks upon scientific materialism, universalism and secularism. These were written in an idiosyncratic, obscure, rhapsodical, sybilline prose, full of at times untraceable allusions, private jokes, elaborate puns, meandering digressions into dark paths, which appear to lead nowhere in particular; all this in language which he doubtless intended to contrast as sharply as possible with the, to him, now detestable elegance and brilliance, shallow clarity and spiritual emptiness of the *habitués* of the Paris *salons* – blind leaders of the blind, men cut off from the true, the inner life of man. He was by temperament not merely indifferent, but deeply opposed, to those who seek to find some intelligible order in the universe, capable of being reduced to, and communicated by means of, a theoretical system. He belonged to those thinkers (perhaps more often found east than west of the Rhine) whose hatred of tidy, rational schemas leads them to look for the exceptional and the irregular, if only because these serve to undermine reliance on general laws, and to confute those who suppose that they can catch and order the teeming variety of reality within their artificial constructions. Monist, dualist, pluralist systems were, for him, equally delusive chimeras, efforts to confine the unconfinable, contain the wildly conflicting, unpredictable, often chaotic, data of direct experience, and reduce them to regularities and symmetries by means of logical or metaphysical links – he describes them as walls of sand built to hold back the waves of an ocean.

A more profoundly anti-scientific or anti-rational outlook can scarcely be conceived: all knowledge for Hamann can be obtained solely through direct confrontation with reality provided by the senses, by instinct, by the imagination, by the immediate, uncontradictable insight of the poet, the lover, the man of simple faith. His favourite quotation is *I Corinthians* 1.27 – 'God hath chosen the foolish things of the world to confound the wise' – that is, Descartes, Voltaire and their disciples in free-thinking Berlin. Like William Blake, Hamann believed that truth is always particular, never general; genuine knowledge is direct, gained through some species of immediate acquaintance; the senses, outer and inner, do not refer: they present data directly, and any attempt to organise such data into systems distorts their concrete actuality. 'To cut the cord between faith and the senses is the first symptom of our upside-down type of thought.' Belief (in Hamann's sense) is a 'basic instinct' (*Grundtrieb*) without which we could not act at all.[1] Words are symbols which convey a voice speaking; they are either a method of communication between real persons, immortal souls, or they are mere mechanical devices, the classifying instruments of an impersonal science. Hamann was a passionate Christian pietist, and believed that men had or could have direct experience of God, everywhere and at all times: the words of the Bible were God's voice speaking directly to them, and so was the whole of nature to those who had eyes to see and ears to hear; so, too, was the history of mankind, which was a divine language to convey spiritual truths to an untrammelled understanding, not corrupted by the formulas of the sophists of Paris. It was not words that were the main obstacle to the vision of reality, as Bacon, Locke, Berkeley had maintained. Direct perception was far more violently distorted by concepts, theories, systems; such book-keeper's devices might have their uses in organising or controlling economic or political activities – regions that no longer interested Hamann – but they failed to reveal the real world. They were mere fictions, *entia rationis*, man-made dummies, mistakenly identified with the real world. Only insight which sprang from feeling – at its height, from love for a person or a thing – could reveal and illuminate. It was not possible to love the ghostly network of formulas, general propositions, laws, concepts and categories that the French philosophers had erected between

[1] Johann Georg Hamann, *Sämtliche Werke*, ed. Joseph Nadler (Vienna, 1949–57) (hereafter *Werke*), vol. 3, p. 190. All references to Hamann's works are to this edition, with the exception of letters: letters from 1751–86 are taken from Johann Georg Hamann, *Briefwechsel*, ed. Walther Ziesemer and Arthur Henkel (Wiesbaden, 1955–75) (hereafter *Briefwechsel*), and later letters from *Johann Georg Hamann's, des Magus im Norden, Leben und Schriften*, ed. C. H. Gildemeister (Gotha, 1857–73) (hereafter *Schriften*).

themselves and reality. The task of the philosopher was to explain life in all its contradictions, all its peculiarities, not to smooth it out, or substitute for it hypostatised abstractions, idealised entities, useful, perhaps, for limited ends, but figments all the same. God is a poet, not a mathematician; only spiders like Spinoza make systems that shut out the real world, 'catch small flies'[1] and build 'castles in the air'.[2] Men have mistaken 'words for concepts, and concepts for realities'.[3] No system, no elaborate construction of scientific generalities, will, in Hamann's view, enable a man to understand what is conveyed by a gesture, a look, a tone, a style, or to understand a line of poetry, a painting, a vision, a spiritual condition, an *état d'âme*, a form of life – how can men, caught in such webs of abstractions, achieve communion with their fellows, still less with God, who speaks to them in the simple human language of the Bible, in the burning words of inspired visionaries, of nature, and of history, if only men knew how to look and to listen?

What is real is always particular; what matters is the unique, the individual, the concrete, that wherein a thing differs from other things; for that is its essence and its point, and not that which it has in common with other things – all that the generalising sciences seek to record. 'Feeling alone gives to abstractions and hypotheses hands, feet, wings.' God speaks to us in poetical words, addressed to the senses, not in abstractions for the learned. Men like Kant (an intimate friend) suffer, he tells us, from 'a gnostic hatred of matter',[4] rearrange reality into artificial patterns and live in a world of figments. Systems, Hamann insists over and over again, are mere prisons of the spirit, they lead not only to false ideas but sooner or later to the creation of huge bureaucratic machines, built in accordance with rules which ignore variety, the unique, asymmetrical lives of men, and force living creations into the mechanism of some repressive political system, in the name of some intellectual chimera, unrelated to the flow of history or the real lives lived by men. To understand a man, a group, a sect, one must grasp what shapes them – the union of language, tradition and history. Every court, every school, every profession, every sect, has its own vocabulary. How does one enter them? With the passion of a friend, like a lover, an intimate, with faith, not by means of rules.

[1] Letter to Kant, 27 July 1759, *Briefwechsel*, vol. 1, p. 378.
[2] Letter to Jacobi, 14 November 1784, ibid., vol. 5, pp. 265–6.
[3] ibid., p. 264.
[4] *Werke*, vol. 3, p. 285.

Reality is an unanalysable, dynamic, changing organism, incapable of being represented by the static metaphors of mathematics and the natural sciences. All absolute rules, all dogmatic precepts are fatal: they may be needed in the conduct of ordinary life, but nothing great was ever achieved by following them.

The English critics, Young above all, had rightly maintained that originality entailed breaking rules, that every creative act, every transforming insight, could be obtained only by setting aside the commandments of the arrogant masters of theory. Hamann declared that rules are like vestal virgins; unless they are violated, there will be no issue. Nature is no ordered whole: so-called sensible men are blinkered beings who walk with a firm tread because they are blind to the true and profoundly disturbing character of reality, sheltered from it by their man-made contraptions; if they glimpsed it as it is – a wild dance – they would go out of their minds. How dare these pathetic pedants impose on the vast world of continuous, fertile, unpredictable, divine creation their own narrow, desiccated categories? There is no knowledge save by direct perception – a direct sense of reality which Hamann calls *Glaube*, faith, the direct capacity which all men have for unquestioning acceptance of *data* and not *ficta*.[1] Faith is analogous to sight or taste – the physical senses offer me my immediate experience of the physical world, while faith – *Glaube* – is needed to reveal to me my inner life, as well as the meaning of what others say to me by means of symbols, gestures, ritual acts, works of art, books or any other expression of the imagination or the passions. *Glaube* is for Hamann a kind of sense; faith, like the senses, cannot be refuted by reason, it is not its creature; its findings need no evidence, it does not rest on grounds, it is not subject to doubt; it may be delusive, but it cannot be corrected by calculation or rational argument, certainly not by the constructions of the scientists, which are, at best, mere practical devices for utilitarian purposes, which say nothing to the soul or the senses, through which alone God and nature speak to us.[2] The wiseacres of Paris, like their allies in Berlin, who dissect nature, deal with dead matter: they know a great deal and understand little. Man is not born to reason, but to eat and drink and procreate, to love and hate, agonise and sacrifice and worship. But they know nothing of this in Paris, where the monstrous *cogito* has obscured the sublime *sum*.

[1] *Schriften*, vol. 5, p. 668. See also *Werke*, vol. 3, p. 190 (cf. p. 167, note 1 above).

[2] *Werke*, vol. 2, pp. 73–4.

Hamann attempted no less than a total reversal of the values of the Enlightenment; in place of the abstract and general he wished to place the particular and the concrete: in place of the theoretical constructions, stylised patterns and idealised entities of the philosophers and scientists – the directly given, the unmediated, the sensuous. He was in the strict sense of the term a reactionary; that is, he wished to return to an older tradition of the ages of faith: quality in place of quantity, primacy of the given, not of the analytic intellect, the immediately perceived secondary qualities, not the inferred primary ones; the free imagination, not logic. His deepest conviction was of the indissolubility of spirit and matter, the sensuous and the spiritual attributes of man, and of the omnipresence of God, transcendent and personal, not the depersonalised world soul of the pantheists, or the remote Clockmaker – the rationally demonstrated, somewhat shadowy Supreme Being of the deists.

I have tried to convey the general drift of this most unsystematic father of German romanticism, with his revulsion against the French *raisonneurs* and his celebration of the irregulars of life, the outsiders and vagabonds, outcasts and visionaries, whom he favours because they are closer to God than liberal theologians who seek to prove his existence by logical methods. 'Whoever seeks to conceive God in his head', wrote a German pietist[1] thirty years earlier, 'becomes an atheist', and this is what Hamann himself believed. Religion was the direct experience of the presence of God, or it was nothing. From *Glaube* – belief or faith – to revelation was but a short step. Hamann's religion was that of the burning bush, not that of Thomist logic or 'natural' semi-Lutheran religion; it sprang from a Dionysiac experience, not Apollonian contemplation. Driven to the extreme to which he drives it, this attack on all generalisation leads inevitably to the denial of the possibility of all language and thought. Hamann ignores this. He is obsessed by the conviction that the fullness of life, the transforming moments of sudden illumination, are lost in analysis and dissection. No wonder that he was greatly admired by Goethe and by the romantics and criticised sternly by Hegel, that he inspired Herder and Jacobi and, most of all, Kierkegaard, who called him 'The Emperor'.

What, you may ask, has all this to do with David Hume, whose temperament, beliefs and entire outlook were exceedingly remote

[1] Count Nikolaus Ludwig von Zinzendorf. See *Zinzendorf: Ueber Glauben und Leben*, ed. Otto Herpel (Sannerz/Leipzig, 1925), p. 16.

from this ecstatic view of life, who was repelled by nothing so much as zeal, fanaticism, religious enthusiasm, against which (so his best biographer tells us) he had reacted so strongly, as a result of his own strict Presbyterian upbringing? And indeed, it *has* nothing to do with Hume. But Hume, so it turned out, had, all unknowing, a good deal to do with it.

II

Hume's works, like those of other British writers, were much read in the mid-eighteenth century by German intellectuals. The *Treatise* was translated into German only in 1790, but translations of some of the moral, political and literary essays, in the form of *Vermischte Schriften*, were published in German in 1754–6, including *An Enquiry concerning Human Understanding* in 1755. A German version of *The Natural History of Religion* was published in 1755, and an anthology of Hume's writings (compiled by J. G. Bremer), perhaps translated from the French, appeared in 1774. A complete version by K. G. Schreiter of the posthumous *Dialogues on Natural Religion* came out in 1781.

Hamann was a lifelong student of Hume. He read him partly in translation, but mainly in English – he certainly read the *Treatise* in the original, probably during his early London sojourn. His first mention of Hume occurs in 1756, after he had read the German translation of the essays. In a letter to Jacobi of 1787 he wrote 'I studied Hume even before I wrote my *Socratic Memoirs* [i.e. before 1759] and this is the source to which I owe my doctrine of faith [*Glaube*] . . . I was full of Hume when I was writing the *Socratic Memoirs* . . . *Our own existence and the existence of all things* outside us must be *believed* and cannot be demonstrated in any other fashion.'[1] It may be an exaggeration to claim that Hamann actually derived his notion of *Glaube* as fundamental to all knowledge and understanding solely from Hume. But equally there is no doubt that Hume's doctrine of belief, particularly such assertions as, for example, the statement in the *Treatise* that '*belief is more properly an act of the sensitive, than of the cogitative part of our natures*',[2] made a profound impression upon

[1] *Schriften*, vol. 5, p. 506. The last sentence is a self-quotation: see *Werke*, vol. 2, p. 73.

[2] David Hume, *A Treatise of Human Nature*, ed. L. A. Selby-Bigge (Oxford, 1888) (hereafter *Treatise*), p. 183.

Hamann, played a part in his return to fervent Christian faith, and certainly reinforced his anti-intellectualism by providing him with an anti-Cartesian weapon of great power. The doctrine that reason is unable to progress by means of purely logical steps from one statement of fact about the world to another – and that consequently the entire ontological structure of the Cartesian, or indeed any other rationalist metaphysics, was built on a central fallacy – that, to Hamann and his followers, was a boon of inestimable value; they used it as a battering-ram against the hated Wolffian philosophy that dominated German universities and that seemed to them to despiritualise the world, to reduce its irregular, living texture to an artificial pattern of bloodless categories, or, alternatively, in its empirical version, to the deathly materialism of Holbach or Helvétius, in which there was, for Hamann, no colour, novelty, genius, thunder, lightning, agony, transfiguration. In the course of this he transformed Hume's psychological and logical concepts into religious ones; for Hamann, belief, faith, revelation, were ultimately one.

Nevertheless, Hume's scepticism, above all his denial of the existence of necessary connections in nature, and his severance of logical relations from those of the real world, which had shocked Kant out of his dogmatic slumber, delighted Hamann, since for him this cleared the path to the existence and power of the basic human faculty of belief, without which there was neither thought nor action, neither an external world nor history, neither God nor other persons, nothing but an unrefuted solipsism. Hamann had no illusions about Hume's general position; no man who had demanded that philosophy, when dealing with the human mind, adopt the methods of the natural sciences, could be anything but an enemy; but Hume was an enemy who, however unintentionally, had uncovered the truth on a crucial issue. 'Hume', Hamann wrote to Herder in 1781 (evidently meaning to contrast him with Kant), 'is always my man, because he at least paid homage to the principle of faith, and incorporated it in his system.'[1] No doubt Hamann unwarrantably identified Hume's doctrine of belief with the full doctrine of Pauline faith in things unseen. Still, belief and acceptance of reality without *a priori* demonstration were the basis of Hume's epistemology. To have so powerful an ally in the camp of the enemy, indeed, in the shape of an unbeliever through whose mouth God had chosen to reveal a central truth, was itself a marvellous gift. Towards the end of the preface to the second edition

[1] Letter of 10 May 1781, *Briefwechsel*, vol. 4, p. 294.

of the *Critique of Pure Reason*, in a famous sentence, Kant says 'it remains a scandal for philosophy and human reason in general that the existence of things outside us . . . must be taken only on faith, and that if it occurs to someone to doubt it, we can produce no counter-argument sufficient to prove it'.[1] What is a scandal for Kant is at the very heart of Hamann's doctrine; in support of it he quotes Hume's words in the *Enquiry*: 'It seems evident, that men are carried, by a natural instinct or prepossession, to repose faith in their senses';[2] and he tells Kant: 'to eat an egg, to drink a glass of water, the Attic philosopher Hume needs faith . . . If he needs faith to eat and drink, why does he belie his own principle when judging of things higher than . . . eating or drinking?'[3] In other words, if the reality of the external world is guaranteed by belief as a form of direct acquaintance, why should this also not hold of our belief in God, the belief or faith of those who daily and hourly see God in His creation, or hear His voice in His sacred books, in the words of His saints and prophets, to be found among the humblest and most unregarded of mankind? Whatever his errors, Hume is surely right about belief; without it, Hamann tells Kant in 1759, there can be no action: 'if you want a proof for everything, you cannot act at all – Hume realises this'.

Even though Hume's concept of belief is none too clear, as he himself admits in the *Treatise*, it is nevertheless far removed from Hamann's quasi-intuitive, infallible, Pauline-Lutheran *Glaube*. Hume at times speaks of belief as a peculiar and not further describable 'feeling'[4] or 'superior *force*, or *vivacity*, or *solidity*, or *firmness*, or *steadiness*'[5] and the like; but the reasonableness or justification of beliefs about reality rests not so much on the evidence of introspection of this kind, as on repeated conjunctions of impressions, and the association of the resultant ideas, that is, on regularities in experience and the construction therefrom of a systematic network of reliable expectations without which neither human thought nor action is possible. Although inductive methods, which rest on the undemonstrable belief that the future will imitate the past, cannot yield certainty, their job

---

[1] *Kant's gesammelte Schriften*, vol. 3 (Berlin, 1911), p. 23, note.

[2] David Hume, *Enquiries*, ed. L. A. Selby-Bigge, 3rd ed., revised by P. H. Nidditch (Oxford, 1975) (hereafter *Enquiries*), p. 151.

[3] *Briefwechsel*, vol. 1, p. 379.

[4] e.g. *Treatise*, p. 624; *Enquiries*, pp. 48–9; *An Abstract of a Treatise of Human Nature*, ed. J. M. Keynes and P. Sraffa (Cambridge, 1938), pp. 18–21.

[5] *Treatise*, p. 629.

is to generate various degrees of probability. It is by these that, for Hume, at least in some moods, rational beliefs (which, in his somewhat loose fashion, he tended to identify with custom, habit, experience, nature and the like) are to be distinguished from mere fantasy or guesswork or prejudice or superstition. Since the existence of one thing can never logically entail the existence of any other, these methods are all that is available to us for building a body of knowledge. It is by applying this criterion to the assertions of theologians, whether orthodox Christians or deists, that Hume justifies his most sceptical and destructive conclusions.

Nothing could be further from Hamann's fervent defence of *Glaube* as the only path to the external world, to other persons, to God. At times he almost acknowledged this. 'I do not know', he wrote in 1787 to Jacobi, 'what Hume or either of us understands by *Glaube* – the more we speak and write about it, the less we shall manage to seize hold of this lump of quicksilver; *Glaube* cannot be communicated like a parcel of goods, it is the kingdom of heaven and hell within us.'[1] This is very remote from Hume's world, something of which, in some sense, Hamann is not unaware, for he systematically ignores everything in Hume which is antipathetic to him, that is, almost all that is most characteristic of the Scottish philosopher. Thus he says nothing about Hume's insistence on the 'received maxims of science, morals, prudence, and behaviour',[2] which Hamann himself looks on as so many philistine obstacles to the authentic vision of truth. Hamann has nothing to say on the crucial distinction made in the *Treatise* between superstition and prejudice, on the one hand, and, on the other, belief supported by direct experience and the evidence of constant conjunction. He ignores Hume's psychology of belief as the effect of nature, custom, tradition and the like; he detests the associationist psychology with its mechanical approach and hair-splitting (as he calls it). As might be expected, he will have nothing to do with Hume's notion of the self as a bundle of sensations, the plaything of desires and passions; Hamann's self is an immortal soul known by

[1] Letter of 27–30 April 1787, *Schriften*, vol. 5, p. 517. On this see W. M. Alexander, *Johann Georg Hamann: Philosophy and Faith* (The Hague, 1966), pp. 130 ff.

[2] Which Shirley Robin Letwin rightly stresses; see her article 'Hume: Inventor of a New Task for Philosophy', *Political Theory* 3 (1975), 134–58. For Hume's phrase see *Hume's Dialogues Concerning Natural Religion*, ed. Norman Kemp Smith (Oxford, 1935) (hereafter *Dialogues*), p. 169.

direct *Glaube*, with an inner life concerned with matters not dreamt of in Hume's philosophy. Hume for Hamann is an unbeliever whose theological views are therefore of no concern to him; consequently he ignores the inconsistency between Hume's apparently deistic argument in *The Natural History of Religion*, and its virtual dissolution in the *Dialogues* (pointed out by Kemp Smith and others) and replacement by Philo's total agnosticism; nor does he pay attention to Hume's violent diatribes against precisely the type of Christianity that he and his friends most fervently espoused.

Hume's positivism and his anti-clericalism are equally remote from Hamann's own spiritual concerns. He mentions neither the celebrated passage in section 12 of the *Enquiry* about committing everything that is neither quantitative nor empirical to the flames, nor the equally famous designation of historical religions as 'sick men's dreams', and 'playsome whimsies of monkies in human shape',[1] about which Hume declared that 'in a future age, it will probably become difficult to persuade some nations, that any human, two-legged creature could ever embrace such principles. And it is a thousand to one, but these nations themselves shall have something full as absurd in their own creed, to which they will give a most implicit and most religious assent.'[2] In theory Hume is speaking only of absurdly irrational systems and religions, but irrationality was not a defect in Hamann's eyes: indeed, he accepted and glorified it. His interest in Hume is intense and lifelong, but narrow, confined to Hume's argument against the conception of reason held by the rationalist thinkers, the followers of Descartes and Leibniz and Spinoza. Hume is acclaimed for showing that reason is not an organ of discovery, and for reducing it to its proper role as a mere capacity for recombination, elucidation, consistency, taxonomy, lacking all power of creation or revelation. Hume, Hamann wrote in 1759, is 'a spirit for tearing down, not building up, that is indeed his glory'.[3] Hume is a destroyer of metaphysical illusions; it was precisely because Kant, in his effort to build a system of his own, to some degree restored the very *a priori* links discredited by Hume, that Hamann clearly preferred Hume to his old Königsberg friend, whom he sometimes calls – whether or not

---

[1] *The Natural History of Religion*, section 15. *Essays Moral, Political and Literary*, ed. T. H. Green and T. H. Grose (London, 1875), vol. 2, p. 362.

[2] ibid., section 12, p. 344.

[3] Letter to Lindner, 21 March 1759, *Briefwechsel*, vol. 1, p. 305.

this is intended as a compliment – 'a Prussian Hume'.[1] Hume is, of course, one of the pillars of the Enlightenment, a fighter on the wrong side of the barricades; nevertheless, Hamann sees him as being, despite himself, a kind of ally. 'Just as nature', Hamann writes to Lindner in 1759, 'furnishes an area of poisonous weeds with antidotes in close proximity, and the Nile knows how to couple the crocodile with his treacherous enemy, so Hume falls on the sword of his own truths';[2] like Socrates, Hume shows how wide is the realm of human ignorance – a very useful weapon, Hamann remarks, against 'our clever heads and scribes'. Hume's immortal service is his destruction of apriorism, the notion of logically or metaphysically guaranteed truths about the world: this, for Hamann, removes the rationalist barriers to direct communication with nature and with God, liberates the creative imagination in which such communication can be embodied, and brings down the house of cards of the builders of metaphysical fictions. Hume's relativism, his phenomenalism, his doctrine of the role of belief in the growth of scientific knowledge – all this is nothing to Hamann. It is the cauterising scepticism which Hume is held to share with Socrates, that confession of ignorance of first causes, or of the ultimate purpose of things, which prepared the soil for the daimon of Socrates, for the revelation of the divine, the Pauline vision, that excited Hamann. His hatred of laws, rules, system, is almost obsessive: it is this love of an open texture, whether of the individual imagination or of social relationships that are spontaneous, founded on natural human feeling, that is echoed in the two centuries that followed by Herder and his disciples – populists, romantics, influenced by Rousseau, nostalgic seekers after a vanished organic society, denouncers of all forms of alienation.

In all this, it is direct contact of the individual with things and persons and God, the movement of both history and nature, which he calls 'faith', that dominates Hamann's thought. He says that faith – *Glaube* – in its most intense form is something which must lead and illuminate us in a fashion far more immediate, more inward, darker and more certain than 'rules' of any kind. This notion of belief is, of course, something very different from that strain in Hume in which he speaks of belief as a more or less mechanical, inescapable acceptance of external reality, which men share with animals; or, indeed, from

[1] Letter to Herder, 10 May 1781, *Briefwechsel*, vol. 4, p. 293 (see also p. 172, note 1 above).
[2] Letter of 3 July 1759, ibid., vol. 1, p. 355.

the epistemology of Reid and the Scottish school. Yet they had the root of the matter in them: 'truth to tell,' Hamann wrote later in his life, 'I look with pity on the philosopher who demands from me evidence that he possesses a body and that there exists a material world. To waste one's time and wit on these kinds of truths and evidences is at once sad and ridiculous.' It is because Hume shows the absurdity of demanding demonstrative proof of the existence of any thing or person, human or divine, and, unlike Kant, does not draw ontological lines between types of reality with no basis in experience, that Hamann claims him as an ally. This accounts for the fact that in his references to Hume he shows no trace of the kind of attitude displayed towards him by his British detractors, nothing resembling Beattie's outburst against the 'vile effusion of a hard and stupid heart', or Warburton's and Hurd's denunciations – evidently he is not, to Hamann, one of the three demons driven by the angel into the bottomless pit of Reynolds's celebrated allegorical painting.

Hamann's particular use of Hume is perhaps best illustrated in his treatment of the words which form the concluding paragraph of the tenth section of the *Enquiry*, entitled 'Of Miracles'. In this, according to Kemp Smith 'probably the most notorious passage in all Hume's writings',[1] Hume asserts that

> upon the whole, we may conclude that the *Christian Religion* not only was at first attended with miracles, but even at this day cannot be believed by any reasonable person without one. Mere reason is insufficient to convince us of its veracity: And whoever is moved by *Faith* to assent to it, is conscious of a continued miracle in his own person, which subverts all the principles of his understanding, and gives him a determination to believe what is most contrary to custom and experience.[2]

No unprejudiced reader could fail to notice, as indeed Kemp Smith points out, that both the content and tone of this passage are ironical and clearly designed to discredit faith in miracles. Hume's general argument is that the probability of human mendacity or delusion or fantasy or credulity is, on the evidence available, far greater than the probability of the events in question, the prodigies and miracles reported in the Old Testament, which are incompatible with the laws of nature as established by experience; and since the testimony of

[1] *Dialogues*, p. 60.
[2] *Enquiries*, p. 131.

those who have claimed to have observed miracles cannot be regarded as being more reliable than the mass of the testimony of observation on which acceptance of the laws of nature is founded, the weight of the former cannot stand up against the weight of the testimony for the latter.

Hamann, and after him Jacobi, did not, as they well might have done, question the *validity* of this argument; they simply turned it round. They seized eagerly upon this very text as an argument for the miraculous nature of faith, a doctrine of which Hamann's most ardent admirer, Kierkegaard, became the most celebrated proponent. For Hamann, miracles are not a breach of the natural order, for he does not believe in causality, either as a relation of real objects or as a category of the mind – a truth for which, again (less plausibly in the latter case), he claims the authority of Hume. For Hamann everything is a work of God, working not through secondary causes, but by the direct action of His will. What is there in nature, he asked, in the commonest and most natural events, which is not a miracle for us, a miracle in the strictest sense? Everything that happens need not have happened unless God had willed it so: we accept it as real because we have been given *Glaube* – in itself a miracle – which indelibly impresses it upon our minds, our senses, imaginations, memories and intellect. Hume's 'continued miracle in his own person' is precisely what the thinkers of the Counter-Enlightenment most passionately believed, or wished to believe. Writing to his friend Lindner in 1759 about this passage, Hamann says 'Hume may have said this scornfully or earnestly, nevertheless it is orthodoxy, and a testimony to the truth from the mouth of an enemy and persecutor of it – all his doubts are but a proof of his proposition.'[1] And three weeks later, in a letter to Kant, he cites the same sentence from Hume's essay – 'a passage which should prove that even in jest, without knowing or wishing to do so, one can tell the truth'.[2] Hume is 'like Saul among the prophets',[3] a witness to a truth which he does not himself understand; for does he not rightly declare that faith – true Christian faith – is neither custom nor common sense, but a miracle of the spirit? Yet Hume did not see that this applied to himself too, did not realise that it undermined his own scepticism; he may have intended these words against Christianity,

[1] Letter cited on p. 176 above, note 2, p. 356.
[2] Letter of 27 July 1759, *Briefwechsel*, vol. 1, p. 380; see Alexander, op. cit. (p. 174, note 1 above), p. 152, note 2.
[3] ibid.

but – such is God's grace – he thereby added to the believers' armoury.

It is probably in this spirit that Hamann began to translate the *Dialogues Concerning Natural Religion*, which Hume's nephew David published in 1779, three years after the author's death. The first edition of the *Dialogues* appeared on 21 July; a year later, on 7 August 1780, Hamann completed his own work on the text. It is not a complete translation, only a résumé and a rendering of about a quarter of Hume's text. He circulated it in manuscript privately to his friends, and it remained unpublished until 1951, when Nadler included it in his edition of Hamann's works. So far as we can tell, this was the only version of Hume's *Dialogues* known to Kant – there is no evidence that he was acquainted with Schreiter's full version of 1781. 'The *Dialogues* is a work full of poetic beauties', Hamann wrote to the publisher Hartknoch in 1780, 'and like Green[1] I consider it not so very dangerous. I am translating it like a fifty-year-old Swabian clergyman, for the benefit of my open-hearted [*freimüthige*] colleagues and countrymen . . .'.[2] Kant is said to have been delighted and influenced by it, although the *Prolegomena* of 1783 shows that he did not fully accept the refutation of the argument from design, which Hume develops in it. As for Hamann, any attack upon rational theology and deism was grist to his mill and that of the other defenders of revelation against both atheists and proponents of natural religion, between whom he and his allies professed to see little difference. The very notion of natural religion angered Hamann, who compared it to the idea of natural language – a typical fiction of the philosophers, logic-choppers who had not enough sense of reality to know that languages were intimately connected with particular places and times, particular environments, particular forms of historical growth, were organic expressions of particular groups of human beings in unique relationships to one another, something which no general formula could convey. The real enemies were the deists, who invented an abstraction, a First Cause, or The Divine Clockmaker who set the universe in motion; but what had this *ens rationis*, this figment of the philosophers, to do with the God who spoke to men's hearts, the God whose only begotten son died to redeem us from our sins? 'It seems evident,' said Hume in the twelfth section of *An Enquiry concerning Human Understanding*, 'that men are carried, by a natural instinct or prepossession, to repose faith in their senses; and that, without any reasoning, or even almost before

---

[1] Kant's friend, the English merchant, who lived in Königsberg.

[2] Letter of 29 July 1780, *Briefwechsel*, vol. 4, pp. 205–6.

the use of reason, we always suppose an external universe . . .'. Even animals do this. 'But this . . . opinion of all men is soon destroyed by the slightest philosophy, which teaches us, that nothing can ever be present to the mind but an image or perception.'[1] For Hume this is an argument against commonsense realism. But to Hamann this and similar passages may well have seemed the very opposite: warnings, the more striking if they were not consciously so intended, against the corrosive touch of philosophy and its delusive constructions, particularly when they touch on matters of ultimate concern, such as the relationship of man to God.

So also with the *Dialogues*. In the concluding passage of the *Dialogues*, in a paragraph added by Hume in one of his final revisions, Philo says

> A person, seasoned with a just sense of the imperfections of natural reason, will fly to revealed truth with the greatest avidity: While the haughty dogmatist, persuaded that he can erect a complete system of theology by the mere help of philosophy, disdains any farther aid, and rejects this adventitious instructor. To be a philosophical sceptic is, in a man of letters, the first and most essential step towards being a sound, believing Christian.[2]

Hamann does not, as far as I know, refer to this passage: yet it is difficult not to think that he could have regarded it as anything but yet another piece of Christian evidence provided by an enemy, unintended testimony to a truth sufficient to destroy the scepticism or agnosticism which is Philo's official position in the *Dialogues*. Hume's scepticism seemed to him to sweep away far more effectively than Kant's cautious arguments the rickety constructions of reason which obstruct the inpouring of faith; into the vacuum so created *Glaube* can enter. In one of his last letters to Jacobi, which I have quoted already, Hamann says 'I was full of Hume when I was writing the *Socratic Memoirs*, and [a passage in] my little book refers to this: *Our own existence and the existence of all things* outside us must be *believed* and cannot be demonstrated in any other fashion.'[3] This is the heart of the *Dialogues* for Hamann. 'One must start *a posteriori*, not *a priori* – that is the mistake of other philosophers.'[4] Causality, determinism, are

---

[1] *Enquiries*, p. 151 (see also p. 173, note 2 above).
[2] *Dialogues*, p. 282.
[3] *Schriften*, vol. 5, p. 506 (see also p. 171, note 1 above).
[4] ibid., p. 232.

barriers to the comprehension of the miraculous nature of reality. 'Do you not realise, philosopher, that there is no physical bond between cause and effect, means and ends, but a mental, ideal one, one of blind faith, as the world's greatest writer of his country's history and of the "natural church" has maintained?'[1] The blind 'faith' is 'the faith that is not the work of reason and not open to attacks by reason, since faith no more happens according to reasons than taste or sight'.[2] That is why 'Hume is always my man', not Kant – 'our fellow-countryman who is constantly blasting away with his causality'[3] (*seine Causalitätsstürmerey*).

III

It is a strange paradox that has thus made Hume one of the patron saints of German fideism and irrationalism. Yet so it was. Hamann's disciple, Friedrich Heinrich Jacobi, continues this line of thought; and since, according to one of the posthumous essays of the late Arthur Lovejoy, Jacobi was one of the most widely read thinkers of his time both in Germany and outside it, it is not a matter for surprise that his views entered the current of German and French philosophical intuitivism, which fed various streams of modern vitalism, irrationalism and existentialism. Jacobi (1743–1818) was not a thinker of the first or even second order. He is more interesting as a philosophical novelist, man of letters, middleman of ideas and indefatigable letter-writer. His correspondence with Kant, Herder, Hamann, Goethe, Mendelssohn, his famous controversy with Mendelssohn about Lessing's real beliefs (the so-called *Pantheismusstreit*), his attacks on Kant, Fichte, Herder and Schelling (and the ferocious counter-attack by the last named), and his rediscovery of such forgotten thinkers as Spinoza and Bruno, stimulated thinkers more gifted than himself and threw a great deal of light on the German philosophical scene at the turn of the eighteenth century. In 1786 he published a book, which he entitled *David Hume über den Glauben, oder Realismus und Idealismus: Ein Gespräch*.[4] In this work, particularly in the introduction to the philo-

---

[1] *Werke*, vol. 3, p. 29.
[2] ibid., vol. 2, p. 74. Cf. p. 169, note 2 above.
[3] Letter cited on p. 172 above, note 1, loc. cit.
[4] I have used the text published in *Friedrich Heinrich Jacobi's Werke* (Leipzig, 1812, 1815) (hereafter *Jacobi's Werke*), vol. 2 (1815), pp. 1–310.

sophical dialogue which forms its main content, there is a paean to
Hume as the apostle of non-rational faith. The mere fact that Hume's
name occurs in the title of this treatise is evidence of the place occupied
by him in the pantheon of early German romanticism. Jacobi was a
realist in epistemology, but he was also a fervent anti-rationalist theist,
brought up, like Kant, Herder and Hamann, in the pietist tradition,
and he faithfully followed Hamann's practice of self-observation as
well as his use of texts from Hume in the campaign against the shallow
materialists and deists in France and their followers in Germany, particularly among liberal Lutheran pastors. His book carries an epigraph
from Pascal: 'Reason refutes the dogmatist; nature refutes the sceptic.'[1] It was the latter position that Jacobi developed at some length.
Philip Merlan, who in a short and interesting article examined the
relations of Hamann, Hume and Jacobi,[2] took the trouble to point
out that nature, unlike reason, could not refute, it could only cause us
to avoid the truth and accept illusions, for truth remained truth, and
illusions remained false, however comforting or indispensable they
might turn out to be.

This, however, is, I believe, a misunderstanding of Jacobi's meaning. His thesis is that there is but one kind of genuine knowledge, and
that is our natural *Glaube*: 'We are born in faith as we are born in
society'; there are forms of intuitive certainty that reason is incapable
of either confirming or refuting, such as my awareness of my own
identity, of my causal efficacy revealed in deliberate effort and action,[3]
and of the freedom of my will. And I am similarly certain of the
existence of God, of the rational world and of other sentient beings.
These beliefs, according to Jacobi, are not merely presupposed in all
that we do or feel or think, but are with us from birth, are all that
bind us to reality, and are wholly independent of hypotheses or postu-
lates or theoretical constructions of any kind, such as, for example,
the hypothesis of the uniformity of nature, which is a necessary postu-
late of the propositions of the natural sciences – for hypotheses are
subject to verification or falsification, from which true *Glaube*, faith
or belief, loss of which is inconceivable, is wholly free. Our certainty
of our own existence and of our own unique personality is a 'feeling' –

---

[1] *Jacobi's Werke*, vol. 2, p. 1.

[2] P. Merlan, 'Kant, Hamann-Jacobi and Schelling on Hume', *Rivista
critica di storia della filosofia* 22 (1967), 484.

[3] Something of this kind used to be argued by Whitehead and Stout, and
it has had its later exponents.

ein Gefühl – a sense of reality; and it guarantees the reality of whatever it reveals. Our infallible conviction of our own self is the touchstone of all other knowledge: we measure the reliability of other beliefs by it, not the other way about, for all inference and evidence cannot be as strong as what we know by acquaintance with our own personality. The task of philosophy is to 'reveal existence', *das Dasein zu enthüllen*; and it is such feelings – *Gefühle* or *Gesinnungen* – that do this; there is no way of establishing the truth 'beyond and above' this. To support this he quotes Hume's *Treatise*,[1] where belief is described as 'something *felt* by the mind, which distinguishes the ideas of the judgment from the fictions of the imagination. It gives them more force and influence; makes them appear of greater importance; infixes them in the mind; and renders them the governing principles of all our actions.' He quotes, too, from section 12 of the *Enquiry* the relevant passage on men's 'natural instinct or prepossession, to repose faith in their senses'. 'This very table, which we see white, and which we feel hard, is believed to exist, independent of our perception, and to be something external to our mind, which perceives it.'[2] Jacobi goes on to say that 'we believe in our senses, and therefore in the existence of a sensible world. And similarly we believe in our inner sense, and therefore in the existence of a world beyond the senses.'[3] This seems to him to follow from Hume's premises; and such belief (he says nothing about Hume's difficulties with solipsism) seems to him, as it does to Hamann, to pass insensibly into *Offenbarung*, that is, revealed truth given directly without benefit of reason. This is then contrasted with the generalisations and abstractions of Plato or Spinoza, builders of logically coherent systems of idealised figments that are death to the sense of reality.

Jacobi's method of drawing sustenance from the enemy's resources is well illustrated by his treatment of Hume's celebrated refutation of the argument from design. Jacobi characteristically turns it on its head in the manner of Hamann, to reinforce his own conception of faith, *Glaube*. Hume in the *Enquiry*[4] argues that since it is an argument from analogy, it cannot be applied to something that, *ex hypothesi*, is unique, namely the deity. Analogies can be sought only between entities which belong to a species containing other actual or possible

[1] *Treatise*, p. 629.
[2] *Enquiries*, p. 151 (see also above, p. 173, note 2, and p. 180, note 1).
[3] *Jacobi's Werke*, vol. 2, p. 152.
[4] *Enquiries*, pp. 144–8.

members. Let me quote Richard Wollheim's succinct formulation of this argument in his edition of Hume on religion :

> the only cases in which we can validly infer from a particular event to its cause, is where the event is one of a series of events which have been observed to be constantly conjoined with events similar in kind to the cause. In other words, we cannot attribute a cause to an event if that event is unique in human experience. But it is obvious that 'the frame of nature' is in this sense unique : therefore the religious hypothesis . . . turns out to be an unwarranted inference.[1]

And this, indeed, is the burden of Hume's three-pronged criticism of what in the *Dialogues* he calls 'the religious hypothesis'.

Jacobi positively welcomes this mode of reasoning. He agrees that ordinary knowledge is founded on what he calls 'comparisons', and since God is unique, no comparison with Him is possible. He is not an instance of a general concept. But neither, Jacobi avers, is my own mind : it, too, is unique, wholly individual, and cannot be reached from any external starting-point. This is precisely why I know God, as I know myself, by an immediate *sense* of their existence; not by analogy or any other kind of inference, nor, in the case of my self-identity, by memory or in any other indirect fashion. I am not to myself an idea capable of being described, still less analysed; my certainty of my own existence cannot be separated from my certainty of what I am, of the mind, indeed the unique substance, that I directly know myself to be. This knowledge is the basis of all other awareness : it is direct and transcendent; no wonder that Hume and Kant, who look for the self in ordinary sense experience or the shadow world of logical categories, cannot find it.

This inversion of Hume's empiricism and scepticism in order to prop up faith is typical of the entire strategy of this group of dogmatic religious transcendentalists : they call in Hume as a kind of outside specialist, expert at demolishing what they most deeply abhor – the theories of knowledge and reality of the rationalist metaphysicians. For Jacobi, reality is revealed by what he sometimes calls *Wesenheitsgefühl* – the immediate feeling of essential being – which he regards as a gift of God. He speaks of *Glaube* – the direct apprehension of God, oneself, the external world – as a kind of *salto mortale*, a leap of faith, without which we remain imprisoned in the imaginary worlds

---

[1] Richard Wollheim (ed.), *Hume on Religion* (London, 1963), pp. 23–4.

of logical, mathematical or metaphysical constructions – Hamann's castles in the air – remote from reality, in which many worthy and respected thinkers live all their lives. From this, Hume's scepticism can save us. That, indeed, Jacobi tells us, is his claim to immortal fame.

IV

To sum up this peculiar relationship: it is doubtful whether the German opponents of the Enlightenment needed Hume to establish their position, but it is a historical fact that their founding fathers, Hamann and Jacobi, were fascinated by his arguments against their principal enemies, the deists, whom they abhorred more than out-and-out atheists, perhaps because the latter at least did not seem to them to vulgarise and dilute that which the existence and presence and direct knowledge of God meant to the true believer. They simply took from Hume's writings what they needed. Shirley Letwin, in a recent essay on Hume,[1] has justly observed that 'every great philosopher has been rendered into diverse characters'. Lessing, Herder, Goethe had done this for Spinoza, who after being the secret inspirer of French materialism was turned into something approaching a pantheistic transcendentalist, the father of German Absolute Idealism. In Hume's case the metamorphosis is no less complete. Represented by some as 'the most devastating sceptic, who not only destroyed the pretences of traditional philosophy but also showed that knowledge of any sort is an illusion', he is turned by others into 'a dogmatic empiricist who believed that mankind could achieve incontrovertible truth'.[2]

Support can be found in Hume's writings for both these interpretations, and for others also. Burke's distrust of philosophical abstractions, his faith in nature, good sense, history, civilisation, and his hostility to absolute rules and *a priori* generalisations, and, still more, to radical reform in the name of eternal principles or unstable, capricious popular passions – all this has its roots in Hume as well as in Montesquieu and Hooker. Mill and, following him, Russell owe him much of their faith in scientific method and their rejection of dogmatism, apriorism and the false analogies drawn by theologians, as well as their suspicion of the tendency to mistake convention and habit for eternal principles, their acceptance of probability as the

[1] op. cit. (p. 174, note 2 above), p. 134.   [2] ibid.

nearest approximation to unattainable empirical certainty, their crusading hatred of irrationalism, their approval of the calmer passions and their inclination towards naturalism and a modified utilitarianism. But for Hamann and his disciples Hume was simply a more destructive critic than Kant of the older rationalism. He seemed to them to have finally undermined the notion of unalterable categories of experience, as well as any form of dualism, the doctrine of two worlds, whether of a Cartesian, Leibnizian or Kantian kind; there was only one world, that of direct confrontation with reality; and although Hume's notion of this world was radically different from their own, the recognition of its unity, and of the Platonic fallacy which underlay all attempts to determine frontiers that divided reality from everyday experience, was of supreme importance to them.

For these mystical nominalists there were no walls between the natural and the spiritual worlds. God spoke to them in symbols which they understood, those of nature, history, sacred books, for their eyes and ears were open to His words. Armed with faith, they needed no proof or evidence of the reality of what they saw before them. They perceived tongues in trees, books in the running brooks, sermons in stones and (by a slight emendation) God in everything. These were not metaphors to them: the God they worshipped was personal; they looked on pantheism as a species of atheism. Hamann and his allies wanted no barriers to the all-penetrating power of faith, a faith which brooked no rules, obeyed no laws, was inconceivably remote from the tiny world of human contrivances — institutional order, utilitarian calculation, the artificial constructions of the logic- and evidence-bounded natural sciences, the clear and sensible organisation sought after, in their various fashions, by the King of Prussia and his officials, by Bentham, by the radical thinkers of Paris, perhaps by Hume too. The ideals of the Enlightenment seemed to at least one of its German opponents, Lenz, no better than a form of postponed death; Holbach's system struck the young Goethe as Cimmerian, grey, corpse-like, the end of all vitality, freedom and imagination. Hume's scepticism was the most devastating weapon against these enemies of the spirit that some among these forerunners of romanticism thought that they had found; Hume had removed the *a priori* bonds needed to guarantee the indestructible validity of the rationalist edifice (and indeed, after him, despite the efforts of later philosophers, the old confidence never fully returned). But to the thinkers of whom I am speaking the eliminating of the *a priori* cement seemed to render one supreme service: to clear the ground for the victory of religious faith.

Nothing could have been further from Hume and his outlook. The history of his influence on a handful of German antinomian thinkers is no more than a footnote in any account of his philosophy, although an exceedingly odd one. It is of somewhat greater importance to the history of irrationalist ideas in Europe, both religious and secular, during the nineteenth and twentieth centuries, of which this revolt against reason marks the modern beginnings. It is strange to reflect that the calm, reasonable, placid, moderate, ironical Hume, with his firm sense of reality, and his lucid and disciplined prose, should have attained semi-canonical status as one of the founding fathers — if not a strictly legitimate one (but then Hamann had an ambivalent attitude to all conventions, and especially to legitimate paternity) — of this turbulent, extravagant, heaven-storming movement, the very existence of whose leaders remained, so far as one can tell, wholly unknown to him. Which was, perhaps, just as well, for he would hardly have approved of them or their views; indeed, he could scarcely have felt anything but his habitual revulsion before such storms of uncontrolled spiritual enthusiasm. If, in addition, he had known of their insistent and admiring acknowledgement to him of a major intellectual debt, he might have looked upon this as one of the unintended, and unwelcome, yet, perhaps, not altogether unpredictable consequences of their own ideas, which even the most reasonable, careful, self-protective and accommodating thinkers cannot always wholly escape.

Herzen and his Memoirs

ALEXANDER HERZEN, like Diderot, was an amateur of genius whose opinions and activities changed the direction of social thought in his country. Like Diderot, too, he was a brilliant and irrepressible talker: he talked equally well in Russian and in French to his intimate friends and in the Moscow *salons* – always in an overwhelming flow of ideas and images; the waste, from the point of view of posterity (just as with Diderot), is probably immense: he had no Boswell and no Eckermann to record his conversation, nor was he a man who would have suffered such a relationship. His prose is essentially a form of talk, with the vices and virtues of talk: eloquent, spontaneous, liable to the heightened tones and exaggerations of the born story-teller, unable to resist long digressions which themselves carry him into a network of intersecting tributaries of memory or speculation, but always returning to the main stream of the story or the argument; but above all, his prose has the vitality of spoken words – it appears to owe nothing to the carefully composed formal sentences of the French *philosophes* whom he admired or to the terrible philosophical style of the Germans from whom he learnt; we hear his voice almost too much – in the essays, the pamphlets, the autobiography, as much as in the letters and scraps of notes to his friends.

Civilised, imaginative, self-critical, Herzen was a marvellously gifted social observer; the record of what he saw is unique even in the articulate nineteenth century. He had an acute, easily stirred and ironical mind, a fiery and poetical temperament, and a capacity for vivid, often lyrical, writing – qualities that combined and reinforced each other in the succession of sharp vignettes of men, events, ideas, personal relationships, political situations and descriptions of entire forms of life in which his writings abound. He was a man of extreme refinement and sensibility, great intellectual energy and biting wit, easily irritated *amour propre* and a taste for polemical writing; he was addicted to analysis, investigation, exposure; he saw himself as an expert 'unmasker' of appearances and conventions, and dramatised himself as a devastating discoverer of their social and moral core. Tolstoy, who had little sympathy with Herzen's opinions, and was not given to excessive praise of his contemporaries among men of letters, especially when they belonged to his own class and country, said towards the end of his life that he had never met anyone with 'so rare a combination of scintillating depth and brilliance'.[1] These gifts make a good many of Herzen's essays, political articles, day-to-day journalism, casual notes and reviews, and especially letters written to intimates or to political correspondents, irresistibly readable even today, when the issues with which they were concerned are for the most part dead and of interest mainly to historians.

Although much has been written about Herzen – and not only in Russian – the task of his biographers has not been made easier by the fact that he left an incomparable memorial to himself in his own greatest work – *My Past and Thoughts* – a literary masterpiece worthy to be placed by the side of the novels of his contemporaries and countrymen, Tolstoy, Turgenev, Dostoevsky. Nor were they altogether unaware of this. Turgenev, an intimate and life-long friend (the fluctuations of their personal relationship were important in the life of both; this complex and interesting story has never been adequately told), admired him as a writer as well as a revolutionary journalist. The celebrated critic Vissarion Belinsky discovered, described and acclaimed his extraordinary literary gift when they were both young and relatively unknown. Even the angry and suspicious Dostoevsky excepted him from the virulent hatred with which he regarded the pro-western Russian revolutionaries, recognised the poetry of his writing, and remained well-disposed towards him until the end of his life. As for Tolstoy, he delighted both in his society and his writings: half a century after their first meeting in London he still remembered the scene vividly.[2]

---

[1] Reported by P. A. Sergeenko in his book on Tolstoy, *Tolstoy i ego sovremenniki* (Moscow, 1911), p. 13.

[2] Sergeenko (ibid., pp. 13–14) says that Tolstoy told him in 1908 that he had a very clear recollection of his visit to Herzen in his London house in March 1861. 'Lev Nikolaevich remembered him as a not very large, plump little man, who generated electric energy. "Lively, responsive, intelligent, interesting," Lev Nikolaevich explained (as usual illustrating every shade of meaning by appropriate movements of his hands), "Herzen at once began talking to me as if we had known each other for a long time. I found his personality enchanting . . . I have never met a more attractive man. He stands head and shoulders above all the politicians of his own and of our time."'

It is strange that this remarkable writer, in his lifetime a celebrated European figure, the admired friend of Michelet, Mazzini, Garibaldi and Victor Hugo, long canonised in his own country not only as a revolutionary but as one of its greatest men of letters, is, even today, not much more than a name in the west. The enjoyment to be obtained from reading his prose – for the most part still untranslated – makes this a strange and gratuitous loss.

Alexander Herzen was born in Moscow on 6 April 1812, some months before the great fire that destroyed the city during Napoleon's occupation after the battle of Borodino. His father, Ivan Alexandrovich Yakovlev, came of an ancient family distantly related to the Romanov dynasty. Like other rich and well-born members of the Russian gentry, he had spent some years abroad, and, during one of his journeys, met, and took back to Moscow with him, the daughter of a minor Württemberg official, Luiza Haag, a gentle, submissive, somewhat colourless girl, a good deal younger than himself. For some reason, perhaps owing to the disparity in their social positions, he never married her according to the rites of the church. Yakovlev was a member of the Orthodox church; she remained a Lutheran.[1] He was a proud, independent, disdainful man, and had grown increasingly morose and misanthropic. He retired before the war of 1812, and at the time of the French invasion was living in bitter and resentful idleness in his house in Moscow. During the occupation he was recognised by Marshal Mortier, whom he had known in Paris, and agreed – in return for a safe conduct enabling him to take his family out of the devastated city – to carry a message from Napoleon to the Emperor Alexander. For this indiscretion he was sent back to his estates and only allowed to return to Moscow somewhat later.

In his large and gloomy house on the Arbat he brought up his son, Alexander, to whom he had given the surname Herzen, as if to stress the fact that he was the child of an irregular liaison, an affair of the heart. Luiza Haag was never accorded the full status of a wife, but the boy had every attention lavished upon him. He received the normal education of a young Russian nobleman of his time, that is to say, he was looked after by a host of nurses and serfs, and taught by private tutors, German and French, carefully chosen by his neurotic, irritable, devoted, suspicious father. Every care was taken to develop his gifts. He was a lively and imaginative child and absorbed knowledge easily

[1] There is evidence, although it is not conclusive, that she was married to him according to the Lutheran rite, not recognised by the Orthodox church.

and eagerly. His father loved him after his fashion: more, certainly, than his other son, also illegitimate, born ten years earlier, whom he had christened Egor (George). But he was, by the 1820s, a defeated and gloomy man, unable to communicate with his family or indeed anyone else. Shrewd, honourable, and neither unfeeling nor unjust, a 'difficult' character like old Prince Bolkonsky in Tolstoy's *War and Peace*, Ivan Yakovlev emerges from his son's recollections a self-lacerating, grim, shut-in, half-frozen human being, who terrorised his household with his whims and his sarcasm. He kept all doors and windows locked, the blinds permanently drawn, and, apart from a few old friends and his own brothers, saw virtually nobody. In later years his son described him as the product of 'the encounter of two such incompatible things as the eighteenth century and Russian life'[1] – a collision of cultures that had destroyed a good many among the more sensitive members of the Russian gentry in the reigns of Catherine II and her successors.

The boy escaped with relief from his father's oppressive and frightening company to the rooms occupied by his mother and the servants; she was kind and unassuming, crushed by her husband, frightened by her foreign surroundings, and seemed to accept her almost oriental status in the household with uncomplaining resignation. As for the servants, they were serfs from the Yakovlev estates, trained to behave obsequiously to the son and probable heir of their master. Herzen himself, in later years, attributed the deepest of all his social feelings (which his friend, the critic Belinsky, diagnosed so accurately), concern for the freedom and dignity of human individuals, to the barbarous conditions that surrounded him in childhood. He was a favourite child, and much spoiled, but the facts of his irregular birth and of his mother's status were brought home to him by listening to the servants' gossip and, on at least one occasion, by overhearing a conversation about himself between his father and one of his old army comrades. The shock was, according to his own testimony, profound: it was probably one of the determining factors of his life.

He was taught Russian literature and history by a young university student, an enthusiastic follower of the new romantic movement, which, particularly in its German form, had then begun to dominate Russian intellectual life. He learned French (which his father wrote

[1] A. I. Herzen, *Sobranie sochinenii v tridtsati tomakh* (Moscow, 1954–65), vol. 8, p. 86. Subsequent references to Herzen's works are to this edition, hereafter called *Sobranie sochinenii*.

more easily than Russian) and German (which he spoke with his mother) and European, rather than Russian, history – his tutor was a French refugee who had emigrated to Russia after the French Revolution. The Frenchman did not reveal his political opinions, so Herzen tells us, until one day, when his pupil asked him why Louis XVI had been executed; to this he replied in an altered voice, 'Because he was a traitor to his country',[1] and finding the boy responsive, threw off his reserve and spoke to him openly about the liberty and equality of men. Herzen was a lonely child, at once pampered and cramped, lively and bored; he read voraciously in his father's large library, especially French books of the Enlightenment. He was fourteen when the leaders of the Decembrist conspiracy were hanged by the Emperor Nicholas I. He later declared that this event was the critical turning-point of his life; whether this was so or not, the memory of these aristocratic martyrs in the cause of Russian constitutional liberty later became a sacred symbol to him, as to many others of his class and generation, and affected him for the rest of his days. He tells us that a few years after this, he and his intimate friend Nick Ogarev, standing on the Sparrow Hills above Moscow, took a solemn 'Hannibalic' oath to avenge these fighters for the rights of man, and to dedicate their own lives to the cause for which they had died.

In due course he became a student in the University of Moscow. He was already steeped in Schiller and Goethe; he plunged into the study of German metaphysics – Kant, and particularly Schelling. And then the new French school of historians – Guizot, Augustin Thierry, and, in addition, the French Utopian socialists, Saint-Simon, Fourier, Leroux, and other social prophets smuggled into Russia in defiance of the censorship, and became a convinced and passionate radical. He and Ogarev belonged to a group of students who read forbidden books and discussed dangerous ideas; for this he was, together with most other 'unreliable' students, duly arrested and, probably because he declined to repudiate the views imputed to him, condemned to imprisonment. His father used all his influence to get the sentence mitigated, but could not save his son from being exiled to the provincial city of Vyatka, near the borders of Asia, where he was not indeed kept in prison, but put to work in the local administration.

To his astonishment, he enjoyed this new test of his powers; he displayed administrative gifts and became a far more competent and perhaps even enthusiastic official than he was later prepared to admit,

[1] *Sobranie sochinenii*, vol. 8, p. 64: 'Parce qu'il a été traître à la patrie.'

and helped to expose the corrupt and brutal governor, whom he detested and despised. In Vyatka he became involved in a passionate love affair with a married woman, behaved badly, and suffered agonies of contrition. He read Dante, went through a religious phase, and began a long and passionate correspondence with his first cousin Natalie, who, like himself, was illegitimate, and lived as a companion in the house of a rich and despotic aunt. As a result of his father's ceaseless efforts, he was transferred to the city of Vladimir, and with the help of his young Moscow friends, arranged the elopement of Natalie. They were married in Vladimir against their relations' wishes. He was in due course allowed to return to Moscow and was appointed to a government post in Petersburg.

Whatever his ambitions at the time, he remained indomitably independent and committed to the radical cause. As a result of an indiscreet letter, opened by the censors, in which he had criticised the behaviour of the police, he was again sentenced to a period of exile, this time in Novgorod. Two years later, in 1842, he was once more permitted to return to Moscow. He was by then regarded as an established member of the new radical intelligentsia, and, indeed, as an honoured martyr in its cause, and began to write in the progressive periodicals of the time. He always dealt with the same central theme: the oppression of the individual; the humiliation and degradation of men by political and personal tyranny; the yoke of social custom, the dark ignorance, and savage, arbitrary misgovernment which maimed and destroyed human beings in the brutal and odious Russian Empire.

Like the other members of his circle, the young poet and novelist Turgenev, the critic Belinsky, the future political agitators Bakunin and Katkov (the first in the cause of revolution, the second of reaction), the literary essayist Annenkov, his own intimate friend Ogarev, Herzen, with most of his intellectual contemporaries in Russia, became immersed in Hegel's philosophy. He composed arresting historical and philosophical essays, and stories dealing with social issues; they were published, widely read and discussed, and created a considerable reputation for their author. He adopted an uncompromising position. A leading representative of the dissident Russian gentry, his socialist beliefs were caused less by a reaction against the cruelty and chaos of the *laissez-faire* economy of the bourgeois west – for Russia, then in its early industrial beginnings, was still a semi-feudal, socially and economically primitive society – than as a direct response to the agonising social problems in his native land: the poverty of the masses, serfdom and lack of individual freedom at all levels, and a lawless and brutal autocracy.[1] In addition, there was the wounded national pride of a powerful and semi-barbarous society, whose leaders were aware of its backwardness, and suffered from mingled admiration, envy and resentment of the civilised west. The radicals believed in reform along democratic, secular, western lines; the Slavophils retreated into mystical nationalism, and preached the need for return to native 'organic' forms of life and faith that, according to them, had been all but ruined by Peter I's reforms, which had merely encouraged a sedulous and humiliating aping of the soulless and, in any case, hopelessly decadent west. Herzen was an extreme 'Westerner', but he preserved his links with the Slavophil adversaries – he regarded the best among them as romantic reactionaries, misguided nationalists, but honourable allies against the tsarist bureaucracy – and later tended systematically to minimise his differences with them, perhaps from a desire to see all Russians who were not dead to human feeling ranged in a single vast protest against the evil regime.

In 1847 Ivan Yakovlev died. He left the greater part of his fortune to Luiza Haag and her son, Alexander Herzen. With immense faith in his own powers, and burning with a desire (in Fichte's words that expressed the attitude of a generation) 'to be and do something in the world', Herzen decided to emigrate. Whether he wished or expected to remain abroad during the rest of his life is uncertain, but so it turned out to be. He left in the same year, and travelled in considerable state, accompanied by his wife, his mother, two friends, as well as servants, and, crossing Germany, towards the end of 1847 reached the coveted city of Paris, the capital of the civilised world. He plunged at once into the life of the exiled radicals and socialists of many nationalities who played a central role in the fermenting intellectual and artistic activity of that city. By 1848, when a series of revolutions broke out in country after country in Europe, he found himself with Bakunin and Proudhon on the extreme left wing of revolutionary socialism. When rumours of his activities reached the Russian government, he was ordered to return immediately. He refused. His fortune in Russia

---

[1] The historical and sociological explanation of the origins of Russian socialism and of Herzen's part in it cannot be attempted here. It has been treated in a number of (untranslated) Russian monographs, both pre- and post-revolutionary. The most detailed and original study of this topic to date is *Alexander Herzen and the Birth of Russian Socialism, 1812–1855* ([Cambridge, Massachusetts], 1961) by Martin Malia.

and that of his mother were declared confiscated. Aided by the efforts of the banker James Rothschild, who had conceived a liking for the young Russian 'baron' and was in a position to bring pressure on the Russian government, Herzen recovered the major portion of his resources, and thereafter experienced no financial want. This gave him a degree of independence not then enjoyed by many exiles, as well as the financial means for supporting other refugees and radical causes.

Shortly after his arrival in Paris, before the revolution, he contributed a series of impassioned articles to a Moscow periodical controlled by his friends, in which he gave an eloquent and violently critical account of the conditions of life and culture in Paris, and, in particular, a devastating analysis of the degradation of the French bourgeoisie, an indictment not surpassed even in the works of his contemporaries Marx and Heine. His Moscow friends for the most part received this with disfavour : they regarded his analyses as characteristic flights of a highly rhetorical fancy, irresponsible extremism, ill suited to the needs of a misgoverned and backward country compared to which the progress of the middle classes in the west, whatever its shortcomings, was a notable step forward towards universal enlightenment. These early works – the *Letters from Avenue Marigny* and the Italian sketches that followed – possess qualities which became characteristic of all his writings : a rapid torrent of descriptive sentences, fresh, lucid, direct, interspersed with vivid and never irrelevant digressions, variations on the same theme in many keys, puns, neologisms, quotations real and imaginary, verbal inventions, gallicisms which irritated his nationalistic Russian friends, mordant personal observations and cascades of vivid images and incomparable epigrams, which, so far from either tiring or distracting the reader by their virtuosity, add to the force and swiftness of the narrative. The effect is one of spontaneous improvisation : exhilarating conversation by an intellectually gay and exceptionally clever and honest man endowed with singular powers of observation and expression. The mood is one of ardent political radicalism imbued with a typically aristocratic (and even more typically Muscovite) contempt for everything narrow, calculating, self-satisfied, commercial, anything cautious, petty or tending towards compromise and the *juste milieu*, of which Louis-Philippe and Guizot are held up to view as particularly repulsive incarnations.

Herzen's outlook in these essays is a combination of optimistic idealism – a vision of a socially, intellectually and morally free society, the beginnings of which, like Proudhon, Marx and Louis Blanc, he saw in the French working class; faith in the radical revolution which alone could create the conditions for their liberation; but with this, a deep distrust (something that most of his allies did not share) of all general formulas as such, of the programmes and battle-cries of all the political parties, of the great, official historical goals – progress, liberty, equality, national unity, historic rights, human solidarity – principles and slogans in the name of which men had been, and doubtless would soon again be, violated and slaughtered, and their forms of life condemned and destroyed.

Like the more extreme of the left-wing disciples of Hegel, in particular like the anarchist Max Stirner, Herzen saw danger in the great magnificent abstractions the mere sound of which precipitated men into violent and meaningless slaughter – new idols, it seemed to him, on whose altars human blood was to be shed tomorrow as irrationally and uselessly as the blood of the victims of yesterday or the day before, sacrificed in honour of older divinities – church or monarchy or the feudal order or the sacred customs of the tribe, that were now discredited as obstacles to the progress of mankind.

Together with this scepticism about the meaning and value of abstract ideals as such, in contrast with the concrete, short-term, immediate goals of identifiable living individuals – specific freedoms, reward for the day's work – Herzen spoke of something even more disquieting, a haunting sense of the ever widening and unbridgeable gulf between the humane values of the relatively free and civilised élites (to which he knew himself to belong) and the actual needs, desires and tastes of the vast voiceless masses of mankind, barbarous enough in the west, wilder still in Russia or the plains of Asia beyond. The old world was crumbling visibly, and it deserved to fall. It would be destroyed by its victims – the slaves who cared nothing for the art and the science of their masters; and indeed, Herzen asks, why should they care? Was it not erected on their suffering and degradation? Young and vigorous, filled with a just hatred of the old world built on their fathers' bones, the new barbarians will raze to the ground the edifices of their oppressors, and with them all that is most sublime and beautiful in western civilisation; such a cataclysm might be not only inevitable but justified, since this civilisation, noble and valuable in the eyes of its beneficiaries, has offered nothing but suffering, a life without meaning, to the vast majority of mankind. Yet he does not pretend that this makes the prospect, to those who, like him, have tasted the riper fruits of civilisation, any less dreadful.

It has often been asserted by both Russian and western critics that Herzen arrived in Paris a passionate, even Utopian idealist, and that it was the failure of the revolution of 1848 which brought about his disillusionment and a new, more pessimistic realism. This is not sufficiently borne out by the evidence.[1] Even in 1847, the sceptical note, in particular pessimism about the degree to which human beings can be transformed, and the still deeper scepticism about whether such changes, even if they were achieved by fearless and intelligent revolutionaries or reformers, ideal images of whom floated before the eyes of his Westernising friends in Russia, would in fact lead to a juster and freer order, or on the contrary to the rule of new masters over new slaves – that ominous note is sounded before the great débâcle. Yet, despite this, he remained a convinced, ultimately optimistic revolutionary. The spectacle of the workers' revolt and its brutal suppression in Italy and in France haunted Herzen all his life. His first-hand description of the events of 1848–9, in particular of the drowning in blood of the July revolt in Paris, is a masterpiece of 'committed' historical and sociological writing. So, too, are his sketches of the personalities involved in these upheavals, and his reflections upon them. Most of these essays and letters remain untranslated.

Herzen could not and would not return to Russia. He became a Swiss citizen, and to the disasters of the revolution was added a personal tragedy – the seduction of his adored wife by the most intimate of his new friends, the radical German poet Georg Herwegh, a friend of Marx and Wagner, the 'iron lark' of the German revolution, as Heine half ironically called him. Herzen's progressive, somewhat Shelleyan, views on love, friendship, equality of the sexes, and the irrationality of bourgeois morality, were tested by this crisis and broken by it. He went almost mad with grief and jealousy: his love, his vanity, his deeper assumptions about the basis of all human relationships, suffered a traumatic shock from which he was never fully to recover. He did what few others have ever done : described every detail of his own agony, every step of his altering relationship with his wife, with Herwegh and Herwegh's wife, as they seemed to him in retrospect ; he

[1] The clearest formulation of this well-worn and almost universal thesis is to be found in E. H. Carr's lively and well-documented treatment of Herzen in his *The Romantic Exiles* (London, 1933). Malia's book (op. cit., p. 194, note 1 above) avoids this error.

noted every communication that occurred between them, every moment of anger, despair, affection, love, hope, hatred, contempt and agonised, suicidal self-contempt. Every tone and nuance in his own moral and psychological condition is raised to high relief against the background of his public life in the world of exiles and conspirators, French, Italian, German, Russian, Austrian, Hungarian, Polish, who move on and off the stage on which he himself is always the central, self-absorbed, tragic hero. The account is not unbalanced – there is no obvious distortion – but it is wholly egocentric.

All his life Herzen perceived the external world clearly, and in proportion, but through the medium of his own self-romanticising personality, with his own impressionable, ill-organised self at the centre of his universe. No matter how violent his torment, he retains full artistic control of the tragedy which he is living through, but also writing. It is, perhaps, this artistic egotism, which all his work exhibits, that was in part responsible both for Natalie's suffocation and for the lack of reticence in his description of what took place : Herzen takes wholly for granted the reader's understanding, and still more, his undivided interest in every detail of his own, the writer's, mental and emotional life. Natalie's letters and desperate flight to Herwegh show the measure of the increasingly destructive effect of Herzen's self-absorbed blindness upon her frail and *exalté* temperament. We know comparatively little of Natalie's relationship with Herwegh : she may well have been physically in love with him, and he with her : the inflated literary language of the letters conceals more than it reveals; what is clear is that she felt unhappy, trapped and irresistibly attracted to her lover. If Herzen sensed this, he perceived it very dimly.

He appropriated the feelings of those nearest him as he did the ideas of Hegel or George Sand : that is, he took what he needed, and poured it into the vehement torrent of his own experience. He gave generously, if fitfully, to others; he put his own life into them, but for all his deep and life-long belief in individual liberty and the absolute value of personal life and personal relationships, scarcely understood or tolerated wholly independent lives by the side of his own; his description of his agony is scrupulously and bitterly detailed and accurate, never self-sparing, eloquent but not sentimental, and remorselessly self-absorbed. It is a harrowing document. He did not publish the story in full during his lifetime, but now it forms part of his memoirs.

Self-expression – the need to say his own word – and perhaps the craving for recognition by others, by Russia, by Europe, were primary needs of Herzen's nature. Consequently, even during this, the darkest period of his life, he continued to pour out a stream of letters and articles in various languages on political and social topics; he helped to keep Proudhon going, kept up a correspondence with Swiss radicals and Russian *émigrés*, read widely, made notes, conceived ideas, argued, worked unremittingly both as a publicist and as an active supporter of left-wing and revolutionary causes. After a short while Natalie returned to him in Nice, only to die in his arms. Shortly before her death, a ship on which his mother and one of his children, a deaf-mute, were travelling from Marseilles, sank in a storm. Their bodies were not found. Herzen's life had reached its lowest ebb. He left Nice and the circle of Italian, French and Polish revolutionaries to many of whom he was bound by ties of warm friendship, and with his three surviving children went to England. America was too far away and, besides, seemed to him too dull. England was no less remote from the scene of his defeats, political and personal, and yet still a part of Europe. It was then the country most hospitable to political refugees, civilised, tolerant of eccentricities or indifferent to them, proud of its civil liberties and its sympathy with the victims of foreign oppression. He arrived in London in 1851.

He and his children wandered from home to home in London and its suburbs, and there, after the death of Nicholas I had made it possible for him to leave Russia, his most intimate friend, Nikolay Ogarev, joined them. Together they set up a printing press, and began to publish a periodical in Russian called *The Pole Star* – the first organ wholly dedicated to uncompromising agitation against the imperial Russian regime. The earliest chapters of *My Past and Thoughts* appeared in its pages. The memory of the terrible years 1848–51 obsessed Herzen's thoughts and poisoned his blood stream : it became an inescapable psychological necessity for him to seek relief by setting down this bitter history. This was the first section of his memoirs to be written. It was an opiate against the appalling loneliness of a life lived among uninterested strangers[1] while political reaction seemed to envelop the

---

[1] Herzen had no close English friends, although he had associates, allies and admirers. One of these, the radical journalist W. J. Linton, to whose *English Republic* Herzen had contributed articles, described him as 'short of stature, stoutly built, in his last days inclined to corpulence, with a grand head, long chestnut hair and beard, small, luminous eyes, and rather ruddy complexion. Suave in his manner, courteous, but with an intense power of irony, witty . . . clear, concise, and impressive, he was a subtle and profound

entire world, leaving no room for hope. Insensibly he was drawn into the past. He moved further and further into it and found it a source of liberty and strength.

This is how the book which he conceived on the analogy of *David Copperfield* came to be composed.[1] He began to write it in the last months of 1852. He wrote by fits and starts. The first three parts were probably finished by the end of 1853. In 1854 a selection which he called *Prison and Exile* – a title perhaps inspired by Silvio Pellico's celebrated *Le mie prigioni* – was published in English. It was an immediate success; encouraged by this, he continued. By the spring of 1855, the first four parts of the work were completed; they were all published by 1857. He revised part IV, added new chapters to it and composed part V; he completed the bulk of part VI by 1858. The sections dealing with his intimate life – his love and the early years of his marriage – were composed in 1857 : he could not bring himself to touch upon them until then. This was followed by an interval of seven years. Independent essays such as those on Robert Owen, the actor Shchepkin, the painter Ivanov, Garibaldi (*Camicia rossa*), were published in London between 1860 and 1864; but these, although usually included in the memoirs, were not intended for them. The first complete edition of the first four parts appeared in 1861. The final sections – part VIII and almost the whole of part VII – were written, in that order, in 1865–7.

Herzen deliberately left some sections unpublished: the most intimate details of his personal tragedy appeared posthumously – only a part of the chapter entitled 'Oceano nox' was printed in his lifetime.

---

thinker, with all the passionate nature of the "barbarian", yet generous and humane . . . Hospitable, and taking pleasure in society . . . a good conversationalist, with a frank and pleasant manner' (*Memories* (London, 1895), pp. 146–7). And in his *European Republicans* (London, 1893) he said that the Spanish radical Emilio Castelar declared that Herzen, with his fair hair and beard, looked like a Goth, but possessed the warmth, vivacity, verve, 'inimitable grace' and 'marvellous variety' of a southerner (pp. 275–6). Turgenev and Herzen were the first Russians to move freely in European society. The impression that they made did a good deal, though perhaps not enough, to dispel the myth of the dark 'Slav soul', which took a long time to die; perhaps it is not altogether dead yet.

[1] '[*Copperfield*] is Dickens's *Past and Thoughts*,' he said in one of his letters in the early 60s; humility was not among his virtues. *Sobranie sochinenii*, vol. 27, p. 394 (letter of 16 December 1863).

He omitted also the story of his affairs with Medvedeva in Vyatka and with the serf girl Katerina in Moscow – his confession of them to Natalie cast the first shadow over their relationship, a shadow that never lifted; he could not bear to see it in print while he lived. He suppressed, too, a chapter on 'The German Emigrants' which contains his unflattering comments on Marx and his followers, and some characteristically entertaining and ironical sketches of some of his old friends among the Russian radicals. He genuinely detested the practice of washing the revolutionaries' dirty linen in public, and made it clear that he did not intend to make fun of allies for the entertainment of the common enemy. The first authoritative edition of the memoirs was compiled by Mikhail Lemke in the first complete edition of Herzen's works, which was begun before, and completed some years after, the Russian Revolution of 1917. It has since been revised in successive Soviet editions. The fullest version is that published in the exhaustive edition of Herzen's works, a handsome monument of Soviet scholarship.[1]

The memoirs formed a vivid and broken background accompaniment to Herzen's central activity: revolutionary journalism, to which he dedicated his life. The bulk of it is contained in the most celebrated of all Russian periodicals published abroad – *The Bell* (*Kolokol*) – edited by Herzen and Ogarev in London and then in Geneva from 1857 until 1867, with the motto (taken from Schiller) 'Vivos voco'. *The Bell* had an immense success. It was the first systematic instrument of revolutionary propaganda directed against the Russian autocracy, written with knowledge, sincerity and mordant eloquence; it gathered round itself all that was uncowed not only in Russia and the Russian colonies abroad, but also among Poles and other oppressed nationalities. It began to penetrate into Russia by secret routes and was regularly read by high officials of state, including, it was rumoured, the Emperor himself. Herzen used the copious information that reached him in clandestine letters and personal messages, describing various misdeeds of the Russian bureaucracy, to expose specific scandals – cases of bribery, miscarriage of justice, tyranny and dishonesty by officials and influential persons. *The Bell* named names, offered documentary evidence, asked awkward questions and exposed hideous aspects of Russian life.

Russian travellers visited London in order to meet the mysterious

---

[1] op. cit. (p. 191, note 1 above).

leader of the mounting opposition to the Tsar. Generals, high officials and other loyal subjects of the Empire were among the many visitors who thronged to see him, some out of curiosity, others to shake his hand, to express sympathy or admiration. He reached the peak of his fame, both political and literary, after the defeat of Russia in the Crimean War and the death of Nicholas I. The open appeal by Herzen to the new Emperor[1] to free the serfs and initiate bold and radical reforms 'from above', and, after the first concrete steps towards this had been taken in 1858, his paean of praise to Alexander II,[2] ending 'Thou hast conquered, O Galilean', created the illusion on both sides of the Russian frontier that a new liberal era was at last dawning, in which a degree of understanding – perhaps of actual cooperation – could be achieved between tsardom and its opponents. This state of mind did not last long. But Herzen's credit stood very high – higher than that of any other Russian in the west: in the late 50s and early 60s, he was the acknowledged leader of all that was generous, enlightened, civilised, humane in Russia.

More than Bakunin and even Turgenev, whose novels formed a central source of knowledge about Russia in the west, Herzen counteracted the legend, ingrained in the minds of progressive Europeans (of whom Michelet was perhaps the most representative), that Russia consisted of nothing save only the government jackboot on the one hand, and the dark, silent, sullen mass of brutalised peasants on the other – an image that was the by-product of the widespread sympathy for the principal victim of Russian despotism, the martyred nation, Poland. Some among the Polish exiles spontaneously conceded this service to the truth on Herzen's part, if only because he was one of the rare Russians who genuinely liked and admired individual Poles, worked in close sympathy with them, and identified the cause of Russian liberation with that of all her oppressed subject nationalities. It was, indeed, this unswerving avoidance of chauvinism that was among the principal causes of the ultimate collapse of *The Bell* and of Herzen's own political undoing.

After Russia, Herzen's deepest love was for Italy and the Italians. The closest ties bound him to the Italian exiles Mazzini, Garibaldi, Saffi and Orsini. Although he supported every liberal beginning in

---

[1] 'Pis'mo k Imperatoru Aleksandru vtoromu', *Sobranie sochinenii*, vol. 12, pp. 272–4.

[2] 'Cherez tri goda', *Kolokol*, 15 February 1858: *Sobranie sochinenii*, vol. 13, pp. 195–7.

France, his attitude towards her was more ambiguous. For this there were many reasons. Like Tocqueville (whom he personally disliked), he had a distaste for all that was centralised, bureaucratic, hierarchical, subject to rigid forms or rules; France was to him the incarnation of order, discipline, the worship of the state, of unity, and of despotic, abstract formulas that flattened all things to the same rule and pattern – something that had a family resemblance to the great slave states – Prussia, Austria, Russia; with this he constantly contrasts the decentralised, uncrushed, untidy, 'truly democratic' Italians, whom he believed to possess a deep affinity with the free Russian spirit embodied in the peasant commune with its sense of natural justice and human worth. To this ideal even England seemed to him to be far less hostile than legalistic, calculating France: in such moods he comes close to his romantic Slavophil opponents. Moreover, he could not forget the betrayal of the revolution in Paris by the bourgeois parties in 1848, the execution of the workers, the suppression of the Roman revolution by the troops of the French Republic, the vanity, weakness and rhetoric of the French radical politicians – Lamartine, Marrast, Ledru-Rollin, Félix Pyat.

His sketches of the lives and behaviour of leading French exiles in England are masterpieces of amused, half-sympathetic, half-contemptuous description of the grotesque and futile aspects of every political emigration condemned to sterility, intrigue and a constant flow of self-justifying eloquence before a foreign audience too remote or bored to listen. Yet he thought well of individual members of it: he had for a time been a close ally of Proudhon, and despite their differences he continued to respect him; he regarded Louis Blanc as an honest and fearless democrat, he was on good terms with Victor Hugo, he liked and admired Michelet. In later years he visited at least one Paris political *salon* – admittedly, it was that of a Pole – with evident enjoyment: the Goncourts met him there and left a vivid description in their journal of his appearance and his conversation.[1]

[1] See entry in the *Journal* under 8 February 1865 – 'Dinner at Charles Edmond's [Chojecki] . . . A Socratic mask with the warm and transparent flesh of a Rubens portrait, a red mark between the eyebrows as from a branding iron, greying beard and hair.

'As he talks there is a constant ironical chuckle which rises and falls in his throat. His voice is soft, melancholy, musical, without any of the harsh sonority one might have expected from his huge neck: the ideas are fine, delicate, pungent, at times subtle, always definite, illuminated by words that

Although he was half German himself, or perhaps because of it, he felt, like his friend Bakunin, a strong aversion from what he regarded as the incurable philistinism of the Germans, and what seemed to him a peculiarly unattractive combination of craving for blind authority with a tendency to squalid internecine recriminations in public, more pronounced than among other émigrés. Perhaps his hatred of Herwegh, whom he knew to be a friend both of Marx and of Wagner, as well as Marx's onslaughts on Karl Vogt, the Swiss naturalist to whom Herzen was devoted, played some part in this. At least three of his most intimate friends were pure Germans. Goethe and Schiller meant more to him than any Russian writers. Yet there is something genuinely venomous in his account of the German exiles, quite different from the high-spirited sense of comedy with which he describes the idiosyncrasies of the other foreign colonies gathered in the 50s and 60s in London – a city, if we are to believe Herzen, equally unconcerned with their absurdities and their martyrdoms.

As for his hosts, the English, they seldom appear in his pages. Herzen had met Mill, Carlyle and Owen. His first night in England was spent with English hosts. He was on reasonably good terms with one or two editors of radical papers (some of whom, like Linton and Cowen, helped him to propagate his views, and to preserve contact with revolutionaries on the continent as well as with clandestine traffic of propaganda to Russia), and several radically inclined Members of

---

take time to arrive, but which always possess the felicitous quality of French as it is spoken by a civilised and witty foreigner.

'He speaks of Bakunin, of his eleven months in prison, chained to a wall, of his escape from Siberia by the Amur River, of his return by way of California, of his arrival in London, where, after a stormy, moist embrace, his first words [to Herzen] were "Can one get oysters here?" '

Herzen delighted the Goncourts with stories about the Emperor Nicholas walking in the night in his empty palace, after the fall of Eupatoria during the Crimean War, with the heavy, unearthly steps of the stone statue of the Commander in *Don Juan*. This was followed by anecdotes about English habits and manners – 'a country which he loves as the land of liberty' – to illustrate its absurd, class-conscious, unyielding traditionalism, particularly noticeable in the relations of masters and servants. The Goncourts quote a characteristic epigram made by Herzen to illustrate the difference between the French and English characters. They faithfully report the story of how James Rothschild managed to save Herzen's property in Russia.

Parliament, including minor ministers. In general, however, he seems to have had even less contact with Englishmen than his contemporary and fellow exile, Karl Marx. He admired England. He admired her constitution; the wild and tangled wood of her unwritten laws and customs brought the full resources of his romantic imagination into play. The entertaining passages of *My Past and Thoughts* in which he compares the French and the English, or the English and the Germans, display acute and amused insight into the national characteristics of the English. But he could not altogether like them: they remained for him too insular, too indifferent, too unimaginative, too remote from the moral, social and aesthetic issues which lay closest to his own heart, too materialistic and self-satisfied. His judgements about them, always intelligent and sometimes penetrating, are distant and tend to be conventional. A description of the trial in London of a French radical who had killed a political opponent in a duel in Windsor Great Park is wonderfully executed, but remains a piece of genre-painting, a gay and brilliant caricature. The French, the Swiss, the Italians, even the Germans, certainly the Poles, are closer to him. He cannot establish any genuine personal relationship with the English. When he thinks of mankind he does not think of them.

Apart from his central preoccupations, he devoted himself to the education of his children, which he entrusted in part to an idealistic German lady, Malwida von Meysenbug, afterwards a friend of Nietzsche and Romain Rolland. His personal life was intertwined with that of his intimate friend Ogarev, and of Ogarev's wife, who became his mistress; in spite of this the mutual devotion of the two friends remained unaltered – the memoirs reveal little of the curious emotional consequences of this relationship.

For the rest, he lived the life of an affluent, well-born man of letters, a member of the Russian, and more specifically Moscow, gentry, uprooted from his native soil, unable to achieve a settled existence or even the semblance of inward or outward peace, a life filled with occasional moments of hope and even exultation, followed by long periods of misery, corrosive self-criticism, and most of all overwhelming, omnivorous, bitter nostalgia. It may be this, as much as objective reasons, that caused him to idealise the Russian peasant, and to dream that the answer to the central 'social' question of his time – that of growing inequality, exploitation, dehumanisation of both the oppressor and the oppressed – lay in the preservation of the Russian peasant commune. He perceived in it the seeds of the development of a non-industrial, semi-anarchist socialism. Only such a solution, plainly influenced by the views of Fourier, Proudhon and George Sand, seemed to him free from the crushing, barrack-room discipline demanded by western communists from Cabet to Marx; and from the equally suffocating, and, it seemed to him, far more vulgar and philistine ideals contained in moderate, half-socialist doctrines, with their faith in the progressive role of developing industrialism preached by the forerunners of social democracy in Germany and France and of the Fabians in England. At times he modified his view: towards the end of his life he began to recognise the historical significance of the organised urban workers. But all in all he remained faithful to his belief in the Russian peasant commune as an embryonic form of a life in which the quest for individual freedom was reconciled with the need for collective activity and responsibility. He retained to the end a romantic vision of the inevitable coming of a new, just, all-transforming social order.

Herzen is neither consistent nor systematic. His style during his middle years has lost the confident touch of his youth, and conveys the consuming nostalgia that never leaves him. He is obsessed by a sense of blind accident, although his faith in the values of life remains unshaken. Almost all traces of Hegelian influence are gone. 'The absurdity of facts offends us . . . it is as though someone had promised that everything in the world will be exquisitely beautiful, just and harmonious. We have marvelled enough at the deep abstract wisdom of nature and history; it is time to realise that nature and history are full of the accidental and senseless, of muddle and bungling.' This is highly characteristic of his mood in the 60s; and it is no accident that his exposition is not ordered, but is a succession of fragments, episodes, isolated vignettes, a mingling of *Dichtung* and *Wahrheit*, facts and poetic licence.

His moods alternate sharply. Sometimes he believes in the need for a great, cleansing, revolutionary storm, even were it to take the form of a barbarian invasion likely to destroy all the values that he himself holds dear. At other times he reproaches his old friend Bakunin, who joined him in London after escaping from his Russian prisons, for wanting to make the revolution too soon; for not understanding that dwellings for free men cannot be constructed out of the stones of a prison; that the average European of the nineteenth century is too deeply marked by the slavery of the old order to be capable of conceiving true freedom, that it is not the liberated slaves who will build the new order, but new men brought up in liberty. History has her own tempo. Patience and gradualism – not the haste and violence of a Peter the Great – can alone bring about a permanent transformation. At such moments he wonders whether the future belongs to the free, anarchic peasant, or to the bold and ruthless planner; perhaps it is the industrial worker who is to be the heir to the new, unavoidable, collectivist economic order.[1] Then again he returns to his early moods of disillusionment and wonders whether men in general really desire freedom: perhaps only a few do so in each generation, while most human beings only want good government, no matter at whose hands; and he echoes de Maistre's bitter epigram about Rousseau: 'Monsieur Rousseau has asked why it is that men who are born free are nevertheless everywhere in chains; it is as if one were to ask why sheep, who are born carnivorous, nevertheless everywhere nibble grass.' Herzen develops this theme.[2] Men desire freedom no more than fish desire to fly. The fact that a few flying fish exist does not demonstrate that fish in general were created to fly, or are not fundamentally quite content to stay below the surface of the water, for ever away from the sun and the light. Then he returns to his earlier optimism and the thought that somewhere – in Russia – there lives the unbroken human being, the peasant with his faculties intact, untainted by the corruption and sophistication of the west.

But this Rousseau-inspired faith, as he grows older, grows less secure. His sense of reality is too strong. For all his efforts, and the efforts of his socialist friends, he cannot deceive himself entirely. He oscillates between pessimism and optimism, scepticism and suspicion of his own scepticism, and is kept morally alive only by his hatred of all injustice, all arbitrariness, all mediocrity as such – in particular by his inability to compromise in any degree with either the brutality of reactionaries or the hypocrisy of bourgeois liberals. He is preserved by this, buoyed up by his belief that such evils will destroy themselves, and by his love for his children and his devoted friends, and his unquenchable delight in the variety of life and the comedy of human character.

On the whole, he grew more pessimistic. He began with an ideal vision of human life, and largely ignored the chasm which divided it from the present – whether the Russia of Nicholas, or the corrupt constitutionalism in the west. In his youth he glorified Jacobin radicalism

[1] This is the thesis in which orthodox Soviet scholars claim to discern a belated approach to those of Marx.

[2] *Sobranie sochinenii*, vol. 6, p. 94.

and condemned its opponents in Russia – blind conservatism, Slavophil nostalgia, the cautious gradualism of his friends Granovsky and Turgenev, as well as Hegelian appeals to patience and rational conformity to the inescapable rhythms of history, which seemed to him designed to ensure the triumph of the new bourgeois class. His attitude, before he went abroad, was boldly optimistic. There followed, not indeed a change of view, but a cooling-off, a tendency to a more sober and critical outlook. All genuine change, he began to think in 1847, is necessarily slow; the power of tradition (which he at once mocks at and admires in England) is very great; men are less malleable than was believed in the eighteenth century, nor do they truly seek liberty, only security and contentment; communism is but tsarism stood on its head, the replacement of one yoke by another; the ideals and watchwords of politics turn out, on examination, to be empty formulas in the name of which devout fanatics happily slaughter hecatombs of their fellows. He no longer feels certain that the gap between the enlightened élite and the masses can ever, in principle, be bridged (this becomes an obsessive refrain in later Russian thought), since the awakened people may, for unalterable psychological or sociological reasons, despise and reject the gifts of a civilisation which will never mean enough to them. But if all this is even in small part true, is radical transformation either practicable or desirable? From this follows Herzen's growing sense of obstacles that may be insurmountable, limits that may be impassable, his empiricism, scepticism, the latent pessimism and despair of the middle 60s.

This is the attitude which some Soviet scholars interpret as the beginning of an approach on his part towards a quasi-Marxist recognition of the inexorable laws of social development – in particular the inevitability of industrialism, above all of the central role to be played by the proletariat. This is not how Herzen's left-wing Russian critics interpreted his views in his lifetime, or for the half century that followed. To them, rightly or wrongly, these doctrines seemed symptomatic of conservatism and betrayal. For in the 50s and 60s, a new generation of radicals grew up in Russia, then a backward country in the painful process of the earliest, most rudimentary beginnings of slow, sporadic, inefficient industrialisation. These were men of mixed social origins, filled with contempt for the feeble liberal compromises of 1848, with no illusions about the prospects of freedom in the west, determined on more ruthless methods; accepting as true only what the sciences can prove, prepared to be hard and, if need be, unscrupulous and cruel, in order to break the power of their equally ruthless oppressors; bitterly hostile to the aestheticism, the devotion to civilised values, of the 'soft' generation of the 40s.

Herzen realised that the criticism and abuse showered upon him as an obsolete aristocratic dilettante by these 'nihilists' (as they came to be called after Turgenev's novel *Fathers and Children*, in which this conflict is vividly presented for the first time) was not altogether different from the disdain that he had himself felt in his own youth for the elegant and ineffective reformers of Alexander I's reign; but this did not make his position easier to bear. What was ill-received by the tough-minded revolutionaries pleased Tolstoy, who said more than once that the censorship of Herzen's works in Russia was a characteristic blunder on the part of the government; the government, in its anxiety to stop young men from marching towards the revolutionary morass, seized them and swept them off to Siberia or prison long before they were even in sight of it, while they were still on the broad highway; Herzen had trodden this very path, he had seen the chasm, and warned against it, particularly in his *Letters to an Old Comrade*. Nothing, Tolstoy argued, would have proved a better antidote to the 'revolutionary nihilism' which Tolstoy condemned than Herzen's brilliant analyses. 'Our Russian life would not have been the same during the last twenty years if [Herzen] had not been kept from the younger generation.'[1] Suppression of his books, Tolstoy went on, was both a criminal, and from the point of view of those who did not desire a violent revolution, an idiotic policy.

At other times, Tolstoy was less generous. In 1860, six months before they met, he had been reading Herzen's writings with mingled admiration and irritation: 'Herzen is a man of scattered intellect, and morbid *amour propre*,' he wrote in his diary, 'but his breadth, ability, goodness, elegance of mind are Russian.'[2] From time to time various correspondents record the fact that Tolstoy read Herzen, at times aloud to his family, with the greatest admiration. In 1896, during one of his angriest, most anti-rationalist moods, he said, 'In spite of his enormous talent, what did he say that was new or useful?'[3] – as for

[1] Letter to N. N. Gay senior of 13 February 1888. See also letter to N. G. Chertkov of 9 February 1888.

[2] Diary entry for 4 August 1860.

[3] Diary entry for 17 May 1896. But on 12 October 1905 he writes in his diary that he is reading Herzen's *From the Other Shore*, and says 'Our intelligentsia has sunk so low that . . . it cannot understand him.'

the argument that the generation of the 40s could not say what it wanted to say because of the rigid Russian censorship, Herzen wrote in perfect freedom in Paris and yet 'managed to say nothing useful'.[1] What irritated Tolstoy most was Herzen's socialism. In a letter to his aunt, Alexandra Tolstoy, he says that he despises Herzen's proclamations, which the Russian police suspect him of harbouring.[2] The fact that he believed in politics as a weapon was sufficient to condemn him in Tolstoy's eyes. From 1862 onwards, Tolstoy had declared his hostility to faith in liberal reform and improvement of human life by legal or institutional change. Herzen fell under this general ban. Moreover, Tolstoy seems to have felt a certain lack of personal sympathy for Herzen and his public position – even a kind of jealousy. When, in moments of acute discouragement and irritation, Tolstoy spoke (perhaps not very seriously) of leaving Russia for ever, he would say that whatever he did, he would not join Herzen or march under his banner : 'he goes his way, I shall go mine'.[3]

He seriously underrated Herzen's revolutionary temperament and instincts. However sceptical Herzen may have been of specific revolutionary doctrines or plans in Russia – and no one was more so – he believed to the end of his life in the moral and social need and the inevitability, sooner or later, of a revolution in Russia – a violent transformation followed by a just, that is a socialist, order. He did not, it is true, close his eyes to the possibility, even the probability, that the great rebellion would extinguish values to which he was himself dedicated – in particular, the freedoms without which he and others like him could not breathe. Nevertheless, he recognised not only the inevitability but the historic justice of the coming cataclysm. His moral tastes, his respect for human values, his entire style of life, divided him from the tough-minded younger radicals of the 60s, but he did not, despite all his distrust of political fanaticism, whether on the right or on the left, turn into a cautious, reformist liberal constitutionalist. Even in his gradualist phase he remained an agitator, an egalitarian and a socialist to the end. It is this in him that both the Russian populists and the Russian Marxists – both Mikhailovsky and Lenin – recognised and saluted.

It was not prudence or moderation that led him to his unwavering support of Poland in her insurrection against Russia in 1863. The wave of passionate Russian nationalism which accompanied its sup-

[1] Diary entry for 17 May 1896.   [2] Letter of 22–3(?) July 1862.
[3] Letter to his aunt, Countess A. A. Tolstaya, 7 August 1862.

pression robbed him of sympathy even among Russian liberals. *The Bell* declined in circulation. The new, 'hard' revolutionaries needed his money, but made it plain that they looked upon him as a liberal dinosaur, the preacher of antiquated humanistic views, useless in the violent social struggle to come. He left London in the late 60s and attempted to produce a French edition of *The Bell* in Geneva. When that too failed, he visited his friends in Florence, returning to Paris early in 1870, before the outbreak of the Franco-Prussian War. There he died of pleurisy, broken both morally and physically, but not disillusioned; still writing with concentrated intelligence and force. His body was taken to Nice, where he is buried beside his wife. A life-size statue still marks his grave.

Herzen's ideas have long since entered into the general texture of Russian political thought — liberals and radicals, populists and anarchists, socialists and communists, have all claimed him as an ancestor. But what survives today of all that unceasing and feverish activity, even in his native country, is not a system or a doctrine but a handful of essays, some remarkable letters, and the extraordinary amalgam of memory, observation, moral passion, psychological analysis and political description, wedded to a major literary talent, which has immortalised his name. What remains is, above all, a passionate and inextinguishable temperament and a sense of the movement of nature and of its unpredictable possibilities, which he felt with an intensity which not even his uniquely rich and flexible prose could fully express.

He believed that the ultimate goal of life was life itself; that the day and the hour were ends in themselves, not a means to another day or another experience. He believed that remote ends were a dream, that faith in them was a fatal illusion; that to sacrifice the present or the immediate and foreseeable future to these distant ends must always lead to cruel and futile forms of human sacrifice. He believed that values were not found in an impersonal, objective realm, but were created by human beings, changed with the generations of men, but were none the less binding upon those who lived in their light; that suffering was inescapable, and infallible knowledge neither attainable nor needed. He believed in reason, scientific methods, individual action, empirically discovered truths; but he tended to suspect that faith in general formulas, laws, prescription in human affairs was an attempt, sometimes catastrophic, always irrational, to escape from the uncertainty and unpredictable variety of life to the false security of our own symmetrical fantasies. He was fully conscious of what he believed. He had obtained this knowledge at the cost of painful, and, at times, unintended, self-analysis, and he described what he saw in language of exceptional vitality, precision and poetry. His purely personal credo remained unaltered from his earliest days: 'Art, and the summer lightning of individual happiness: these are the only real goods we have,' he declared in a self-revealing passage of the kind that so deeply shocked the stern young Russian revolutionaries in the 60s. Yet even they and their descendants did not and do not reject his artistic and intellectual achievement.

Herzen was not, and had no desire to be, an impartial observer. No less than the poets and the novelists of his nation, he created a style, an outlook, and, in the words of Gorky's tribute to him, 'an entire province, a country astonishingly rich in ideas',[1] where everything is immediately recognisable as being his and his alone, a country into which he transplants all that he touches, in which things, sensations, feelings, persons, ideas, private and public events, institutions, entire cultures, are given shape and life by his powerful and coherent historical imagination, and have stood up against the forces of decay in the solid world which his memory, his intelligence and his artistic genius recovered and reconstructed. *My Past and Thoughts* is the Noah's ark in which he saved himself, and not himself alone, from the destructive flood in which many idealistic radicals of the 40s were drowned. Genuine art survives and transcends its immediate purpose. The structure that Herzen built in the first place, perhaps, for his own personal salvation, built out of material provided by his own predicament – out of exile, solitude, despair – survives intact. Written abroad, concerned largely with European issues and figures, these reminiscences are a great permanent monument to the civilised, sensitive, morally preoccupied and gifted Russian society to which Herzen belonged; their vitality and fascination have not declined in the hundred years and more that have passed since the first chapters saw the light.

---

[1] M. Gorky, *Istoriya russkoy literatury* (Moscow, 1939), p. 206.

The Life and Opinions of Moses Hess

MOSES HESS was both a communist and a Zionist. He played a decisive role in the history of the first movement, he virtually invented the second. Indeed this remarkable fact is his chief, perhaps his sole, claim to fame. Nevertheless, in the course of his troubled and dedicated life, Hess uttered some highly original and telling judgements, that have not, even now, obtained the recognition that they seem to me to deserve. He was a prophet without much honour in his own generation, certainly none in his own country. Yet much of what he said was new and, as it has turned out, both important and true. In particular he detected in the life both of European society in general, and of the European Jews in particular, symptoms of what, he feared, was a fatal disease; or, if not fatal, at any rate dangerous. Against it he offered remedies which, whether or not they were effective, were at any rate specific proposals capable of being realised, and not cries of self-pity, or empty forms of words, or vague and idle dreams. His theses were indeed dismissed at the time of their utterance, as being some, or all, of these things. But this verdict seems to me wholly unjust. The counter-thesis that I should like to offer is that Hess was, at any rate after 1848, an exceptionally penetrating and independent thinker who understood and formulated the problems with which he was dealing more clearly than the majority of his critics, whose rival diagnoses, admired for their wisdom in their own day, have stood up badly to the test of time. But even if I am mistaken about this, the questions that Hess raised, in the form in which he raised them, are exceedingly live issues today, and have become, if anything, more critical than they were in his own lifetime. Even if he had no other claim on our attention, this would, I think, be sufficient in itself.

I

Moses Hess was born in 1812, in the city of Bonn, into a Jewish family whose forbears may have come from Poland. His parents belonged to that generation of German Jews which had been freed by the French wars of liberation. Between 1795 and 1814 Bonn was under French rule; the gates of the Jewish ghetto were flung wide open, and its inmates, after centuries of being driven in upon themselves, were permitted to emerge into the light of day. Personal freedom (or at any rate an enlarged measure of it), economic opportunity, secular knowledge, liberal ideas, acted like a heady wine upon the children of the newly emancipated Jews. When, in 1815, after the final defeat of Napoleon, the Rhineland was annexed to Prussia, and King Frederick William III made an attempt to return to ancient ways, the reimposition of most of the old restrictions on the Jews of his kingdom produced a crisis among the newly liberated. Some among them could not bear the thought of a return to their former degraded status, and accepted baptism with varying degrees of sincere conviction. The radical journalist, Ludwig Börne, changed his name and his faith on the same day; so too did Heinrich Marx, the father of Karl Marx. The poet Heine, the jurist Eduard Gans, Ludwig Stahl (who later founded the Christian Social Party), the children of the philosopher Moses Mendelssohn, were the best known converts to Christianity. Others reacted in the opposite direction. For reasons both of genuine piety and of pride, they became even more fiercely attached to their ancient religion. Amongst these were the members of Hess's family. In 1817 his father moved to Cologne, where he established a sugar refinery, soon grew prosperous, and in due course became head of the Jewish community of the city. The boy, aged five, was left behind in Bonn, where his devoutly religious maternal grandfather gave him a traditional Jewish upbringing, and a solid knowledge of the Bible, the Talmud and the medieval commentaries. Almost half a century later Hess gave a moving account of this single-minded old merchant, who could not hold back his tears when he spoke of the destruction of the temple in Jerusalem and the dispersion of the Jews. There is no doubt that his early education affected Hess indelibly: images and symbols drawn from the history of the Jews remained with him to the end of his life. One may, perhaps, permit oneself to wonder about the consequences to the world, had Karl Marx, the grandson of a rabbi, been brought up in this fashion, and not (as in fact he was) on a diet of eighteenth-century rationalism by a father who was a mild follower of Voltaire.

Hess's mother died when he was fourteen, and he then went to live in his father's house in Cologne. When he was eighteen, he was reluctantly allowed by his father to go to the university of Bonn. There is no evidence of what happened to him there. Indeed, it is dubious whether he even matriculated. At any rate, the experience seems to have left no impression upon him. We know little about him at this time; only that, in common with a good many other idealistic young men in Germany, he was deeply affected by the mystical nationalism and romanticism which then was sweeping over the German intelligentsia.

His father wished him to enter his own expanding business. Moritz Hess, as he was called at this time, flatly declined. He appears to have had no clear idea of what he wanted to do. He wished only to serve mankind, help the destitute, liberate the oppressed and, above all, not make money, since this appeared to him bourgeois egotism in its most repulsive form. He quarrelled with his father, and left his parents' house with a very small sum of money in his pocket, to see the world, or at any rate Europe. He went to England, where he starved miserably, then to Holland and France. He was in Paris in 1832, and it was perhaps among the poor German émigrés – mostly left-wing exiles – that he imbibed the radical ideas then in vogue in that relatively free capital.[1] The revolution of 1830 had created immense hopes among the liberals of Europe, and Paris was fermenting with socialist sects and ideas, especially those affected by Saint-Simonian and Fourierist doctrines, which, by and large, called upon men to recognise and fight the evils of cut-throat competition and individual enterprise and the strife and destruction of both the bodies and the souls of men inevitably entailed by them, and instead to cooperate in collective undertakings that would release the great productive energies of mankind in a planned and harmonious manner, and create universal prosperity, justice and happiness on earth. Some of these men were confused dreamers. Others were acute and highly practical organisers who understood the revolutionary consequences of technological progress. Idealistic and short-lived communist colonies in America and elsewhere sprang from the former strain. From the latter grew the Suez and Panama canals, the new railway system of France, and novel technocratic notions and institutions of many sorts, from the industrial monopolies to the New Deal, from vast cartels and state-owned

---

[1] Doubt is thrown upon this by Edmund Silberner, 'Der junge Moses Hess im Lichte bisher unerschlossener Quellen', *International Review of Social History* 3 (1958), 43–70, 239–68.

enterprises to five-year plans and the welfare state. The most radical of these trends was the continuing underground tradition of out-and-out communism, preached by the proscribed followers of the executed revolutionary Babeuf, who declared that not merely the love, but the possession, of private property was the root of all evil, and that justice or liberty were not possible without complete social and economic equality which, in its turn, depended upon the total abolition of inheritance and of virtually all private ownership.

Hess accepted these doctrines fervently, adding to them his own enthusiastic faith in the romantic intuitionism preached by the disciples of Fichte and Schelling, together with what he understood of Spinoza, whom the romantics affected to admire; and, like other radical young intellectuals of his generation, tried to cast this odd amalgam into the mould of the great dominant philosophy of that time – the Hegelian system. Totally destitute, he returned to Cologne on foot, made his peace with his father, and was appointed a clerk in the family sugar refinery. This, as might have been foreseen, ended in complete failure.

He finally abandoned his father's house, scraped together a sum of money sufficient to keep him alive for a few months, and, anxious to say his own, personal word in the metaphysical debates that (partly as a result of government censorship) took the place of political discussion in Germany in his day, composed a treatise embodying his entire *Weltanschauung*. This metaphysical philosophy of history, full of Hegelian clichés, published in 1837, was called *The Sacred History of Mankind by a Young Disciple of Spinoza*, and today is virtually unreadable. Although the title claims the inspiration of Spinoza, apart from a vague rationalism, and belief in the unity of all creation, the text has little to do with the great seventeenth-century master; its inspiration is more that of romantic Protestant theology: the spirit is that of Schleiermacher. The central thesis is that in the beginning men lived in an undifferentiated unity of spirit and matter – a condition of primitive communism that preceded the invention of property. This period is carefully divided by the author into fourteen subperiods each dominated by a great leader. This original unity was broken by Christianity, which began by reconciling spirit with matter, but, in its distorted medieval form, exaggerated the spirit, and led to a one-sided mysticism. The dynamic process of the Hegelian historical dialectic will, however, set this right. It is the task of modern man, armed with consciousness of his historic mission, to create a rational harmony of matter and spirit, as preached by Schelling in Germany –

though, in the author's view, with too much emphasis on spirit; and by Saint-Simon in France – though with too much emphasis on matter. This harmony is to be embodied in a new dispensation – 'social humanity' – in which the evil institution of private property – the social form of covetous greed – together with competition and the division of labour by which men are brutalised and dehumanised into the semblance of mere animate property – so much raw material to be exploited by an élite of capitalists – will at long last be abolished. Thus the Hebrew prophets – the truest heralds of the new world – will at last be vindicated. To achieve this ideal men must (in the spirit of Fichte) obey the moral imperative of seeking after the holy life of reciprocal self-sacrifice. The Jews are mentioned by Hess only to be dismissed as embodying a preliminary stage superseded by Christianity. The ancient Jewish state is to be admired, indeed, as representing a unity – a fusion of state, church, religion, and political and social life – a single set of principles regulating the whole of human life. Men have wandered from God, but they will return to Him, and 'the ancient law will rise again, transfigured. . .'. In this way the Jews will disappear as a people, but not before they have conquered the world spiritually. Thereby their special mission will be fulfilled. Indeed their part is over already, for they have been rendered obsolete by Christianity, and they are counselled to leave the stage of history. 'The people chosen by their God must disappear for ever, that out of its death might spring a new, more precious life.'

All this was no worse, but certainly no better, than the farrago of metaphysics, social messianism, and personal ardour that constituted the normal matter of the innumerable historico-theological systems with which German universities were at this time flooding the philosophical public. Most of these treatises were deeply religious in spirit and purpose, being attempts to find in art or science the path to individual or national salvation which the orthodox Christian churches seemed no longer capable of providing for critical minds. Some sought substitutes for religion in literature, in music, in varieties of mystical experience. Others, perhaps the majority of such spiritually *désoeuvrés*, at any rate in countries under German influence, sought for the answer in history as the progressive revelation of the ways of God or the Absolute Spirit, and this led to the schools of what is best called historiosophy – the attempt to make history do the work of theology or speculative metaphysics – of which the most celebrated are the movements associated with the names of Schelling, Hegel, Comte,

Spengler, and to some degree, Marx and the disciples of Darwin. Arnold Toynbee was the leading, it may be the last, representative of this type of secular messianism in our day.

The Sacred History of Mankind found no readers, and is today deservedly forgotten. It is of interest only because it shows that, even in this early phase, Hess was a fully-fledged socialist, indeed the earliest German socialist – the first faithful German disciple of the French egalitarians – a belated, somewhat idealistic, German Babouvist. Moreover, it established Hess as a member of the avant-garde philosophical left – the Young Hegelians of extreme radical views. All the disciples of Hegel believed that their master had discovered the true pattern of human history, which lay in perpetual movement towards increasing rationality and freedom, that is to say, a state in which more and more men would comprehend more and more clearly what the logically inevitable purposes of the Universal Spirit must be – whither history, revealing its nature and direction to itself, in the form of the critical and creative human spirit, was developing. This growth of self-awareness on the part of the universe conceived as an active subject – a spirit or organism – takes the form of the increase of rational knowledge among men, and therefore of their power over nature and over themselves, that is, their freedom, and thereby brings the millennium nearer. According to Hegelians of all shades of opinion this process consisted in the perpetual struggle and collision of forces at every 'level' – social, intellectual, economic, political, physical – leading to crises (that sometimes took the form of social revolutions), each of which marked a stage in the ascent of the 'World Spirit'. The left-wing Hegelians interpreted this as meaning that the essential function of the most advanced elements in society – the most rational, the most conscious of what they were, what stage they had reached, and whither the next inevitable step in the ascent of the Spirit must lead – was essentially destructive, destructive of whatever was static, dead, literally stupid, frozen, irrational, whatever obstructed self-criticism and thereby the progress of humanity towards its goal. In their view absolute rationality meant the attainment by humanity of absolute freedom over itself and over its environment; and this could be achieved only by actively removing the obstacles to such emancipation – a view that carried plainly revolutionary implications. Some young Hegelians confined their radicalism to the realms of theory, and spent their energies on subverting traditional beliefs – mainly religious and metaphysical – like David Friedrich Strauss with his boldly iconoclastic

Life of Jesus, or Feuerbach and the brothers Bauer who, in their different ways, interpreted religion in terms of social mythology. Others went farther, and, like the eighteenth-century materialists, held that unless the social and psychological conditions which had kept men in ignorance, and given birth to the religious or social or political illusions that had reconciled humanity to its helplessness and misery, were themselves destroyed, no true progress could be made. Among these were such young philosophical amateurs as Arnold Ruge, Friedrich Engels and, the best known of all, Karl Marx.

Hess felt it craven to be anywhere but in the forefront of this battle for the soul of mankind. He was twenty-five years old, a generous, high-minded, kindly, touchingly pure-hearted, enthusiastic, not over-astute young man, ready, indeed eager, to suffer for his ideas, filled with love of humanity, optimism, a passion for abstractions, and aversion from the world of practical affairs towards which the more hard-headed members of his family were trying to steer him. His marriage tells us more of his character and temperament than anything else. He met in Cologne, and married, a poor seamstress – sometimes referred to as a prostitute in the writings about him[1] – not, apparently, because he had fallen in love with her, but in order to redress the injustice perpetrated by society; he wished to perform an act expressive of the need for love among men and for equality between them. So far as we know he lived in complete harmony and happiness with his wife for the rest of his days. Sibylle Hess, who was a gentile, worshipped him to the end of his life, occasionally deceived him (against which he protested, but not very strongly), and shared his poverty with the greatest devotion. It was perhaps this childlike quality – Hess's unworldliness and purity of character, rising at moments to genuine saintliness[2] – that so deeply irritated the tough-minded 'realists' among his fellow socialists, who looked on him as a benevolent ass. Yet even

---

[1] Sibylle Pesch was described as a street-walker in a Cologne police dossier of 1854, and Hess's family seems to have believed something of this kind. Edmund Silberner, in his definitive biography of Hess, throws some doubt on this and finds that the evidence is inconclusive. All that we know is that Sibylle was and remained a pious Catholic, and that Hess did not marry her until his father's death, perhaps for fear of upsetting him too deeply.

[2] Hess's moral character has a strong affinity with Dostoevsky's ideal of the 'positively good man' embodied in the heroes of *The Idiot* and *The Brothers Karamazov*. A Jewish communist is the last human type in which Dostoevsky would have looked for any semblance to his ideal.

Marx, who utterly despised him, could discover no moral view or fault to cast in his teeth.

Hess spent the next four years in intensive reading of books about philosophy and social theory, still supported, we must surmise, by his irritated, but far from heartless family. His next volume, which appeared in 1841, attracted more attention. *The European Triarchy* is a primarily political treatise, an answer to a now even more forgotten work called *The European Pentarchy* that advocated the parcelling out of Europe between the five great powers; and it represents an advance in its author's social and political views. The only salvation of mankind lies, we are told, in the universal adoption of socialism, in particular in the abolition of private property.[1] The reason for this is not the need for economic efficiency, nor the inexorable demands of history, nor the emergence of a particular class – the proletariat – at war with other classes, which is destined inevitably to destroy or supersede all its rivals, but quite simply that socialism alone is just. Hess, in sharp contrast to Marx and his school, even while he fully accepts the analysis of society into social-economic classes, does not believe that class conflict is either desirable or inevitable. He is a socialist, indeed a communist, because he thinks that all egoism – like all domination – is destructive of the human personality and frustrates master and slave alike, inasmuch as individual faculties can never be developed fully in conditions of competition, but only in harmonious collaboration with others, as the French socialists – Saint-Simon and Fourier – had conclusively shown. Communism for Hess was the sole form of social altruism realisable in the historical conditions of the age. (In 1843 he describes it as being simply 'practical ethics'.) He did not attempt to give a detailed analysis of the structure or needs of the proletariat, largely because (like his fellow radicals, Marx, Ruge, Engels, Grün, Feuerbach and the brothers Bauer) he had personally met too few members of this class, and was a good deal more honest than most of his allies. History for him is a struggle of

[1] Edmund Silberner, in his very illuminating article on Moses Hess in *Historia Judaica* 13 (1951), 3–28, describes the doctrine of this book, despite its advocacy of the abolition of private inheritance and the community of ownership, as not quite tantamount to socialism. I am not sure that I understand what, in his opinion, distinguishes Hess's doctrine from, at any rate, the stock French socialism of his time. Hess does not, it is true, go so far as Cabet, but he is certainly at least as socialist as, say, Louis Blanc, and more so than the Fourierists or Proudhon.

self-assertive egoism (of individuals or classes or nations) with the opposite principles of altruism, love and social justice. The fact that the belief in equality, solidarity and justice had always represented, at any rate, the professed aspirations of men, proves that these qualities flow from man's true nature. Rational and harmonious cooperation between men is possible (sometimes appeal is made to the authority of Spinoza or Hegel, sometimes to the theses of the French *philosophes*) but it must always be fought for. Human happiness lies in human hands, and if enough individuals can be convinced of the truth of the propositions advanced by the author, human beings will be enabled to create their own happiness. The 'scientific' socialists – Marx and his tough-minded followers – later poured derision on this 'Utopian', 'rose-water', 'humanitarian' doctrine as an absurdly idealistic, ineffective kind of socialism, suspended in a timeless void, abstract, unhistorical, not evolved out of insight into concrete social conditions; and represented their own brand of socialism as superior, if only in virtue of the fact that it was 'deduced' from the concrete facts – that it was not something the realisation of which turned on luck or accident, on what might or might not happen, that depended upon the precarious goodwill of this or that group of men, or on this or that set of unpredictable circumstances. Marx genuinely believed (as in a sense Hegel believed before him) that what alone made a cause worth fighting for was that it represented the inevitable next stage in the social evolution of men as rational beings, a stage that could be determined accurately only by means of scientific analysis and prediction. The social revolution – the expropriation of the owners of property and their replacement by public ownership, and the victory of the propertyless class – was, on this view, in any case inevitable; for this reason it was what rational men would pursue simply because they knew that to seek after anything else, to identify themselves with any other group of persons, was automatically to ignore the social 'reality' by which any individual, and his ideas, were determined, and consequently to court destruction by the forces of history – something that only fools or madmen could want.

Hess would have none of this. He believed that social equality was desirable because it was just, not because it was inevitable; nor was justice to be identified with whatever was bound, in any case, to emerge from the womb of time. All kinds of bad and irrational conditions had been produced before now, and persisted. Nothing was to be accepted merely because it had occurred – but solely because it was objectively good. Hegelian historicism had evidently not struck so deep in him after all; heretical as this was, he stoutly maintained that the only way to achieve social justice, the abolition of poverty and the equitable distribution of the ever more plentiful goods (which, owing to maldistribution, were breeding more misery than happiness) was by the conscious will of men convinced of the moral necessity of their action. One could, and one had a duty to, convince men by rational argument that if they turned their resources into productive and harmonious channels, they would be better off both materially and morally; this was Hess's 'True Socialism' – the Utopian sentimentalism for which Marx and Engels mocked him so bitterly.[1] They called him Rabbi Moses and Rabbi Hess, and laughed his theses to scorn.

And yet, in the light of our later experience, it almost seems as if Hess, with his *naïveté*, his traditional Jewish morality, his pleas for justice and his quotations from Spinoza and the Bible, may not, after all, have been as profoundly mistaken as the more celebrated founders of 'scientific' socialism. The exacerbation of the class war, as predicted and encouraged by Marx and Engels, has in due course occurred. The revolution for which they worked has, in one form or another, transformed the lives of large portions of the human race. But it seems clear that where this occurred in accordance with Marxist principles and tactics, that is to say by means of the violent expropriation of the property-owning classes, the mere fact of the abolition of private property and the creation of the dictatorship of the communist party (or a committee of it) claiming to represent the proletariat, have not, by themselves, brought about internal or external harmony, or economic equality, or personal liberty or social justice. And, on the other hand, wherever these ideals have been realised or, at any rate, approached, this seems to have been, almost invariably, the result of the conscious effort of individuals working for them as ends in themselves, under no illusion that they embodied the inexorable forces of history or any other agency; least of all the work of men disposed to deceive themselves or others by systematically representing what would normally be recognised as acts of cruelty, exploitation, injustice

---

[1] His views at this time (1843) are very clearly set out in two articles, 'Sozialismus und Kommunismus' and 'Philosophie der That', in an émigré anthology called *Einundzwanzig Bogen aus der Schweiz*, as well as in his articles in the Paris *Vorwärts*, the *Deutsch-Französische Jahrbücher*, and *Der Sprecher*, edited by Karl Grün in Wesel.

and oppression as being mysteriously transformed into virtuous actions, or at least means to virtue, by the sanctifying process of historical necessity – the inexorable march of 'God in history' – the historical dialectic.

Throughout his life Hess's socialism remains founded on purely moral premises. In this respect his opinions resemble those of the nineteenth-century Christian socialists, or the Russian Socialist-Revolutionaries, or the British and Scandinavian socialists of our time, far more than those of Marxists and other 'realists'. Hess wants the abolition of private property because he thinks that men will not cease to fight and oppress one another, and will not cease to be themselves poisoned by the injustice they breed, unless they live a social or communal life; and to this type of life he thinks private property to be a fatal obstacle. Private property must be abolished. But unless the reform is carried out with full moral realisation of what its purpose is, it will achieve nothing. Mere mechanical abolition of private property is certainly not enough. There must be a change of heart. But this cannot happen until the material and institutional conditions which have hardened men's hearts are themselves altered. Yet the mere alteration of this framework will not by itself produce the required spiritual transformation, unless the moral principles which alone are worthy of free men are understood and consciously applied.

These moral principles belong to all men as such, and are recognised even if they are not acted upon by all men in some degree, but most clearly by the best and wisest. These principles are not necessarily those of only one given class, even though the demands of an oppressed class embody them more genuinely than the demands of those who gain by such oppression. This is the notion of 'abstract humanity' with which Marxists charge Hess and the other Utopians; as if the concept of the 'class of the exploited' is any less abstract. Hess's creed derived from these principles from first to last. His socialism, and later his Zionism, are direct consequences of it. Those who find the concept of class rights more real than that of human rights, as well as those who find comfort in believing men to be agents of impersonal forces that will secure the victory for their own group soon or late, whatever their opponents may wish or think, that is to say, all natural Hegelians, Marxists, Calvinists, and other extreme determinists, particularly in the fields of politics or social life, will inevitably find Hess both unrealistic and unsympathetic.

The European Triarchy in particular advocated the union of the three civilised powers in Europe: Germany, the home of ideas and the champion of religious liberty; France, the battlefield on which effective social reform and political independence had been won; and England, the home of economic freedom, and moreover itself the synthesis of the French and German spirit – neither 'over-speculative' like Germany, nor 'vulgarly' materialistic like France. These three powers must unite against Russia, the reservoir of reaction, the home of barbarian repression threatening to engulf Europe and trample upon its liberties. Appeals for union against Russia as an enemy of the west were, by then, common enough in Germany and, indeed, elsewhere in Europe. The only originality of Hess's book consisted in the fact that it tied this familiar proposal to the necessity for radical social reform, and of 'peaceful revolution' (he believed that violence bred violence and destroyed the soil for peaceful reconstruction), as being alone likely to save Europe from collapsing under the weight of the contradictions of its capitalist system of production and distribution.

The book attracted some attention. Hess was revealed to the German intellectual world as an eloquent left-wing agitator, and in the course of the next two years was offered, and accepted, various journalistic posts, which brought him into close contact with other like-minded young men, notably Engels, Marx and Ruge. The first and fieriest German Hegelian to turn communist, Hess converted the young Friedrich Engels to his creed.[1] He met Marx in 1841, and although the latter had had some inkling of current communist doctrines from the book published in Germany by Lorenz Stein which gave an account of the views of the leaders of the French communist sects, it was most probably Hess's hot eloquence that first shook the foundations of his faith in Hegelian political theory with its deification of the bureaucratic state as the expression of human reason and discipline, and turned him on to the path of militant social collectivism. There were of course passages in Hess's book which cannot have satisfied Marx even then. The ethical tone, but, even more, the frequent references to the Hebrew prophets, and the prevalence of Hebraic motifs generally, had never been to his taste. Marx himself, as is only too plain, decided to eliminate this particular source of embarrassment once and for all from his life. He had no intention of

[1] In an article in the Owenite journal *The New Moral World*, Engels says that Hess was the first young Hegelian to become a communist. *New Moral World* No 21, 18 November 1843: see Karl Marx, Friedrich Engels, *Collected Works* (London/New York/Moscow, 1975–), vol. 3 (1975), p. 406.

going through the torments of an ambivalent status such as afflicted more sensitive and less ruthless natures, such Jews as Börne, for instance, or Heine or Lassalle or Disraeli, throughout their mature lives. All his bitter and exasperated feeling against the discrimination practised against himself he transferred by a bold, if not altogether conscious, stroke to a much vaster field : by identifying his own grievances with those of the insulted and the oppressed everywhere, and in particular with those of the proletariat, he achieved his own psychological emancipation. It was in the name of the oppressed workers that he thundered, of a great symbolic multitude – impersonal, remote from his own world and his own wounds – not of his own painful humiliation as a former Jew denied a professorial chair; it was for them alone that he demanded and prophesied justice, revenge, destruction. As for the Jews, in an essay written two years after he met Hess, he declared them simply to be a repellent symptom of a social *malaise* of the time, an excrescence upon the social body – not a race, or a nation, or even a religion to be saved by conversion to some other faith or way of life, but a collection of parasites, a gang of money-lenders rendered inevitable by the economically self-contradictory and unjust society that had generated them – to be eliminated as a group by the final solution to all social ills – the coming, inescapable, universal, social revolution. The violently anti-Semitic tone of this essay, which Engels more feebly echoes (anti-Semitism was not uncommon among socialists of that, or indeed later, time), became more and more characteristic of Marx in his later years. It affected the attitudes of communists, particularly Jewish communists, towards the Jews, and is one of the most neurotic and revolting aspects of his masterful but vulgar personality. The tone adopted by Hess was profoundly different. Hess's actual opinions were not very different from those of Marx or any other young Hegelian radical of this time. Like them, he identified emancipated Jews of his time with capitalism and its evils. He refers to them with open dislike and contempt as so many grasping financiers – 'moneybags': they are for him the epitome of the acquisitive spirit. Nevertheless, the tone is different from that of either the tormented Heine or the troubled Marx. But he did not suffer from a self-hatred that made him wish to commit acts of violence against his nature. He did not try to cut the traces of his origins out of himself, because he did not feel it as a malignant growth that was suffocating him and of which he was ashamed. In *The European Triarchy* he merely repeated what he had said some four years earlier – that the task of the Jews was to disperse and assimilate – they had served their turn in making first Christianity, and after that (inasmuch as Judaism stresses social ties more than Christianity) social regeneration by communism possible; they had acted as a 'goad' and a 'ferment' that has promoted the 'mobility' of the west and prevented it from stagnating like China, but this function was now over. Because they had rejected Christianity, they were now a mere ghostly presence 'unable either to die or to come to life', a mere skeleton, a fossil, and it was time that they married gentiles and disappeared. The 'Triarchy' of the civilised great powers would emancipate them fully, and give them the rights of men and citizens; but their real emancipation would occur only when all hatred and contempt for them on the part of others disappeared. In short he repeated the noble commonplaces that have formed the staple doctrine of liberal assimilationists everywhere and at all times.

The act of apostasy constituted by this creed precipitated the final rupture between him and his devotedly Jewish father. Yet this is not the whole story of Hess's feelings about the Jews even at this time. In 1840, in Damascus, a Jew was accused and convicted of committing an act of ritual murder. Anti-Jewish disorders followed. The repercussions of this terrible and ancient slander led to agitation by the horrified Jews of France and England, scandalised their sympathisers everywhere, and ended in some redress for this injustice obtained by the Montefiore-Crémieux mission. Hess reacted painfully to this incident, and for the first time, so he tells us later, began to wonder whether the general solution that he advocated for all human ills would, in fact, automatically cure those of the Jews also. In the same year, during the great wave of anti-French chauvinism which passed over Germany at that time, he came across a Francophobe hymn by the poet Becker, and in a burst of patriotic feeling set it to music and sent his composition to the author. Becker sent an icily polite reply with an anti-Semitic scribble[1] in a disguised, but still recognisable, hand on the back of the envelope. Hess was dreadfully upset; but as a rationalist and socialist, decided to conquer his feelings both about Damascus and about Becker. These, he tried to say to himself, were the aberrations of a society in its death throes. The social regeneration of mankind would make them for ever impossible.

[1] 'Du bist ein Jud.' *Rom und Jerusalem, die Nationalitätsfrage* (Leipzig, 1862) (hereafter *R.J.*), letter 5, p. 25. Subsequent references to the letters of *R.J.* are given by letter and page, thus: V 25.

There was no room in the universal society of the future for sectional religions or interests. The Jews must scatter and vanish as a historical entity. A universal religion must replace a purely national one. If the Jews could not bring themselves to accept baptism for themselves, at least they must baptise their children; in this way the 'Judaeo-Christian tradesmen's world' would end in dignified dissolution. In any case the sufferings of the proletariat were surely a greater and more urgent cause than those of the Jews, however painful and undeserved. Hess repressed his wounded feelings, at any rate for the time being. Doctrine – helped out with special pleading – triumphed over the direct evidence of experience.[1] This is the prototype of the story of many a Jewish socialist and communist since his day. It is to Hess's eternal credit that he was among the few to recognise, before his life was done, that this comforting theory rested on a fallacy; not an ignoble fallacy, perhaps, but still delusive. Twenty years later, having diagnosed it as such, he proclaimed his results to the world, with great simplicity and courage. At no moment in his life did he have anything to hide. He made mistakes, since he was often naïve and uncritical. He was saved by his moral insight, which remained uncontaminated by personal vanity or dogma. And his conscience was always clear.

The time of disenchantment was still to come. In 1841 Hess fell under the spell of the brilliance and boldness of Karl Marx's views. He met Marx in August of that year, preached communism to him, and early in September wrote[2] to his sceptical friend Auerbach:

---

[1] But not entirely. In *R.J.*, Hess mentions a manuscript composed at this time proclaiming the need for self-determination as a solution for the Jewish problem. The fate of this *esquisse* is unknown: most probably Hess incorporated it in *R.J.* But there does survive a fragment of this early period, which, as Edmund Silberner, its discoverer, has been good enough to tell me, declared the need for a Jewish nationhood. This demonstrates that Hess did not, as might otherwise have been suspected, unconsciously antedate the moment at which he first conceived the idea of the Jewish state. But at this stage it was probably no more than a bold fantasy. The young Lassalle, too, toyed with the notion of a new Judaea at this time. The 1830s and 40s are rich in extravagant political schemes. Nevertheless, despite occasional moods of this kind, Hess was wholly anti-nationalist at this period, and consciously rejected the Zionist ideas which had suggested themselves insistently to him and to which he was later to return.

[2] Cologne, 2 September 1841. See Karl Marx, Friedrich Engels, *Historisch-kritische Gesamtausgabe*, Abteilung 1, Band 1. 2 (Berlin, 1929), pp. 260–1.

He is the greatest, perhaps the only true philosopher actually now alive . . . Dr Marx – that is the name of my idol – is still a very young man (about twenty-four at the most), and will strike the final death blow at medieval religion and politics. He combines philosophical depth with a most biting wit: imagine Rousseau, Voltaire, Holbach, Lessing, Heine and Hegel – not thrown together anyhow, but fused into a single personality – and you will have Dr Marx.

With Marx he collaborated on the radical *Rheinische Zeitung,* until things became too hot for him in the Rhineland. Accused – justly enough – of being the original fountainhead of violent communist agitation in Germany (a strange historical responsibility to bear for a peace-loving idealist deeply opposed to the use of force), he was sent off to the security of Paris as a correspondent for his journal. In Paris he took a hand in the conversion of the celebrated Russian revolutionary, Mikhail Bakunin, to the revolutionary communism that preceded the anarchism of his later life, and for a time became an enthusiastic supporter of Proudhon. He admired Proudhon and Cabet – the most fanatical of all the socialists of that time – for making their appeal directly to the poor and the oppressed, and not waiting, like Saint-Simon or Fourier, for some enlightened despot or millionaire to put through their social schemes for them. In 1843 he returned to Cologne, agitated among the workers, published routine left-wing articles attacking private property, religion, and the tyranny of the state; he seems to have occupied a political position intermediate between communism and anarchism.[1] He was at this time an active member of a faithful band of brothers, which included Proudhon, Bruno Bauer, Karl Grün, Max Stirner, all afterwards condemned by Marx as mere abstract moralists – men who denounced capitalism for no better reason than that they believed it to be evil – which was mere subjectivism disguised as objective judgement. Marx maintained that since all men were in fact conditioned by the position of their class, and their position in their class, and since their moral and political opinions were a rationalisation of their interests (that is to say, of what their class at a given stage of its evolution needed and desired, or was endangered by and feared), to suppose that one could praise or condemn from some neutral vantage point, above the battle, above the class struggle, was to fall into a fatal 'metaphysical' illusion. The only truly objective ground from which one could rationally attack, or act

[1] See p. 222, note 1 above.

to destroy, a given view, institution, regime, was that of the new dialectical science of historical development. Rational politics was the
support of what history – the class struggle – would bring forth, and
the condemnation of what it could not but destroy; to resist the
movement of history, operating through objective material factors
and their effects on – and reflections in – human consciousness, was
therefore arbitrary, irrational, literally suicidal. Proudhon, Cabet,
Hess, were in this sense 'idealists' and Utopians, and had condemned
themselves to impotence, to what Trotsky was later to call 'the
rubbish heap of history'.

Nevertheless, despite their contempt for their former mentor (and
perhaps their jealousy of a forerunner), Marx, and especially Engels,
preserved relatively good relations with Hess, made some use of his
draft (if only to condemn it) for the *Communist Manifesto* which they
composed late in 1847,[1] and treated him with a mixture of patronising
irony and ill-tempered impatience that was due to what all Marxists
were later in a chorus to describe as 'sentimental and idealistic communism'. Hess was too simple and free from *amour propre* to react to,
or even notice, this insulting attitude. He tended to return good for
evil, and treated the fathers of 'scientific' socialism with deep respect
and even loyalty to the end of his life. He saw in them, whatever their
faults, indefatigable workers in the cause of justice for the oppressed
workers. That was enough for him. Whoever resisted injustice and
fought for a freer and better life for all men was his friend and ally.

After a precarious existence in Paris, eked out by hack work in
various German émigré journals, he went to Brussels in 1845 and
stayed there, on and off, until 1848. He paid visits to Germany, helped
Engels to edit a left-wing journal, *Der Gesellschaftsspiegel*, in Elberfeld,
and to agitate (they won converts everywhere except among the
workers), wrote on the evils inherent in capitalism as the cause of
overproduction and misery in the midst of plenty, condemned money
as itself a factor in the process of *Entmenschlichung* – turning human
beings into goods bought and sold for a price – and was finally dismissed by Marx as a 'feeble echo of French socialism and communism
with a slight philosophical flavour'.

[1] As also, somewhat earlier, in their *German Ideology*, unpublished in their
lifetime, of which with his customary disinterestedness Hess, who was reviled
in other parts of the work, may actually have written a section. See Eduard
Bernstein, 'Vorbemerkung', in *Dokumente des Sozialismus* (Berlin, 1901–5),
vol. 3, p. 17f.

The revolution of 1848 broke out while he was in Germany. His widow later maintained that he had been condemned to death for his part in it, but this is probably a pious invention. The defeat of the revolution did not break his spirit or diminish his faith in mankind. Unlike most of his radical allies in France and Germany, whom the easy victories of Bismarck, the Emperor of Austria and Prince Napoleon over the forces of democracy left morally and intellectually bankrupt, he neither crossed over to the enemy, nor retreated into the typically émigré condition of resentful inactivity broken by occasional efforts to justify one's own conduct and condemn that of everyone else. He wandered over, and starved in, Switzerland, Belgium, Holland, opened a brush shop in Marseilles, and finally returned to Paris, in 1854, where after more than twenty years of nomadic life, he finally settled. Living in poverty (alleviated for a short while by an inheritance left him by his father, who died in 1851) and supporting himself by casual journalism, the father of German communism continued to believe unswervingly in the classless society, the perfectibility of all mankind, and the part to be played in this by the progress of empirical discovery and invention. He studied anthropology, physiology and the natural sciences in general – for he was convinced that mankind would be regenerated by scientific knowledge applied by men of skill and public spirit. Politically he sympathised with whatever seemed to him to move towards the light. He won the friendship and respect of Ferdinand Lassalle – 'the man with the head of Goethe on Jewish shoulders' – and cooperated with him in the creation of his new General Federation of German Workers – the foundation of all organised social democracy in Europe. At the same period he ardently acclaimed the Italian struggle for unity and independence. The Italians, especially Mazzini and his friends, represented the principle of nationalism as he had always understood and believed in it. Hess did not accept the Marxist doctrine of the unreality of nationalism as a basic factor in history. He condemned cosmopolitanism as the deliberate and unnatural suppression of real historical differences which enriched mankind. But he did not see what right any nation had to regard itself as superior to another, and he sharply rejected the Hegelian distinction between the 'historic' nations, and those unfortunate 'submerged' nationalities, which the more bellicose nations, chosen to 'play a historic role' in virtue of their superiority, had a 'historic' right to absorb and dominate. Like the eighteenth-century humanist Herder, he believed in the natural differentiation of mankind into separate races or nations. He did not bother to define these concepts, since he thought that they signified something that all sane men recognised, and which had only acquired disreputable associations because of the brutal acts that had been, and still were, committed in their names. He condemned Prussian chauvinism without reserve. He detested Russian expansionism and tyranny. But the desire of the Italians to establish themselves as a free nation in their own land evoked his warmest sympathy. He saw in the papacy, rather than in foreign invasions, the major cause of Italian backwardness, disunity, and economic and spiritual misery, echoing, in this respect, the views of Italian patriots from Machiavelli to our own day. As he reflected about the problems of Italian nationalism, and followed the career of the Italian patriotic movement with the devoted sympathy and admiration that every liberal in Europe (and particularly in England) felt for the followers of Garibaldi and Mazzini, the nature and destiny of his own scattered and 'submerged' people – the Jews – once again began to preoccupy his thoughts. In 1861 he returned to Cologne under a political amnesty granted by the King of Prussia. In 1862 he published his best and most famous book, *Rome and Jerusalem*, in which his new doctrine was expounded.

Whether Lassalle's national brand of socialism – Hess was collaborating closely with Lassalle at this time – had influenced him, or whether his ideas grew according to some inner pattern of their own, there is no doubt that he spoke and wrote thereafter like a man who had had a transfiguring experience. Scarcely any notice of his book was taken then, or subsequently, by political specialists or the general European reader. It remained, like Hess himself, outside the central currents of its time. Upon the educated German Jews, however, it fell like a bombshell, as, indeed, it was intended to do. Even today, more than a hundred years after its publication, when much of it is necessarily obsolete, and a great deal that must once have seemed wildly Utopian and fanciful has in fact, sometimes by scarcely perceptible steps, come to pass, it still impresses one as a bold and original masterpiece of social analysis. It is a clear, penetrating, candid, uncompromising book, at once a collection of disturbing home truths calculated to cause acute discomfort to liberal assimilationists among Jews everywhere, and at the same time, and despite its occasional rhetoric, a direct, simple and exceedingly moving profession of faith. It contains a description of the condition of the Jews in the west, a diagnosis of their ills, and a programme for the future. The pinpricks of his cosmopolitan socialist friends evidently no longer affected Hess. He gave expression to a dominant conviction which he had for many years repressed, and which finally proved too strong to stifle, and felt at peace.

II

Rome and Jerusalem consists of a preface, twelve letters written to a bereaved lady,[1] an epilogue, and ten supplementary notes. It deals with a wide variety of aspects of the same central subject – the Jews, what they are, and what they should be. The essential tone is given near the beginning of the book, in the first letter, in which the author says:

> Here I am again, after twenty years of estrangement, in the midst of my people. I take part in its days of joy and sorrow, in its memories and hopes, its spiritual struggles within its own house, and among the civilised peoples in whose midst it lives, but with which, despite two thousand years of common life and effort, it cannot achieve complete unity. One thought which I believed I had extinguished for ever within my breast is again vividly present to me: the thought of my nationality, inseparable from the heritage of my fathers and from the Holy land – the eternal city, the birthplace of the belief in the divine unity of life and in the future brotherhood of all men.[2]

Hess goes on to assert that nationality is real. Nations are a natural historical growth, like families, like physical types. To deny this is merely to falsify the facts, and springs from unworthy motives of fear and cowardice. In the case of the Jews the ringing phrases that some among them use against nationalism and medieval prejudice are only an attempt to conceal their desire to dissociate themselves from their 'unhappy, persecuted, ridiculed people . . . The modern liberal Jew is to be despised with his fine words about humanity and enlightenment, intended only to disguise his disloyalty to his brothers.'[3] This creates a false situation that becomes increasingly unbearable to everyone. Europeans have always regarded the existence of Jews as an

[1] The lady was, in fact (as Edmund Silberner has established), a genuine friend of Hess, but the genre is a common vehicle in the nineteenth century for political *pensées*.

[2] I 1 (see p. 226, note 1 above).

[3] V 27–8.

anomaly. It may well be that the progress of justice and humanity will
one day lead to justice for the Jews : they will perhaps be emancipated,
but they will never be respected so long as they act on the principle of
'Ubi bene, ibi patria.'[1] Denial of nationality forfeits everyone's respect.
Assimilation is no solution : 'It is not the pious old Jew, who would
rather have his tongue cut out than misuse it by denying his nationality :
it is the modern Jew who is despicable for disowning his race because
the heavy hand of fate oppresses it.'[2] The banner of enlightenment
will not save him from the stern verdict of public opinion. 'It is no use
pleading various geographical or philosophical alibis.'[3] The modern
Jew is merely despised for trying to leave what he thinks to be a sinking
ship. 'You may don a thousand masks, change your name and your
religion and your mode of life, creep through the world incognito so
that nobody notices that you are a Jew. Yet every insult to the Jewish
name will wound you more than a man of honour who remains loyal
to his family and defends his good name.'[4] Some Jews in Germany
think that they can save themselves by modernising their religion, or,
finally, by conversion. But this will not help them. 'Neither reform,
nor baptism, neither education nor emancipation, will completely open
before the Jews of Germany the doors of social life.'[5] He says again
and again that the Germans are anti-Jewish racially. The tall, blond
Germans are much too conscious of the small, dark Jews as being
something intrinsically different from themselves. What the Germans
hate is not so much the Jewish religion or Jewish names as the Jewish
noses ;[6] change of faith or name evidently does not help : consequently
what the Jews are tempted to deny is not so much their religion as
their race. But their noses will not vanish, their hair will remain curly,
their type has, after all, remained unaltered since the ancient Egyptian
bas-reliefs in which the Semitic type, as we know it, is quite unmis-
takable.[7] They are 'a race, a brotherhood, a nation, whose own existence is unfortunately denied by its own children, and one which every
street urchin considers it his duty to despise, so long as it is homeless'.[8]
Homelessness is the heart of this problem : for without soil 'a man sinks
to the status of a parasite, feeding on others'.[9] All betrayal is base as
such. 'If it is true that Jewish emancipation is not compatible with
adherence to the Jewish nation, a Jew ought to sacrifice the former
for the latter.'[10] And, still more violently : 'Jews are not a religious

---

[1] 'Where I do well, there is my country.' V 27.   [2] ibid.
[3] V 28.   [4] ibid.   [5] IV 14.   [6] ibid.
[7] IV 15.   [8] V 31.   [9] XII 110.   [10] IV 17.

group, but a separate nation, a special race, and the modern Jew who denies this is not only an apostate, a religious renegade, but a traitor to his people, his tribe, his family.'[1] Racial chauvinism – nationalism in any form – is condemned by Hess in the most passionate terms, then and later. But to deny one's nation or race is at least as repulsive as to proclaim its superior rights or powers. The German Jews cannot understand this. They are genuinely puzzled by German anti-Semitism. They feel that they are true patriots, soldiers who have fought for Germany, 'Teutomaniacs'[2] as fiercely hostile to the French as other Germans. They sing popular patriotic German songs as fervently as any Germans; yet when Becker, the author of one of these, insulted him, Hess, for attempting to set it to music, this was a brutal and deplorable act, as he declares he now realises, but in a sense almost instinctive – a natural reaction. Intolerant nationalism is certainly a vice, but one must realise that it is a racial vice; for races exist, and Jews belong to a race which is not that of the Germans. To deny this is to falsify the facts. To be a race or a nation is not to desire racial or national mastery. It is a disease of nationalism to seek to dominate others: but Jews, like other peoples, need a normal national life. Hess goes on to say that the great French historian Augustin Thierry at the beginning of the nineteenth century rightly maintained that history is dominated by the struggles not only of classes, but also of races and nationalities. 'Semites' and 'Teutons' are not mere linguistic categories, although they carry no titles to superiority in themselves. Each race has different and incommensurable gifts, and they can all contribute to the enrichment of mankind. The Aryan race, according to Hess, has the gift of explanation – that of science – and the gift of creating beauty, a capacity for art. The Semites' genius lies elsewhere – in their ethical insight and in their sense of holiness – in the sanctifying of the world by religion. There are no superior and inferior races. All races must be made free, and then only will they cooperate as equals. Like others, like many Christian and Moslem peoples, the Jews have slept a deep sleep under gravestones upon which various preachers have inscribed their soporific formulas, but the crowing of the Gallic cock has awakened the kingdom of the sleepers, and the French, the soldiers of progress, will break the gravestones, and the peoples will begin to rise from their graves.[3] Just as Rome, which since Innocent III has been the city of eternal sleep, is today gradually being resurrected as the city of eternal life by the stout-hearted

[1] IV 17.   [2] V 26.   [3] V 28–9.

patriots who fight for Italian freedom, so Jerusalem too will awake. The waters of the Tiber – the sound of the victories in North Italy – awake the Jews from their slumbers, and resound in the hills of Zion. He declares that he too had been living his life in a dream. It was only in 1840, when the charge of ritual murder was made against the Jews in Damascus, that he himself suddenly realised where the truth lay. 'It dawned on me for the first time, in the midst of my socialist activities, that I belonged to my unfortunate, slandered, despised and dispersed people',[1] and he goes on to say that he stifled his cry of pain, because of the greater sufferings of the European proletariat to which he thought that he ought to devote his life.

Polish nationalism had evidently made little impression on Hess, since it was bound up with Roman Catholicism, and Rome had been an inexhaustible well of anti-Semitic poison. But the awakening of Italy – secular and humanist – had made him realise that the last of all the great national questions, the Jewish question, must finally obtain its solution too. He declares that this question has too long been concealed behind the fantastic illusions of rationalists and philanthropists who deny the national character of the Jewish religion. The religious reform movement among the German Jews has done nothing but bring emptiness into Jewish life, and break off boughs from the Jewish tree. With a shameful lack of pride its leaders tell the Jews to conceal themselves among the other nations. With what result? They change their names, only so that the anti-Semites might dig up their original Jewish names, and fling them in their faces; so that poor Meyerbeer, the composer, is now always called by them Jacob Meyer Lippmann Beer; and Ludwig Börne is always called Baruch, which is, indeed, his real name.[2] Socialists in Germany[3] indulge in this pastime no less than others. This situation is deeply humiliating. Jews have been persecuted and massacred, but in the Middle Ages, by remaining steadfast and faithful to their ancestral values, they at least avoided degradation. Modern Jews, especially those who have changed their names, deserve the contumely which openly or secretly is heaped upon them.

Hess proceeded to be as good as his word. He declared that his first name was henceforth not Moritz but his Hebrew name, Moses.[4] He

---

[1] V 23. [2] VI 42.

[3] And, he might have added, France, Russia, and a good many other countries.

[4] His works continued to appear under the non-committal 'M. Hess'.

said that he regretted that he was not called Itzig; nothing was worse than flying under false colours.[1] In a moving passage, early in the book, he says that Moses was not buried in the Holy Land, whereas the bones of Joseph were carried there, because, according to the rabbis,[2] when Moses presented himself before his future father-in-law, Jethro the priest of Midian, to sue for his daughter's hand, he did not reveal his true origin: he allowed it to be assumed that he was an Egyptian; whereas Joseph revealed himself to his brethren, and never disavowed anyone or anything. One moment of weakness deprived Moses of his right to burial in the land of the ancestors whom he had by his silence denied; so that, according to the Scriptures, no man knows the place of his grave.

What, then, are the Jews to do if they are not to remain sorry hypocrites or worthless nonentities among the nations? Hess affirms that Jews are made Palestinian patriots by their very religion. When his grandfather wept as he read to him Jeremiah's vision of Rachel, in her tomb in Ramah, lamenting over her children as they were carried off before her eyes to the Babylonish captivity;[3] and when he showed him olives and dates, saying with shining eyes, 'These come from *Eretz Israel*,'[4] he was many miles from his native Rhineland. Jews buy Palestine earth, he goes on to say, on which to rest their head when they are buried; they carry sprigs of palm bound in myrtle during the Feast of the Tabernacles; and, he might have added, they pray for rain or dew at the seasons at which their forefathers did so in the Holy Land. This is more than a superstition or a dogma. Everything that comes from Palestine, everything that reminds them of it, moves them and is dear to them as nothing else. If the Germans are prepared to accept them only at the price of denying their race, their religion, their temperament, their historical memories, their essential character – then the price is not only morally too high, but not capable of being paid at all: the proposal is both disgusting and impracticable.

Nor is the solution to be found among those fanatical fundamentalists who, with their heads buried in the sand, denounce all science, all aspects of modern secular life. How, he asks, are the Jews to build a bridge between the nihilism of the reform rabbis who have learned

---

[1] VI 42.

[2] He gives as his source the *Midrash Rabba* on Deuteronomy, II 8, p. 37 in the English translation by J. Rabbinowitz (London, 1939).

[3] IV 19–20.

[4] 'Yisróel', as in fact they called it. IV 18.

nothing and the conservatism of the orthodox who have forgotten nothing? There is only one solution, and it awaits the Jews upon the banks of the Jordan. The French nation will aid them. France the great liberator, the first to break the ancient shackles and herald the civil liberties of the Jews like those of other peoples – France must, once she has built the Suez canal, make it possible for the Jews to establish colonies on its shores, for without soil (Hess repeats this over and over again) there is no national life. But who will go to this barren eastern country? Not, it is certain, the Jews of the west. They will stay in the various European lands in which they have gained education, culture, honourable positions in society. They are too deeply bound up with western civilisation. They have lost their vitality as Jews. They will not wish to emigrate to a remote and barren land. They may place their knowledge, their wealth, their influence, at the disposal of the immigrants, but they will not go themselves. For them Palestine will be at best what Hess calls 'a spiritual nerve centre'.[1] Universities will arise there, and a common language which all these immigrants will speak. Who, then, will go? There can be no doubt of that. The Jews of eastern Europe and the other lands where the ancient faith has kept them solid and insulated from their environment, it is these and only these that will move.[2] Their vitality is like that of the corn seeds sometimes found in the graves of Egyptian mummies: given soil and light and air, they grow and become fertile again.[3] Western Jewry is encrusted by the dead residues of the obsolete products of a decayed rationalism which no inner force – only a shock from without – can remove; but the rigid crust of orthodoxy that stunts the progress of eastern Jewry will be melted when the sparks of national feeling that smoulder beneath it are kindled into the sacred fire which heralds the new spring, and the resurrection of their nation into a new life.[4] The Jewish assimilationists who detest what they call religious obscurantism desire to root out these superstitions. But to crush the rabbinical shell in which Judaism is contained is to crush the seed within. It needs not destruction but earth to grow in.

There is also an extraordinary excursus[5] on the Hassidic movement. Whereas the reform movement inspired by Moses Mendelssohn is an attempt to dilute Judaism and to free the Jewish people on foreign

---

[1] *R.J.*, note 9, p. 234.

[2] This surely constitutes one of the most exact true prophecies ever made about events three-quarters of a century later.

[3] V 29–30.   [4] XII 121.   [5] VI note 5 (on pp. 208–11).

soil – which is patently impossible – the great revivalist sect of the Hassidim is a genuine development of the Jewish religion, a response to the authentic need for life on the part of the devout masses, for fresh significance for old symbols, and therefore destined for a great future. Unlike the reformers who are using the timber of Judaism for non-Jewish ends, and secretly share Heine's view that the Jewish religion is a misfortune rather than a religion, forgetting that even converted Jews, whether they want it or not, are painfully affected by the condition of the Jewish masses, the Hassidim are a living spiritual force. It is true that Hess confuses the name of the founder of the *Chabad* Hassidim, and speaks of a Samuel of Wilno instead of Shneur Zalman. But what is remarkable is that an émigré communist agitator should have heard of this movement at all, and have realised at so early a date that the founder of this movement – the Baal Shem – was destined, in the end, to triumph over Moses Mendelssohn. For Hassidism and Zionism were, and are, living forces, as the reform movement, with all its humanity, civilisation and learning, is not.

It is the benighted beings of whom there are millions in the dominions of the Russian, Prussian, Austrian and Turkish empires, the Jews of these backward provinces, that will, according to Hess, immigrate to Palestine and create the new state. There the existence of Jewish self-identity will neither 'need to be demonstrated, nor to be demonstrated away'.[1] As for the other Jews, they will, if they wish it, assimilate to the countries of their birth; and in this way, as men who recognise themselves to be of foreign origin and have, by an act of free choice, decided to change their nationality, will obtain more respect than those who pretend that they have no nationality to exchange. Even the Germans who today (that is to say, in the 60s of the last century) despise all 'the painstaking efforts of their Jewish fellow citizens to Germanise themselves', and care nothing for all their 'cultural achievements' the catalogue of which the latter are forever reciting, will, once the Jews are a nation on their own ancestral soil, give them as a nation that which they refuse to give them as individuals.[2]

But that day may not be near: and in the meanwhile religion is the great preservative of Judaism, and must on no account be diluted or brought up to date. For Hess the Jewish religion is, in its secular aspect, the foundation of all egalitarianism and socialism: for it recog-

[1] IV 17.   [2] ibid.

238

nises no castes or classes, and assumes the unity of all creation. It allows no feudalism, no social hierarchy, it is just and equal and the true source of the noblest social movements of modern times. It does recognise the principle of nationality, but (so Hess maintained) it excludes chauvinistic nationalism, such as that of Prussia, as morally wrong; yet equally it leaves no room for its contrary – empty and artificial cosmopolitanism which, by denying even the just claims of nationality, falsifies the facts, sets up illusory ideals, and with its bogus prospectus lures innocent men to their doom. The first condition of true internationalism is that there should be nationalities. Internationalism is a movement not to abolish, but to unite, nations. Consequently Hess welcomes the renaissance of Jewish historiography among the German Jews and quotes with approval the names of Weill, Kompert, Bernstein, Wihl, and, above all, Graetz, who became his friend, and from whose history of the Jewish people – 'people, let it be noted, not church or religion' – he copiously and happily quotes.

Everything that had been suppressed by Hess for over twenty years now came welling up. He constantly returns to beliefs instilled in him by his father and grandfather. 'I myself, had I a family, would, in spite of my dogmatic heterodoxy, not only join an orthodox synagogue, but would also observe in my home all the feast and fast days, so as to keep alive in my heart, and in the hearts of my children, the traditions of my people.'[1] He denounces all forms of adulteration and compromise, all forms of adaptation to meet the needs of modern times. Prayers must on no account be shortened, nor German versions used instead of Hebrew; Jewish preachers must be held in the greatest honour. What he fears above everything is what he calls 'nihilism'.[2] The reform movement he regards as thin and unconvincing, a pathetic and vulgar imitation of Christianity, a counterfeit modern substitute for something ancient and unique. If he must choose, he would rather keep all the six hundred and thirteen rules of the *Shulchan Aruch*; one day a new Sanhedrin, meeting in Jerusalem, may change or abrogate them; until then, the Jews must preserve what they possess – their authentic spiritual heritage – unmodified. He mocks at the fictitious 'missions'[3] which some Jews persuade themselves that they have been called to perform among the nations – to teach toleration to other religions, or propagate the doctrine of 'pure theism',[4] or

[1] VII 50.   [2] *R.J.*, *passim*, e.g. VII 52, VIII 63.
[3] VIII 66.   [4] VIII 65.

even the arts of commerce. 'It is better for the Jew who does not believe in a national regeneration of his people to labour, like an enlightened Christian of today, for the dissolution of his religion. I can understand how one can hold this view; what I do not understand is how one can believe simultaneously in "enlightenment" and in the Jewish mission in exile, that is to say, in the ultimate dissolution and the continued existence of Judaism at one and the same time.'[1] Do the Jews who wish to sacrifice their historical past to such abstractions as 'Liberty' and 'Progress' really imagine that anyone will be taken in?[2] Does Meyerbeer really think that anyone besides himself is deceived because he so carefully avoids Biblical themes in his operas?

Having settled his account with the German Jews, Hess turned to the practical problem of the colonisation of Palestine. He noted that Rabbi Hirsch Kalischer of Thorn had already drafted a plan for precisely such a movement;[3] he noted, too, that a Monsieur Ernest Laharanne, in a book called *The New Oriental Question*, supported this view. Laharanne, who was employed in the private office of the Emperor Napoleon III, was a Christian and a passionate advocate of Zionism. He denounced the rich emancipated Jews for their indifference, the pious Jews for defeatism, and declared a state in Palestine to be the only solution of the Jewish problem; the Sultan and the Pope would doubtless resist this plan, but he felt sure that free French democracy would ultimately prevail against both. He spoke of the fundamental right of the Jews to a historic home, and believed, too optimistically, that the Turks would, for a handful of gold tossed them by Jewish bankers (or, perhaps, obtained by the nobler expedient of a democratic subscription from the entire Jewish people), admit large Jewish colonisation. He spoke lyrically of the infinite mystery of Jewish survival, of the fact unparalleled in the history of mankind, that faced by enemies in every age – Alexandrian Greeks, Romans, Asiatics, Africans, barbarians, feudal kings, grand inquisitors, Jesuits, modern tyrants – they yet survived and multiplied. The French and the Jews must march together, together they must revitalise the parched land of Palestine and rescue it from the terrible Turk. French democracy, Jewish genius, modern science, that was to be the new

[1] VIII 67.　　　　　　　　　　[2] IX 74.

[3] Kalischer's *Drishath Zion* appeared a few months before *R.J.*; like Newton and Leibniz, the two authors knew little of one another's lines of thought.

triple alliance that would at once save an ancient people and revive an ancient land.

Hess, as may be imagined, welcomed this with great enthusiasm. In a characteristically apocalyptic mood, he prophesied that the national solidarity and unity that was the basis of Jewish religion would gradually make all men one. Natural science would liberate the workers, racial struggles would come to an end, and so, too, would those of classes. Jewish religion and Jewish history (a vast amalgam in which he included the teachings of the Old Testament and the Talmud, the Essenes and Jesus) said to men : 'Be of the oppressed and not of the oppressors; receive abuse and return it not; let the motive of all your actions be the love of God, and rejoice in suffering.'[1] By this gospel the world would be regenerated; but the first requirement was the establishment of the Jewish state in Palestine. The rich Jews must buy the land and train agricultural experts. The *Alliance Israélite* – a philanthropic body of French Jews – must help Rabbi Natonek of Stuhl-Weissenburg in Hungary, who was ready to interview the Sultan about this plan, armed with a letter of recommendation from the Turkish Ambassador in Vienna. Jewish colonists must be led by men trained in modern methods of thought and action and not by obscurantist rabbis. The plan was capable of being realised; it must be realised; nothing stood in the way but bigotry and artificial cosmopolitanism, from both of which the majority of the Jews recoiled instinctively. Hess ends his extraordinary sermon on a note of high enthusiasm.

The language of *Rome and Jerusalem*, after a hundred years, seems antiquated. The style is by turns sentimental, rhetorical, and at times merely flat; there are a good many digressions and references to issues now totally forgotten. And yet it is a masterpiece. It lives because of its shining honesty, its fearlessness, the concreteness of its imagination, and the reality of the problem that it reveals. The morbid condition that Hess seeks to diagnose and cure has not vanished; on the contrary, it is as widespread now as in his day, but its symptoms are better known. Consequently the book is, despite its lack of literary talent, not dated. And because it is simple, and not encumbered by the dead formulas and the (by now often meaningless) Hegelian patter that mars some of the most original pages of Marx and his followers, its

[1] He refers to the passages in the tractates *Sabbath* 88b, *Yoma* 23a and *Gittin* 36b, as cited in H. Graetz, *Geschichte der Juden*, 2nd ed., vol. 3 (Leipzig, 1863), p. 226, note 1. See *R.J.*, p. 137, note.

impact is still exceedingly fresh and direct; it can still provoke sympathy or violent opposition; it remains an analytic and polemical essay of the first order. No one concerned with its central theme can read it with indifference.

III

Hess had travelled a long way from the violently anti-religious communism and anti-nationalism of his younger days. The fierce attack upon the assimilationist reformers was in part, of course, an attack on his own dead self. The solution consisting in a dignified national dissolution by means of systematic intermarriage and the education of children in a faith different from one's own, which he now so ferociously denounced, was the very conduct that he himself had earlier advocated. The conscientious internationalism of his young Hegelian days was replaced by the realisation (it seems destined to come, late or soon, to almost every Jewish social thinker, whatever his views) that the Jewish problem is something *sui generis*, and seems to need a specific solution of its own, since it resists the solvent of even the most powerful universal panaceas. Nor was this in Hess's case the final reaction of a persecuted and exhausted old socialist, who, tired of waiting for the realisation of his universalist dreams, settles for a more limited national solution as a temporary expedient, or returns to the happy, conformist days of his youth as an escape from the excessive burden of the universal social struggle. To think this is to misunderstand Hess profoundly. He was a man who abandoned no belief unless he had convinced himself by rational methods that it was false. His Zionism did not cause him to abandon socialism. He evidently felt no incompatibility between communist ideals and belief in a Jewish national Risorgimento. Hess was not, like Hegel or Marx, a historical thinker of genius who broke with previous tradition, perceived relationships hitherto unnoticed (or at least not clearly described), imposed his vision on mankind, and transformed the categories in terms of which human beings think of their situation, their past and their destiny. But neither did he suffer from the defects of these despotic system-builders. He was intellectually (as indeed in every other respect) a man of complete integrity and did not, for any psychological or tactical reason, try to force the facts into some preconceived dogmatic pattern. The strongest single characteristic of his writings, especially

242

of his later works, is a pure-hearted devotion to the truth, expressed with candid, at times childlike, simplicity. It is this that makes his words often devastating, and causes them to linger in the memory longer than the richer and weightier sentences of the more celebrated prophets of the age.

Hess abandoned neither socialism nor Zionism because he saw no incompatibility between them. His socialism – which was nothing but desire for social justice and a harmonious life – did not, any more than Lassalle's, preclude nationality. He could conceive of no inevitable collision between purposes or policies that seemed true, responded to genuine needs, and were morally good. It did not so much as occur to him that modern Jews should be prevented or even dissuaded from, let us say, the celebration of the Feast of the Passover, or the fulfilment of other religious duties, because these were obsolete survivals or superstitions that had nothing in common with an enlightened scientific outlook. He took it for granted that one truth and one value could not require the suppression of another; hence the moral values of socialism, and the truths embodied in a sense of one's individual social national human past, could not possibly, if correctly conceived, ever clash. Life would be sadly and quite gratuitously impoverished by the sacrifice of anything good or true or beautiful. It is this 'idealism', this *'naïveté'*, that the tougher-minded revolutionaries derided in his day much as they do in ours.

After being Lassalle's representative in Cologne, and five years after publishing *Rome and Jerusalem* – to the theses of which he remained unwaveringly faithful to the end of his days – in 1867 Hess joined the International Workingmen's Association, founded, as everyone knows, by his old comrade in arms and remorseless denigrator, Karl Marx. He represented the workers of Berlin in the First International, and in 1868 and 1869, as a Marxist delegate, fought the representatives of Proudhon and of Bakunin, old friends whom he deeply admired, because he thought that their doctrines would disrupt working-class unity. He never became an orthodox Marxist. He still did not believe in violence or class warfare as an inescapable historical category; and he was a full-fledged Zionist *avant la parole*. But he was a socialist, and when he spoke of the Jewish state in Palestine, he declared that the soil of that country must be acquired by the Jews acting as a single national whole in order to prevent private exploitation. Similarly he regarded full legal protection of labour among the future colonists as a *sine qua non*, and declared that the organisation of industry, agriculture and trade must follow Mosaic – which for him was synonymous with socialistic – principles. He wanted to see in the new Jewish state workers' cooperatives of the type organised by Lassalle in Germany, state-aided until such time as the proletarians formed a majority of the inhabitants of Palestine, when the state would automatically, peacefully, and without revolution, become a socialist commonwealth.

All these ideas met, it may well be imagined, with an exceedingly hostile reception among educated Jews, particularly those German liberal Jews against whom Hess's sharpest sallies were directed. Such words had certainly never before been addressed to them. Jews in Germany had for almost a century been much adjured and much discussed. Mendelssohn and his followers had accused them of clinging senselessly to the ghetto for its own sake, of blind avoidance of the magnificent opportunity of entering the world of western culture that was at last open to receive them. The orthodox charged them with godlessness, with heresy and sin. They were told to cling to their ancient faith; to abandon it; to adjust it to modern life; to dilute it; to emulate German culture by critical examination of their own antiquities; to be historians, scholars, higher critics; to enter western civilisation by their own door; by doors already built by others; not to enter it at all. But in this great babel of voices, no one had yet proposed to them to recognise themselves for what they were – a nation: odd, *sui generis*, but still a nation; and therefore to give up nothing, avoid self-deception, not to seek to persuade themselves that what was not theirs and had never been theirs was dearer to them than what was truly their own, not to offer up, with pain and an unbearable sense of shame, what alone they could truly love, their own habits, outlook, memories, traditions, their history, their pride, their sense of identity as a nation, all that they, like other peoples, were and lived by, everything, indeed, that they could respect in themselves or others respected in them. Others – Englishmen, Frenchmen, Italians – probably understood this better than the emancipated Jews to whom Hess spoke. No people struggling for its country can deny the Jewish people the right to its own land without the most fatal inconsistency, he wrote. And so, in the twentieth century, it duly and honourably turned out. But in the circumstances of the time his words were wounding to many, not least because they were true. 'Educated *parvenus* in Christian society'[1] he called his opponents with more bitterness than justice.

[1] *R.J.*, note 9, p. 234.

He poured vinegar in their wounds with the bitter zeal of a convert turning upon the blind mass from which he is sprung. Their reaction may well be imagined. The most eminent German-Jewish scholar of the day, Steinschneider, expressed himself with comparative moderation, and called Hess a repentant sinner,[1] adding the hope that the book would not be exploited by the enemies of the Jews already in Palestine. The celebrated scholar and publicist, the advocate of reform Judaism, Abraham Geiger, whose disavowal of nationality and intense efforts to feel and think like a Hegelian German of Jewish persuasion Hess had pilloried in telling language, reacted with understandable hostility: in an anonymous review entitled 'Old Romanticism, New Reaction', he condemned Hess's book root and branch. He called the author 'an almost complete outsider, who, after bankruptcy as a socialist, and all kinds of swindles, wants to make a hit with nationalism . . . and along with the questions of restoring Czech, Montenegrin and Szekler nationality, etc. . . . wants to revive that of the Jews'.[2] The *Allgemeine Zeitung des Judenthums* said, '. . . we are first and foremost Germans, Frenchmen, Englishmen and Americans, and only then Jews'.[3] The growth of civilisation would cause desire for Palestine to evaporate among the eastern Jews.

So the debate — which even now is by no means closed — began, more than thirty years before the word 'Zionism' had been so much as heard of. The *Alliance Israélite Universelle* cautiously opened its journal, the *Archives Israélites*, to Hess, and offered tepid support. The *Alliance* was attracted by the notion of having so well known a publicist on its side, but was frightened of the notion of organised immigration to Palestine, although it was prepared to support such Jews as had already found their way there as the result of such minor efforts to colonise Palestine as were already, at that time, beginning to be made.

The scandal caused by the book duly died down. Like Hess's earlier works, it had, as far as can be determined, no influence at all. The return of the Jews to Palestine had, after all, been spoken of not

---

[1] 'Ein Baal Teshuvah'. Quoted by Theodor Zlocisti, *Moses Hess, Der Vorkämpfer des Sozialismus und Zionismus 1812–1875* (Berlin, 1921), p. 312.

[2] *Jüdische Zeitschrift für Wissenschaft und Leben* 1 (1862), 252.

[3] *Allgemeine Zeitung des Judenthums* 26 (1862), 610. See further a valuable article by Israel Cohen, to which I owe these quotations, 'Moses Hess: Rebel and Prophet', *Zionist Quarterly* (Fall 1951), 45–56, especially pp. 51–2.

only by pious Jews or Christian visionaries, but by the great Napoleon himself at the time of his Egyptian campaign, by Fichte, by the Russian revolutionary Decembrist Pestel, who, like Fichte, wished to rid Europe of the Jews, by the French-Jewish publicist Joseph Salvador, by the eccentric English traveller Laurence Oliphant, by Rabbi Kalischer, and by other more obscure figures. It is possible that George Henry Lewes, who had met Hess in Paris, had spoken of his views to George Eliot and so inspired her novel *Daniel Deronda*, with its Jewish nationalist hero. But all this was of no account in a world where no one except, perhaps, a few groups of Jews scattered in eastern Europe (and, oddly enough, Australia) took such matters seriously. Hess was not destined to see in his own lifetime even the beginning of the fulfilment of his ideals.

The rest of his life is characteristic enough. Like other impoverished émigré journalists, he acted as correspondent of various German and Swiss journals, as well as the Chicago German weekly *Die Illinois Staats-Zeitung*, for which he wrote from 1865 a series of despatches which show a grasp of European affairs scarcely inferior to those of the *New York Tribune*'s European correspondent – Karl Marx – and far greater powers of accurate prediction of events.[1] He was dismissed from it in 1870, ostensibly for excessive interest in politics in which his German-American readers were held to have too little interest. In the same year, on the outbreak of the Franco-Prussian war, he was expelled from Paris as a Prussian citizen, although, as may be imagined, he denounced Bismarck's aggression with all his might, and called upon the Jews to give their sympathies to France – the cradle of liberty and fraternity, the home of revolution and all humane ideals. He went to Brussels where he called for an alliance of all free peoples against 'Russianised Germany', a country intent on destroying France, only because France wanted to make humanity happier. In 1875 he died, as for the most part he had lived, in obscurity and poverty, an unworldly, isolated figure, and by his own wish was buried in the Jewish cemetery in Deutz by the side of his parents. His posthumous work, *Die Dynamische Stofflehre*, was published in Paris by his devoted wife in 1877 as a pious monument to his memory.

[1] The evidence of Hess's gifts as a political prophet, as well as much else of interest, may be found in Helmut Hirsch, 'Tribun und Prophet. Moses Hess als Pariser Korrespondent der Illinois Staats-Zeitung', *International Review of Social History* 2 (1957), 209–30. See also the admirable *Denker und Kämpfer* (Frankfurt, 1955) by the same author.

She declared it to be his life's work, but it is a confused, half philosophical, half scientific, speculation of no interest or value today.[1] His real life's work is the simple and moving book which still contains more truth about the Jews, both in the nineteenth century and in our own, than any comparable work. Like its author, it was all but forgotten until events themselves rescued both from unjust oblivion. Today streets are called after him in the two principal cities of the state of Israel: nothing would have surprised or delighted him more greatly. After 1862 he was a Jew first and a Marxist second; he would, I suspect, have considered the systematic disparagement of his ideas and personality by Engels and his imitators as more than made up for by the recognition given him by the Jewish state in which he believed with his whole being. Yet nothing seemed less likely during his lifetime.

IV

Like other intellectually honest, morally sensitive and unfrightened men, Moses Hess turned out to have a deeper understanding of some essential matters than more gifted and sophisticated social thinkers. In his socialist days – and they only ceased with his death – he said that the abolition of property and the destruction of the middle classes did not necessarily and automatically lead to paradise; for they did not necessarily cure injustice or guarantee social or individual equality. This was a bold and original view for a socialist of those days. His allies were, for the most part, men dominated by a desire for a clear-cut social structure, and a rationalist, rather than rational, desire to solve social problems in almost geometrical, black-and-white terms. Like their forerunners in the eighteenth century, but armed with different hypotheses, they tried to treat history as an exact science, and to deduce from the study of it some unique plan of action guaranteed to make men for ever free, equal, happy and good. In this dogmatic and intolerant milieu Hess permitted himself to doubt whether any solution could, in principle, achieve this, unless and until the men who built the new world themselves lived by the principles of justice, and felt benevolence and love towards individual human beings and not

[1] Hess's earliest biographer, Theodor Zlocisti, thinks otherwise, and calls him a forerunner of modern atomic theory: op. cit. (p. 245, note 1 above), p. 412.

merely humanity at large, that is to say, were endowed with a character and an outlook which no amount of social and political reform could of itself secure. It is surely a sign of immaturity (even though it may be evidence of a noble and disinterested nature) to stake everything on any one final solution to social problems. When to such immaturity there is added a ruthless will, and a genius for organisation which enables its possessor to force human beings into patterns unrelated to their nature and their own wishes, then what starts as pure and disinterested idealism, inevitably ends in oppression, cruelty and blood. A sense of symmetry and regularity, and a gift for rigorous deduction, that are prerequisites of aptitude for some natural sciences, will, in the field of social organisation, unless they are modified by a great deal of sensibility, understanding and humanity, inevitably lead to appalling bullying on the one side and untold suffering on the other. Even though he knew that he would be mercilessly denounced for stupidity, ignorance and irresponsible Utopianism by his admired, tyrannical comrades in arms, Marx and Engels, Hess could not bring himself to view the world through their distorting spectacles. He did not accept their view of man's nature. He believed in the permanent and universal validity of certain general human values. To the end of his days he firmly believed that human feeling, natural affections, the desire for social justice, individual freedom and solidarity within historically continuous groups – families or religious associations or nationalities – were to be valued as being good in themselves. He did not think that these deep human interests, however they might be modified in space or time, were necessarily altered by historical evolution or conditioned by class consciousness or by any other relatively transient phenomenon to anything like the decisive extent of which the so-called scientific Marxists spoke. As for the relative value and importance of the desire for national independence, it is perhaps enough to point to recent events in Hungary, in Poland and elsewhere[1] for evidence that the orthodox Marxist interpretation of national feeling and its lack of influence upon the working classes of a nation conspicuously no longer capitalist, contains fallacies that have proved tragic enough to many of those involved in them. These are merely the latest and most spectacular examples of truths which Hess saw more clearly than his comrades, without the slightest trace of chauvinism or morbid nationalism, and, let it be added, in the context of the extreme left-wing socialism of which he was one of the purest

[1] This was written in 1957.

and most eloquent proponents. This alone seems to me to establish that his claims, even as a social theorist, as against his critics, are not too difficult to sustain, and that his significance has been for many years systematically underestimated by faithful Marxists[1] to the greater glory of their own creed, but at the expense of the facts of history.

v

In his view of the Jewish question (as it used to be called) Hess's predictions have proved to be almost uncannily accurate. Thus, in one of his more sibylline passages, he declares that the liberal Jews of Germany will one day suffer a cataclysm the extent of which they cannot begin to conceive. Nobody will deny that, at any rate, this prophecy has proved to be only too horribly verified. Similarly Hess preached against assimilation in its heyday, and all that he said about the false position into which the assimilators had put both themselves and their victims seems to me to have been wholly vindicated by the events that followed. No one can today pretend not to know what Hess had meant by his references to 'various geographical or philosophical alibis'[2] behind which Jews (or other human beings) try to make out that they are not what they most conspicuously are because they cannot face embarrassing truths about themselves; thereby deceiving only themselves, causing discomfort or shame to their friends, and amusement or contempt, and, in the end, hatred, on the part of their enemies. Hess had observed that the Jews were in fact a nation, however skilfully definitions were juggled to prove that they were not, and he said so in simple, and, to some, startling and even shocking language. Yet it seems clear that the state of Israel, whatever

---

[1] e.g. by Auguste Cornu, who in his scholarly and lucid *Moses Hess et la gauche Hégélienne* (Paris, 1934) treats Hess as a minor and somewhat slow-witted precursor of Marx, whose views had been rendered obsolete by Marxism. Cornu's later works go even farther in this respect. This is in effect also the view of Georg Lukács in his article 'Moses Hess und die Probleme der idealistischen Dialektik', *Archiv für die Geschichte des Sozialismus und der Arbeiterbewegung* 12 (1926), 105–55. Irma Goitein in her *Probleme der Gesellschaft und des Staates bei Moses Hess* (Leipzig, 1931), shows far more insight.

[2] V 28 (cf. p. 233, note 3 above).

attitude may be adopted towards it, could not have come into being if the Jews had in fact been not such as he, but as his opponents supposed them to be, whether they were orthodox rabbis, or liberal assimilationists, or doctrinaire communists. He has, furthermore, proved to be right in supposing that the western Jews would not, of their own volition, choose to emigrate, whatever the difficulties they encountered in their various communities, because, in the end, they were too happy, too comfortable, too well integrated in them. Although, like his friend Heine, he had to some degree anticipated the development of German barbarism, yet Hitler was far beyond anything that either had imagined; and Hess had, therefore, on the evidence available in his day, correctly assumed that it was the eastern and not the German Jews who would be driven both by their internal solidarity and by economic desperation to new worlds, and in particular to the creation of an autonomous community in Palestine.

He believed in natural science applied to create social welfare; he believed in cooperatives, communal endeavour, state ownership, or, at any rate, public ownership. To a large degree – larger than is pleasing to those who favour other forms of social organisation – these principles have today been realised in the state of Israel. He believed deeply in the faithful preservation of historical tradition. He spoke about this in language scarcely less fervent, but a good deal less biassed and irrational, than Burke or Fichte. He did so not because he feared change – he was after all a radical and a revolutionary – but because through his most extreme and radical beliefs there persists a conviction that there is never any duty to maim or impoverish oneself for the sake of an abstract ideal; that nobody can, or should, be required to vivisect himself, to throw away that which affords him the deepest spiritual satisfaction known to human beings – the right to self-expression, to personal relationships, to the love of familiar places or forms of life, of beautiful things, or the roots and symbols of one's own, or one's family's, or one's nation's past. He believed that nobody should be made to sacrifice his own individual pattern of the unanalysable relationships – the central emotional or intellectual experiences – of which human lives are compounded, to offer them up, even as a temporary expedient, for the sake of some tidy solution, deduced from abstract and impersonal premises, some form of life derived from an alien source, imposed upon men by artificial means, and felt to be the mechanical application of some general rule to a concrete situation for which it was not made. All that Hess, towards the end of his life, wrote or said, rests on the assumption that to deny what inwardly one knows to be true, to do violence to the facts for whatever tactical or doctrinal motive, is at once degrading and doomed to futility. The foundations of his beliefs, both socialist and Zionist, were unashamedly moral. He was convinced, moreover, as a matter of empirical knowledge, that moral beliefs played a major role in human affairs.

The socialist morality that he so pure-heartedly preached, as well as the type of nationalism that he idealised, have, on the whole, proved more enduring and productive of human freedom and happiness than the more 'realistic' solutions of his more Machiavellian rivals, both on the right and on the left. For this reason he is to be counted among the genuine prophets of our own day who said much that was novel, true and still of the first importance. This is the title to immortality of 'the communist rabbi', the friend of Heine and Michelet, the man whom Karl Marx, in his rare moments of high good humour, used to call 'the donkey, Moses Hess'.

Benjamin Disraeli, Karl Marx and the Search for Identity

I

ALL Jews who are at all conscious of their identity as Jews are steeped in history. They have longer memories, they are aware of a longer continuity as a community than any other which has survived. The bonds that unite them have proved stronger than the weapons of their persecutors and detractors; and stronger than a far more insidious weapon: the persuasions of their own brothers, fellow Jews who, at times, with much sincerity and skill try to argue that these bonds are not as strong or as peculiar as they seem, that the Jews are united by no more than a common religion, or common suffering, that their differences are greater than their similarities, and therefore that a more enlightened way of life – liberal, rationalist, socialist, communist – will cause them to dissolve peacefully as a group into their social and national environment – that at most their unity may come to be no greater than that of, say, Unitarians, Buddhists, vegetarians, or any other world-wide group, sharing certain common, not always too passionately held, convictions. If this had been true, there would not have been enough vitality, not enough desire to live a common life, to have made colonisation of Palestine, and ultimately the state of Israel, possible. Whatever other factors may have entered into the unique amalgam which, if not always Jews themselves, at any rate the rest of the world instantly recognises as the Jewish people, historical consciousness – sense of continuity with the past – is among the most powerful.

The nineteenth-century Russian revolutionary, Herzen, said of his own country that its strength lay not in history, of which it did not have a great deal, but in geography – the extent of its territory, barbarous but vast. The Jews could reasonably say that what they have lacked at all times is geography – enough soil to live on and develop – for of history they have had, if anything, more than enough. The late

Lewis Namier once told me that upon being asked by a splendid English peer why he, a Jew, devoted himself to writing English history, and not Jewish history, he replied : 'Derby! There *is* no modern Jewish history. There is only a Jewish martyrology, and that is not amusing enough for me.' This was in character and no doubt was mainly intended to put the thoughtless peer in his place. But there is a certain truth in it. The annals of the Jews between the destruction of the Second Temple and comparatively recent times is indeed largely a story of persecution and martyrdom, weakness and heroism, an unbroken struggle against greater odds than any other human community has ever had to contend with. Nevertheless, from the point of view of the historian of the Jews, the task was rendered relatively easier by the fact that inasmuch as systematic and concerted persecution, mainly by Christians, but to some degree also by Moslems, drove the Jews into the confined spaces of ghettos, Pales of Settlement, and the like, their communal history was made thereby only too painfully easy to identify, describe and analyse. It certainly seemed to have been so in Europe at any rate until the eighteenth century. Individual Jews left their communities and lived among gentiles; sometimes they accepted baptism, at other times they secretly practised the whole or some part of their ancestral religion, or, like Spinoza, were open heretics, abjured by their own community, and treated with, at best, nervous respect by the larger society in which they lived, but with which they never became wholly identified. There were not many of these. Hence the question of who was and who was not a Jew in the ancient world or the Middle Ages, or during the Renaissance and its aftermath, is not a grave historical problem.

If we are to attempt a rough periodisation of Jewish history, we could say that there are at least three main periods in it : (1) while they lived in their own land, with colonies dispersed not very widely in Asia Minor or North Africa; (2) the medieval Diaspora, where they lived in insulated groups and where their fortunes, at least in theory, can, for this very reason, be followed without too much difficulty; (3) after emancipation. Here genuine difficulties for historians arise: what is, and what is not, Jewish history? Who belongs to it, and who does not? The social, intellectual and religious history of the eastern communities clearly does. So does that of the Russo-Polish Pale of Settlement. But what are we to say of the western Jews? Is it possible to trace the history of their institutions as a community? In England, where their history is one of the most fortunate in this period, it is least dramatic and of least interest to those like Namier, who like colour and movement and the play of complex personalities and situations. Happy periods, as Hegel said, are blank pages in the volume of history.

But now a problem arises: is the history of individuals of Jewish origin, or even the Jewish faith, also part and parcel of Jewish history? Most historians of the Jews mention such figures as, say, Joseph of Naxos, or Spinoza, when historians of Italy would scarcely count Cardinals Mazarin or Alberoni or Marie de Médicis as figures in Italian history. This is rendered plausible because, until modern times, serious problems of identification scarcely arise: Plutarch was not faced with the question of whether he was a Greek or a Roman; Josephus was in no doubt about his identity; Spinoza did not ask himself whether he was or was not truly a Dutchman. The dissolution of corporations by the European nation-states and their claim to total allegiance altered this picture and led to conflicts of loyalty. This crisis began for the Jews later than it did for their neighbours; it became explicit when the gates of the ghettos were opened, and Jews began, timidly at first, then with growing confidence and success, to mingle with their fellow-citizens of other faiths, and increasingly to share in their common life, both public and private. Where, in recent history, are we to draw the line between the history of the Jews as such and the history of the larger societies of which they happen to be members? We are all familiar with those somewhat pathetic lists of contributions to general culture with which apologists for the Jews have sought to remind their detractors how much Christian civilisation owes them. Are the lives and the achievements of Heine, Felix Mendelssohn, Ricardo, part of the history of the Jews? Or, if these are excluded on the ground of their baptism, what are we to say of – to take random examples from the last century – Lassalle, Meyerbeer, Pissarro, who were not baptised but had special bonds with institutional Jewish life? We do not speak of Francis Bacon or John Stuart Mill or Russell as Christian thinkers, however dissident; should we, nevertheless, look upon Husserl or Beigson or Freud as Jewish thinkers in some special sense?

This very question raises the ancient problem, which has been brought home to us so directly now, as a result both of the most fearful genocide in history and the creation of a Jewish state – the problem, 'What is a Jew?' What is his relation to the rest of his society? In what sense is it, and in what sense is it not, 'his' society? Are the differences between him and other members of it analogous to other, more familiar differences, which divide classes, professions, churches and other social groups, within what are normally regarded as single social wholes – states, nations, countries?

This problem became particularly acute after the French Revolution for those who were released from the ancient prison house and were moving into the light of day, out of the confinement of the ghettos – or what were so in fact if not in name – of the western world. The liberation had been relatively sudden : the problems of adjustment had not been prepared for. Some recoiled before the prospect of a strange, wider world, and preferred to linger in the shadows of the narrow but familiar place of ancient confinement. Others, the most eager, the most ambitious and most idealistic and optimistic, went towards the light with passionate hopes. Some successfully assimilated with their new brothers, changed their faith, or, at any rate, their habits, with evidently no great agony or expense of spirit, like the Jewish banker Gideon in eighteenth-century England, whose name is all but forgotten today; like the economist David Ricardo or those eminent financiers and railway-builders, the Sephardic disciples of Saint-Simon. Others, for a variety of reasons, but often psychological causes – some unsurrendering quality in their temperament – sometimes against their conscious wills, felt incapable of assimilation, incapable of the degree of accommodation which those who seek to alter their habits radically must achieve, and at times remained betwixt and between, unmoored from one bank without reaching the other, tantalised but incapable of yielding, complicated, somewhat tormented figures, floating in midstream, or, to change the metaphor, wandering in a no-man's-land, liable to waves of self-pity, aggressive arrogance, exaggerated pride in those very attributes which divided them from their fellows; with alternating bouts of self-contempt and self-hatred, feeling themselves to be objects of scorn or antipathy to those very members of the new society by whom they most wished to be recognised and respected. This is a well-known condition of men forced into an alien culture, by no means confined to the Jews; it is a well-known neurosis in an age of nationalism in which self-identification with a dominant group becomes supremely important, but, for some individuals, abnormally difficult. Anyone who reads the letters, for example, of Ferruccio Busoni, the half-Italian, half-German-Jewish musician, will realise that his life was torn by such tensions. Hilaire Belloc's exaggerated violence of style and opinion is traceable to his insecure position in English society, something of which he was not unaware. There are a great many less-known figures who belong to what in the United States are called hyphenated groups,[1] recent immigrants not fully integrated into the new life of a foreign land. But the most vivid examples of this malaise can be found among the most famous and gifted of all the wandering tribes of men – the Jews of the west who had lost the supporting framework of the rigorous discipline of their faith, and stood facing a new and by no means friendly world, marvellous but dangerous, in which any untoward step might be fatal, but the rewards were correspondingly great, where ignorance, anxiety, ambition, danger, hope, fear, all fed the imagination. Over-anxiety to enter into a heritage not obviously one's own can be self-defeating, lead to over-eager desire for immediate acceptance, hopes held out, then betrayed: to unrequited love, frustration, resentment, bitterness, although it also sharpens the perceptions, and, like the grit which rubs against an oyster, causes suffering from which pearls of genius sometimes spring.

This was the fate of the first generation of gifted and ambitious Jews to seek admission to the outer world. Everyone knows the story of Ludwig Börne and Heinrich Heine,[2] to whom their anomalous status became a kind of obsession. The more they insisted that they were Germans, true heirs of German culture, concerned only about German values, or at any rate about bringing the fruits of enlightenment to their compatriots, the less German they seemed to these same Germans. The search for security seems to those who are secure a symptom of abnormality, and often irritates them. Less temperamental and quieter personalities among the Jews slipped through the doors of the European world unperceived. Their children mingled peacefully and naturally with its inhabitants. The bolder spirits hammered upon the gates, attracted unwelcome attention, were admitted grudgingly, and never attained to complete ease in their new surroundings. They resorted to various expedients in order to keep going, to triumph over their disabilities, to convince the others of their good faith, of their

[1] Italian-American, Greek-American etc.

[2] Heine, of course, identified himself with the Jewish community to a far greater extent than Börne ever did, at any rate before his baptism; but even after it, in his alternating moods of mocking irony and sentimental attachment to the old religion, and in particular the Old Testament, he never severed himself spiritually from it, as other Jewish converts of his time, for example Stahl or Mendelssohn's daughters and their brother who changed his name to Bartholdy, clearly did.

loyalty, of their genius, of their eligibility to the club. The more they protested, the more evidence they provided of the nature of the problem which they constituted and of the difficulties of any simple solution.

It is with two cardinal representatives of this peculiar historical and psychological predicament that I am concerned in this essay. I have chosen two men, both famous, influential, exceptionally gifted, to point my moral. They differ vastly from each other in obvious respects; yet they share in the particular qualities which I have touched upon, and were involved in a common situation.

It was Herder, the German philosopher of history, who first drew wide attention to the proposition that among elementary human needs – as basic as those for food, shelter, security, procreation, communication – is the need to belong to a particular group, united by some common links – especially language, collective memories, continuous life upon the same soil, to which some added characteristics of which we have heard much in our time – race, blood, religion, a sense of common mission, and the like. However greatly we may deplore the appalling consequences of the exaggeration or perversion of what in Herder was a peaceful and humanitarian doctrine, there can be no doubt that the world which succeeded the French Revolution in Europe was dominated by the principle of conscious cohesion, and the emergence of hitherto relatively suppressed groups – national, social, religious, political, and the like. In this age of the self-conscious solidarity of nations, of ethnic and linguistic minorities, of classes, parties, social orders, the question of what group a given individual belonged to, where he was naturally at home, became increasingly acute. The Jews were emancipated under the great banner of humanism, equality, toleration, internationalism, enlightened ideals in the name of which men rose against kings and priests, ignorance and privilege. Yet, as all students of history discover, the Revolution and the wars that followed unchained the aggressive forces of submerged nations, classes, movements, individuals. The Europe into which the victims of injustice and inequality were admitted was a world more and more dominated by the violent struggles of hitherto suppressed groups for liberty and self-determination, by nationalism, by ferocious competition for status, power, acquisition. The desire on the part of the most discriminated-against minority in history to be integrated, to be at one with respected members of mankind, was naturally overwhelming. The great eighteenth-century apostle of secular education for the

Jews, Moses Mendelssohn, had wished them to attain to the social and educational and cultural level of their neighbours : to be as others are. The fact that one of his sons and both his daughters became Christian is not altogether surprising ; how much Christian doctrine they believed remains uncertain. What is clear is that they wished to be at one with the enviable part of humanity, the upper, civilised, liberated section of it. Cultural and political unity, national, so-called 'organic', solidarity, these were among the watchwords of the day. To some of those who were outside this development, it seemed at times bathed in a golden light. It is a well-known psychological phenomenon that outsiders tend to idealise the land beyond the frontier on which their gaze is fixed. Those who are born in the solid security of a settled society, and remain full members of it, and look upon it as their natural home, tend to have a stronger sense of social reality : to see public life in reasonably just perspective, without the need to escape into political fantasy or romantic invention. This tendency to idealisation is most frequently found among those who belong to minorities which are to some degree excluded from participation in the central life of their community. They are liable to develop either exaggerated resentment of, or contempt for, the dominant majority, or else over-intense admiration or indeed worship for it, or, at times, a combination of the two, which leads both to unusual insights and — born of overwrought sensibilities — a neurotic distortion of the facts.

This has often been noticed in the case of political leaders who come from outside the society that they lead or, at any rate, from its edges, the outer marches of it. Napoleon's vision of France was not that of a Frenchman ; Gambetta came from the southern borderlands, Stalin was a Georgian, Hitler an Austrian, Kipling came from India, de Valera was only half-Irish, Rosenberg came from Estonia, Theodor Herzl and Jabotinsky, as well as Trotsky, from the assimilated edges of the Jewish world — all these were men of fiery vision, whether noble or degraded, idealistic or perverted, which had its origin in wounds inflicted upon their *amour propre* and upon their insulted national consciousness, because they lived near the borders of the nation, where the pressure of other societies, of foreign civilisations, was strongest. Hugh Trevor-Roper has justly remarked that the most fanatical nationalism arises in centres where nationalities and cultures mingle, where friction is sharpest, in, for example, Vienna — to which could be added the Baltic provinces which formed Herder, the independent Duchy of Savoy, in which de Maistre, the father of French chauvinism, was born and bred, or Lorraine, in the case of Barrès or de Gaulle. It is in these outlying provinces that the ideal vision of the people or the nation as it should be, as one sees it with the eyes of faith, whatever the actual facts, is generated and grows fervent.

It is, therefore, not surprising to find this same process in the case of the newly emancipated members of a community which, being a minority everywhere, longed to identify itself with the majority, men who saw themselves in their daydreams as being recognised at last, granted equality and status, or, in the case of more passionate temperaments, as lifted from the status of liberated slaves to that of masters who determine the fate of others. But even if the imagination of such members of excluded groups did not reach this pitch of ardour, they looked for liberation from their anomalous, and often inferior, social status. This tended to take two forms: either conscious demands for equality or superiority, struggles for self-determination and independence on the part of submerged nations, for conquest and glory on the part of rising empires, for social or economic recognition or domination by militant classes, religious communities, churches, and other human groups. That was one form. The history of nationalism, of socialism, of clerical and anti-clerical movements, of imperialism, militarism, fascism, racial conflict and the like, is familiar enough to us today.

But there is also another form of this craving for recognition: and that is an effort to escape from the weakness and humiliation of a depressed or wounded social group by identifying oneself with some other group or movement that is free from the defects of one's original condition: consisting in an attempt to acquire a new personality, and that which goes with it, a new set of clothing, a new set of values, habits, new armour which does not press upon the old wounds, on the old scars left by the chains one wore as a slave. That is indeed the point of armies, discipline, uniforms. Men who feel lost and defenceless in their original condition are transformed into brave and disciplined fighters when they are given a brand new cause to fight for, especially one which can historically be connected with real or imaginary past glories. Irishmen, demoralised in conquered Ireland, fought magnificently in British or American armies. Bohemians, crushed by Austria, performed feats of valour in the Czech Legion. Theodor Herzl knew what he was about when he compelled his bewildered followers at the first Zionist Congress to wear the most formal possible dress in order to rise to the dignity and historical grandeur of the occasion – an occasion which was to lead to their spiritual and material metamorphosis from a collection of disorganised individuals into a national movement. Herzl's demand for ceremonial was regarded by the more doubting delegates from eastern Europe, including Weizmann, with ill-disguised irony and scepticism. Weizmann recognised his error in due course. To acquire a new persona, to shed the emblems of servitude and inferiority, and don the garments and badges, acquire the gestures and habits and style of life, of free men – that was the natural craving of a good many members of hitherto oppressed groups standing on the threshold – so at any rate they hoped – of a new life of equality, dignity, and a career open to their hitherto frustrated talents. Such was the new hope given by Napoleon's victories to the Jews of the Rhineland, a great storm blowing down the ancient feudal restrictions, destroying ghettos, raising their denizens to their full stature as human beings; a new beginning which Heine, who lived through it, half-celebrated, half-derided, as he did everything. The winds of change, unleashed by events abroad, began to blow in England too. It is the psychological peculiarity of this situation that I should like to illustrate by the reactions of the two very dissimilar men, Benjamin Disraeli and Karl Marx.

II

At first the contrast between them must seem very sharp: the first a somewhat fantastic figure, an ambitious opportunist, a social and political adventurer, flamboyant, over-dressed, the epitome of dandyism and artificiality: rings on his gloved fingers, elaborate ringlets of hair falling about his pale, exotic features, with his fancy waistcoats, his rococo eloquence, his epigrams, his malice, his flattery, and his dazzling social and political gifts, admired but distrusted and by some feared and loathed, a Pied Piper leading a bemused collection of dukes, earls, solid country gentlemen, and burly farmers, one of the oddest and most fantastic phenomena of the entire nineteenth century. And on the other side, a grim and poverty-stricken subversive pamphleteer, a bitter, lonely and fanatical exile, hurling imprecations against the rich and the powerful, a remorseless plotter, preparing the doom of the accursed class of exploiters and enemies of the workers; a single-minded and solitary worker in the British Museum, who with his pen has caused a greater transformation in the world than heads of state and soldiers and men of action. And yet there is a certain parallel to which I should like to call attention.

Their origins were not wholly dissimilar; neither came of celebrated ancestors. Disraeli's family appears to have come from Italy, and before that, if Cecil Roth is allowed his plausible conjecture, from the Levant. As for Karl Marx, his ancestors on both sides of his family were German, Hungarian and Polish rabbis. His paternal grandfather and great-grandfather were both rabbis in his native city of Trier. Karl Marx's father was the son of the rabbi Meier Halevy Marx, or Marx Levi, who married the daughter of Moses Lwow. Moses Lwow's father, Heschel Lwow, was chosen Rabbi of Trier in 1723, and was descended from rabbis in the Polish city whose name he bore; other ancestors were rabbis in Padua, Cracow and Mainz. Karl's earliest traceable ancestor migrated to Italy from Germany in the early fifteenth century. His maternal grandfather moved from Hungary to Holland, where he became a rabbi in Nijmegen. One daughter married Heschel Marx, Karl's father. The other married a banker named Philips, grandfather of the founder of the electrical firm which today has grown to world size. In both cases the families benefited socially from the opportunities offered by the Enlightenment in the second half of the eighteenth century.

There is, too, a certain psychological similarity between the fathers of these greatly, though perhaps unequally, gifted men. Isaac d'Israeli, who refused to enter the commercial career intended for him by his father Benjamin, was by all accounts a gentle and amiable minor man of letters, a bookish and unassuming compiler of entertaining miscellanies of anecdotes and odd English literary bric-à-brac. He was a good-natured and unpretentious man, and it was by these characteristics rather than by literary distinction that he won the patronage of eminent men of letters – Scott, Lockhart, Byron, Samuel Rogers – as well as the friendship of the publisher John Murray II, and became a welcome figure in the literary London society of his time. An affable host, almost a country gentleman,[1] an enlightened Tory with a passion for Charles I, he was irritated by the reiterated demands that he perform administrative functions in the Sephardi synagogue of London; he left it, and the Jewish community, easily. He seems to have been remote from any kind of passionate belief. If anything, he was

---

[1] André Maurois in his biography of Benjamin Disraeli seems to me to make too much of this. His book – *La Vie de Disraëli* (Paris, 1927) – reveals more about the author than about the subject.

probably something of an eighteenth-century deist, neither particularly pleased nor displeased at being born a Jew. He was an easy-going man, not bothered with spiritual problems – a state of mind which he shared with a great many of the liberal agnostics of his civilised age and milieu. His friend, Sharon Turner, persuaded him to baptise his children; he did this, as many similar persons have done since, in order to let them have an easier path in the world, unencumbered by burdens which, in any case, he saw no good reason to bear or make others carry. His son Benjamin was baptised in 1817. In this same year, Heschel Marx, Karl's father, was received into the Lutheran church and baptised Heinrich. Like Isaac d'Israeli, the elder Marx came of an orthodox family – his father and brother were, after all, rabbis in Trier – but he too had been brought up on the works of anti-clerical writers, Voltaire and Rousseau. He was thirty-four or thirty-five when the restoration of Prussian rule in the Rhineland, after the defeat of Napoleon, placed a barrier to the employment of Jews as lawyers. Since he wished to continue his career, and had evidently long lost his Jewish faith, and probably looked on official Protestantism as not so very different from the vague deism of many of the founders of the Enlightenment, he too painlessly crossed the frontier, and baptised Karl and his other children in August 1824. Mild, respectful to authority, anxious to please, he wished to stand well with his fellow-citizens. He was devoted to Karl, worried by his headstrong character, eager that he should pursue a successful career and not irritate important persons. Kindly, tremulous, anxious to do what is right, he was a model Prussian citizen, as Isaac d'Israeli was a model British one. Both of these gentle, middle-class fathers gave to the world sons driven on by an inner dynamism remote from their own constitution, passionate, imperious, with fiery temperaments, unbending wills, and considerable contempt for most of the human beings by whom they were surrounded: determined to be and do something, and, in their very different ways, successful in this ambition. In both cases, bonds of affection united son to father. Benjamin Disraeli always spoke in the most touching terms of Isaac; Karl Marx all his life carried with him a picture of his father; he was never as intimate with anyone else, not even with Engels. The famous letter he wrote to his father in November 1837, when he was nineteen years old, is the most complete, indeed the only, self-disclosure that we have of him. Both looked on their mothers with relative indifference. What this shows about either I must leave to psychologists to consider.

Profoundly as Marx and Disraeli differed in outlook as well as circumstances and temperament, they did evidently have something in common: above all, both were filled with a passionate desire to dominate their society. Marx wished to alter it, Disraeli to be accepted by it and lead it. Both wrote extravagant, romantic fantasies in their youth; both, each in his own fashion, turned against the milieu into which they had been born; both discovered the proletariat as its victim: Marx saw it as the carrier of revolution; Disraeli as an object of concern to the landed classes and their ally against the bourgeoisie.[1]

As for Christian doctrine, it was rejected by Marx quite early in life, by the time he was a university student. It meant a good deal to Disraeli. He was not in the least cynical about religion in general, nor about Christianity in particular. All his life he seems to have believed in a quasi-mystical, somewhat literary Christianity of his own, a religion deeply tinged by a sense of historical continuity and a faith sanctified by tradition which Burke and Coleridge had done much to reinvigorate. In spite of this he was, of course, thought of as a Jew by almost everyone, and more or less thought of himself as one at all times. He was no more like an average Englishman in appearance or bearing than Marx was like an average German. Both were outsiders, both took steps to rid themselves of the disadvantages of their origins; Disraeli took one path, Marx another.

Disraeli's position was thoroughly ambivalent. He was not in any ordinary sense an Englishman, that was clear; what, then, was he? Others did not need to answer this question. To them he was an odd, anomalous being, an object of admiration or disdain, envy or ridicule, found irresistibly attractive or vulgarly exhibitionistic, the 'Jew d'esprit', as he was known in certain London circles in the earlier part of the century. But to himself he was a problem. If he was to be effective – and he made no secret of the intense ambition that drove him on – he must find his place in a deeply class-ridden and, despite the rapid social transformation produced by the Industrial Revolution, still very hierarchical English society. What was he? What interest, class, social structure, did he represent? He could float on as an amusing and exotic literary dilettante – the author of *Vivian Grey*, a *roman-à-clef*, a sparkling and ironical account of the London society of his time. He began as an outsider, a forerunner of Oscar Wilde, Proust, Evelyn Waugh, fascinated by the aristocracy, half in love with it, half mocking it, an amusing young artist, the inventor of

[1] I owe this point to Yigal Allon.

the political novel, a brilliant talker and diner-out, thought something of a bounder by men, and found attractive by women – in that easy world he could continue without identifying himself with any particular segment of society, a cool observer from the outside, whose sense of perspective came from his very distance from the material of his art. But this was not enough for him. He wanted power, and he wanted recognition by those on the inside, as one of them, at least as an equal if not as a superior. Hence the psychological need to establish an identity for himself, for which he would secure recognition, an identity that would enable him to develop his gifts freely, to their utmost extent. And in due course he did create a personality for himself, at least in his own imagination. He saw before him a society of aristocrats, free, arrogant and powerful, which, however sharply he may have seen through it, he nevertheless viewed with bemused eyes as a rich and marvellous world. His novels make this very clear. A man may not be sincere in his political speeches or his letters, but his works of art are himself and tell one where his true values lie. He did not set himself to conquer this world solely because it was politically important. Perhaps the new order of manufacturers and technicians, the still rising middle class which was creating the wealth of England, was, as he well knew, more important in terms of present and future power. But Disraeli was hopelessly fascinated by the aristocracy as a class and a principle. It was by it that he wished to be recognised, it that he admired, and of it that he wished to govern the universe; he describes it with the most loving devotion, even at his most malicious and ironical.

Disraeli was always drawn to the non-rational sides of life. He was a genuine romantic not merely in the extravagance and flamboyance of his works, the poses that he struck, and the many vanities of his private and political life – these could be regarded as relatively superficial. He was a romantic in a deeper sense, in that he believed that the true forces that governed the lives of individuals and societies were not intelligible to analytical reason, not codifiable by any kind of systematic, scientific investigation, but were unique, mysterious, dark and impalpable, beyond the reach of reason. He believed deeply in the vast influence of superior individuals – men of genius lifted high over the head of the mob – masters of the destinies of nations. He believed in heroes no less than his detractor Carlyle. He despised equality, mediocrity, and the common man. He saw history as the story of conspiracies by men of hidden power everywhere, and delighted in the thought.

Utilitarianism, sober observation, experiment, mathematical reasoning, rationalism, common sense, the astonishing achievements and constructions of scientific reason – the true glory of humanity since the seventeenth century – these were almost nothing to him. His contempt for Bentham or Mill was not stimulated by the mere fact that he was conservative and they were not; it was rooted in his particular vision which made their values seem to him dreary and vulgar, as, say, Bertrand Russell's values appeared to T. S. Eliot (another 'alien' Tory). He was passionately convinced that intuition and imagination were vastly superior to reason and method. He believed in temperament, blood, race, the unaccountable leaps of genius. He was an antirationalist through and through. Art, love, passion, the mystical elements of religion, meant more to him than railways or the transforming discoveries of the natural sciences, or the industrial might of England, or social improvement, or any truth obtained by measurement, statistics, deduction. A man of this outlook, which remained unaltered from the beginning to the end of his days, could not but be dazzled by the aristocracy, as Balzac, or Wilde, or Proust were, as many a sensitive, imaginative, inferiority-ridden boy of plebeian or middle-class origin must have been, when he came into contact with what seemed, and perhaps was, a freer, gayer, more confident world.

Given these characteristics, and an overwhelming desire to enter this exhilarating society and play a great part in it, Disraeli gave free rein to his fantasy, not indeed consciously, but all the more passionately. He came to see himself lifted high above the milling multitude – the middle and lower classes, the masses of men of limited vision; for he was not of them, he was a brilliant high-born figure. How could this be? It was, it must be so, because he was a member of an élite, an ancient race which had given the world its most precious possessions – religion, laws, social institutions, its sacred books, and finally its Divine Saviour, who completed the work of the great lawgiver Moses, his own family being among the noblest and proudest of the ancient race. The race was indeed ancient; as for his ancestors, in 1849, in his edition of his father's works, Disraeli told his readers this:

> My grandfather . . . was an Italian descendant from one of those Hebrew families whom the Inquisition forced to emigrate from the Spanish Peninsula at the end of the fifteenth century, and who found a refuge in the more tolerant territories of the Venetian Republic. His ancestors had dropped their Gothic surname . . . and grateful to the God of Jacob who had sustained them through

unprecedented trials and guarded them through unheard-of perils, they assumed the name of DISRAELI, a name never borne before or since by any other family, in order that their race might be for ever recognised. Undisturbed and unmolested, they flourished as merchants for more than two centuries under the protection of the lion of St Mark . . .[1]

And so on. There is, it seems, no word of truth in this. Lucien Wolf[2] and Cecil Roth[3] have torn it all to shreds, and Lord Blake in his admirable biography accepts their findings.[4] It is probably all pure fiction. There is no evidence that Disraeli's family came from Spain, nor that they had settled in Venice; his grandfather came to England from the Papal States, from Cento, near Ferrara, and two poor relatives of his did live in the Venetian ghetto in his own lifetime, but that is all. There are no records of any earlier d'Israelis in Spain or Venice. Nor was the well-known De Lara family, with whom he claimed kinship, related to him; and so, I am afraid, it goes on. But he evidently persuaded himself of all this, and this belief buoyed him up. The reality was too embarrassing: he needed a role to act, otherwise he could not perform. He was the most brilliant performer of his age, and if he had not half-believed in the reality of his own invention he could scarcely have mounted the public stage. It was as a fellow-aristocrat that he led the dukes and the baronets against the manufacturers and the Benthamites. His opponents, and many a later observer, thought him no better than a cunning and cynical impostor. Yet this cannot possibly be anywhere near the whole truth. Certainly he invented; but he was, as happens with imaginative men, largely taken in by his own inventions. His achievement and his ascendancy are not intelligible without this. He was an actor, and he became one with his act: the mask became one with his features: second nature replaced first – otherwise the gestures would have been too hollow, and in the end would have deceived no one. Yet, despite all the artifice and rhetoric and exotic airs, he carried conviction. He did so because

[1] 'On the Life and Writings of Mr Disraeli', in Isaac Disraeli, *Curiosities of Literature* (London, 1881), vol. 1, p. viii.

[2] Lucien Wolf, 'The Disraeli Family', *The Times*, 20 (p. 6) and 21 (p. 12) December 1904; repr. in *Transactions of the Jewish Historical Society of England* 5 (1902–5), 202–18.

[3] Cecil Roth, *Benjamin Disraeli: Earl of Beaconsfield* (New York, 1952), chapter 1.

[4] Robert Blake, *Disraeli* (London, 1966), p. 4.

he had convinced himself: his ideas, his political ideals, his religious views may have struck some both then and later as tawdry, theatrical or even wicked, but they were not sham. Disraeli was an adventurer and an exhibitionist, but he was not, in politics or religion, either a cynic or a hypocrite.

There is a puzzle here. Even if the Tory party, after it was split by Peel over the repeal of the Corn Laws, needed a clever man to restore its fortunes, since it was not too well endowed with able men itself ('The Conservatives [are] the stupidest party,'[1] said John Stuart Mill; and, when attacked for this, 'I never meant to say that the Conservatives are generally stupid. I meant to say that stupid people are generally Conservative'),[2] and even if the country squires and the dukes, and even the burly farmers, thought that they needed this oriental-looking spellbinder to save them from follies and blunders, yet the fact that he became their undisputed leader, that he achieved this astonishing symbiosis with men so utterly different from himself, with men who suffered from every possible prejudice against all that he was and stood for, cannot be explained unless he truly believed himself called upon to be the champion of their cause, genuinely believed in their attributes, idealised them as something far superior to qualities and interests represented by the Whigs and the radicals with whom he had begun life. More than this. The most intimate political associates of his middle years were those members of Young England who believed profoundly in an organic national society, in the duties of aristocratic landowners to their dependents, in the restoration of a Christian neo-feudal order, young men with a horror of industrialism and a desire to restore the broken texture of faith and community, a sense of social dedication, a spirit of loyalty and duty directed against the bleak individualism and self-interest of the manufacturers and shopkeepers and the market society which Carlyle and Ruskin, Kingsley and William Morris denounced with equal fury, despite all their profound differences. How could these deeply earnest, deeply Christian, sensitive, fastidious young noblemen, how could they, of all people, not only accept as one of themselves but faithfully follow as their leader a clever Levantine manipulator, a kind of hired mercenary *condottiere*, without principles or ideals, the kind of soulless leprechaun that Disraeli has

---

[1] *Considerations on Representative Government*, chapter 7, note.

[2] W. L. Courtney, *Life of John Stuart Mill* (London, 1889), p. 147. See also J. S. Mill, *Autobiography* (London, 1873), p. 289.

from time to time been represented as being by unsympathetic biographers and historians? It is as a diabolical figure, false through and
through, a deadly opponent of all that was right and good, that Gladstone, for instance, or the Duke of Argyll saw him. This is the viper
whom Lord John Manners and Lord George Bentinck pressed to
their bosom; whom, despite their parents' warnings, these young
Tory lords followed and never repented of their allegiance.

But there is no need to be too deeply puzzled by this. Disraeli's
novels afford all the evidence needed to show that his faith in aristocracy, in race, in genius, his hatred of industrial exploitation, his
belief in blood and soil (before these words had become degraded by
the use made of them by insane German nationalists), his adoring
devotion to history, the land, the continuity that breeds distinction,
to ancient institutions – however irrational, fanciful, reactionary all
this may have been – were, at any rate, genuine. This was the material
out of which his own historical, or pseudo-historical, imagination
constructed the personality with which he faced England and the
world. Unlike some of the assimilated Jews of his time, baptised and
unbaptised, he did no violence to what he felt to be true of himself.
No one can fail to notice that he boasted of his Jewish origins almost
too insistently, and mentioned them in and out of season at some risk
to his political career, and this despite his eccentric but genuine Christianity. No doubt the fact that he was born a Jew offered an obstacle
to his career: he overcame it by inflating it into a tremendous claim
to noble birth. He needed to do this in order to feel that he was dealing
on equal terms with the leaders of his family's adopted country, which
he so profoundly venerated. Hence the extraordinary fantasies in his
novels.

It is plain that at school he was, or came near to being, mocked and
persecuted. The famous passage in his early novel, *Vivian Grey*, in
which the usher at school speaks of the hero, namely himself, as a
'seditious stranger'[1] (he made no secret that his novels were largely
autobiographical) gives us the key. And again:

> They were called my brothers, but Nature gave the lie to the re-
> iterated assertion. There was no similitude between us. Their blue
> eyes, their flaxen hair, and their white visages claimed no kindred
> with my Venetian countenance. Wherever I moved I looked around

[1] Book 1, chapter 4, p. 9: page references are to the Bradenham Edition
of the Novels and Tales of Benjamin Disraeli, 1st Earl of Beaconsfield
(London, 1926–7).

me, and beheld a race different from myself. There was no sympathy between my frame and the rigid clime whither I had been brought to live.

This is a passage from *Contarini Fleming*[1] and it tells its own tale. How was he to get even with these people? Why, by asserting, and over-asserting, his true origin. Who were these people who set themselves up above him? He describes them as 'A troop of Norman knights, whose fathers were wreckers, Baltic pirates.'

Was then this mixed population of Saxons and Normans, among whom he had first seen the light, of purer blood than he? Oh no, he was descended in a direct line from one of the oldest races in the world, from that rigidly separate and unmixed Bedouin race who had developed a high civilisation at a time when the inhabitants of England were going half-naked and eating acorns in their woods.

He goes on to declare that he was of pure blood, and yet, strange to say, they regarded his race as of lower caste, and nevertheless they had adopted most of the laws, and many of the customs, which constituted the peculiarity of this caste in their 'Arabian' home. They had appropriated all the religion and all the literature of his father. The heritage of the Jews was the basis of all subsequent civilised society. They revered the literature, the Sabbath, the sacred history of the Jewish people, its hymns, laments and praises, finally, 'the son of a Jewish woman as their God'. 'Yet, nevertheless, they excluded with disdain from their society and their parliament, as if they were the off-scourings of the earth, the race to which they owed their festivals, their psalms, their semi-civilisation, their religion and their God. He racked his brains.'

I need not rehearse again all the passages quoted by Disraeli's many biographers, particularly by the Jews among them, of all those lyrical outbursts in which he speaks of the ancient Hebrews and of the Jews in general. In his early fantasy, *The Wondrous Tale of Alroy*, the hero restores the Jews to their ancient land, conquers the whole of Asia Minor, and finally perishes in glorious fashion. In *Coningsby*, the mysterious and omnipotent figure of Sidonia, benevolent, powerful, all but omniscient, is a representative of the 'pure Asian breed'[2] that makes Jews and Arabs cousins, and causes Disraeli to describe

[1] Part 1, chapter 2, p. 5.
[2] Book 4, chapter 10, p. 232.

the Arabs as merely 'Jews upon horseback'.[1] Sidonia explains that the
Jews have triumphed over time and persecution because of their
Caucasian blood[2] and the wise laws that segregate them from lower
races.[3] He compares them favourably with 'some flat-nosed Frank,
full of bustle and puffed-up with self-conceit (a race spawned perhaps
in the morasses of some Northern forest hardly yet cleared)'.[4] There
is the strange vision of the feverish *Lothair*. There is the epiphany in
Tancred when 'the angel of Arabia' addresses the hero in Palestine in
mystical phrases.[5] This novel, Disraeli's favourite, is more than any
of his other works penetrated by the notion that all that is eastern is
good, noble, fine, destined to triumph. This is not Jewish nationalism
in any simple sense. To suppose that Disraeli was a Zionist is anachronistic and not plausible.[6] The eastern melodies were called into
being in response to the need to construct a persona, an inner image of
himself with which he could establish for himself a place in the world,
and play a part in history and in society.

That is what is meant by the search for identity contained in my
title. As the son of a minor littérateur, an Italianate stranger, who
clearly did not belong to any of the normal social groups which composed British political society in the nineteenth century, he could not
easily make his way without some decisive act of psychological self-
transformation, if he was not to be consumed by the painful consciousness that he was out of place, did not belong, was a foreign body, stared
at and dismissed as a mountebank, Carlyle's 'superlative Hebrew Con-
juror',[7] a foreign adventurer of whom E. T. Raymond declared that
'his heart was not that of an Englishman'.[8] He was, therefore, driven
to invent a role for himself, to find a desirable class of persons with

[1] *Tancred*, book 4, chapter 3, p. 261.

[2] *Coningsby*, book 4, chapter 15, pp. 263–7.

[3] ibid., chapter 10, p. 232.

[4] *Tancred*, book 3, chapter 7, p. 233.

[5] Book 4, chapter 7, pp. 299–300.

[6] The story of the Austrian journalist Chlumiecki that Disraeli was the
author of a Zionist tract which only Bismarck persuaded him not to place
before the Congress of Berlin does not seem, to say the least, plausible enough
to deserve closer scrutiny. See Cecil Roth, op. cit. (p. 266, note 3 above),
pp. 159–62.

[7] Thomas Carlyle, 'Shooting Niagara: and After?', *Critical and Miscel-
laneous Essays* (London, 1899), vol. 5, p. 11.

[8] E. T. Raymond (pseudonym of E. R. Thompson), *Disraeli: The Alien
Patriot* (London, [1926]), p. 5.

whom he could worthily identify himself. This was accomplished by a mysterious, unconscious sleight of mind: 'the influence of a great race will be felt'. Hence 'it is impossible to destroy the Jews'.[1] All Jews were aristocrats: their peers were the ancient landed gentry who were being done down, defeated and destroyed by ill-bred upstarts, Burke's utilitarian sophisters, economists and calculators, heartless industrial exploiters who were destroying the bodies and souls of their fellow-men in mines and factories, vulgarians unaware of history, men who did not know what their feet were trampling, atheists, utilitarians, Manchester individualists, materialists remote from all spiritual values, from the sacred mystery of being, blind leaders of the blind, dead to the spiritual bonds that united men to each other and to God. This fantasy was fed by his luxuriant imagination and, growing round the older doctrine derived from the Anglican tradition, Burke and the romantics, became one of the roots of that mystique which is still at the heart of what remains of English Conservative thought.

In the course of developing this splendid vision, Disraeli invested the British Empire, and in particular its oriental possessions, India and the dominion over Egypt still to come, with the same opulent imagination that was intrinsically so foreign to ordinary empirical, cautious British thought. The combination of this richly coloured fantasy with more traditional strains affected British political thought, and shaped it for many fateful decades. When Disraeli presided over the elevation of Queen Victoria to the throne of the Empress of India, and all that went with it, the gorgeous trappings of empire, the elephants and the durbars, and all those eastern splendours which had succeeded the realistic, hard-headed rule of the East India Company and inspired the vast and occasionally hollow periods of later imperialist rhetoric, it is difficult to resist the impression that something of this stemmed from Disraeli's genuine orientalism. There is, after all, none of it in Dutch or French or Spanish or Portuguese imperialism – nor are any native British roots perceptible. So, too, Disraeli's relationship to the Queen, those enormous compliments which seemed so shameless to his rivals, were a natural expression of this vision. Doubtless there was a good dose of irony, not to say cynicism, in his courtship of the Queen. But it sprang no less from the craving for splendour and glory with which hard-headed, shrewd, even ruthless personalities – even Victoria herself – need to comfort themselves to compensate

[1] *Lord George Bentinck: A Political Biography* (London, 1852), pp. 494, 495.

for the hollow qualities of public life. Like all those whose lives are in part a fantasy, yet not wholly cut off from reality, Disraeli knew that some of this was make-believe, that *Alroy*, as he once said, was not to be taken too seriously, for it was but a legend. Yet it also penetrated his being. His vision of his relationship to Queen Victoria was an imaginative creation in which he believed, even while he was aware of the element of sheer invention. He did half genuinely see Victoria as a great empress and himself as her vizier; she was Semiramis and Titania, Empress of the East and Queen of the Fairies.

His own rise must have seemed incredible and marvellous to him; when he played his part in the pantomime, he was transported by it; his mockery of it did not make it unreal to him; it is like the jokes that believers make about their own faith. If he had not at least half-believed in the world he conjured up, he could scarcely have carried it all through. The hypnotist half-hypnotised himself. If this is not recognised, his whole career is not intelligible. It is not enough, as some of his biographers are apt to do, to describe his outer gestures; the inner dynamism must be grasped, and this is bound up with the identity that he invented for himself, that seemed gimcrack and false to the Gladstonian Duke of Argyll, whom Cecil Roth quotes as saying of Disraeli that, having as a Jew no opinions of his own and no traditions with which to break, he 'was free to play with prejudices in which he did not share, and to express passions which were not his own, except insofar as they were tinged with personal resentment'.[1] This seems to me a false diagnosis: Disraeli may not have shared the prejudices, but the passions had indeed been made his own; if he had no relevant traditions of his own, he constructed them, and in the end believed in them, lived by them. Of course any life founded on as much Byronic fantasy as Disraeli's is bound to seem 'deceitful', 'politically dishonest', immoral and cynical, to high-minded and unsympathetic observers. But when Disraeli says, as he does in *Coningsby*, 'An unmixed race of a firstrate organisation are the true aristocracy of Nature',[2] he clearly believes this. His advocacy of race, nationality, tradition, his distaste for liberal cosmopolitanism, and so, too, for atheism, rationalism, free trade, is the genuine faith he lived by. The only way in which he could avoid what was irregular in his own position was by clothing himself in the play of a transforming fancy.

[1] Cecil Roth, op. cit. (p. 266, note 3 above), p. 85.
[2] Book 4, chapter 10, p. 232.

How limited is human reason [he makes Sidonia exclaim], the profoundest inquirers are most conscious. We are not indebted to the Reason of man for any of the great achievements which are the landmarks of human action and human progress. It was not Reason that besieged Troy; it was not Reason that sent forth the Saracen from the Desert to conquer the world; that inspired the Crusades; that instituted the Monastic orders; it was not Reason that produced the Jesuits; above all, it was not reason that created the French Revolution. Man is only truly great when he acts from the passions; never irresistible but when he appeals to the imagination. Even Mormon counts more votaries than Bentham.

This comes from *Coningsby*.[1] 'Mormon counts more votaries than Bentham.' This is certainly an irrationalist creed. It is this that enabled him to say, 'I am not disposed for a moment to admit that my pedigree is not as good [as] and even superior to that of the Cavendishes',[2] a remark he made during the election of 1847; and again, 'Fancy calling a fellow an adventurer when his ancestors were probably on intimate terms with the Queen of Sheba.'[3] His religious feeling, without which his involvement with Tory England is inexplicable, springs from the same source: when in the lecture at Oxford he said against Darwin and Huxley that he was on the side not of the apes but of the angels, I feel sure that this was more than a *bon mot*. It was typical of him: amusing, ironical, not intended to be taken seriously, and yet his deepest belief. There are those who can only bear to say what they most deeply feel in language purged of all solemnity. This sort of flippant irony may be defensive, but it is not therefore frivolous or superficial.

Unable to function in his proper person, as a man of dubious pedigree in a highly class-conscious society, Disraeli invented a splendid fairy tale, bound its spell upon the mind of England, and thereby influenced men and events to a considerable degree. Instead of ignoring or concealing his origins, which must have irked him when he was a schoolboy, and which were constantly cast in his face by his enemies (including Gladstone, who spoke of his fanaticism in the Jewish cause and called him a crypto-Jew), he went too far. He harps on it, exaggerates its importance, introduces it irrelevantly in his novels, and inserts a long excursus on the Jews in his life of Lord George Bentinck, which, he himself admits, has little to do with Bentinck's acts

[1] Book 4, chapter 13, p. 253.
[2] Cecil Roth, op. cit. (p. 266, note 3 above), p. 60.   [3] ibid.

or opinions: by way of preface to a lengthy refutation of the doctrine that the Jewish dispersion is a punishment for deicide, as being both theologically and historically unsound, he writes:

> The toiling multitude rest every seventh day by virtue of a Jewish law; they are perpetually reading, 'for their example', the records of Jewish history and singing the odes and elegies of Jewish poets; and they daily acknowledge on their knees, with reverent gratitude, that the only medium of communication between the Creator and themselves is the Jewish race. Yet they treat that race as the vilest of generations . . .[1]

as they did 'the Attic race' before the restoration of Greece as a modern state. Such excursuses may crop up anywhere in his works. The idea of Jews grows obsessive: the world is for him populated with imaginary Jews: not only the all-powerful slightly sinister Sidonia, and the bizarre figures in *Tancred*, but a host of strange and surprising figures, early Jesuits and German professors, Russian diplomatists, Italian composers and prima donnas – all are Jews: they pull all the strings, they dominate all countries. 'All is race; there is no other truth,' says Sidonia;[2] 'progress and reaction are but words to mystify the millions . . . All is race,' he says in his life of Bentinck,[3] and the Jews are the quintessence of race. He was possessed by the idea of race, and, indeed, by that of his own origins. He denounced the 'pernicious doctrine of modern times, the natural equality of man',[4] the doctrine of cosmopolitanism, of mingling with 'inferior' races. Not socialism or internationalism but 'religion, property, and natural aristocracy' – these are the Jewish 'bias'.[5] Jews do become revolutionaries, as in 1848, but only because of wounds inflicted on them by 'ungrateful Christendom'.[6] He declares that

> The political equality of a particular race is a matter of municipal arrangement and depends entirely on political considerations and circumstances; but the natural equality of man now in vogue, and taking the form of cosmopolitan fraternity, is a principle which, were it possible to act on it, would deteriorate the great races and destroy all the genius of the world.[7]

If the 'great Anglo-Saxon republic' allowed itself to 'mingle with their

---

[1] op. cit. (p. 271, note 1 above), pp. 482–3.
[2] *Tancred*, book 2, chapter 14, p. 153.
[3] op. cit. (p. 271, note 1 above), p. 331.
[4] ibid., p. 496. [5] ibid., p. 497. [6] ibid., p. 498. [7] ibid., p. 496.

negro and coloured populations' they would decline and 'probably be reconquered' by the very 'aborigines whom they have expelled and who would then be their superiors'.[1] But this will not be: 'it is in vain for man to attempt to baffle the inexorable law of nature which has decreed that a superior race shall never be destroyed or absorbed by an inferior'.[2] That is why the Jews have survived: 'for none but one of the great races could have survived the trials which it has endured'.[3] The basis of Disraeli's claims on behalf of the Jews is their 'Arabian' faith and the glories of their sacred history. It is arguable that such an argument could not have originated in, or been addressed to, any society less given to veneration of the past or intimate knowledge of Biblical texts, than that of Victorian England (and Scotland). Fichte and Arndt, Gobineau and Danilevsky, based their racist or biological fantasies on very different grounds.

Disraeli was one of the most troubled and most gifted of these 'alienated' men, whose problems today worry politicians, sociologists, educators, psychologists and all those who are concerned with the disintegrating effects of centralisation and industrialism. Of all the uprooted individuals and groups whom the nineteenth century generated, the Jews were, perhaps, the most striking and tragic example. It became clear that some way out of their dilemmas would have to be found, if they were not to be driven out of their minds, or drive others out of theirs. Assimilation, socialism, nationalism, redoubled efforts to preserve the ancient Jewish faith in all its rigour and purity, all these solutions have been proffered. The life of Benjamin Disraeli, the least Victorian of the Victorian age, a man out of his proper element, yet subduing it by sheer power of will and imagination, is one of the most vivid illustrations of a desperate search for a set of operative ideas, a plan of action, but above all, for a group loyalty, a regiment with which he could identify himself, in whose name he could speak and act, because he could not face the awful prospect of speaking in his own – indeed, he could not be certain that, if he tried to find what was his own, he would find an answer. The very doubt was unbearable. If the answer could not be found, it would have to be invented. Disraeli's conceptions of England, Europe, Jews, himself, were bold romantic fantasies. 'When I want to read a novel,' he once declared, 'I write one.'[4] His entire life was a sustained attempt to live a fiction, and to cast its spell over the minds of others.

[1] ibid. [2] ibid., p. 495. [3] ibid., p. 490.
[4] See Wilfrid Meynell, *The Man Disraeli* (London, 1927), p. 220.

III

I shall not dwell at length on Disraeli's diametrical opposite, Karl Marx, whose case is better known. Karl Marx, as we all know, took a path directly contrary to that of Disraeli. So far from spurning reason, he wished to apply it to human affairs. He believed himself to be a scientist, Engels saw him as the Darwin of the social sciences. He wished to perform a rational analysis of what caused social development to occur as it did, why human beings had hitherto largely failed, and why they could and would in the future succeed in attaining to peace, harmony, cooperation and, above all, the self-understanding which is a prerequisite of rational self-direction.

This was remote from Disraeli's mode of thought; indeed it was what he most deeply abhorred. Yet there is something analogous about their social environment. Marx was directly descended from two long generations of rabbis. His father belonged, as Disraeli's did, to the first generation of emancipated Jews: both were mild conformists against whom their sons seemed to react violently, even while they retained affection for them, if no deep respect. Since Marx was baptised, he did not suffer from the disabilities of the Jews in Germany. But he was subject to anti-Semitic gibes from fellow socialists and radicals during the greater part of his life – he was taunted on this account by the Russian anarchist Bakunin, and he could scarcely have been unaware of Proudhon's violent hatred of the Jews, or of the similar views held by Arnold Ruge and Eugen Dühring. He attacks these men with violence; but there is no hint about his own Jewish origins. On this he is silent. His only contact with Jews as such is mentioned in a letter to Ruge, in 1843,[1] in which he writes that 'the President of the Israelites here [in Cologne] has just come to see me to get my help in the matter of a petition from the Jews addressed to the Diet. I will do it for them, repugnant as the Israelite faith is to me.' He explains this on the ground that the inevitable rejection of Jewish petitions, by causing resentment to grow, might be a blow at the Christian state. He mentions his origins, we are told by Marxologists, only once: in a letter to his uncle in Holland, Lion Philips, in 1864, he refers – as it happens – to Disraeli as a man coming 'from our common stock'.[2]

[1] Letter of 13 March 1843, Karl Marx, Friedrich Engels, *Werke* (East Berlin, 1956–) (hereafter *Werke*), vol. 27 (1973), p. 418.

[2] 'Unser Stammgenosse'. Letter of 29 November 1864, *Werke*, vol. 31 (1975), p. 432.

This is all. He comments casually and not unsympathetically on the conditions of the poor Jews in Jerusalem, who, Disraeli had remarked earlier in the century, were being converted by Christian missionaries at twenty piastres a head. He sent a dedicated copy of *Das Kapital* to the Jewish historian Heinrich Graetz. Apart from this, his attitude to Jews is uncompromisingly hostile. In a celebrated passage in his essay *On the Jewish Question* of 1844, he says that the secular morality of the Jews is egoism, their secular religion is huckstering, their secular god is money. The real God of the Jews is the bill of exchange. 'Money is the zealous God of Israel, before whom no other god may be',[1] and this is, in effect, repeated in the summary of the argument in *The Holy Family*. His specific argument against Bruno Bauer's objections to Jewish emancipation is not relevant: what is striking is the ferocity of his language, which resembles that of many later anti-Semitic tracts, both right- and left-wing, German, French, Russian, English: chauvinistic and Fascist, anarchist and communist, in the past and in growing measure in our own time.

In the *Theses on Feuerbach* of 1845, Marx speaks of a mistaken conception of praxis in its 'dirty Jewish manifestation'.[2] He calls the Paris Bourse the 'stock exchange synagogue', suggests that the tenth muse is Hebraic – 'the muse of stock exchange quotations'. He omits no opportunity of stressing the Jewish origin of the Foulds, the Rothschilds, and other financiers in Paris, and in 1856, in one of his articles in the New York *Tribune*, remarks: 'every tyrant is backed by a Jew and every Pope by a Jesuit'. His language rises to a climax of real hatred when he speaks of Lassalle (who remained unbaptised and did not conceal his Jewish sentiments). In a letter to Engels,[3] he calls him 'the Jewish nigger', and advances the hypothesis that Negro blood must have entered his veins as the result of the racial admixtures acquired by the Jews during the exodus from Egypt.[4] In another letter he complains of Lassalle's typically 'Jewish whine'.[5] Lassalle is usually

---

[1] *Werke*, vol. 1 (1974), p. 374.

[2] *Werke*, vol. 3 (1969), p. 5.

[3] Letter of 30 July 1862, *Werke*, vol. 30 (1974), pp. 257–9.

[4] ibid., p. 259: 'As the shape of his head and the texture of his hair suggest, he is descended from the negroes who joined Moses in his exodus from Egypt (unless his mother or paternal grandmother were crossed with a nigger). This union of Jew and German with its negro source was bound to produce a strange hybrid. The fellow's importunity is also negro.'

[5] *Werke*, vol. 30 (1974), p. 164.

referred to as Itzig, or Baron Itzig. (There was a real person of this name, a banker, in the eighteenth century, much mocked by Heine, but here the name is used as a derogatory nickname for a Jew. Itzig is a swindler, a usurer, in Gustav Freytag's *Soll und Haben*, and, like Lassalle, a Silesian Jew.) There is therefore something odd, to say the least, in the assertion made in a publication of the Marx-Engels Institute in 1943 that 'Marx denounced anti-Semitism in the strongest terms.' It is difficult to resist Thomas Masaryk's judgement that Marx is justly described as anti-Semitic. Yet it is clear that the issue was not one of complete indifference to him. When his son-in-law, Longuet, in his obituary of Marx's wife, Jenny von Westphalen, written for the socialist journal *La Justice* in 1881,[1] wrote of her hard fight against the resistance of her family to her marriage to him, and attributed this to racial prejudice, Marx was furious. He wrote to his daughter, Longuet's wife, that no such prejudice existed in the Westphalen family, and said that Monsieur Longuet would oblige him if he never mentioned his name again. That no anti-Semitic feeling at all existed even among enlightened aristocrats in the Rhineland at that period is not probable. The testimony of both Heine and Hess scarcely supports this. Even if the Westphalens were wholly untouched by anti-Semitism, Marx's reaction seems, on the face of it, over-violent. This was evidently a painfully sensitive area. What does seem clear is that Marx was a man of strong will and decisive action, who decided once and for all to destroy within himself the source of the doubts, uneasiness and self-questioning which tended to torment men like Börne, Heine, Lassalle and a good many others, including the founders of reform Judaism, and – until he resolved the problem in a Zionist sense – the first German communist, Moses Hess, whose origins and intellectual formation resembled Marx's own.

Marx contemptuously swept this question out of the way and decided to treat it as unreal. No doubt he would have found this more difficult if he had not been genuinely remote from Judaism. Yet he, too, was faced with the difficulty that the youthful Disraeli had encountered: he wished not merely to describe society but to alter it. He wanted to make his mark. He was a fighter, and wished to destroy those whom he conceived as obstacles to human progress. Germany in his day was more acutely nationalistic, after her humiliation by the French, not only under Napoleon but continuously during the two preceding centuries, than England or Holland or Italy or even France.

[1] *La Justice*, 7 December 1881.

278

Extreme German chauvinism had taken pathologically anti-Semitic forms in the years before Marx's birth. This occurred in the Rhineland no less than elsewhere in Germany. Anti-Jewish feeling was not confined to religious intolerance. In the powerful propaganda of Arndt, Jahn, Goerres, and for that matter also Fichte, and in the outbreaks of patriotic student associations, it was openly racialist. Lassalle once said, with penetrating candour, that if he had not been born a Jew he would probably have become a right-wing nationalist. Indeed, one of the traits which made the socially ambitious, at times intolerably showy and vain, Lassalle so astonishingly effective as an agitator and organiser of German socialism was his complete personal integrity. It was this as much as anything that enabled him to exercise a moral influence over the German workers scarcely ever again attained by anyone else.

Marx's systematic omission of all references to his own origins and the taunts with which his references to Jews were accompanied are attributed by the eminent Russo-Jewish historian Simon Dubnov to the natural hatred of a renegade for the camp which he has deserted – which need not prevent him from attacking others, for example Joseph Moses Levy, the proprietor of the London *Daily Telegraph*, for concealing their Jewish origins. But I suspect that Werner Blumenberg comes nearer the truth when he attributes this notorious fact to a peculiar form of self-hatred to which others among the newly emancipated Jews were also liable.[1] Disraeli, in describing his grandmother Sarah Shiprut, once said that she 'had imbibed that dislike for her race which the vain are too apt to adopt when they find that they are born to public contempt'.[2] This, it seems to me, does something to explain the attitude to his former brethren of the otherwise rational and realistic Karl Marx. Self-hatred is not a mysterious phenomenon. Most human beings are affected by opinions prevalent in their environment, especially when these are long and widely held. Anti-Semitism was, after all, a universal sentiment in Europe long before Marx's day, and became exceedingly virulent in Napoleonic and post-Napoleonic Germany. It naturally breeds self-contempt and self-hatred among its victims, who cannot but judge themselves in the light of the normal values prevalent in their society. This was less general while the Jews were insulated in the ghetto; the two ways of life touched at the edges, but did not collide. But contact and mingling with their fellows

[1] Werner Blumenberg, *Karl Marx* (London, 1972), p. 60.
[2] op. cit. (p. 266, note 1 above), p. x.

exposed the Jews to new modes of thought and, as part of these, to systems of values in terms of which they stood condemned.

The term *juedischer Selbsthass* – Jewish self-hatred (as opposed to self-criticism or realistic analysis) – was appropriately enough coined by a German-Jewish writer, Theodor Lessing, and describes a feeling with the peculiar manifestations of which all Heine's readers are familiar. It is, after all, in Germany that a Jewish party,[1] however small and today justly forgotten, accepted Hitler's estimate of the Jewish character, and declared the Jews to be their own greatest misfortune. Perhaps the most violent of all forms of Jewish self-abasement is to be found in the one Jewish writer admired by the Nazis, the once celebrated Otto Weininger, who suffered from paroxysms of Jewish self-hatred. There is painful evidence of a neurotic distortion of the problem in the diaries of Rathenau, with his ecstatic admiration for the anti-Semitic nationalists who ultimately murdered him; there are symptoms of it in the high-minded and deeply tormented essays of Simone Weil, and in the works of some living Jewish writers whom it would be uncharitable to mention. This is the kind of milieu in an early phase of which Marx grew to manhood. But he had a stronger and harsher nature than those who grappled with what, at times, developed into a psychosis that lasted all their lives. The baptised Jewish intellectual, still regarded as racially a Jew by his fellows, could not hope to be politically effective so long as nationalism remained a problem for him. It had somehow to be eliminated as an issue. Consciously or not, Marx all his life systematically underestimated nationalism as an independent force – an illusion which led his followers in the twentieth century to a faulty analysis of Fascism and National Socialism, for which many of them paid with their lives, and which led to a good deal of false diagnosis and prediction of the course of human history in our own time. Despite the depth and originality of his major theses, Marx failed to give an adequate account of the sources and nature of nationalism, and underestimated it, as he underestimated the force of religion, as an independent factor in society. This is one of the major weaknesses of his great synthesis.

Once again an effort to escape from intolerable reality is observable. As Disraeli, faced with a similar predicament, identified himself with the British landed aristocracy and gentry, and worked his magic on the squires and the great landowners until they all but accepted his metamorphosis, so Marx, too, donned a uniform that liberated him

[1] Verband deutschnationaler Juden, led by Max Naumann.

from his own oppressive garments and entered and transformed a movement and a party that bore none of the scars of the highly vulnerable social group in which he was brought up. In short, as all the world knows, Marx identified himself with a social force, the great international class of the disinherited workers, in whose name he could thunder his anathemas, the class which his writings would arm for inevitable victory, inasmuch as its triumph seemed to him to embody the promise of all that he truly believed in : reason in action, the establishment of a harmoniously, rationally organised society, the end of the self-destructive struggles that distorted the vision and the acts of mankind – in a word, the proletariat. Marx had as little affinity with individual proletarians – individual unskilled factory workers or miners or landless labourers – as Disraeli with the inner core of the British upper class. That is to say, the group in question was an intensive object of study to Disraeli and Marx respectively; it was their subject and the ark of their covenant; they had made themselves its poets and its priests, even though Marx claimed scientific status; but they remained outside it, observers, analysts, propagandists, allies, champions, leaders, but not of it, not its kith and kin.

The proletariat remains an abstract category in Marx. Despite all his accusations against other thinkers of ignoring history, of indulging in timeless abstractions, of erecting idealised entities and then treating them as real men engaged in the processes of real life, he himself is not wholly innocent in this respect. His proletarians are a body of men without national allegiance, utterly deprived of all but the barest means of life, mere machine fodder, men so destitute as to have almost no individual needs of their own, starving, brutalised, scarcely at the minimum subsistence level. This concept of the workers, even in the terrible nineteenth century, even today in countries where conditions are still abominable, is nevertheless an abstraction. The picture is too stylised, too undifferentiated. Marx knew poverty and he knew humiliation; he grasped the dynamics of modern industrialism as a world-wide system, in all its guises and disguises, as no one had done before him. He understood the mentality and activities of capitalists in his own time, both in general and in specific cases, with an accuracy of vision sharpened by indignation and hatred, and with a degree of intellectual and prophetic power, not hitherto brought to bear on fully developed industrial society. But when he speaks of the proletariat, he speaks not of real workers but of humanity in general, or, at times, of his own indignant self. When he denies that any armistice or compromise between the classes can be reached, when he denounces appeals for understanding, and prophesies that the last shall be first, that the arrogant enemy who lords it today will bite the dust when the day of the revolution comes, it is the oppression of centuries of a people of pariahs, not of a recently risen class, that seems to be speaking in him. The insults he is avenging and the enemies he is pulverising are, as often as not, his own: the adversary, the bourgeoisie and its executives – governments, judges, policemen – are the persecutors of the rootless cosmopolitans, the revolutionary Jewish intellectuals, the cosmopolitan avengers of insulted mankind. This it is that lends passion and reality to his words, and for that very reason they appeal most deeply to other persons like himself, alienated members of a world-wide intelligentsia, the dispossessed *révoltés* children of bourgeois or aristocratic parents, outraged by the injustice or the irrationality and vulgarity of the order supported by their own class. Marx spoke to such men, and speaks to them still, more directly than to operatives in the factories of industrialised countries in whose name he is ostensibly addressing mankind. Marx's proletariat is a class to some extent constructed after Marx's own specifications, as a vessel to carry the vials of his justified wrath. Its function in his system is similar to that of its exact opposite – the racial élites of *Coningsby* and *Tancred* and *Lothair* and *Contarini Fleming* in Disraeli – as the voice of the author, the idealised human beings with whom and with whose ills the author identifies himself, the platform, as it were, from which he can direct his fire. The class, which embodies the vision of the writer, despite all talk of concreteness, remains idealised.

Let me repeat my thesis. When Marx speaks for the proletariat, in particular when he alters the history of socialism (and of mankind) by asserting that there is no common interest between the proletarians and the capitalists, and therefore no possibility of reconciliation; when he insists that there is no common ground, and therefore no possibility of converting the opponents of mankind by appeals to common principles of justice, or common reason or common desire for happiness, for there are no such things; when, by the same token, he denounces appeals to the humanity or sense of duty of the bourgeois as mere pathetic delusion on the part of their victims, and declares a war of extermination against capitalism, and prophesies the triumph of the proletariat as the inexorable verdict of history itself, of the triumph of human reason over human irrationality – when he says all that (and is virtually the first to say it, for the Puritans and Jacobins did, at least in theory, allow the possibility of persuasion and agreement), it is difficult not to think that the voice is that of a proud and defiant pariah, not so much of the friend of the proletariat as of a member of a long humiliated race. *The German Ideology, The Communist Manifesto*, the polemical pages of *Das Kapital*, are the works of a man who is shaking his fist at the establishment and, in the manner of an ancient Hebrew prophet, who speaks in the name of the elect, pronouncing the burden of capitalism, the doom of the accursed system, the punishment that is in store for those who are blind to the course and goal of history, and therefore self-destructive and condemned to liquidation. Marx's idealisation of the proletariat, despite all his own preaching against illusions of this kind, is itself the idealised image of a man craving to identify himself with a favoured group of men who do not suffer from his particular wounds.

I am here not concerned with the validity of Marx's analysis of industrial society and culture: only with its psychological roots in his own personality and predicament. His metamorphosis generates from the role of an itinerant radical journalist that of an organiser and leader of an army of men wholly distinct from his own milieu, at least partly because he needs it, because he is an outsider, because his credentials are doubtful, particularly suspect in a society acutely conscious of social and national origins. His baptism rendered him what Donna Louisa in Sheridan's *The Duenna* describes as 'the blank leaves between the Old and New Testament'[1] (a quip which Disraeli once applied to himself), and he therefore needed to find a secure platform from which to deliver his shafts, from which to organise his forces. Marx did meet members of the proletariat during his life, but not very many; and never became truly intimate with any. He preached to them; he told them what to do; he impressed British trade union leaders, dominated the First International; but his friends, those to whom he could speak, were *déclassés* figures like himself: Engels, Freiligrath, Heine. Particularly Heine, because his antecedents and social and personal outlook resembled his own; they shared an intolerable irritation about their origins, not turned to exaggerated pride like Disraeli's, but viewed as a maddening fact (as it was by other gifted and acutely sensitive men, caught and isolated in a similar impasse, by Pasternak in *Dr Zhivago*, for example, who suffered from similar ancestral trouble). It is one thing not to believe in the dominant importance of race, tradition, nationality, religion; still less not to wish to

[1] Act I, scene 3.

make a fetish of them. It is another fiercely to deny their intrinsic importance, to relegate them (desperately) to the role of superstructure or by-product, with no independent role in history – phenomena which, with the inevitable change in the economic base, will vanish like the evil dreams and irrational fantasies that the wise can recognise in them already.

My thesis is not that anything that either Disraeli or Marx said is false, or even dubious. I do, indeed, think that Disraeli's social and historical views were shot through with extraordinary and, at times, absurd, deeply reactionary, and dangerous fancies; and also that Marx laid too little stress on the play of non-economic factors in history. But that is not the point at issue here. I am concerned with a personal, not a universal, topic: the social predicament in which these exceptionally intelligent, imaginative, ambitious and energetic men of similar antecedents found themselves, and its effect upon them. Even if all that either said turned out to be wholly correct, my thesis – and I advance it cautiously and tentatively, for I am no psychologist – is that one of the sources of the vision of both Disraeli and Marx – what made the former see himself as a natural leader of an aristocratic élite, and the latter as the teacher and strategist of the world proletariat – was their personal need to find their proper place, to establish a personal identity, to determine, in a world in which this question was posed much more insistently than it had ever been posed before, what section of mankind, what nation, party, class they properly belonged to. It was an attempt on the part of those whom history and social circumstances had cut off from their original establishment – the once familiar, safely segregated Jewish minority – to replant themselves in some new and no less secure and nourishing soil. The unambitious, those who merely wished to get by, Isaac d'Israeli, Heinrich Marx, against whose view of life their sons so sharply reacted, managed, like many before and after them, to assimilate peacefully without worrying over-much about who they were and what they were. Their sons, the ironical (and passionate) political romantic, Disraeli, the no less passionate moralist and social theorist, Karl Marx, needed firmer moorings and, since they were not born with them, invented them. They did this only at the price of ignoring a good deal of reality seen by less agonised, more ordinary, but saner men.

The fact that men seek to belong to some group, and that the need for this is a basic need, and that they seek for the recognition by their fellows of their status and their rights – these facts, together with the abnormal position of the children and grandchildren of the ghetto in the early nineteenth century, faced, as they were, by an alien and none too welcoming world, do much to explain both the irrationalist fantasies of Disraeli and the rationalist ideals of Marx. Both were outsiders, with no accepted place in society. Both rebelled against the middle-class society of their time, which their fathers were only too anxious to enter; rebelled perhaps largely because of this. Both turned vehemently against the social class from which they came. Disraeli set himself against the tide of what Mill called collective mediocrity,[1] by seeking to preserve and promote the aristocratic élite with which he identified his imaginary ancestors, and offering it a morally acceptable role as defender against the predatory bourgeoisie of the poor, the simple and the weak. Marx more realistically identified the Jews with the bourgeoisie, and attacked it from below, in the name of the insulted and the oppressed. Their origins irked both; they could not accept them, or their own selves, for what they were. Disraeli was obsessed by this. He brought the Jews into everything, irrelevantly and compulsively, and transformed them into something rich and strange in the fantasy which sustained him all his life. Marx virtually shut out all awareness of his ancestors from his conscious thought. When nevertheless it broke through the crust, it did so in the form of violent caricature, the nightmarish product of powerful repression, something that modern psychologists would find it all too easy to interpret.

As Disraeli wrapped himself in the mantle of a mysterious princely being, moving among other superior spirits, lifted high above the teeming multitude by the genius of a 'great' race, so Marx identified himself with an idealised proletariat, the heir to the perfect human society, remote from his own origins and from his environment as a bourgeois intellectual, a purifying source of strength and integrity. Both, at least spiritually, lived at a distance from the class they idealised. Both sought to dominate and guide, identifying themselves with the group conceived in general terms, rather than the real members of it who were to be met in the drawing-rooms and the factories. The doctrines which gave intellectual form to these visions evoked passionate dedication, fervent loyalties, religious worship. Neither Disraeli's mystical conservatism nor Marx's vision of a classless society were, as a rule, viewed by them as testable hypotheses, liable to error,

[1] *On Liberty*, chapter 3: p. 195 in *Utilitarianism, On Liberty, Essay on Bentham*, ed. Mary Warnock (London, 1962).

correction, modification, still less to radical revision in the light of experience. This could not but be so if, as I wish to suggest, these doctrines sprang, to a degree, from psychological needs to which they were the response: their function was not primarily to describe or analyse reality, but rather more to comfort, strengthen resolution, compensate for defeat and weakness, generate a fighting spirit principally in the authors of the doctrines themselves. Disraeli's open aversion to the rational methods of scientific inquiry, and Marx's identification of scientific method with his own dialectical teleology, and consequent disdain for the more objective, if less transforming recourse to empirical techniques, seem to me to spring from similar psychological roots.

Self-understanding is man's highest requirement. If there is any substance in this thesis, the story of these two sons of newly emancipated fathers, men of dissimilar character, unequal gifts, but placed in a common predicament, may serve as a moral tale, to inspire some and warn others.

The *'Naïveté'* of Verdi

for W. H. Auden

MY topic is Verdi's *'naïveté'*. I hope that this phrase will not be misunderstood. To say that Verdi was naïve in any ordinary sense is an absurd suggestion. But it seems to me that he was so in a very special – now forgotten – sense, in which this term was once used by Friedrich Schiller. Verdi greatly admired Schiller's dramatic works, which inspired four of his operas. But it is not this – the affinity of Verdi and Schiller which has often been remarked – that I wish to discuss. My thesis is concerned with a different link between them.

In his once celebrated essay, published in 1795, which he called *Über Naive und Sentimentalische Dichtung*,[1] Schiller distinguished two types of poets: those who are not conscious of any rift between themselves and their milieu, or within themselves; and those who are so conscious. For the first, art is a natural form of expression; they see what they see directly, and seek to articulate it for its own sake, not for any ulterior purpose, however sublime. Let me quote his own words:

> Such poets occur in the youth of the world and later: they are severe and chaste, like the virgin goddess Diana in her woods . . . The dry, truthful way in which such a poet treats his material often resembles lack of feeling. The object possesses him entirely. His heart does not, like a cheap metal, lie on the very surface, but, like gold, must be sought in depths. He is concealed by his works like God by the world He has created. He is his work, for the work is himself. Only someone who is unworthy of a work, or does not understand it, or is satiated by it, will look in it only for the creator.[2]

Homer, Aeschylus, Shakespeare, even Goethe, are poets of this kind. They are not, as poets, self-conscious. They do not, like Virgil or Ariosto, stand aside to contemplate their creations and express their

[1] See *Schillers Werke*, ed. Ernst Jenny, vol. 10 (Basel, 1946), pp. 208–321.
[2] ibid., p. 232.

own feelings. They are at peace with themselves. Their aim is limited, and they are able, if they have genius, to embody their vision fully. These Schiller calls *naiv*. With them he contrasts those poets who come after the Fall. Let me quote again : 'When man enters the stage of culture, and art has laid its hand on him, the primordial, sensuous unity is gone . . . The harmony between sense and thinking, which in the earlier state was *real*, now exists only as an *ideal*. It is not *in* a man, as a fact of his life, but outside him, as an ideal to be realised.'[1] The unity has been broken. The poet seeks to restore it. He looks for the vanished, harmonious world which some call nature, and builds it from his imagination, and his poetry is his attempt to return to it, to an imagined childhood, and he conveys his sense of the chasm which divides the day-to-day world which is no longer his home from the lost paradise which is conceived only ideally, only in reflection. Hence this ideal realm is bounded by nothing; it is in its very essence indefinable, unattainable, incapable of being embraced by means of any finite medium, no matter how great the poet's capacity for finding, moulding, transforming his material. Let me quote Schiller again : 'Visual art reaches its goal in the finite; that of the imagination . . . in infinity.'[2] And again, 'The poet . . . *is* either himself nature, or he *seeks* her.'[3] The first of these, Schiller calls *naiv*, the second, *sentimentalisch*.

For Schiller as for Rousseau, once ideas enter, peace, harmony, joy, are gone for ever. The artist becomes conscious of himself, of his ideal aims, of their infinite distance from his own divided nature, that is, of the estrangement of his society and himself from the original and unbroken whole of thought and action, feeling and expression. The characteristic poetry of the 'sentimental' is satire, that is, negation, an attack on that which calls itself real life but is in fact a degradation of it (what is now called alienation from it), artificial, ugly and unnatural; or it is elegy – the affirmation of the lost world, the unrealisable ideal. This distinction is not at all the same as that between the classical and the romantic (whatever that may be), if only because it is not concerned with the presence or absence of objective rules, universal standards, fixed criteria, or an eternal ideal order. Aeschylus, Cervantes, Shakespeare, Ossian, the heroes of romanticism, condemned by the classical school as undisciplined and wild, are *naiv*; the models of classicism – the authors of dramatic, or idyllic, or satirical, or epic poetry – Euripides, Virgil, Horace, Propertius, the neo-

---

[1] op. cit. (p. 287, note 1 above), p. 238.   [2] ibid., p. 242.   [3] ibid., p. 237.

classical poets of the Renaissance – are nostalgic, self-conscious, deeply *sentimentalisch*.

The naïve artist is happily married to his muse. He takes rules and conventions for granted, uses them freely and harmoniously, and the effect of his art is, in Schiller's words, 'tranquil, pure, joyous'. The sentimental artist is in a turbulent relationship to his muse: married to her unhappily. Conventions irk him, although he may defend them fanatically. He is Amfortas and seeks peace, salvation, the healing of his own or his society's secret and patent wounds. He cannot be at rest. Of him Schiller says:

> His observation is forcibly pushed aside by fancy, his sensibility by ideas, he closes his eyes and ears so that nothing may disturb his self-absorption in his own thoughts . . . His soul suffers no impression without at once turning to contemplate its own play . . . In this manner we never receive the object itself, only what the reflective understanding of the poet made of the object; and even when the poet is himself this object, when he wants to portray his feelings to us, we do not apprehend his feelings directly, at first hand, but only their reflection in his soul, what he thought about them as a spectator of himself.[1]

Hence the effect of the sentimental artist is not joy and peace, but tension, conflict with nature or society, insatiable craving, the notorious neuroses of the modern age, with its troubled spirits, its martyrs, fanatics and rebels, and its angry, bullying subversive preachers, Rousseau, Byron, Schopenhauer, Carlyle, Dostoevsky, Flaubert, Wagner, Marx, Nietzsche, offering not peace, but a sword.

Schiller's distinction, like all dichotomies, can, if taken literally, be carried much too far. But it is very original and very suggestive. If we ask whether in modern times there are artists who in Schiller's sense are naïve – at peace with their medium – integral as men and artists, as tranquil and solid and free from self-consciousness or obsession and fulfilled artistically as, say, Cervantes, Bach, Handel, Rubens, Haydn, men whose art culminates in its object and is not used for some spiritual end beyond itself – to reach out for some unattainable ideal, or as a weapon in a war against philistines and traitors, we could answer, 'Yes, indeed: Goethe, Pushkin, Dickens, at times Tolstoy (when he forgets his doctrine and his guilt), certainly these, Rossini and Verdi.' Among composers of genius, Verdi is perhaps the last complete, self-fulfilled creator, absorbed in his art; at one with it; seeking

[1] ibid., pp. 257–8.

to use it for no ulterior purpose, the god wholly concealed by his works, severe, farouche, like Schiller's Diana, suspicious of anyone curious about his inner life, wholly, even grimly, impersonal, dryly objective, at one with his music. A man who dissolved everything in his art, with no more personal residue than Shakespeare or Tintoretto. In Schiller's sense, the last great naïve poet of our time.

Of course, anyone who has any knowledge of Verdi's life knows that it was intertwined with that of his country : that his name became the very symbol of the Risorgimento, that 'Viva Verdi' (not for political or monarchist reasons alone) was the most famous revolutionary and patriotic cry in Italy : that he admired both Mazzini and Cavour, both the revolutionary democrats and the King, and in this way united in his person the diverse strands which made the Italian nation. He always (to use Herder's metaphor) lived near the centre of gravity of his nation, and spoke to his countrymen and for them, as no one else did, not even Manzoni or Garibaldi, to both of whom he was close. His convictions, whether they moved to the right or the left, moved with those of popular feeling; he responded deeply and personally to every twist and turn in the Italian struggle for unity and freedom. The Hebrews of *Nabucco* were Italians in captivity. *Va Pensiero* was the national prayer for resurrection. The performance of *Battaglia di Legnano* evoked scenes of indescribable popular excitement in the revolutionary Rome of 1849. *Rigoletto*, no less than *Don Carlo*, *Forza del Destino* and *Aida*, is inspired by a hatred of oppression, inequality, fanaticism and human degradation. The hymn which Verdi wrote for Mazzini is only an episode in a single great campaign. For half a century he was the living symbol of all that was most generous and universal in Italian national feeling.

All this is so. Nevertheless, it is not at the centre of Verdi's art. Insight into his music does not require us to know all, or any, of this. Of course all knowledge of what a man of genius was and felt is interesting, but it is not always essential. The point is, however, that it is essential in the case of the great 'sentimental' masters : no one who does not realise what Beethoven felt about tyranny can fully understand the *Eroica*, or *Fidelio*, the first great political opera; no one who is ignorant of the relevant social movements in Russia can understand the significance of *Boris Godunov*, or *Khovanshchina*. Schumann's aesthetic outlook, Wagner's mythology, the romantic theories that dominated Berlioz, are indispensable to the understanding of their masterpieces; but it is not necessary to know Shakespeare's political views to understand his historical plays; it might help, but it is not required. It is so with Verdi. Anyone who is acquainted with primary human passions: paternal love, and the full horror of the humiliation of men by other men in a dehumanised society, will understand *Rigoletto*; insight into a hero destroyed by jealousy is sufficient for understanding *Otello*. Knowledge of basic human emotions is virtually all the extra-musical equipment that is needed to understand Verdi's works, early or late, great or small, *Suoni la Tromba* as much as *La Traviata*; *Attila* or *Luisa Miller* no less than *Forza del Destino* or *Aïda*; *Il Corsaro* or *Ernani* as much as *Il Trovatore*, the *Requiem* or *Otello*, or even *Falstaff*. *Falstaff* is musically and artistically absolutely unique. Nevertheless the requirements needed to do it justice do not include, as indispensable *sine quibus non*, knowledge of the personal views or attributes of the composer, or the historical circumstances of his life or those of his society. This is not needed in his case any more than in those of Bach or Mozart or Rossini, of Shakespeare or Goethe or Dickens. From *Oberto, Conte di Bonifazio* to the *Quattro Pezzi Sacri*, the character of Verdi's creations is, in Schiller's special sense, wholly *naiv*: they spring from a direct vision of the object. There is no effort to reach beyond, to an infinite and unattainable empyrean, and lose oneself in it, no ulterior aim, no impossible attempt to fuse antagonistic worlds – music and literature, the personal and the public, concrete reality and a transcendent myth. Verdi never seeks to close a breach, to compensate for the imperfections of human life, or heal his own wounds or overcome his society's inner cracks, its alienation from a common culture or from the ancient faith, by using magical means, by conjuring up an infernal, or a celestial vision as a means of escape or revenge or salvation. This is as true of *Falstaff* as it is of *Un Giorno di Regno* or the String Quartet. Desire, said Bishop Butler, culminates in its object. Verdi belongs to this tradition, and represents its finest flowering. Verdi's art, like that of Bach, is objective, direct and in harmony with the conventions which govern it. It springs from an unbroken inner unity, a sense of belonging to its own time and society and milieu, which precludes the *nostalgie de l'infini*, the conception of art as therapy which lies at the heart of what Schiller calls *sentimentalisch*. In this sense Virgil, Propertius and Horace were *sentimentalisch*: 'sentimental' and also models of classicism; while the *Song of the Niebelungs* or *Don Quixote*, idealised by the romantics, are *naiv*.

Verdi was the last of the great naïve masters of western music, in an age given over to the *Sentimentalisches*. He remained scarcely affected by it. He may have been interested in, or even influenced by, Wagner, or Liszt, or Meyerbeer; but the influence was confined to method, technical innovations. Their worlds and their doctrines remained alien to him. After him *naïveté* is to be found, in the west at any rate, only in the borderlands, outside the central movement – among the composers of the Slav countries, Spain, perhaps Norway, where social conditions resemble an earlier Europe.

Verdi is, of course, not without an ideology. But it is that of vast numbers of mankind across large stretches of history: this is, indeed, one of the central meanings of the term 'humanism'. Alberto Moravia traces it to his peasant origin and upbringing, which triumphed over the bourgeois society of his time. Peasants are an ancient and universal social class, and if it is this that worked in Verdi, it is not irrelevant to what Rousseau and Schiller meant by relatively uncorrupted relationship with nature.

The attacks on Verdi are notorious. They came from many quarters. In England, Mr Chorley found him too noisy, that is, too vulgar, compared to Rossini, Boieldieu etc. Nor was the wish to return to Rossini and Bellini confined to the conservatives of the north – it came from Italians too; least of all, let it be noted, from Rossini himself. Naturally the principal onslaught came from the champions of the new music: the Wagnerians and the Lisztians, the protagonists of all that was most self-conscious, extra-musical, 'sentimental', from faith in music as a messianic rebirth of the spirit. Boito, who was later to denounce Wagner as a false prophet, was in his day deeply caught by this. His explosion against Verdi is too well known to cite.

This is as it should be. Verdi was indeed the greatest, most triumphant obstacle to the new aesthetic religion: it was not worth wasting powder and shot on Pacini or Mercadante, even on Meyerbeer, Auber or Halévy, while Verdi was dominant: he was the archenemy, the traditionalist of power and genius. Still more violent were the attacks from the east: delivered by the great new national school of the Slav world, in particular the Russians. Balakirev and Borodin, Mussorgsky and Stassov, detested Verdi: not for his occasional platitudes and vulgarities – not for *Questa o Quella* or *O tu Palermo* – but for the very qualities in which his strength resided, his acceptance of, and his identification with, the hateful *formula* – the conventions of opera. The Russians, inspired by populist ideals, disciples of the unknown master Dargomyzhsky (whom they regarded as a genius of the first order), believed in musical realism, in the most intimate inter-relation of words, plot, expression, music, historical and social con-sciousness. They virtually invented the expressive semi-recitative to convey the finest psychological nuances of the 'real' inner and outer life of both individuals and masses. When Busoni declared that love scenes should not occur on the stage – because what is intimate should not take place in public – this most sophisticated man echoed, however unconsciously (he would have been horrified to be told this), this literal realism. The Russians were in open revolt against the Italian opera of Paisiello, Cherubini, Rossini, Donizetti, Bellini. At long last the miserable crew of operatic purveyors showed signs of going under; but Verdi had breathed new life into the tradition and recon-quered the musical public for the beastly *formula*, the mechanical succession of detachable operatic 'numbers', the bits and pieces which could be performed in any order, from, for example, the *Requiem*, with which Verdi and his singers toured Europe. They denounced all those self-contained arias, duets, trios, quintets, choruses, the inevitable appoggiaturas and artificially stuck-on cabalettas and cavatinas, the mechanism of the all too predictable orchestral accompaniment, the terrible hurdy-gurdy that killed the living expression of real experi-ence. *Prince Igor* seemed to them spontaneous and 'real', whereas *Don Carlo* and *La Traviata* were Christmas trees decked out with meretricious baubles. Not that they liked Wagner any better – he seemed to them one of the 'pompous disseminators of clamorous con-fusion',[1] to use Boito's phrase. Serov, their colleague who admired and imitated this master, was duly drummed out of the nationalist regiment. Their gods were Liszt and Berlioz. The greatest enemy was always Verdi, upon whom they looked as the early German romantics looked on the French arbiters of taste in the eighteenth century: shallow, pompous, stilted, artificial, utterly predictable, utterly worth-less. Liszt and Berlioz were Rousseau – the return to the colours and sounds of nature, to real individual feeling from the corrupt, commer-cialised sophistication of the standardised authors, Marivaux, Crébillon, Marmontel, above all Voltaire, the dancing masters, with their pow-dered wigs and rhymed couplets and carefully contrived epigrams amid the bric-à-brac of the trivial and heartless *salons*.

This (as in the case of the Germans and the French a century earlier) was the attack of the *Sentimentalisch* on the *Naiv*: equally

[1] Arrigo Boito, 'Mendelssohn in Italia', *Tutti gli scritti*, ed. Piero Nardi (Verona, 1942), p. 1256.

inevitable, perhaps, and equally exaggerated and wrongheaded. Verdi went his way, wounded, but ultimately serene and unperturbed. Doubtless, he did not belong to the new world of Baudelaire, Flaubert, Liszt, Wagner, Nietzsche, Dostoevsky, Mussorgsky. There is no reason to think that he was aware of this, or would have cared if he had been. He was the last great voice of humanism not at war with itself, at any rate in music.

No matter how sophisticated his scores, there is no trace, right to the end, of self-consciousness, neurosis, decadence. For that, in Italian music, we must wait for Boito, Puccini and their followers. He was the last master to paint with positive, clear, primary colours, to give direct expression to the eternal, major human emotions: love and hate, jealousy and fear, indignation and passion; grief, fury, mockery, cruelty, irony, fanaticism, faith, the passions that all men know. After him, this is much more rare. From Debussy onwards, whether music is impressionist or expressionist, neo-classical or neo-romantic, diatonic or chromatic, dodecaphonic, aleatoric or concrete, or a syncretism of these, innocence is gone.[1]

To escape from the inflation and the appalling elephantiasis of late German romanticism, a variety of astringent, deflationary styles came into being. But the return to Bach or to Pergolesi, or to Gesualdo, or to Machaut, is a conscious attempt to look for antidotes. This has indeed generated much original and fascinating music, anti-*sentimentalisch*, and thereby itself *sentimentalisch*, inasmuch as it is self-regarding, self-conscious, doctrine-influenced music, accompanied by theories and manifestos, neo-Catholic (Solesmes), atonal, surrealist, socialist-realist (neo-diatonic) etc. to justify it. We expect ideological declarations, programmatic statements, anathemas from Wagner or Berlioz or Debussy or the Russian composers in the twentieth century. But just as we should have regarded a manifesto on the function of literature signed by Dickens or Dumas *père* as almost inconceivable, so a *profession de foi* by Verdi on the aesthetic or social significance of Italian opera or its relation to the *commedia dell'arte* (of the kind to be

---

[1] There is a sense in which, for instance, Bruckner can be called naïve. But that is the ordinary, not Schiller's, sense. In Schiller's sense of the word, Bruckner's visionary mysticism, the combination of sensuousness and effort at self-transcendence (as in the even acuter case of César Franck and the Schola Cantorum), is the deepest imaginable *Sentimentalität*. So is the very notion of the *Gesamtkunstwerk*, with its striving for an unattainable integration of all the elements.

found in the writings of, say, Boito or Busoni) would rightly be suspected of being an exceptionally unplausible forgery. Manifestos are a symptom of revolt or reaction, personal or collective; that is to say, of an acute phase of 'sentimentality'. The remoteness of Verdi, who is so often and, in a sense, so justly described as one of the most deeply characteristic and representative artists of the nineteenth century, from this particular condition, which is usually held to be a central feature of that period – its typical *malaise* – is, perhaps, what is most arresting in his personality, both as an artist and as a man. In this respect he has no successors. In music at least, he is the last naïve artist of genius. The desire to 'go back' to Verdi itself becomes a form of incurable nostalgia, of acutely non-Verdian 'sentimentality', from which he was himself wholly and peacefully free.

It is natural enough that what during the high tide of the *sentimentalisch* movement, from, say, the 1870s to the 1930s, was looked upon both by the German and the anti-German (i.e. Franco-Russian) musical public (and its critics) as Verdi's popular, vulgar style, should have re-emerged during the last quarter-century, as the last direct voice of the great tradition. It is felt to be so in conscious contrast with the quest for the remote and the exotic – symptoms of recession, the desire to obtain comfort or derive new life from traditions remote in space and time – the music of the Middle Ages or of the Age of Reason, or the relics of the folk tradition in eastern Europe, Asia, Africa and the islands of the Pacific.

Noble, simple, with a degree of unbroken vitality and vast natural power of creation and organisation, Verdi is the voice of a world which is no more. His enormous popularity among the most sophisticated as well as the most ordinary listeners today is due to the fact that he expressed permanent states of consciousness in the most direct terms: as Homer, Shakespeare, Ibsen and Tolstoy have done. This is what Schiller called *naiv*. After Verdi this is not heard in music again. Verdi's assured place, in the high canon of the musical art, which nobody now disputes, is a symptom of sanity in our time. The sociology of this phenomenon, like that of Verdi's own position in his own time, is itself a fascinating topic, but not one with which I am qualified to deal.

Georges Sorel

SOREL remains an anomalous figure. The other ideologists and prophets of the nineteenth century have been safely docketed and classified. The doctrines, influence, personalities of Mill, Carlyle, Comte, Darwin, Dostoevsky, Wagner, Nietzsche, even Marx, have been safely placed on their respective shelves in the museum of the history of ideas. Sorel remains, as he was in his lifetime, unclassified; claimed and repudiated both by the right and by the left. Was he a bold and brilliant innovator of devastating genius as his handful of disciples declare? Or a mere romantic journalist, as George Lichtheim calls him? A pessimist 'moaning for blood',[1] in G. D. H. Cole's contemptuous phrase? Or, with Marx, the only original thinker (according to Croce) socialism has ever had? Or a notorious muddle-head, as Lenin unkindly described him? I do not volunteer an answer: I only wish to say something about his principal ideas, and also – to employ that much-abused word – the relevance of these ideas to our time.

I

Georges Sorel was born in 1847 in Cherbourg. His father was an unsuccessful businessman, and the family was forced to practise extreme austerity. According to his cousin, the historian Albert Sorel, Georges Sorel early showed exceptional mathematical gifts. In 1865 he became a student at the École Polytechnique in Paris, and five years later entered the Department of Public Works (Ponts et Chaussées) as an engineer. During the next twenty years he was posted to various provincial towns. During the débâcle of 1870 and 1871 he was in Corsica. In 1875 he fell ill in an hotel in Lyon, and was nursed by a servant called Marie David, a devoutly religious, semi-literate peasant from the borders of Savoy, with whom he set up a household.

[1] G. D. H. Cole, *The Second International* [*A History of Socialist Thought*, vol. 3], part 1 (London, 1956), p. 387.

In his letters he refers to her as his wife, but in fact he appears never to have married her, probably out of deference to the wishes of his family, which was evidently shocked by this *mésalliance*. It appears to have been an entirely happy relationship. He taught her, and learnt from her, and, after her death in 1898, wore a sacred image that she had given him and worshipped her memory for the rest of his days.

Until the age of forty, his life had been that of a typical minor French government official, peaceful, provincial and obscure. In 1889 his first book was published. In 1892, being then forty-five years old, having attained the rank of Chief Engineer and been rewarded with the rank of Chevalier of the Légion d'Honneur, he suddenly resigned. From this moment his public life began. His mother had left him a small legacy, and this enabled him to move to Paris. He settled in a quiet suburb, Boulogne-sur-Seine, where he lived until his death, thirty years later, in 1922. In 1895 he started to contribute to left-wing journals, and from then on became one of the most controversial political writers in France.

He appeared to have no fixed position. His critics often accused him of pursuing an erratic course: a legitimist in his youth, and still a traditionalist in 1889, he was by 1894 a Marxist. In 1896 he wrote with admiration about Vico. By 1898, influenced by Croce, and also by Eduard Bernstein, he began to criticise Marxism and at about the same time fell deeply under the spell of Henri Bergson. He was a Dreyfusard in 1899, a revolutionary syndicalist during the following decade. By 1909 he was a sworn enemy of the Dreyfusards, and, in the following two or three years, an ally of the royalists who edited the *Action française* and a supporter of the mystical nationalism of Barrès. He wrote with admiration about Mussolini's militant socialism in 1912, and in 1919 with still greater admiration about Lenin, ending with whole-hearted support for Bolshevism and, in the last years of his life, an unconcealed admiration for the Duce.

What credence could be placed in the thought of a man whose political views veered so violently and unpredictably? He did not claim to be consistent. 'I write from day to day', he wrote in 1903 to his faithful correspondent, the Italian philosopher Benedetto Croce, 'following the need of the moment.'[1] Sorel's writings have no shape or system, and he was not impressed by it in those of others. He was a compulsive and passionate talker, and, as is at times the case with famous talkers – Diderot, Coleridge, Herzen, Bakunin – his writings

[1] Letter of 28 April 1903, *La critica* 25 (1927), 372.

remained episodic, unorganised, unfinished, fragmentary, at best sharp, polemical essays or pamphlets provoked by some immediate occasion, not intended to be fitted into a body of coherent, developed doctrine, and not capable of it. Nevertheless, there is a central thread that connects everything that Sorel wrote and said, if not a doctrine, then an attitude, a position, the expression of a singular temperament, of an unaltering view of life. His ideas, which beat like hailstones against all accepted doctrines and institutions, fascinated both his friends and his opponents, and do so still not only because of their intrinsic quality and power, but because what in his day was confined to small coteries of intellectuals has now grown to world-wide proportions. In his lifetime Sorel was looked on as, at best, a polemical journalist, an autodidact with a powerful pen and occasional flashes of extraordinary insight, too wayward and perverse to claim for long the attention of serious and busy men. In the event, he has proved more formidable than many of the respected social thinkers of his day, most of whom he ignored or else regarded with unconcealed disdain.

II

The ideas of every philosopher concerned with human affairs in the end rest on his conception of what man is and can be. To understand such thinkers, it is more important to grasp this central notion or image (which may be implicit, but determines their picture of the world) than even the most forceful arguments with which they defend their views and refute actual and possible objections. Sorel was dominated by one *idée maîtresse*: that man is a creator, fulfilled only when he creates, and not when he passively receives or drifts unresisting with the current. His mind is not a mechanism or organism responsive to stimuli, analysable, describable and predictable by the sciences of man. He is, for Sorel, in the first place, a producer who expresses himself in and through his work, an innovator whose activity alters the material provided by nature, material that he seeks to mould in accordance with an inwardly conceived, spontaneously generated, image or pattern. The productive activity itself brings this pattern to birth and alters it – as it fulfils itself freely, obedient to no law, being conceived as a kind of natural spring of creative energy which can be grasped by inner feeling and not by scientific observation or logical analysis. All other views of what men are, or could be, are fallacious. History shows that men are essentially seekers not of happiness or peace or knowledge or power over others, or salvation in another life – at least these are not men's primary purposes; where they are so, it is because men have degenerated from their true humanity, because education or environment or circumstances have distorted their ideas or character or rendered them impotent or vicious.

Man, at his best, that is, at his most human, seeks in the first place to fulfil himself, individually and with those close to him, in spontaneous, unhindered creative activity, in work that consists of the imposition of his personality on a recalcitrant environment. Sorel quotes his political enemy Clemenceau as saying: 'Everything that lives, resists.'[1] He believed in this proposition as strongly as he believed in anything in his life. To act and not be acted upon, to choose and not be chosen for, to impose form on the chaos that we find in the world of nature and the world of thought – that is the end of both art and science and belongs to the essence of man as such. He resists every force that seeks to reduce his energy, to rob him of his independence and his dignity, to kill the will, to crush everything in him that struggles for unique self-expression and reduce it to uniformity, impersonality, monotony, and, ultimately, extinction. Man lives fully only in and by his works, not by passive enjoyment or the peace and security that he might find by surrender to external pressures, or habit, or convention, by failure to use for his own freely conceived goals the mechanism of the laws of nature to which he is inevitably subject.

This is, of course, not a new idea. It lies at the heart of the great revolt against rationalism and the Enlightenment, identified particularly with French civilisation, that animated the more extreme German Protestant sects after the Reformation, and which, towards the end of the eighteenth century, took the form of celebrating the primacy of the human will against material forces and calm, rational knowledge alike. This is not the place in which to discuss the origins of romanticism. But one cannot understand Sorel, or the impact of his views, unless one realises that what caused the ferment in his mind was a passionate conviction which he shares with some of the early romantic writers, that the pursuit of peace or happiness or profit, and concern with power or possessions or social status or a quiet life, is a contemptible betrayal of what any man, if he takes thought, knows to be the true

---

[1] *Réflexions sur la violence* (Paris, 1972) (hereafter *R.V.*), p. 80.

end of human life : the attempt to make something worthy of the maker, the effort to be and do something, and to respect such effort in others. The notion of the dignity of labour, of the right to work as opposed to the mere Pauline duty to engage in it, which is at the heart of much modern socialism, springs from this romantic conception, which German thinkers, notably Herder and Fichte, brought up in earnest Lutheran pietism, impressed upon the European consciousness.

Sorel's violent and lifelong disgust with the life of the Parisian bourgeoisie of his time, in its own way as ferocious as that of Flaubert, with whom temperamentally he has something in common, is bound up with a Jansenist hatred of the twin evils of hedonism and materialism. The opportunism and corruption of French political life in the early years of the Third Republic, together with the sense of national humiliation after 1870, may have been a traumatic experience for him, as for many Frenchmen. But it seems unlikely that he would have felt differently in the greedy and competitive Paris of Louis-Philippe or the plutocratic and pleasure-seeking Paris of the Second Empire. An agonised sense of suffocation in the commercialised, jaunty, insolent, dishonourable, easy-going, cowardly, mindless, bourgeois society of the nineteenth century fills the writings of the age : the works of Proudhon, Carlyle, Ibsen, Marx, Baudelaire, Nietzsche, almost the whole of the best known Russian literature of the time, are one vast indictment of it. This is the tradition to which Sorel belongs from the beginning to the end of his life as a writer. The corruption of public life appears to him to have gone deeper than during the decadence of classical Greece, or the end of the Roman Empire. Parliamentary democracy, with its fraudulence and hypocrisy, appeared to him to be an odious insult to human dignity, a mockery of the proper ends of men. Democratic politics resembled a huge stock exchange in which votes were bought and sold without shame or fear, men were bamboozled or betrayed by scheming politicians, ruthless bankers, crooked businessmen, *avocasserie et écrivasserie* – lawyers, journalists, professors, all scrambling for money, recognition, power, in a world of contemptible fools and cunning knaves, deceivers and deceived, living off the exploited workers 'in a democratic bog' in a Europe 'stupefied by humanitarianism'.[1]

[1] *R.V.*, p. 101.

The western tradition of social thought has been sustained by two central doctrines. The first taught that the ultimate causes of human misery, folly and vice were ignorance and mental laziness. Reality, it was held by rationalists from Plato to Comte, is a single, intelligible structure: to understand it and explain it, and to understand one's own nature and place in this structure – this alone can reveal what, in a specific situation, can, and what cannot, be realised. Once the facts and the laws that govern them are known to him, no man, desiring as he does happiness or harmony or wisdom or virtue, can pursue any but the sole correct path to his goal that his knowledge reveals to him. To be a rational, even a normal, human being, is to seek one, or several, of the limited number of the natural ends of human life. Only ignorance of what they are, or of what are the correct means for their attainment, can lead to misery or vice or failure. The scientific or naturalistic version of this doctrine animated the Enlightenment and the forms which it took in the two centuries that followed – until, indeed, our own day.

Sorel rejected this entire approach. He saw no reason for believing that the world was a rational harmony, or that man's true perfection depended on understanding of the proper place assigned to him in it by his creator – a personal deity or an impersonal nature. Influenced by both Marx and the half-forgotten Italian thinker, Vico, of whom he was one of the few perceptive readers in the nineteenth century, Sorel believed that all that man possessed he owed to his own unflagging labour. Certainly natural science was a triumph of human effort; but it was not a transcription or map of nature, as the positivists had claimed in the eighteenth century; they, and their modern disciples, were mistaken about this. There were two natures: artificial nature, the nature of science – a system of idealised entities: atoms, electric charges, mass, energy and the like – fictions compounded out of observed uniformities, particularly in regions relatively remote from man's daily concerns, like the contents of the world of astronomy, deliberately adapted to mathematical treatment that enabled men to identify some of the furniture of the universe, and to predict and, indeed, control parts of it. The concepts and categories in terms of which this nature had been constructed were conditioned by human aims: they abstracted from the universe those aspects that were of interest to men and possessed sufficient regularity to make them capable of generalisation. This, of course, was a stupendous achievement, but an achievement of the creative imagination, not an accurate reproduction of the structure of reality, not a map, still less a picture, of what there was. Outside this set of formulas, of imaginary entities and mathematical relationships in terms of which the system was constructed, there was 'natural' nature – the real thing – chaotic, terrifying, compounded of ungovernable forces, against which man had to struggle, which, if he was to survive and create, he had at least in part to subdue; with the help, indeed, of his sciences; but the symmetry, the coherence, were attributes of the first, or artificial nature, the construction of his intellect, something that was not found but made. The assumption that reality was a harmonious whole, a rational structure whose logical necessity is revealed to reason, a marvellously coherent system which a rational being cannot think or wish to be otherwise and still remain rational, and in which, therefore, it must feel happy and fulfilled – all this is an enormous fallacy. Nature is not a perfect machine, nor an exquisite organism, nor a rational system; it is a savage jungle: science is the art of dealing with it as best we can. When we extend such manipulation to men as well, we degrade and dehumanise them, for men are not objects but subjects of action. If Christianity has taught us anything, it has made us realise that the only thing of absolute value in the universe is the human soul, the only thing that acts, that imagines, that creates, that resists the impersonal forces which work against it and, unless they are resisted, enslave us and ultimately grind us into dust. This is the menace that perpetually hangs over us. Consequently life is a perpetual battle.

To deny this truth is shallow optimism, characteristic of the shallow eighteenth century for which Sorel, like Carlyle, felt a lifelong contempt. The laws of nature are not descriptions, they are, as he came to learn from William James (and perhaps also from Marx), strategic weapons. Croce had taught him that our categories are categories of action, that they alter what we call reality as the purposes of our active selves alter: they do not establish timeless truths as the positivists maintained. 'We consider as matter, or as the base, that which escapes, less or more completely, from our will. The form is rather what corresponds to our freedom.'[1] Systems, theories, unrelated to action, attempting to transcend experience, that which professors and intellectuals are so good at, are only abstractions into which men escape to avoid facing

---

[1] 'Osservazione intorno alla concezione materialista della storia', in *Saggi di critica del marxismo* (Palermo, 1902), p. 44.

the chaos of reality; scientific (and political) Utopias are compounded out of them; the pseudo-scientific predictions about our future by which such Utopias are bolstered are nothing but modern forms of astrology. When such schemes are applied to human beings they can do dreadful damage. To confuse our own constructions and inventions with eternal laws or divine decrees is one of the most fatal delusions of men: this is what had happened in the French Revolution. The confusion of the two natures, the real and the artificial, is bad enough. But the *philosophes* were not, by and large, even genuine scientists: only social and political theorists who talked about science without practising it; the *Encyclopédie* had not improved one's real knowledge or skill. Ideological patter, optimistic journalism about the uses of science, were not science. They only lead to positivism and bureaucracy, *la petite science*; and when theory is ruthlessly applied to human affairs, its result is a fearful despotism. Sorel speaks almost the language of William Blake. The Tree of Knowledge has killed the Tree of Life. Robespierre and the Jacobins were fanatical pedants who tried to reduce human life to rules that seemed to them based on objective truths; the institutions they created crushed spontaneity and invention, enslaved and maimed the creative will of man.

Men, whose essence, for Sorel, is to be active beings, are perpetually menaced by two equally fatal dangers: a Scylla and a Charybdis. Scylla is weariness, the loss of nerve, decadence, when men relax from effort, return to the fleshpots, or else fall into quietism and become the victims of the trickery of the clever operators who destroy all honour, energy, integrity, independence, and substitute the rule of cunning and fraud, the dead hand of bureaucracy, laws that can be turned to their advantage by unscrupulous operators, aided and abetted by an army of experts – prostitutes and lackeys of those in power, or idle entertainers and sycophantic parasites, like Voltaire and Diderot, the 'buffoons of a degenerate aristocracy',[1] bourgeois who aspire to ape the tastes of an idle and pleasure-loving nobility. Charybdis is the despotism of fanatical theorists – 'the bloodthirsty frenzy of an optimist maddened by sudden resistance to his plans',[2] who is ready to butcher the present to create the happiness of the future on its bones. These alternations mark the unhappy eighteenth century.

How are men to be rescued from the horns of this dilemma? Only by moral strength: by the development of new men, fully-formed

[1] *Les Illusions du progrès*, 5th ed. (Paris, 1947), p. 133.
[2] *R.V.*, p. 14.

303

human beings not obsessed by fear and greed, men who have not had their imagination and emotion fettered by doctrinaires or rotted by intellectuals. Sorel's vision resembled that of Tolstoy and Nietzsche when they were young – of the fullness of life, as it was once lived by the Homeric Greeks, free from the corrosive effect of civilised scepticism and critical questioning. It is not the possession of common ideas, convictions bred by reasoning, that creates true human bonds, but common life and common effort. The true basis of all association is the family, the tribe, the *polis*, in which cooperation is instinctive and spontaneous and does not depend on rules or contracts or invented arrangements. Associations for the sake of profit or utility, resting on some artificial agreement, as the political and economic institutions of the capitalist system plainly do, stifle the sense of common humanity and destroy human dignity by generating a spirit of competitive opportunism. Athens created immortal masterpieces until Socrates came, and spun theories, and played a nefarious part in the disintegration of that closely knit, once heroic, community by sowing doubt and undermining established values which spring from the profoundest and most life-enhancing instincts of men.

Sorel began to write in this fashion when he was still a municipal engineer in Perpignan; his friend Daniel Halévy assures us that he had not then read a line of Nietzsche, whom he later came to admire. But their charge against Socrates is identical: both Nietzsche and Sorel take the side of his accusers: it was Socrates, and his disciple Plato, arch-intellectuals, who planted the life-destroying seeds that led to the glorification of abstractions, academies, contemplative or critical philosophies, Utopian schemes, and so to the decline of Greek vitality and Greek genius.

Can decadence be averted? Where is permanent salvation to be sought? There is another ancient doctrine in which men have traditionally sought reassurance: teleology. History, it was thought, would be meaningless – merely a causal sequence, or a chaos of unrelated episodes – if it lacked some ultimate purpose. This was considered unthinkable: reason rejects the notion of a mere collocation of 'brute' facts; there must be advance or growth towards the fulfilment of some goal or pattern; the mind demands some guarantee that, despite all accidents and collapses, the story will have a happy ending; either Providence is leading us towards it in its own inscrutable fashion; or else history is conceived as the self-realisation from stage to stage of the great cosmic spirit of which all men and all their institutions, and perhaps all nature, is the changing and progressive expression. Or, perhaps, it is human reason itself that cannot and will not for ever be frustrated, and must, late or soon, triumph over all obstacles, both external and self-generated, and build a world in which men have become everything that, as rational creatures, they consciously or unconsciously seek to be. In its metaphysical or mystical or secular forms this amalgam of Hebraic faith and Aristotelian metaphysics dominated the ideas of the last three centuries and gave confidence to many who might otherwise have despaired.

These central intellectual traditions to which men have pinned their hopes – the Greek doctrine of salvation by knowledge and the Judaeo-Christian doctrine of history as theodicy – were all but rejected by Sorel. All his life he believed in two absolutes: that of science, and that of morality. Science, even though, or perhaps because, it is a human artifice, enables us to classify, predict, control certain events. The concepts and categories in terms of which science puts its questions may vary with cultural change: the objectivity and reliability of the answers do not. But it is a weapon, not an ontology, not an analysis of reality. The great machine of science does not yield answers to problems of metaphysics or morality: to reduce the central problems of human life to problems of means, that is, of technology, is not to understand what they are. To regard technical progress as being identical with, or even as a guarantee of, cultural progress, is moral blindness. Sorel devoted a series of essays to demonstrating the absurdity of the idea of general human progress which springs from confusion of technology with life, or of the preposterous claim, first advanced by men of letters in the late seventeenth century, of their inevitable superiority to the ancients. As for theological or metaphysical beliefs in human perfectibility, they are only a pathetic clutching at straws, a refuge of the weak.

Neither science nor history offers comfort: Turgot and Condorcet and their nineteenth-century disciples are poor, deluded optimists who believe that history is on our side; so it will be, but only if we make it so, if we fight the good fight against the oppressors and exploiters, the dreary, life-destroying levellers, the masters and the slaves, and protect the sublime and the heroic against democrats and plutocrats, pedants and philistines.

Sorel has no doubt about what is health, and what is disease, whether in individuals or in societies. The Homeric Greeks lived in the light of values without which a society could not be creative or possess a sense of grandeur. They admired courage, strength, justice, loyalty, sacrifice, above all the struggle itself; freedom for them was not an ideal but a reality: the feeling of successful effort. Then (and this probably comes from Vico) came scepticism, sophistry, ease of life, democracy, individualism, decadence. Greek society disintegrated and was conquered. Rome, too, was once heroic, but it had given in to legalism and the bureaucratisation of life; the late Empire was a cage in which human beings felt stifled.

It was the early church that had once held high the flag of man. What the early Christians believed is less important than the intensity of a faith that did not allow the corrosive intellect to penetrate it. Above all, these men refused to compromise. The early Christians could have saved themselves from persecution by coming to terms with the Roman bureaucrats. They preferred faith, integrity and sacrifice. Concessions, Sorel repeats, always, in the end, lead to self-destruction. The only hope lies in ceaseless resistance to forces that seek to weaken what one instinctively knows that one lives by. When the church triumphed and made its peace with the world, it became infected by it and therefore degenerated: the barbarians were converted to Christianity, but to a worldly Christianity, and so fell into decay.

The heroic Christianity of the martyrs is a defence against the decadent state, but it is itself intrinsically socially destructive. Christians (and Stoics too) are not producers: the Gospels, unlike the Old Testament or Greek literature, are addressed to paupers and anchorites. A society indifferent to riches, content with its daily bread, allows no room for vigorous, creative life. Christianity, like every ideology, like its secular imitation – the Utopian socialism of a later day – 'cut the links between social life and the spirit, sowing everywhere germs of quietism, despair, death'.[1] Too little was accorded to Caesar, too much to the church – an organisation of consumers, not (in Sorel's sense) of producers. Sorel wishes to return to the firm values of the hardy Judaean peasants or the Greek *polis*, where merely to question them was considered subversive. He is concerned neither with happiness nor salvation: only with the quality of life itself, with what used to be called virtue (which in his case much resembles Renaissance *virtù*). Like the Jansenists, like Kant and the romantics, he values motive and character, not consequences and success.

The accumulation of public wealth in the hands of priests and monks played its part in the exhaustion and fall of the Roman west.

[1] *La Ruine du monde antique*, 3rd ed. (Paris, 1933), p. 44.

But after decay there is always hope of a revival: does not Vico speak of a *ricorso* – when one cycle of history has ended in moral weakness and decadence, a new one, barbarian, fresh and simple and pious and strong, begins the story again? Sorel dwells on this with the enthusiasm of Nietzsche. He is fascinated by every example of resolute moral resistance to decay, and consequently by the story of the church under persecution and of the church militant; he takes little interest in the church triumphant. It is in connection with movements of resistance and renewal that he develops (increasingly after falling under the influence of Bergson) the theories of which he became the most famous upholder: of the social myth, of permanent class war, of violence, of the general strike.

Even in the darkest moments of decadence, the social organism develops antibodies to resist the disease – men who will not give in, who will stand up and save the honour of the human race. The dedicated monastic orders, the saints and martyrs who preserved mankind from total contamination by late Roman society – what men today embody such qualities, possess the *virtù* of the great *condottieri* and artists of the Renaissance? There may be something of it in the American men of business, bold, enterprising, creative captains of industry who make their will prevail over nature and other men; but they are tainted by the general corruption of capitalism of which they are the leaders. There was, it seemed to Sorel, only one true body of this kind: those who are saved by work – the workers, the only genuinely creative class of our day. The proletarians, who are not morally caught in the toils of bourgeois life, appear to Sorel heroic, endowed with a natural sense of justice and humanity, morally impregnable, proof against the sophistries and casuistries of the intellectuals.

In the last years of the century, during the united front of the left created by the Dreyfus Affair, and perhaps influenced by the reformist socialism of Bernstein in Germany which seemed to him to be at any rate based on economic realities, Sorel supported the idea of a political party of the working class. But soon he accepted the position of the syndicalist journalist, Lagardelle, in whose journal, *Le Mouvement socialiste*, a good many of his articles appeared, that it is not opinions that truly unite men, for beliefs are a superficial possession, blown about by ideologists who play with words and ideas, and can be shared by men of different social formation who have basically nothing in common with each other. Men are truly made one only by real ties, by the family – the unchanging unit of the moral life, as Proudhon and

Le Play had insisted – by martyrdom in a common cause, but above all by working together, by common creation, united resistance to the pressures both of inanimate nature, which provides the workers with their materials, and of their masters, who seek to rob them of the fruits of their toil. The workers are not a party held together by lust for power or even for material goods. They are a social formation, a class. It was the genius of Marx that discovered the true nature of classes defined in terms of their relationship to the productive processes of a society torn, but also driven forward, by conflict between capitalist and proletarian. Sorel never abandoned his belief in Marx, but he used his doctrines selectively.

Sorel derives from Marx (reinforced by his own interpretation of Vico) his conception of man as an active being, born to work and create; from this follows his right to his tools, for they are an extension of his nature. The working tools of our day are machines. Machinery is a social cement more effective, he believes, than even language. All creation is in essence artistic, and the factory should become the vehicle of the social poetry of modern producers. Human history is more than the impersonal story of the evolution of technology. Inventions, discoveries, techniques, the productive process, are activities of human beings endowed with minds but, above all, wills. Men's values, their practice, their work, are one dynamic, seamless whole. Sorel follows Vico in insisting that we are not mere victims or spectators of events, but actors and originators. Marx, too, is appealed to, but he is, at times, too determinist for Sorel, especially in the versions of his more positivist interpreters – Engels, Kautsky, Plekhanov, men inclined to *la petite science*, like bourgeois economists and sociologists. Social and economic laws are not chains, not a constricting framework, but guidelines to possible action, generated and developed by, and in, action. The future is open. Sorel rejects such determinist phraseology as 'tendencies working with iron necessity towards inevitable results' and the like, of which *Das Kapital* is full. Marxism 'is a doctrine of life good for strong peoples; it reduces ideology to the role of a mere instrument'.[1] History for Sorel is what it was for Hegel, a drama in which men are authors and actors; above all it is a struggle between the forces of vitality and those of decay, activity and passivity, dynamic energy versus cowardice and surrender.

Marx's deepest single insight, for Sorel, is his notion of the class war as the matrix of all social change. Creation is always a struggle:

[1] loc. cit. (p. 306, note 1 above).

Greek civilisation for Sorel is symbolised by the sculptor who cuts the marble – the resistance of the stone, resistance as such, is essential to the process of creation. In modern factories the struggle is not merely between men – workers – and nature, which provides raw material, but between workers and employers, who seek to extract surplus value by exploiting other men's labour power. In this struggle men, like steel, are refined. Their courage, their self-respect, their solidarity with each other, grow. Their sense of justice develops too, for justice, according to Proudhon (to whom Sorel's debt is greater than even to Marx), is something that springs from the feeling of indignation aroused by the humiliation inflicted on others. What is insulted is what is common to all men – their humanity which is ours; the insult to human dignity is felt by the offender, by the injured man, and by the third party; this common protest which they all feel within them is the sense of justice and injustice. It is this that united some among the socialists with the liberal bourgeoisie against the chicanery of the army and the church during the Dreyfus case, and created Sorel's bond with Charles Péguy, who was never a Marxist but was prepared to work with anyone who did not wish to see France dishonoured by a cynical miscarriage of justice. In 1899 he speaks of the 'admirable ardour' with which the Allemanist workers are marching for 'truth, justice, morality'[1] by the side of Jaurès whom he was soon to attack so violently for lacking these very qualities.

Justice in particular is for Sorel an absolute value, proof against historical change. His conception of it may, as in the case of Kant and Proudhon, be rooted in a severe upbringing. Sorel dreaded sentimental humanitarianism; when people cease to feel horror at human crimes this will, he thinks, mean a collapse of their sense of justice. Better wild retribution than indifference or a sentimental tendency to forgiveness characteristic of humanitarian democracy. It is his indignation with what he saw as the dilution in the public life of France in his day of the sense of justice – to him a kind of intuitive sense of absolute moral pitch – that drove him from one extreme remedy to another and caused him to reject anything that he suspected of inclining towards compromise with stupidity or wickedness. It is the absence of the sense of absolute moral values, and of the decisive part played in human life by the moral will, that, for Sorel, is Marx's greatest single

[1] 'L'Éthique du socialisme', *Revue de metaphysique et de morale* 7 (1899), 301.

weakness: he is too historicist, too determinist, too relativist. Sorel's uncompromising voluntarism is at the heart of his entire outlook; there is in Marx too much emphasis on economics, not enough ethical doctrine.

The carrier of true moral values today is the proletariat. Only workers have true respect for work, for family, for sacrifice, for love. They are frugal, dignified, honest. For him, as for Fernand Pelloutier, the true founder of French syndicalism, they are beings touched by grace. For Sorel they were what peasants were for Herzen, what 'the folk' was for Herder and the populists, what 'the nation' was for Barrès. It is this traditionalism, which he shared with a certain type of conservative, and the quality of his domestic life with the simple and religious Marie David, that may have deepened his sense of the gulf between the moral dignity of the workers and the character and values of the pliable and the clever who rose to success in democracies. He found, or thought he found, this farouche integrity in Proudhon, in Péguy, in Pelloutier and other uncompromising fighters for justice or independence at whatever cost; he looked for it in the royalist *littérateurs*, in ultra-nationalists, in all resistance to time-serving supporters of the Republic and its demagogues. Hence his lack of sympathy for the populist nationalism of Déroulède, as for the entire Boulangist front. He might have approved of the *Croix de Feu*, but never of Poujadism.

Sorel's relationship to Marx is harder to define: classes and the class war as the central factor in social change; universal, timeless ideals as disguises for temporary class interests; man as a self-transforming, creative, tool-inventing being; the proletariat – the producers – as the bearer of the highest human values; these ideas he never abandoned. But he rejected the entire Hegelian-Marxist teleology which fuses facts and values. Sorel believed in absolute moral values: the historicism of the Hegelian-Marxist tradition was never acceptable to him, still less the view that issues of basic moral or political principle can be solved by social scientists, psychologists, sociologists, anthropologists; or that techniques based on imitation of the methods of natural science can explain and explain away ideas or values, to the permanence and power of which all history and art, all religion and morality, testify; or can, indeed, explain human conduct in mechanistic or biological terms, as the positivists, the blinkered adherents of *la petite science*, believe.

Sorel regards values, both moral and aesthetic, though their forms and applications may alter, as being independent of the march of events. Hence he regards sociological analysis of works of art, whether by Diderot or Marxist critics, as evidence of their profound lack of aesthetic sense, blindness to the mystery of the act of creation, and to the part that art plays in the life of mankind. Yet he shows little consistency when engaged in exposing the motives of the enemy; then he is more than ready to use all the tools of psychological or sociological analysis provided by those who probe for true springs of action by 'unmasking' interests disguised as unalterable laws or disinterested ideals. Thus he fully accepts the Marxist view that economic laws are not laws of nature, but human arrangements, created, whether consciously or not, in the interests of a given class. To look upon them as objective necessities, as bourgeois economists do, is to reify them, an illusion that plays into the hands of that class to whose advantage it is to represent them as being eternal and unchangeable. But then he draws the un-Marxist, voluntarist corollary that freely chosen effort and struggle can change a great deal; and parts company with the orthodox who insist on a rigorous and predictable causal correlation between productive forces and the superstructure of institutions and ideas. The moral absolutes must not be touched: they do not alter with changes in the forces or relations of production.

History for Sorel is more of a wild flux than Marx supposed: society is a creation, a work of art, not (as, perhaps, the state is) a mere product of economic forces. Marx's economism he regards as overstated; this may have been necessary (as Engels, in effect, admitted) in order to counter idealistic or liberal-individualist theories of history. But in the end such theories may, he thinks, lead to a belief in the possibility of predicting the social arrangements of the future. This is dangerous and delusive Utopianism. Such fantasies may stimulate the workers, but they can arm despotisms too. Even if the workers win their fight against the bourgeoisie, yet, unless they are educated to be creative, they too may generate an oppressive élite of doctrinaire intellectuals from within their own class. He accuses Marx of relying altogether too much on that Hegelian maid-of-all-work, the world spirit, although Marx is credited with understanding that science (and especially economic science) is not a 'mill' into which you can drop any problem facing you, and which yields solutions.[1] Methods of application are everything. Did not Marx himself once declare,

[1] *R.V.*, p. 173.

'Whoever composes a programme for the future is a reactionary'?[1] Nor, according to Sorel, did Marx believe in a political party of the working class; for a party, once in the saddle, may well become tyrannical and self-perpetuating, no matter what its manifestos state. Marx, after all, Sorel tells us, believed in the reality of classes alone.

This is a greatly Sorelified Marx: Sorel rejects everything in Marx that seems to him political – his notion of the workers' party, his theory of, and practical measures for, the organisation of the revolution, his determinism, above all the doctrine of the dictatorship of the proletariat which Sorel regards as a sinister recrudescence of the worst elements of repressive Jacobinism. Even the anarchist classless society with which true human history is to begin is virtually ignored by Sorel: evidently it is too much of a conceptual, ideological construction. 'Socialism is not a doctrine,' he declared, 'not a sect, not a political system; it is the emancipation of the working classes who organise themselves, instruct themselves and create new institutions.'[2] The proletariat is for him a body of producers at once disciplined and inspired by the nature of the labour they perform. It is this that makes them a class and not a party. The proletarians are not simply the discontented masses; the proletarian revolution is not merely a revolt of poor against rich, of the *popolo minuto* of the Italian communes, organised and led by a self-appointed general staff, the kind of rising advocated by Babeuf or Blanqui; for this can happen anywhere and at any time. The true social revolution of our day must be the revolt of a heroic class of producers and makers against exploiters and their agents and parasites, something that cannot happen unless – this was Marx's crucial discovery – a society has reached a certain stage of technological development, and the truly creative class has developed a moral personality of its own. (It is this emphasis on the intrinsic value and revolutionary character of the culture of the producers – the proletariat – that appealed to Gramsci and caused him to defend Sorel against his detractors.) Sorel does not seem to have contemplated a society so mechanised as to generate a technocratic bureaucracy in-

---

[1] *R.V.*, p. 168. This letter, by Marx, which Professor L. J. Brentano reported as having been sent to Marx's English friend, Professor Beesly, in 1869, has never, so far as I know, been found. Nor does the sentiment sound very Marxian, although Eduard Bernstein is reported to have said that it seemed to him to be so. See *Mouvement socialiste*, 1 September 1899, p. 270.

[2] 'La Crise du socialisme', *Revue politique et parlementaire* 18 (1898), 612.

volving both managers and workers, in which social dynamism is stifled by the organisation required by the sheer size of the industrial system. According to Daniel Halévy, France at the turn of the century, and in particular Paris and its environs, were relatively unindustrialised compared with England or Germany. Sorel is closer to Proudhon's world than to that of General Motors or I.C.I.

Only conflict purifies and strengthens. It creates durable unity and solidarity; whereas political parties, which anyone, of whatever social formation, can enter, are ramshackle structures, liable to opportunist coalitions and alliances. This is the vice of democracy. Not only is it the sham denounced by Marxists, a mere front for capitalist control; but the very ideal of democracy – national unity, reconciliation of differences, social harmony, devotion to the common good, Rousseau's General Will raised above the battle of the factions – all this destroys the conditions in which alone men can grow to their full stature – the struggle, the social conflict. The most fatal of all democratic institutions are parliaments, since they depend on compromise, concessions, conciliation; even if we forget about the ruses, equivocation, hypocrisy of which the syndicalists speak, political combinations are the death of all heroism, indeed of morality itself. The member of parliament, no matter how militant his past, is inevitably driven into peaceful association, even cooperation, with the class enemy, in committees, in lobbies, in the chamber itself. The representative of the working classes, Sorel observed, becomes an excellent bourgeois very easily. The hideous examples are before our eyes – Millerand, Briand, Viviani, the spellbinding demagogue Jean Jaurès with his easily acquired popularity. Sorel had once hoped for much from these men, but was disillusioned. They all turned out to be squalid earthworms, rhetoricians, grafters and intriguers like the rest.

Sorel goes even farther. Creative vitality cannot exist where everything gives, where it is too soft to resist. Unless the enemy – not the parasitic intellectuals and theorists, but the leaders of the capitalist forces – are themselves energetic and fight back like men, the workers will not find enemies worthy of their steel, and will themselves tend to degenerate. Only against a strong and vigorous opponent can truly heroic qualities be developed. Hence Sorel's characteristic wish that the bourgeoisie might develop stronger sinews. No serious Marxist could begin to accept this thesis, not even the mildest reformist, not even those who, like Bernstein, denied the validity of the Marxist historical libretto and declared in language worthy of Sorel himself:

'The goal is nothing: the movement is everything.'[1] Sorel averts his gaze from the aftermath of the ultimate victory of the working class. He is concerned only with rises and falls, creative societies and classes and decadent ones. No perfection, no final victory, is possible in social existence; only in art, in pure creation, can this be achieved. Rembrandt, Ruysdael, Vermeer, Mozart, Beethoven, Schumann, Berlioz, Liszt, Wagner, Debussy, Delacroix, the impressionist painters of his own day – these were capable of reaching an unsurpassable summit in their art. Hence his attack on those who sell their genius for fame or money. Meyerbeer can be despised but not blamed: he was a true child of his age and milieu: his gift was as vulgar as the audience which he knew how to please; not so Massenet, who prostituted his more genuine talent to please the bourgeois public. Something of this kind, he seems to think, is true of Anatole France too.

The total fulfilment that is possible in art, in science, in the case of individual men of genius, cannot occur in the life of society. Hence Sorel's distrust of the entire Marxist scenario: the expropriation of the expropriators, the dictatorship of the proletariat, the reign of plenty, the withering away of the state. He ignores practical problems; he is not interested in the way in which production, distribution, exchange, will be regulated in the new order, nor in whether there is any possibility of abolishing scarcity without performing at least some tasks that can hardly be described as creative. Marxists can scarcely be blamed if they did not regard as their own a man who wished to preserve the enemy in being lest the swords of his own side rusted in their scabbards, who had nothing to say about the ideal of a free society of associated producers combining to fight inanimate nature, but, on the contrary, declared, 'Everything may be saved if the proletariat, by its use of violence . . . restores to the middle class something of its former energy',[2] a man who did not seem to care about the problems of poverty and misery as such, and protested against sabotage of factories, because this was wilful destruction of the fruits of someone's creative labour. No man could claim to be a Marxist if he condemned revolutionary terror as a political act and damned Jacobins as tyrants and fanatics – men on whom Marx, to some degree, and even more Lenin, looked as their legitimate ancestors. Sorel denounces activity that springs from morally impure feelings, from motives infected by bourgeois poisons: 'The fierce envy of the impoverished intellectual,'

[1] Quoted by Sorel, op. cit. (p. 309, note 1 above), p. 296.
[2] *R.V.*, p. 110.

314

he declares, 'who would like to see the rich merchant guillotined, is a vicious feeling that is not in the least socialist.'[1] He cares only for the preservation of heroic vitality and courage and strength which may decline if total victory leaves the victor no enemy.

Sorel was aware of the oddity of his position, and took perverse and somewhat malicious pleasure in exposing the weakness or confusions of his allies. He pronounced socialism to be dead in the early years of our century. He made no effort to influence any active social or political group. He remained true to his professions: isolated, independent, a man on his own. If he has any parallel within the socialist movement, it is with the equally independent and unpredictable Viennese critic and journalist Karl Kraus, also concerned with morality, and the preservation of style in life and literature.[2] Even Bernard Shaw, who admired vitality, style, Napoleonic qualities, the 'life force', had a greater affinity with him than learned theorists like Kautsky, Plekhanov, Guesde, Max Adler, Sidney Webb, and the other pillars of European socialism. To him they were everything that he despised most deeply – arid, cerebral, latter-day sophists, clerks and glossators who turned every vital impulse into abstract formulas, Utopian blueprints, learned dust. He poured the vials of his scorn upon them. They repaid him by ignoring him completely.

Jaurès called Sorel the metaphysician of syndicalism. And, indeed, Sorel believed that in every human soul there lay hidden a metaphysical ember glowing beneath the cinders. If one could blow this into a flame, it would kindle a conflagration that would destroy mediocrity, routine, cowardice, opportunism, corrupt bargains with the class enemy. Society can be saved only by the liberation of the producers, that is, the workers, particularly those who work with their hands. The founders of syndicalism were right: the workers must be protected against domination by experts and ideologists and professors – the intellectual élite of Plato's hideous dream – what Bakunin (with Marx in mind) had called 'pedantocracy'. 'Can you conceive', asked Sorel, 'of anything more horrible than government by professors?'[3] In these days such men, he observes, tend to be, as often as not, *déraciné* intellectuals, or Jews without a country – men who have no

---

[1] *Matériaux d'une théorie du prolétariat*, 2nd ed. (Paris, 1921), p. 98, note 1.

[2] Marxism is in danger of becoming 'a mythology founded on the maladies of language', he wrote in a letter to Croce of 27 December 1897 (*La critica* 25 (1927), 50–2).

[3] *Le Procès de Socrate* (Paris, 1889), p. 183.

home, no hearth of their own, 'no ancestral tombs to protect, no relics to defend against the barbarians'.[1]

This is, of course, the violent rhetoric of the extreme right – of de Maistre, of Carlyle, of German nationalists, of French anti-Dreyfusards, of anti-Semitic chauvinists – of Maurras and Barrès, Drumont and Déroulède. But it is also, at times, the language of Fourier and Cobbett, Proudhon and Bakunin, and would later be spoken by Fascists and National Socialists and their literary allies in many countries, as well as those who thunder against critical intellectuals and rootless cosmopolitans in the Soviet Union and other countries of eastern Europe. No one was closer to this style of thought and expression than the so called left-wing Nazis – Gregor Strasser and his followers in the early days of Hitler, and in France men like Déat and Drieu la Rochelle.

There is an anti-intellectual and anti-Enlightenment stream in the European radical tradition, at times allied with populism, or nationalism, or neo-medievalism, that goes back to Rousseau and Herder and Fichte, and enters agrarian, anarchist, anti-Semitic and other anti-liberal movements, creating anomalous combinations, sometimes in open opposition to, sometimes in an uneasy alliance with, the various currents of socialist and revolutionary thought. Sorel, whose hatred of democracy, the bourgeois republic, and above all the rational outlook and liberal values of the intelligentsia, was obsessive, fed this stream, indirectly at first, but towards the end of the first decade of our century more violently and openly until, by 1910, this caused a breach between him and his left-wing allies.

Doubtless his devout upbringing, his deep roots in traditional, old-fashioned French provincial life, his unspoken but profoundly felt patriotism, played their part: what seemed to him the demoralisation and disintegration of traditional French society plainly preoccupied him throughout his life and intensified his basic xenophobia and hostility to those who seemed to him to wander beyond the confines of the traditional culture of the west. His anti-intellectualism and anti-Semitism sprang from the same roots as those of Proudhon and Barrès. But there was also the decisive influence of the philosophy of Henri Bergson. With his friend Péguy, Sorel attended Bergson's lectures, and, like Péguy, was deeply and permanently affected.

It was from Bergson that he derived the notion, which he could equally well have found in the francophobe German romantics a

[1] op. cit. (p. 315, note 3 above), p. 158.

century earlier, that reason was a feeble instrument compared with the power of the irrational and the unconscious in the life both of individuals and societies. He was profoundly impressed by Bergson's doctrine of the unanalysable *élan vital*, the inner force that cannot be rationally grasped or articulated, which thrusts its way into the empty and unknowable future, and moulds both biological growth and human activity. Not theoretical knowledge but action, and only action, gives understanding of reality. Action is not a means to preconceived ends, it is its own policy-maker and pathfinder. Prediction, even if it were possible, would kill it. We have an inner sense of what we are at, very different from, and incompatible with, the outside view, that is, calm contemplation that classifies, dissects, establishes clear structures. The intellect freezes and distorts. One cannot render movement by rest, nor time by space, nor the creative process by mechanical models, nor something living by something still and dead – this is an old romantic doctrine that Bergson revivified and developed. Reality must be grasped intuitively, by means of images, as artists conceive it, not with concepts or arguments or Cartesian reasoning. This is the soil which gave birth to Sorel's celebrated doctrine of the social myth which alone gives life to social movements.

There is another source, too, whence the theory of myth may have sprung – the teachings of the founder of modern sociology, Émile Durkheim, who stood at the opposite extreme from Bergson. Rational and sternly positivist, he believed, like Comte, that science alone could answer our questions; what science could not do, no other method could achieve; he was implacably opposed to Bergson's deep irrationalism. Durkheim, who became the leading ideologist of the Third Republic, taught that no society could remain stable without a high degree of social solidarity between its members; this in its turn depended on the prevalence in it of dominant social myths bound up with appropriate ritual and ceremonial; religion had in the past been by far the most powerful of the forms in which this sense of solidarity found natural expression. Myths are not for Durkheim false beliefs about reality. They are not beliefs about anything, but beliefs *in* something – in descent from a common ancestor, in transforming events in a common past, in common traditions, in shared symbols enshrined in a common language, above all in symbols sanctified by religion and history. The function of myths is to bind a society, create a structure governed by rules and habits, without which the individual may suffer from a sense of isolation and solitude, may experience anxiety, feel lost; and this in its turn leads to lawlessness and social chaos. For Durkheim myths are ultimately a utilitarian, if uncontrived, spontaneous and natural, response to a quasi-biological need; his account of their function is treated by him as an empirical discovery of a Burkean kind, of a necessary condition for social stability. Sorel abhorred utilitarianism, and in particular the quest for social peace and cohesion by cautious republican academics, as an attempt to muffle the class war in the interests of the bourgeois republic.

For Sorel, the function of myths is not to stabilise, but to direct energies and inspire action. They do this by embodying a dynamic vision of the movement of life, the more potent because not rational, and therefore not subject to criticism and refutation by university wiseacres. A myth is compounded of images that are 'warmly coloured',[1] and affect men not as reason does, nor education of the will, nor the command of a superior, but as ferment of the soul which creates enthusiasm and incites to action, and, if need be, turbulence. Myths need have no historical reality; they direct our emotions, mobilise our will, give purpose to all that we are and do and make; they are, above all, not Utopias, which from Plato onward are descriptions of impossible states of affairs, fantasies in the heads of intellectuals remote from reality, evasion of concrete problems, escape into theory and abstraction. Sorel's myths are ways of transforming relationships between real facts by providing men with a new vision of the world and themselves: as when those who are converted to a new faith see the world and its furniture with new eyes. A Utopia is 'the product of intellectual labour; it is the work of theorists who, after observing and discussing the facts, seek to build a model against which to measure existing societies . . . it is a construction which can be taken to pieces',[2] its parts can be detached and fitted into other structures — bourgeois political economy is just such an artificial entity. But myths are wholes perceived instantaneously by the imagination. They are, in effect, political aspirations presented in the form of images 'made warm' by strong feeling. They reveal, as mere words cannot, hitherto invisible potentialities in the past and present, and so drive men to concerted efforts to bring about their realisation. The effort itself breeds new vitality, new effort and militancy in an endless dynamic process, spiralling upwards, which he called 'giving an aspect of reality to hopes of immediate action'.[3]

The Christian vision of the Second Coming that is at hand is, for

[1] *R.V.*, p. 184. [2] *R.V.*, p. 38. [3] *R.V.*, p. 149.

Sorel, a myth of this kind – in its light men accepted martyrdom. The Calvinist belief in the renovation of Christianity was a vision of a new order that was not of this world, but fired by it the believers successfully resisted the advance of secular humanism. The idea of the French Revolution, referred to with fervour at civic gatherings in French provincial towns, lives on as a vague but ardent image that commands loyalty and stimulates action of a particular kind, but a myth that cannot, any more than a hymn, or a flag, be translated into a specific programme, a set of clear objectives. 'When masses of men become aroused, then an image is formed which constitutes a social myth.'[1] This is how the Italian Risorgimento presented itself to the followers of Mazzini. It is by means of myths that socialism can be converted into a kind of social poetry, can be expressed in action but not in prose, not in treatises intended merely to be understood. The French revolutionary armies in 1792 were inspired by an ardent myth, and won; the royalist forces lacked it, and were defeated. The Greeks lived and flourished in a world filled with myths until they were subverted by the sophists, and after them by rootless oriental cosmopolitans who flooded into Greece and ruined her. The analogy with the present is all too patent.

Sorel's myth is not a Marxist idea. It has a greater affinity with the modernist psychologism of Loisy or Tyrrell, William James's doctrine of the will, Vaihinger's 'philosophy of "as if"', than with Marx's rationalist conception of the unity of theory and practice. The notion of 'the people', 'the folk' – good, simple and true, but unawakened, as it is conceived by populists, both radical and reactionary, of the eternal 'real nation' in the thought of nationalists, as opposed to its corrupt or craven representatives – Barrès's 'la terre et les morts' – these are Sorel's, not Durkheim's myths. Unsympathetic critics might say the same of most Marxists' use of the concept of the true, dialectically grasped interests of the proletariat, as opposed to its actual 'empirical' wishes, perhaps even of the notion of classless society itself, provided that its outlines remain blurred. The function of a myth is to create 'an epic state of mind'. Sorel's insistence on its irrationality is, perhaps, what caused Lenin to dismiss him so curtly and contemptuously.

What is to be the myth of the workers? What is to raise them to the state of heroic grandeur, above the grey routine of their humdrum lives? Something which, Sorel believes, already inspires those activists

[1] *R.V.*, p. 36.

in the French *syndicats* who have found their leader in the admirable
Fernand Pelloutier, who has rightly kept them from contamination by
democratic politics – the myth of the general strike. The syndicalist
general strike must not be confused with the ordinary industrial or
'political' strike which is a mere effort to extort better conditions or
higher wages from the masters, and presupposes acquiescence in a
social and economic structure common to owner and wage slave.
This is mere haggling and is the very opposite of the true class war.
The myth of the syndicalist general strike is a call for the total overthrow of the entire abominable world of calculation, profit and loss,
the treatment of human beings and their powers as commodities, as
material for bureacratic manipulation, the world of illusory consensus and social harmony, of economic or sociological experts no
matter what master they serve, who treat men as subjects of statistical
calculations, malleable 'human material', forgetting that behind such
statistics there are living human beings, not so much with normal
human needs – to Sorel that does not appear to matter much – but
free moral agents able collectively to resist and create and mould the
world to their will.

The enemy for Sorel is not always the same : during the Dreyfus
affair it was the nationalist demagogues with their paranoiac, Jacobin
cries of treason, their fanatical search for scapegoats and wicked incitement of the mob against the Jews,[1] who play this role. After their
defeat, it is the victors – the 'counter-church' of the intellectuals, the
intolerant, dehumanising, republican 'politico-scholastic' party, led by
academic despots, bred in the École Normale – who increasingly
become the principal targets of his fury. The general strike is the
climax of mounting militancy and 'violence', when, in an act of concentrated collective will, the workers, in one concerted move, leave
their factories and workshops, secede to the Aventine, and then arise
as one man and inflict a total, crushing, permanent, 'Napoleonic'
defeat upon the accursed system that shuffles them into Durkheim's
or Comte's compartments and hierarchies, and thereby all but robs
them of their human essence. This is the great human uprising of the
children of light against the children of darkness, of fighters for freedom against merchants, intellectuals, politicians – the miserable
crew of the masters of the capitalist world with their mercenaries, men
promoted from the ranks, bought off and absorbed into the hierarchy,

[1] Destined, Sorel declared in 1901, to become a formidable weapon. See
De l'église et de l'état (Paris, 1901), pp. 54–5.

careerists and social planners, right-wing and left-wing power- or status-seekers, promoters of societies based on greed and competition, or else on the stifling oppression of remorselessly tidy rational organisation.

Did Sorel believe, did he expect the workers to believe, that this final act of liberation would, or could, in fact, occur as a historical event? It is difficult to tell. He had nothing favourable to say of the general strikes, designed to secure specific concessions, that broke out (during his most syndicalist phase) in Belgium in 1904, above all in the abortive Russian revolution of 1905. This, for him, was Péguy's *mystique* reduced to mere *politique*. Moreover, if he believed, as he appeared to, that if the enemy weakened so would the class of producers, would not total victory lead to the elimination of the tension without which there is no effort, no creation? Yet without a myth it is impossible to create an energetic proletarian movement. Empirical arguments against the possibility or desirability of the general strike are not relevant. It is, one suspects, not intended as a theory of action, still less as a plan to be realised in the real world.

The weapon of the workers is violence. Although it gives its name to Sorel's best-known work ('my standard work',[1] as he ironically referred to it), its nature is never made clear. Class conflict is the normal condition of society, and force is continuously exerted against the producers, that is, the workers, by the exploiters. Force does not necessarily consist in open coercion, but in control and repression by means of institutions which, whether by design or not, have the effect, as Marx and his disciples have made clear, of promoting the power of the possessing class. This pressure must be resisted. To resist force by force is likely to result, as in the case of the Jacobin revolution, in the replacing of one yoke by another, the substitution of new masters for old. A Blanquist *putsch* could lead to mere coercion by the state – the dictatorship of the proletariat, perhaps even of its own representatives, as the successor to the dictatorship of capitalists. Dogmatic revolutionaries easily become oppressive tyrants: this theme is common to Sorel and the anarchists. Camus revived it in his polemic with Sartre. Force, by definition, represses; violence, directed against it, liberates. Only by instilling fear in the capitalists can the workers break their power, the force exerted against them.

This, indeed, is the function of proletarian violence: not aggression, but resistance. Violence is the striking off of chains, the prelude to

[1] Letter to Croce of 25 March 1921, *La critica* 28 (1930), 194.

regeneration. It may be possible to secure a more rational existence, better material conditions, a higher standard of living, security, even justice for the workers, the poor, the oppressed, without violence. But the renewal of life, rejuvenation, the liberation of creative powers, return to Homeric simplicity, to the sublimity of the Old Testament, to the spirit of the early Christian martyrs, of Corneille's heroes, of Cromwell's Ironsides, of the French revolutionary armies – this cannot be attained by persuasion, without violence as the weapon of liberty.

How the use of violence can in practice be distinguished from the use of force is never made clear. It is merely postulated as the only alternative to peaceful negotiation which, by presupposing a common good, common to workers and employers alike, denies the reality of class war. Marx, too, talked about the need for revolution to purify the proletariat from the filth of the old world and render it fit for the new. Herzen spoke of the cleansing storm of the revolution. Proudhon and Bakunin spoke in similarly apocalyptic terms. Even Kautsky declared that revolution raises men from degradation to a more exalted view of life. Sorel is obsessed by the idea of revolution. For him, faith in revolutionary violence and hatred of force entails, in the first place, the stern self-insulation of the workers. Sorel fervently agrees with the syndicalist organisers of the *bourses de travail* (a peculiar combination of labour exchanges, trades councils, and social and educational centres of militant workers) that proletarians who allow themselves any degree of cooperation with the class enemy are lost to their own side. All talk of responsible and humane employers, reasonable and peace-loving workers, nauseates him. Profit-sharing, factory councils that include both masters and men, democracy which recognises all men as equal, are fatal to the cause. In total war there can be no fraternisation.

Does violence mean more than this? Does it mean occupation of factories, the seizing of power, physical clashes with police or other agents of the possessing class, the shedding of blood? Sorel remains unclear. The conduct of the Allemanist workers who marched with Jaurès (then still well thought of) at a certain moment of the Dreyfus affair, is one of his very few allusions to the correct use of proletarian violence. Anything that increases militancy, but does not lead to the formation of power structures among the workers themselves, is approved. The distinction between force and violence appears to depend entirely on the character of its function and motive. Force imposes chains, violence breaks them. Force, open or concealed, enslaves; violence, always open, makes free. These are moral and metaphysical, not empirical, concepts. Sorel is a moralist and his values are rooted in one of the oldest of human traditions. That is why Péguy listened to him, and why his theses do not belong only to their own times but retain their freshness. Rousseau, Fichte, Proudhon, Flaubert, are Sorel's truest modern ancestors; as well as Marx the destroyer of rationalisations, the preacher of class war and of the proletarian revolution; not Marx the social scientist, the historical determinist, the author of programmes for a political movement, the practical conspirator.

IV

The doctrine of myths and its corollary, the emphasis on the power of the irrational in human thought and action, is a consequence of the modern scientific movement, and the application of scientific categories and methods to the behaviour of men. The relatively simple models of human nature which underlay the central ideas of social and political philosophers until quite far into the nineteenth century were gradually being superseded by an increasingly complicated and unstable picture as new and disturbing hypotheses about the springs of action were advanced by psychologists and anthropologists. The rise of doctrines, according to which men were determined by nonrational factors, some of them refracted in highly misleading ways in men's consciousness, directed attention to actual social and political practice and its true causes and conditions, which only scientific investigation could uncover, and which severely limited the area of free will or even made it vanish altogether. This naturalistic approach had the effect of playing down the role of conscious reasons by which the actors mistakenly supposed themselves, and appeared to others, to be motivated. These may well have been among the most decisive causes of the decline of classical political theory, which assumes that men who are, to some degree, free to choose between possibilities, do so for motives intelligible to themselves and others, and are, *pro tanto*, open to conviction by rational argument in reaching their decisions. The penetration of the 'disguises', of concealed factors – psychological, economic, anthropological – in individual and social life by examination of their actual role, transformed the simpler model of human nature with which political theorists from Hobbes to J. S. Mill had operated, and shifted emphasis from political argument to the less or more deterministic descriptive disciplines that began with Tocqueville and Taine and Marx, and were carried on by Weber and Durkheim, Le Bon and Tarde, Pareto and Freud, and their disciples in our time.

Sorel rejected determinism, but his theory of myths belongs to this development. His social psychology is an odd amalgam of Marxism, Bergsonian intuitionism, and Jamesian psychology, in which men, once they realise that they are, whether they know it or not, shaped by the class conflict (which he treats as a historical datum), can, by an effort of the will reinforced by the inspiration of the appropriate myth, freely develop the creative sides of their nature, provided they do not attempt to do so as mere individuals but collectively, as a class. Even this is not entirely true of individual men of genius – especially of artists, who are capable of creation in adverse social conditions by the strength of their own indomitable spirit. Of this dark process James and Croce and Renan seemed to him to show a deeper understanding than the blinkered sociological environmentalists. But Sorel is not a consistent thinker. His desperate lifelong search for a class, or group, which can redeem humanity, or at least France, from mediocrity and decay, is itself rooted in a quasi-Marxist sociology of history as a drama in which the protagonists are classes generated by the growth of productive forces, a doctrine for which he claims objective validity.

v

The effect of Sorel's doctrine upon the revolutionary syndicalist movement was minimal. He wrote articles in journals, collaborated with Lagardelle, Delesalle and Péguy, offered homage to Fernand Pelloutier, and talked and lectured to groups of admirers in Paris. But when Griffuelhes, the strongest personality since Pelloutier among the syndicalists, was asked whether he read Sorel, he replied, 'I read Dumas.'[1] Sorel was himself what he most despised in others – too intellectual, too sophisticated, too remote from the reality of the workers' lives. He looked for biblical or Homeric heroes capable of the epic spirit and was constantly disappointed. During the Dreyfus case, he denounced the anti-Dreyfusards who seemed to him to stand for lies, injustice,

[1] Quoted by Michael Curtis, *Three Against the Third Republic: Sorel, Barrès, and Maurras* (Princeton, 1959), p. 53.

and unscrupulous demagoguery. But after the Dreyfusards had won, he was in turn disgusted by the ignoble political manoeuvring, cynicism and dissimulation of the friends of the people. Jaurès's humanity and eloquence seemed to him mere self-interested demagoguery, democratic claptrap, dust in the workers' eyes, no better than Zola's rodomontades, or the silver periods of Anatole France, or betrayals by false friends of the workers, the worst of whom was Aristide Briand, once the fervent champion of the general strike.

He continued to live quietly in Boulogne-sur-Seine. For ten years, until 1912, he took the tram to attend Bergson's lectures, and on Thursdays came to the gatherings in the offices of Péguy's *Cahiers de la Quinzaine*, which he dominated. There he delivered those vast monologues about politics and economics, classical and Christian culture, art and literature, which dazzled his disciples. He drew on a large store of unsystematic reading; but what lingered in his listeners' memories were his mordant paradoxes. Péguy listened reverently to *le père Sorel*, but in the end, when Sorel, disillusioned with the syndicalists who had gone the way of all workers into the morass of social democracy, began to look for new paladins against political impurity, and denounced the radical intellectuals, especially the Jews among them, too violently, even he became uncomfortable. When Sorel's anti-Semitism became more open and more virulent, and he did an unfriendly turn to Julien Benda (a ferocious critic of Bergson and of every form of nationalism, whom Péguy nevertheless greatly admired), and finally entered into an alliance with the militant royalists and chauvinists led by Maurras and the mystical Catholic nationalists grouped round Barrès, men who alone seemed to him independent, militant, and not tainted by the republican blight, this proved too much for Péguy, and he requested Sorel not to return. Sorel was deeply wounded. He preferred talk to writing. The audience of gifted writers and intellectuals was necessary to him. He began to frequent the bookshop of a humbler follower, and went on talking as before.

The flirtation with the reactionaries in the so-called Cercle Proudhon did not last long. In 1912 Sorel acclaimed Mussolini, then a flamboyant socialist militant, as a *condottiere* who, one day, 'will salute the Italian flag with his sword'.[1] By 1914 he was once again on his own. When war broke out he felt abandoned; Bergson, Péguy,

[1] In a conversation with Jean Variot reported by Variot in *L'Éclair*, 11 September 1922. Quoted by Gaetan Pirou, *Georges Sorel* (Paris, 1927), p. 53.

Maurras, even Hervé, all rallied to the defence of the Republic. During the war he was depressed and silent. He corresponded with Croce, who seemed to him critical and detached, and told his friend Daniel Halévy that the war was nothing but a fight between Anglo-American finance and the German General Staff. He did not seem to care greatly which gang emerged victorious.

After the war, in his letters to Croce, he criticised the beginnings of Fascism, but, perhaps under the influence of Pareto, and Croce's initial pro-Fascist moment, pronounced Mussolini a 'political genius'.[1] Lenin excited him far more. He saw him as a bold and realistic rejuvenator of socialism, the greatest socialist thinker since Marx, who had roused the Russian masses to an epic plane of revolutionary feeling. Lenin was Peter the Great or Robespierre, Trotsky was Saint-Just; their concept of the Soviets seemed to him pure syndicalism : he took it at its face value, as he did, perhaps, Mussolini's denunciation in 1920 of 'the state in all its forms and incarnations ; the state of yesterday, of today and of tomorrow'.[2] He applauded the Bolsheviks' contempt for democracy, and, still more, their ferocious attitude to intellectuals. He declared that the mounting terror of the Bolshevik Party was less harmful than the force which it was designed to repress ; in any case it was probably the fault of its Jewish members. He averted his eyes from the strengthening of the party apparatus, and would not speak of Russia as a socialist state, since this concept seemed to him, as it had seemed to Marx, a blatant contradiction in terms.

To use the state as a weapon against the bourgeoisie was, he declared, like 'Gribouille who threw himself into the water to avoid getting wet in the rain'.[3] He still thought well of Mussolini, but he thought better of Lenin, to whom he wrote a passionate paean. By this time few listened to him ; he was living in solitude and poverty – he had invested too much of his property in tsarist and Austrian bonds. His death, a few weeks before Mussolini's march on Rome, passed unnoticed. His last uttered word is said to have been 'Napoleon . . .'.

Of the two heroes of his declining years, Lenin ignored him ; Mussolini, in search of distinguished intellectual ancestry, claimed him as a spiritual father. Fascist propaganda found useful ammunition in Sorel's writings : the mockery of liberal democracy, the violent

[1] J. Variot, *Propos de Georges Sorel* (Paris, 1935), p. 55.
[2] Quoted by Gaudens Megaro, *Mussolini in the Making* (London, 1938), p. 319.
[3] *R.V.*, p. 144.

anti-intellectualism, the appeal to the power of irrational forces, the calls to activism, violence, conflict as such, all this fed Fascist streams.[1] Sorel was no more a Fascist than Proudhon, but his glorification of action, honour, defiance, his deep hatred of democracy and equality, his contempt for liberals and Jews, are, like Proudhon's brand of socialism, not unrelated to the language and thought of Fascism and National Socialism; nor did his closest followers fail to note (and some among them to be duly influenced by) this fact. The ideological link of his views with what is common to romantic Bolshevism and left-wing strains in Fascism is painfully plain. 'The cry "Death to the Intellectuals",' he wrote hopefully in his last published collection of articles, 'so often attributed to the Bolsheviks, may yet become the battle-cry of the entire world proletariat.'[2]

At this point, one might be tempted to bid Sorel goodbye as an eccentric visionary, a penetrating and cruel critic of the vices of parliamentary democracy and bourgeois humanitarianism – of what Trotsky once called 'Kantian-Quaker-liberal-vegetarian nonsense' – a writer chiefly read in Italy, both in leftist and nationalist circles, duly superseded by Pareto, Mosca and Michels, a friend of Croce, a minor influence on Mussolini, the inspirer of a handful of radicals both of the right and the left, a half-forgotten extremist safely buried in the pages of the more capacious histories of socialist doctrines. Yet his ghost, half a century later, is by no means laid.

VI

Sorel, like Nietzsche, preached the need for a new civilisation of makers and doers, what is now called a counter-culture or an alternative society. The progressive left in the nineteenth century believed in science and rational control of nature and of social and individual life, and on this based their attacks upon tradition, prejudice, aestheticism, clericalism, conservative or nationalist mystiques, whatever could not be defended by rational argument – these men have, to some

---

[1] A romantic, bitterly anti-democratic nineteenth-century Russian reactionary once declared that when he thought of the bourgeois in their hideous clothes scurrying along the streets of Paris, he asked himself whether it was for this that Alexander the Great, in his plumed helmet, had ridden down the Persian hosts at Abela. Sorel would not have repudiated this sentiment.

[2] op. cit. (p. 315, note 1 above), p. 53.

extent, won. The technocratic, post-industrial society in which we are said to be living is governed by men who make use of skilled, scientific experts, rational planners, technocrats. The theory of convergence used to inform us, in its heyday, now evidently past, that societies on both sides of the Iron Curtain are conditioned by similar forces in all essential respects, whatever the differences in kind or degree of individual liberty enjoyed by their members.

This is the kind of order – democracy both real and sham – based on respect for blueprints and specialists, that Sorel most deeply feared and detested. A society of consumers without authentic moral values of their own, sunk in vulgarity and boredom in the midst of mounting affluence, blind to sublimity and moral grandeur, bureaucratic organisation of human lives in the light of what he called *la petite science*, positivist application of quasi-scientific rules to society – all this he despised and hated. Who would revolt against it? The workers had not fulfilled his expectations. They failed to respond to his trumpet calls; they continued to be preoccupied with their material needs; their mode of life remained hopelessly similar to that of the *petite bourgeoisie*, one day to be the main recruiting-ground of Fascism, a class which Sorel regarded as the greatest source of moral contamination. He died a disappointed man.

Yet, if he were alive today, the wave of radical unrest could scarcely have failed to excite him. Like Fanon and the Black Panthers, and some dissenting Marxist groups, he believed that the insulted and the oppressed can find themselves and acquire self-identity and human dignity in acts of revolutionary violence. To intimidate the cowardly bourgeoisie (or, in Fanon's case, imperialist masters) by audacious acts of defiance, though Sorel did not favour terrorism or sabotage, is in tune with his feeling and his rhetoric. Che Guevara's or Fanon's concern about poverty, suffering and inequality was not at the centre of Sorel's moral vision; but they would have fulfilled his ideal of revolutionary pride, of a will moved by absolute moral values.

The idea of repressive tolerance, the belief that toleration of an order that inhibits 'epic' states of mind is itself a form of repression, is an echo of his own view. The neo-Marxist dialectic according to which all institutions and even doctrines are frozen forms of, and therefore obstacles to, the ever-flowing, ever-creative, human praxis, a kind of permanent revolution, might have seemed to him, even if he had understood the dark words of Hegelian neo-Marxism, mere incitement to anarchy. The metaphysics of the School of Frankfurt, and of Lukács (who was in his youth affected by Sorel's views), would surely have been roundly condemned by him as the latest Utopian and teleological nostrums of academic pedants, visionaries or charlatans.

In England anti-liberal critics – Wyndham Lewis and T. E. Hulme – took an interest in his ideas. Hulme translated the *Réflexions*. They found his emphasis on self-restraint and self-discipline sympathetic. Like them he hated disorder, bohemianism, the lack of self-imposed barriers, as symptoms of self-indulgence and decadence. But the revolt of those whom a German writer has recently described as the anabaptists of affluence, the preachers of an alternative society uncontaminated by the vices of the past, might well have made an appeal to him. He would have been disturbed by their sexual permissiveness; chastity was for him the highest of virtues; their slovenly habits, their exhibitionism, their addiction to drugs, their formless lives would have enraged him; and he would have denounced their neo-primitivism, the Rousseauian belief that poverty and roughness are closer to nature than austerity and civilised habits, and therefore more authentic and morally pure. He regarded this as false and stupid and attacked it all his life. But the present state of western society would have seemed to him a confirmation of Vico's prophecy of social disintegration as a prelude to a second barbarism, followed by a new, more virile civilisation, a new beginning in which men would again be simple, pious and severe. Barbarism did not frighten him.

He might have found reasons for acclaiming the Cultural Revolution in China. 'If socialism comes to grief,' he once observed, 'it will evidently be in the same way [as Protestantism], because it will be alarmed at its own barbarity,'[1] with the implication that it must not stop but plunge on – barbarism is, after all, an antidote to decay. This is instinctively believed by all those today who have opted out of a wicked society, as Sorel, who admired the early Christians and Puritans for their renunciation, so ardently wished the workers to do. Sparta rather than Athens. This alone created an unbridgeable gulf between Sorel and the easy-going, generous, humane Jaurès. It is this very quality that appeals to the grimmer dynamiters of the present.

But the strongest single link with the revolutionary movements of our day is his unyielding emphasis on the will. He believed in absolute moral ends that are independent of any dialectical or other historical pattern, and in the possibility, in conditions which men can themselves

[1] *R.V.*, p. 19, note 1.

create, of realising these ends by the concerted power of the free and deliberate collective will. This, rather than a sense of the unalterable timetable of historical determinism, is the mood of the majority of the rebels, political and cultural, of the past two decades. Those who join revolutionary organisations, and those who abandon them, are more often moved by moral indignation with the hypocrisy or inhumanity of the regime under which they live (or alternatively with similar vices in the revolutionary party which, disillusioned, they leave), than by a metaphysical theory of the stages of history – of social change by which they do not wish to be left behind. The reaction is moral more than intellectual, of will rather than reason; such men are against the prevailing system because it is unjust or bestial rather than irrational or obsolescent. More than seventy years ago Eduard Bernstein became convinced that Marxism failed to provide an acceptable view of the ends of life, and preached the universal values of the neo-Kantians. So did Karl Liebknecht, who could not be accused of lack of revolutionary passion. This is far closer to Sorel's position, and connects him with modern revolutionary protest.

Yet, of course, this anti-rationalism was, to some degree, self-refuting. He knew that if faith in reason is delusive, it is only by the use of rational methods, by knowledge and self-knowledge and rational interpretation of the facts of history or psychology or social behaviour, that this could be discovered and established. He did not wish to stop invention and technology; he was no Luddite, he knew that to break machines is to perpetuate ignorance, scarcity and poverty. He might have admitted that the remedies offered by the modern insurgents are delusions; but this would not have troubled him. He proposed no specific economic or social policies. Like Hegel's opponents in post-Napoleonic Germany he appealed to love, solidarity, community; this, in due course, offered sustenance to 'extra-parliamentary' oppositions both of the right and of the left. If Fanon, or the militants of the Third World, or the revolutionary students, were not healers, he might have recognised them as the disease itself. This is what Herzen said about himself and the nihilists of his own generation. His lifelong effort to identify and distinguish the pure from the impure, the physicians from the patients, the heroic few who should be the saviours of society – workers, or radical nationalists, or Fascists, or Bolsheviks – ended in failure. Would he have tried to find them in colonial peoples, or black Americans or students who have mysteriously escaped contamination by the false values of their society? We cannot tell. At any rate, the dangers of which he spoke were, and are, real. Recent events have shown that his diagnosis of the malaise is anything but obsolete.

He was almost everything that he so vehemently denounced, an alienated intellectual, a solitary thinker isolated from men of action who achieved no relationship with the workers and never became a member of any vigorous, cooperative group of producers. He, whose symbol of creation was the cut stone, the chiselled marble, was productive only of words. He believed implicitly in family life and for twenty-five years had none. The apostle of action felt at home only in bookshops, among purveyors of words, talkers cut off, as he had always been, from the life of workers and artists. He remained eccentric, egocentric, an outsider of outsiders. This is an irony that, one may be sure, could scarcely have escaped him.

No monument to him exists. Ten years after his death, so Daniel Halévy tells us, Rolland Marcel, the director of the Bibliothèque Nationale in Paris, came to Halévy with an odd story. He had recently met the Ambassador of Fascist Italy who informed him that his Government had learnt that Sorel's grave was in a state of disrepair : the Fascist Government offered to put up a monument to the eminent thinker. Soon after this, the Ambassador of the U.S.S.R. approached him with an identical proposal on behalf of the Soviet Government. Halévy promised to get in touch with Sorel's family. After a long delay he received a communication which said that the family regarded the grave as its own private affair, and that of no one else. Halévy was delighted. The message was dry, brusque and final. It might have come from Sorel himself.

The prophet of concerted collective action, of pragmatic approaches, prized only absolute values, total independence. He was to be the modern Diogenes bent on exploding the most sacred dogmas and respected beliefs of all the establishments of his enlightened age. Sorel is still worth reading. The world about and against which he was writing might be our own. Whether he is, as he wished to be, 'serious, formidable and sublime',[1] or, as often as not, perverse, dogmatic and obsessed, with all the moral fury of perpetual youth (and this fiery, not wholly adult, outraged feeling may in part account for his affinity with the young revolutionaries of our time), his ideas come at us from every quarter. They mark a revolt against the rationalist ideal of

[1] *R.V.*, p. 170.

frictionless contentment in a harmonious social system in which all ultimate questions are reduced to technical problems, soluble by appropriate techniques. It is the vision of this closed world that morally repels the young today. The first to formulate this in clear language was Sorel. His words still have power to upset.

Nationalism

Past Neglect and Present Power

I

THE history of ideas is a rich, but by its very nature an imprecise field, treated with natural suspicion by experts in more exact disciplines, but it has its surprises and rewards. Among them is the discovery that some of the most familiar values of our own culture are more recent than might at first be supposed. Integrity and sincerity were not among the attributes which were admired – indeed, they were scarcely mentioned – in the ancient or medieval worlds, which prized objective truth, getting things right, however accomplished. The view that variety is desirable, whereas uniformity is monotonous, dreary, dull, a fetter upon the freely-ranging human spirit, 'Cimmerian, corpse-like', as Goethe described Holbach's *Système de la nature*, stands in sharp contrast with the traditional view that truth is one, error many, a view scarcely challenged before – at the earliest – the end of the seventeenth century. The notion of toleration, not as a utilitarian expedient to avoid destructive strife, but as an intrinsic value; the concepts of liberty and human rights as they are discussed today; the notion of genius as the defiance of rules by the untrammelled will, contemptuous of the restraint of reason at any level – all these are elements in a great mutation in western thought and feeling that took place in the eighteenth century, the consequences of which appear in various counter-revolutions all too obvious in every sphere of life today. This is a vast topic which I shall not directly discuss: I wish to draw attention to, at most, only one corner of it.

An earlier version of some of the theses in this essay, although in a different form, was included in an article entitled 'The Bent Twig: a Note on Nationalism' in *Foreign Affairs* 51 (1972), 11–30.

The nineteenth century, as we all know, witnessed an immense growth of historical studies. There are many explanations of this: the revolutionary transformation of both life and thought brought about by the rapid and triumphant development of the natural sciences, in particular by technological invention and the consequent rise of large-scale industry; the rise of new states and classes and rulers in search of pedigrees; the disintegration of age-old religious and social institutions, as a result of Renaissance secularism and the Reformation; all this riveted attention upon the phenomena of historical change and novelty. The fillip given to historical, and, indeed, to all genetic studies, was incalculably great. There was a new sense of continuous advance, or at any rate of movement and change in the life of human society. It is not, therefore, surprising that major thinkers in this period set themselves to discover the laws which governed social change. It seemed reasonable to suppose that the new methods of the natural sciences, which proved capable of explaining the nature and the laws of the external world, could perform this service for the human world also. If such laws could be discovered at all, they must hold for the future as well as for the past. Prediction of the human future must be rescued from mystical prophets and interpreters of the apocalyptic books of the Bible, from the astrologers and dabblers in the occult, and become an organised province of scientific knowledge.

This hope spurred the new philosophies of history, and brought into being an entire new field of social studies. The new prophets tended to claim scientific validity for their statements about both the past and the future. Although much of what some of them wrote was the fruit of luxuriant and unbridled and sometimes egomaniacal imaginations, or at any rate highly speculative, the general record is a good deal more respectable than is commonly supposed. Condorcet may have been too optimistic in prophesying the development of a comprehensive and systematic natural science of man, and with it the end of crime and folly and misery in human affairs, all due to indolence and ignorance and irrationality. In the darkness of his prison in 1794 he drew a glowing picture of a new, virtuous and happy world, organised by the application of scientific method to social organisation by intellectually and morally liberated men, leading to a harmonious society of nations, unbroken progress in the arts and sciences and perpetual peace. This was plainly over-sanguine, yet the fruitfulness of applying mathematical, and in particular statistical, techniques to social problems was a prophecy at once original and important.

Saint-Simon was a man of genius who, as everyone knows, predicted the inevitable triumph of a technocratic order. He spoke of the coming union of science, finance and industrial organisation, and the replacement, in this new world of producers aided by scientists, of clerical indoctrination by a new race of propagandists – artists, poets, priests of a new secular religion, mobilising men's emotions, without which the new industrial world could not be made to function. His disciple, Auguste Comte, called for and predicted the creation of an authoritarian church to educate and control the rational, but not democratic or liberal, society and its scientifically trained citizens. I will not enlarge upon the validity of this prophecy: the combination of technological skills and the absolute authority of a secular priesthood has been realised only too successfully in our day. And if those who believed that prejudice and ignorance and superstition, and their embodiment in irrational and repressive laws, economic, political, racial and sexual, would be swept away by the new enlightenment, have not had their expectations realised, this does not diminish the degree of their insight into the new paths which had opened in western European development. This was the very vision of a rational, swept and garnered, new order, heralded by Bentham and Macaulay, which troubled Mill and Tocqueville and deeply repelled both Carlyle and Disraeli, both Ruskin and Thoreau, and, before them, some among the early German romantics at the turn of the nineteenth century. Fourier, in his turn, together with much nonsense, thundered against the evils of trade and industry, engaged in unbridled economic competition, tending to wanton destruction or adulteration of the fruits of human labour by those who wished to increase their own profits; he protested that the growth of centralised control over vast human groups led to servitude and alienation, and advocated the end of repression and the need for the rational canalisation of the passions by careful vocational guidance which would enable all human desires, capacities, inclinations, to develop in a free and creative direction. Fourier was given to grotesque fantasies: but these ideas were not absurd, and much of what he predicted is now conventional wisdom.

Everyone has recognised the fatal accuracy of Tocqueville's uneasy anticipation of the conformity and the monotony of democratic egalitarianism, whatever may be thought of the nostrums by which he sought to modify its effects. Nor do I know of anyone who would deny that Karl Marx, whatever his errors, displayed unique powers of prognosis in identifying some of the central factors at work in his day that were not obvious to his contemporaries – the concentration and centralisation of the means of production in private hands, the inexorable march of industrialisation, the rise and vast development of big business, then in its embryo, and the inevitable sharpening of social and political conflicts that this involved. Nor was he unsuccessful in unmasking the political and moral, the philosophical and religious, liberal and scientific disguises under which some of the most brutal manifestations of these conflicts and their social and intellectual consequences were concealed. These were major prophets, and there were others. The brilliant and wayward Bakunin predicted more accurately than his great rival Marx the situations in which great risings of the dispossessed would take place, and foresaw that they were liable to develop not in the most industrialised societies, on a rising curve of economic progress, but in countries in which the majority of the population was near subsistence level and had least to lose by an upheaval – primitive peasants in conditions of desperate poverty in backward rural economies where capitalism was the weakest, such as Spain and Russia. He would have had no difficulty in understanding the causes of the great social upheavals in Asia and Africa in our own day. I could go on: the poet Heine, addressing the French in the early years of the reign of Louis Philippe, saw that one fine day their German neighbours, spurred by a combination of historical memories and resentments with metaphysical and moral fanaticism, would fall upon them, and uproot the great monuments of western culture: 'Like early Christians, whom neither physical torture nor physical pleasure could break, restrained neither by fear nor greed', these ideologically intoxicated barbarians would turn Europe into a desert. Lassalle preached, and perhaps foresaw, state socialism – the people's democracies of our day, whether one calls them state communism or state capitalism, a hybrid which Marx utterly condemned in his notes on the Gotha programme.

A decade or so later Jakob Burckhardt anticipated the military-industrial complexes which would inevitably control the decadent countries of the west; Max Weber had no doubts about the growing power of bureaucracy; Durkheim warned of the possibility of anomie; there followed all the nightmares of Zamyatin, Aldous Huxley, Orwell, half satirists, half prophets of our own time. Some remained pure prophecies, others, notably those of the Marxists and Heine's barbarians who dominated the imagination of racialists and neo-pagan irrationalists, were, perhaps, to some degree self-fulfilling. The nineteenth century generated a great many other Utopias and prognoses, liberal, socialist, technocratic and those that were filled with neo-medieval nostalgia, craving for a largely imaginary *Gemeinschaft* in the past – systems for the most part justly forgotten. In all this great array of elaborate, statistically-supported mass of futurology and fantasy, there is one peculiar lacuna. There was one movement which dominated much of the nineteenth century in Europe and was so pervasive, so familiar, that it is only by a conscious effort of the imagination that one can conceive a world in which it played no part: it had its partisans and its enemies, its democratic, aristocratic and monarchist wings, it inspired men of action and artists, intellectual élites and the masses: but, oddly enough, no significant thinkers known to me predicted for it a future in which it would play an even more dominant role. Yet it would, perhaps, be no overstatement to say that it is one of the most powerful, in some regions the most powerful, single movement at work in the world today; and that some of those who failed to foresee this development have paid for it with their liberty, indeed, with their lives. This movement is nationalism. No influential thinker, to the best of my knowledge, foresaw its future – at any rate, no one clearly foretold it. The only exception known to me is the underrated Moses Hess, who, in 1862, in his book *Rome and Jerusalem*, affirmed that the Jews had the historic mission of uniting communism and nationality. But this was exhortation rather than prophecy, and the book remained virtually unread save by Zionists of a later day.

There is no need to emphasise the obvious fact that the great majority of the sovereign states represented at the Assembly of the United Nations today are actuated in a good deal of their behaviour by strong nationalist passions, even more than their predecessors of the League of Nations. Yet I suspect that this fact would have surprised most of the prophets of the nineteenth century, no matter how intelligent and politically intuitive. This is so because most social and political observers of that time, whether or not they were themselves nationalists, tended in general to anticipate the decline of this sentiment. Nationalism was, by and large, regarded in Europe as a passing phase. The desire on the part of most men to be citizens of a state coterminous with the nation which they regarded as their own, was considered to be natural or, at any rate, brought about by a historical-political development of which the growth of national consciousness was at once the cause and the effect, at any rate in the west. Nationalism as a sentiment and an ideology was not (in my opinion, rightly) equated with national consciousness.

The need to belong to an easily identifiable group had been regarded, at any rate since Aristotle, as a natural requirement on the part of human beings: families, clans, tribes, estates, social orders, classes, religious organisations, political parties, and finally nations and states, were historical forms of the fulfilment of this basic human need. No one particular form was, perhaps, as necessary to human existence as the need for food or shelter, security or procreation, but some form of it was indispensable, and various theories were offered to account for the historical progression of these forms, from Plato and Polybius to Machiavelli, Bossuet, Vico, Turgot, Herder, Saint-Simon, Hegel, Comte, Marx and their modern successors. Common ancestry, common language, customs, traditions, memories, continuous occupancy of the same territory for a long period of time, were held to constitute a society. This kind of homogeneity emphasised the differences between one group and its neighbours, the existence of tribal, cultural or national solidarity, and with it, a sense of difference from, often accompanied by active dislike or contempt for, groups with different customs and different real or mythical origins; and so was accepted as both accounting for and justifying national statehood. The British, French, Spanish, Portuguese and Scandinavian peoples had achieved this well before the nineteenth century; the German, Italian, Polish, Balkan and Baltic peoples had not. The Swiss had achieved a unique solution of their own. The coincidence of the territory of the state and nation was regarded as, on the whole, desirable, save by the supporters of the dynastic, multinational empires of Russia, Austria, Turkey, or by imperialists, socialist internationalists, anarchists, and perhaps some ultramontane Catholics. The majority of political thinkers, whether they approved of it or not, accepted this as an inevitable phase of social organisation. Some hoped or feared that it would be succeeded by other forms of political structure; some seemed to regard it as 'natural' and permanent. Nationalism – the elevation of the interests of the unity and self-determination of the nation to the status of the supreme value before which all other considerations must, if need be, yield at all times, an ideology to which German and Italian thinkers seemed particularly prone – was looked on by observers of a more liberal type as a passing phase due to the exacerbation of national consciousness held down and forcibly repressed by despotic rulers aided by subservient churches.

By the middle of the nineteenth century the aspirations for political unity and self-rule of the Germans and Italians seemed well on the way to realisation. Soon this dominant trend would liberate the oppressed peoples of the multinational empires too. After this, nationalism which was a pathological inflammation of wounded national consciousness would abate : it was caused by oppression and would vanish with it. This seemed to be taking longer than the optimists anticipated, but by 1919 the basic principle of the right to national self-government seemed universally accepted. The Treaty of Versailles, recognising the right to national independence, whatever else it might fail to achieve, would at any rate solve the so-called national question. There was, of course, the question of the rights of various national minorities in the new national states, but these could be guaranteed by the new League of Nations – surely if there was anything these states could be expected to understand, if only from their own historical experience, it was the need to satisfy the craving for autonomy on the part of ethnic or cultural groups within their borders. Other problems might still rack mankind – colonial exploitation, social and political inequality, ignorance, poverty, injustice, corruption, privilege; but most enlightened liberals, and, indeed, socialists, assumed that nationalism would decline, since the deepest wounds inflicted upon nations were on the way to being healed.

Marxists and other radical socialists went further. For them, national sentiment itself was a form of false consciousness, an ideology generated, consciously or not, by the economic domination of a particular class, the bourgeoisie, in alliance with what was left of the old aristocracy, used as a weapon in the retention and promotion of the class control of society, which, in its turn, rested on the exploitation of the labour power of the proletariat. In the fullness of time the workers, whom the process of production itself would inevitably organise into a disciplined force of ever-increasing size, political awareness and power, would overthrow their capitalist oppressors, enfeebled as they would be by the cut-throat competition among themselves that would undermine their capacity for organised resistance. The expropriators would be expropriated, the knell of capitalism would sound, and with it of the entire ideology of which national sentiment, religion and parliamentary democracy, were so many particular aspects. National differences might remain, but they would, like local and ethnic characteristics, be unimportant in comparison with the solidarity of the workers of the world, associated producers freely cooperating in the harnessing of the forces of nature in the interests of all mankind.

What these views had in common was the belief that nationalism was the ephemeral product of the frustration of human craving for self-determination, a stage of human progress due to the working of impersonal forces and the ideologies thereby generated by them. On the nature of these forces, theorists were not agreed, but for the most part they supposed that the phenomenon of nationalism itself would disappear with its causes, which in their turn would be destroyed by the irresistible advance of enlightenment, whether conceived in moral or technological terms – the victory of reason or of material progress or of both – identified with changes in the forces and relations of production, or with the struggle for social equality, economic and political democracy and the just distribution of the fruits of the earth ; with the destruction of national barriers by world trade or by the triumphs of science and a morality founded on rational principles, and so the full realisation of human potentialities which sooner or later would be universally achieved.

In the face of all this, the claims and ideals of mere national groups would tend to lose importance, and would join other relics of human immaturity in ethnological museums. As for the nationalists among peoples who had achieved independence and self-government, they were written off as irrationalists – and, with Nietzscheans, Sorelians, neo-romantics, out of account. It was difficult to ignore mounting nationalism after national unity had been largely achieved – for instance, German chauvinism after 1871, or French integralism or Italian *sacro egoismo* or the rise of racial theories and other anticipations of Fascism. None of these, however accounted for, were, so far as I know, regarded by the futurologists of the late nineteenth century or the early years of our own as harbingers of a new phase of human history ; and this seems equally true of conservatives, liberals and Marxists. The age of *Kriege, Krisen, Katastrophen*, which, for instance, Karl Kautsky predicted, he attributed to causes, and described in terms, in which nationalism, if it appears at all, figures only as a by-product, an element in the 'superstructure'. No one, so far as I know, so much as hinted that nationalism might dominate the last third of our own century to such a degree that few movements or revolutions would have any chance of success unless they came arm-

340

in-arm with it, or at any rate not in opposition to it. This curious failure of vision on the part of otherwise acute social thinkers seems to me a fact in need of explanation, or, to say the least, of wider discussion than it has so far obtained. I am neither a historian nor a social psychologist, and do not volunteer an explanation of it: I should merely like to throw out a suggestion which may cast some light on this odd phenomenon.

III

Before doing so, however, I should like to say something on the origins of European nationalism as a state of mind. I do not mean by this national sentiment as such – that can probably be traced to tribal feeling in the earliest period of recorded history. I mean its elevation into a conscious doctrine, at once the product, articulation and synthesis of states of consciousness, that has been recognised by social observers as a force and a weapon. In this sense, nationalism does not seem to exist in the ancient world, nor in the Christian Middle Ages. The Romans may have despised the Greeks, Cicero said disparaging things about the Jews, and Juvenal about Orientals in general; but this is mere xenophobia. There is passionate patriotism in Machiavelli or Shakespeare – and a long tradition of it long before them. I do not mean by nationalism a mere pride of ancestry – we are all sons of Cadmus, we all come from Troy, we are descended from men who made a covenant with the Lord, we spring from a race of conquerors, Franks or Vikings, and rule over the progeny of Gallo-Romans or Celtic slaves by right of conquest.

By nationalism, I mean something more definite, ideologically important and dangerous: namely the conviction, in the first place, that men belong to a particular human group, and that the way of life of the group differs from that of others; that the characters of the individuals who compose the group are shaped by, and cannot be understood apart from, those of the group, defined in terms of common territory, customs, laws, memories, beliefs, language, artistic and religious expression, social institutions, ways of life, to which some add heredity, kinship, racial characteristics; and that it is these factors which shape human beings, their purposes and their values.

Secondly, that the pattern of life of a society is similar to that of a biological organism; that what this organism needs for its proper

341

development, which those most sensitive to its nature articulate in words or images or other forms of human expression, constitutes its common goals; that these goals are supreme; in cases of conflict with other values, which do not derive from the specific ends of a specific 'organism' – intellectual or religious or moral, personal or universal – these supreme values should prevail, since only so will the decadence and ruin of the nation be averted. Furthermore, that to call such patterns of life organic is to say that they cannot be artificially formed by individuals or groups, however dominating their positions, unless they are themselves penetrated by these historically developing ways of acting and thinking and feeling, for it is these mental and emotional and physical ways of living, of coping with reality, above all the ways in which human beings deal with one another, that determine everything else and constitute the national organism – the nation – whether it takes the form of a state or not. Whence it follows that the essential human unit in which man's nature is fully realised is not the individual, or a voluntary association which can be dissolved or altered or abandoned at will, but the nation; that it is to the creation and maintenance of the nation that the lives of subordinate units, the family, the tribe, the clan, the province, must be due, for their nature and purpose, what is often called their meaning, are derived from its nature and its purposes; and that these are revealed not by rational analysis, but by a special awareness, which need not be fully conscious, of the unique relationship that binds individual human beings into the indissoluble and unanalysable organic whole which Burke identified with society, Rousseau with the people, Hegel with the state, but which for nationalists is, and can only be, the nation, whether its social structure or form of government.

Thirdly, this outlook entails the notion that one of the most compelling reasons, perhaps the most compelling, for holding a particular belief, pursuing a particular policy, serving a particular end, living a particular life, is that these ends, beliefs, policies, lives, are *ours*. This is tantamount to saying that these rules or doctrines or principles should be followed not because they lead to virtue or happiness or justice or liberty, or are ordained by God or church or prince or parliament or some other universally acknowledged authority, or are good or right in themselves, and therefore valid in their own right, universally, for all men in a given situation; rather they are to be followed because these values are those of *my* group – for the nationalist, of *my* nation; these thoughts, feelings, this course of action, are good or right, and I shall achieve fulfilment or happiness by identifying myself with them, because they are demands of the particular form of social life into which I have been born, to which I am connected by Burke's myriad strands, which reach into the past and future of my nation, and apart from which I am, to change the metaphor, a leaf, a twig, broken off from the tree, which alone can give it life; so that if I am separated from it by circumstance or my own wilfulness, I shall become aimless, I shall wither away, being left, at best, with nostalgic memories of what it once was to have been truly alive and active, and performing that function in the pattern of the national life, understanding of which alone gave meaning and value to all I was and did.

Florid and emotive prose of this kind was used by Herder, Burke, Fichte, Michelet, and after them by sundry awakeners of the national souls of their dormant peoples in the Slav provinces of the Austrian or Turkish empires or the oppressed nationalities ruled by the tsar; and then throughout the world. There is a distance between Burke's assertion that the individual may be foolish but the species is wise, and Fichte's declaration, a dozen or so years later, that the individual must vanish, must be absorbed, sublimated, into the species. Nevertheless the general direction is the same. This kind of value-laden language may at times affect to be descriptive, aimed only at illuminating the concept of nationhood or historical development. But its influence on conduct has been – and has by those who use it been intended to be – as great as that of the language of natural law or of human rights or of the class war or of any other idea which has shaped our world.

Finally, by a development which need cause no surprise, full-blown nationalism has arrived at the position that, if the satisfaction of the needs of the organism to which I belong turns out to be incompatible with the fulfilment of the goals of other groups, I, or the society to which I indissolubly belong, have no choice but to force them to yield, if need be by force. If my group – let us call it nation – is freely to realise its true nature, this entails the need to remove obstacles in its path. Nothing that obstructs that which I recognise as my – that is, my nation's – supreme goal, can be allowed to have equal value with it. There is no over-arching criterion or standard, in terms of which the various values of the lives, attributes, aspirations, of different national groups can be ordered, for such a standard would be super-national, not itself immanent in, part and parcel of, a given social organism, but deriving its validity from some source outside the life of a particular society – a universal standard, as natural law or natural justice are conceived by those who believe in them. But since, on this view, all values and standards must of necessity be those intrinsic to a specific society, to a national organism, and its unique history, in terms of which alone the individual, or the other associations or groups to which he belongs, if he understands himself at all, conceives all values and purposes, such appeals to universality rest on a false view of the nature of man and of history. This is the ideology of organicism, loyalty, the *Volk* as the true carrier of the national values, integralism, historic roots, *la terre et les morts*, the national will : it is directed against the forces of disruption and decay categorised in the pejorative terms used to describe the application of methods of the natural sciences to human affairs – of critical, 'analytic' reason, 'cold' intellect, destructive, 'atomising' individualism, soulless mechanism, alien influences, shallow empiricism, rootless cosmopolitanism, abstract notions of nature, man, rights, which ignore differences of cultures and traditions – in short, the entire typology and catalogue of the enemy, which begins in the pages of Hamann and Burke, reaches a climax in Fichte and his romantic followers, is systematised by de Maistre and Bonald, and reaches a new height in our own century in the propagandist writings of the First and Second World Wars, and the anathemas of irrationalist and Fascist writers, directed at the Enlightenment and all its works.

The language and the thought behind them, charged with emotion as they tend to be, are seldom wholly clear or consistent. The prophets of nationalism sometimes speak as if the superior, indeed, the supreme claims of his nation upon the individual, are based on the fact that its life and ends and history alone give life and meaning to all that he is and does. But this seems to entail that other men stand in a similar relation to their own nations, with claims upon them equally valid and no less absolute, and that these may conflict with full realisation of the ends or 'mission' of another, for example, a given individual's own nation, and this in its turn appears to lead to cultural relativism in theory, which ill accords with the absolutism of the premise, even if it does not formally contradict it ; as well as opening the door to war of all against all.

There are nationalists who seek to escape this by efforts to demonstrate that a given nation or race – say, the German – is superior to other peoples, and its goals transcend theirs, as measured by some objective, trans-national standard ; that its particular culture breeds beings in whom the true ends of men as such come closer to full realisation than in men outside its culture. This is how Fichte speaks in his later writings (and the same thesis is to be found in Arndt and other German nationalists of this period). This, too, is the sense of the idea of the superior mission of historic nations, each in its appointed time and place, to be found in the thought of Hegel. One can never feel completely certain whether these nationalist writers acclaim their own nation because it is what it is, or because its values alone approximate to some objective ideal or standard which, *ex hypothesi*, only those fortunate enough to be guided by them can even so much as understand, while other societies remain blind to them, and may always remain so, and are therefore objectively inferior. The line between the two conceptions is often blurred; but either leads to a collective self-worship, of which European, and perhaps American, nationalism has tended to be a powerful expression.

The nation is, of course, not the only focus of such worship. Similar language and rhetoric have historically been used in identifying the true interests of the individual with those of his church, his culture, his caste, his class, his party; sometimes these have overlapped or been fused into a unified ideal; at other times they have come into conflict. But the most powerful appeal of all these centres of devotion and self-identification has historically been the nation state. The revelation of its hold on its citizens in 1914, when it proved so much stronger than class solidarity of the international working-class movement, exhibited this truth in a peculiarly devastating and tragic fashion.

Nationalism has assumed many forms since its birth in the eighteenth century, especially since its fusion with *étatisme*, the doctrine of the supremacy in all spheres of the state, in particular the nation state, and after its alliance with forces making for industrialisation and modernisation, once its sworn enemies. But it seems to me, in all its guises, to retain the four characteristics which I tried to outline above: the belief in the overriding need to belong to a nation; in the organic relationships of all the elements that constitute a nation; in the value of our own simply because it is ours; and, finally, faced by rival contenders for authority or loyalty, in the supremacy of its claims. These ingredients, in varying degrees and proportions, are to be found in all the rapidly growing nationalist ideologies which at present proliferate on the earth.

It may be true that nationalism, as distinct from mere national consciousness – the sense of belonging to a nation – is in the first place a response to a patronising or disparaging attitude towards the traditional values of a society, the result of wounded pride and a sense of humiliation in its most socially conscious members, which in due course produce anger and self-assertion. This appears to be supported by the career of the paradigm of modern nationalism in the German reaction – from the conscious defence of German culture in the relatively mild literary patriotism of Thomasius and Lessing and their seventeenth-century forerunners, to Herder's assertion of cultural autonomy, until it leads to an outburst of aggressive chauvinism in Arndt, Jahn, Körner, Goerres, during and after the Napoleonic invasion. But the story is plainly not so simple. Continuity of language, customs, occupation of a territory, have existed since time immemorial. External aggression, not merely against tribes or peoples but against large societies unified by religion, or obedience to a single constituted authority, has, after all, occurred often enough in all parts of the globe. Yet neither in Europe, nor in Asia, neither in ancient times nor medieval, has this led to a specifically nationalist reaction : such has not been the response to defeat inflicted on Persians by Greeks, or on Greeks by Romans, or on Buddhists by Muslims, or on Graeco-Roman civilisation when it was overrun by Huns or Ottoman Turks, quite apart from all the innumerable smaller wars and destruction of native institutions by conquerors in either continent.

It seems clear, even to me who cannot pretend to be a historian or a sociologist, that while the infliction of a wound on the collective feeling of a society, or at least of its spiritual leaders, may be a necessary condition for the birth of nationalism, it is not a sufficient one; the society must, at least potentially, contain within itself a group or class of persons who are in search of a focus for loyalty or self-identification, or perhaps a base for power, no longer supplied by earlier forces for cohesion – tribal, or religious, or feudal, or dynastic, or military – such as was provided by the centralising policies of the monarchies of France or Spain, and was not provided by the rulers of German lands. In some cases, these conditions are created by the emergence of new social classes seeking control of a society against older rulers, secular or clerical. If to this is added the wound of conquest, or even cultural disparagement from without, of a society which has at any rate the beginnings of a national culture, the soil for the rise of nationalism may be prepared.

Yet one more condition for it seems necessary: for nationalism to develop in it, a society must, in the minds of at least some of its most sensitive members, carry an image of itself as a nation, at least in embryo, in virtue of some general unifying factor or factors – language, ethnic origin, a common history (real or imaginary) – ideas and sentiments which are relatively articulate in the minds of the better educated and more socially and historically minded, a good deal less articulate, even absent from, the consciousness of the bulk of the population. This national image, which makes those in whom it is found capable of resentment if it is ignored or insulted, also turns some among them into a conscious intelligentsia, particularly if they are faced by some common enemy, whether within the state or outside it – a church or a government or foreign detractors. These are the men who speak or write to the people, and seek to make them conscious of their wrongs as a people – poets and novelists, historians and critics, theologians, philosophers and the like. Thus resistance to French hegemony in all spheres of life began in the apparently remote region of aesthetics and criticism (I do not here wish to go into the question of what it was in particular that stimulated the original reaction against French neo-classicism in England, or Switzerland). In the German lands it became a social and political force, a breeding ground of nationalism. Among the Germans it took the form of a conscious effort by writers to liberate themselves – and others – from what they felt to be asphyxiating conditions – at first from the despotic dogmas of the French aesthetic legislators, which cramped the free development of the spirit.

But besides the arrogant French, there were domestic tyrants, social and not merely aesthetic. The great outburst of individual indignation against the rules and regulations of an oppressive and philistine society, which goes by the name of the 'Storm and Stress', had as its direct objective the knocking down of all the walls and barriers of social life, obsequiousness and servility below and brutality, arbitrariness, arrogance and oppression above, lies and 'the gibberish and cant of hypocrisy', as Burke calls it, at every level. What began to be questioned was the validity of any laws – the rules, supposedly enjoined by God or by nature or by the prince, that conferred authority and required universal obedience. The demand was for freedom of self-expression, the free expression of the creative will, at its purest and strongest in artists, but present in all men. For Herder, this vital energy was incarnated in the creations of the collective genius of peoples : legends, heroic poetry, myths, laws, customs, song, dance, religious and secular symbolism, temples, cathedrals, ritual acts – all were forms of expression and communication created by no individual authors or identifiable groups, but by the collective and impersonal imagination and will of the entire community, acting at various levels of consciousness; thus, he believed, were generated those intimate and impalpable bonds in virtue of which a society develops as a single organic whole.

The notion of a creative faculty, working in individuals and entire societies alike, replaced the notion of timeless objective truths, eternal models, by following which alone men attain to happiness or virtue or justice or any proper fulfilment of their natures. From this sprang a new view of men and society, which stressed vitality, movement, change, respects in which individuals or groups differed rather than resembled each other, the charm and value of diversity, uniqueness, individuality, a view which conceived of the world as a garden where each tree, each flower, grows in its own peculiar fashion and incorporates those aspirations which circumstances and its own individual nature have generated, and is not, therefore, to be judged by the patterns and goals of other organisms. This cut athwart the dominant *philosophia perennis*, the belief in the generality, uniformity, universality, timeless validity of objective and eternal laws and rules that apply everywhere, at all times, to all men and things, the secular or naturalistic version of which was advocated by the leaders of the French Enlightenment, inspired by the triumph of the natural and mathematical sciences, in terms of which German culture, religious, literary, inward-looking, liable to mysticism, narrowly provincial, at best feebly imitative of the west, made such a poor showing.

I do not wish to imply that this crucial contrast was, at any rate at first, more than a vision in the heads of a small group of German poets and critics. But it was these writers who felt most acutely displaced by the social transformation through which Germany, and in particular Prussia, was passing under the westernising reforms of Frederick the Great. Barred from all real power, unable to fit themselves into the bureaucratic organisation which was imposed on traditional ways of life, acutely sensitive to the incompatibility of their basically Christian, Protestant, moralistic outlook with the scientific temper of the French Enlightenment, harried by the petty despotism of two hundred princes, the most gifted and independent among them responded to the undermining of their world, which had begun with the humiliations inflicted upon their grandfathers by the armies of Louis XIV, by a growing revolt. They contrasted the depth and poetry of the German tradition, with its capacity for fitful but authentic insights into the inexhaustible, inexpressible variety of the life of the spirit, with the shallow materialism, the utilitarianism, and the thin, dehumanised shadow play of the worlds of the French thinkers. This is the root of the romantic movement, which in Germany, at any rate, celebrated the collective will, untrammelled by rules which men could discover by rational methods, the spiritual life of the people in whose activity – or impersonal will – creative individuals could participate, but which they could not observe or describe. The conception of the political life of the nation as the expression of this collective will is the essence of political romanticism – that is, nationalism.

Let me repeat once again that even though nationalism seems to me in the first place to be a response to a wound inflicted upon a society, this, although it is a necessary, is not a sufficient cause of national self-assertion. The wounds inflicted upon one society by another, since time immemorial, have not in all cases led to a national response. For that, something more is needed – namely, a new vision of life with which the wounded society, or the classes or groups which have been displaced by political and social change, can identify themselves, around which they can gather and attempt to restore their collective life. Thus both the Slavophil and the populist movements in Russia, like German nationalism, can be understood only if one realises the traumatic effect of the violent and rapid modernisation imposed on the country by Peter the Great, as it had been, on a smaller scale, by Frederick the Great in Prussia – that is, the effect of technological revolutions or the development of new markets and the decay of old ones, the consequent disruption of the lives of entire classes, the lack of opportunity for the use of their skills by educated men psychologically unfit to enter the new bureaucracy, and, finally, in the case of Germany, occupation or colonial rule by a powerful foreign enemy which destroyed traditional ways of life and left men, and especially the most sensitive and self-conscious among them – artists, thinkers, whatever their professions – without an established position, insecure and bewildered. There is then an effort to create a new synthesis, a new ideology, both to explain and justify resistance to the forces working against their convictions and ways of life, and to point in a new direction and offer them a new centre for self-identification.

This is a familiar enough phenomenon in our own time, which has not lacked in social and economic upheavals. Where ethnic ties and common historical experience are not strong enough to have created a sense of nationhood, this new focus can be a social class, or a political party, or a church, or, most often, the centre of power and authority – the state itself, whether or not it is multinational – which raises the banner under which all those whose traditional modes of life have been disrupted – landless peasants, ruined landowners or shopkeepers, unemployed intellectuals, unsuccessful professionals in various spheres – can gather and regroup themselves. But none of these have, in fact, proved as potent, whether as a symbol or as a reality, as capable of acting as a unifying and dynamic force, as the nation; and when the nation is one with other centres of devotion – race, religion, class – its appeal is incomparably strong.

The first true nationalists – the Germans – are an example of the combination of wounded cultural pride and a philosophico-historical vision to stanch the wound and create an inner focus of resistance. First a small group of educated, discontented Francophobes, then, under the impact of the disasters at the hands of the French armies and Napoleon's *Gleichschaltung*, a vast popular movement, the first great upsurge of nationalist passion, with its wild student chauvinism and book-burnings and secret trials of traitors, a sorcerer's apprentice who got out of hand and excited the disgust of calm thinkers like Goethe and Hegel. Other nations followed, partly under the influence of German rhetoric, partly because their circumstances were sufficiently similar to create a similar malaise and generate the same dangerous remedy. After Germany, Italy and Poland and Russia, and in due course the Balkan and Baltic nationalities and Ireland, and after the débâcle the French Third Republic, and so to our own day, with its republics and dictatorships in Asia and Africa, the burning nationalism of regional and ethnic groups in France and Britain, Belgium and Corsica, Canada and Spain and Cyprus, and who knows where else.

None of the prophets of the nineteenth century, so far as I can tell, anticipated anything of this kind. If anyone had suggested it, it would surely have been regarded as too improbable to be worth consideration. What is the reason for overlooking the likelihood of this cardinal development of our day?

Among the assumptions of rational thinkers of the liberal type in the nineteenth and for some decades in the twentieth century were these: that liberal democracy was the most satisfactory – or at least, the least unsatisfactory – form of human organisation; that the nation-state was, or at least had historically come to be, the normal unit of independent, self-governing human society; and finally, that once the multinational empires (which Herder had denounced as ill-assorted political monstrosities) had been dissolved into their constituent parts, the yearning for union of men with common language, habits, memories, outlooks, would at last be satisfied, and a society of liberated, self-determined nation-states – Mazzini's Young Italy, Young Germany, Young Poland, Young Russia – would come into existence, and, inspired by a patriotism not tainted by aggressive nationalism (itself a symptom of a pathological condition induced by oppression), would live at peace and in harmony with each other, no longer impeded by the irrational survivals of a servile past. The fact that a representative of Mazzini's movement was invited to, and attended, the meeting of the First International Workingmen's Association, however little Marx may have liked it, is significant in this respect. This conviction was shared by the liberal and democratic founders of the succession states after the First World War, and was incorporated in the constitution of the League. As for Marxists, although they regarded nationalism as historically reactionary, even they did not demand the total abolition of national frontiers; provided that class exploitation was abolished by the socialist revolution, it was assumed that free national societies could exist side by side until, and after, the withering away of the state conceived as an instrument of class domination.

Neither of these ideologies anticipated the growth of national sentiment and, more than this, of aggressive nationalism. What, I think, was ignored was the fact which only, perhaps, Durkheim perceived clearly, namely, that the destruction of traditional hierarchies and orders of social life, in which men's loyalties were deeply involved, by the centralisation and bureaucratic 'rationalisation' which industrial progress required and generated, deprived great numbers of men of social and emotional security, produced the notorious phenomena of alienation, spiritual homelessness and growing anomie, and needed the creation, by deliberate social policy, of psychological equivalents for the lost cultural, political, religious values on which the older order rested. The socialists believed that class solidarity, the fraternity of the exploited, and the prospect of a just and rational society which the revolution would bring to birth, would provide this indispensable social cement; and indeed, to a degree it did. Moreover, some among the poor, the displaced, the deprived, emigrated to the New World. But for the majority the vacuum was filled neither by professional associations, nor political parties, nor the revolutionary myths which Sorel sought to provide, but by the old, traditional bonds, language, the soil, historical memories real and imaginary, and by institutions or leaders which functioned as incarnations of men's conceptions of themselves as a community, a *Gemeinschaft* – symbols and agencies which proved far more powerful than either socialists or enlightened liberals wished to believe. The idea, sometimes invested with a mystical or messianic fervour, of the nation as supreme authority, replacing the church or the prince or the rule of law or other sources of ultimate values, relieved the pain of the wound to group consciousness, whoever may have inflicted it – a foreign enemy or native capitalists or imperialist exploiters or an artificially imposed, heartless bureaucracy.

This sentiment was, no doubt, deliberately exploited by parties and politicians, but it was there to be exploited, it was not invented by those who used it for ulterior purposes of their own. It was there, and possessed an independent force of its own, which could be combined with other forces, most effectively with the power of a state bent on modernisation, as a defence against other powers conceived of as alien or hostile, or with particular groups and classes and movements within the state, religious, political and economic, with which the bulk of the society did not instinctively identify itself. It developed, and could be used, in many different directions, as a weapon of secularism, industrialisation, modernisation, the rational use of resources, or in an appeal to a real or imaginary past, some lost, pagan or neo-medieval paradise, a vision of a braver, simpler, purer life, or as the call of the blood or of some ancient faith, against foreigners or cosmopolitans, or 'sophisters, economists and calculators', who did not understand the true soul of the people or the roots from which it sprang, and robbed it of its heritage.

It seems to me that those who, however perceptive in other respects, ignored the explosive power generated by the combination of unhealed mental wounds, however caused, with the image of the nation as a society of the living, the dead and those yet unborn (sinister as this could prove to be when driven to a point of pathological exacerbation), displayed insufficient grasp of social reality. This seems to me to be as true of the present as of the last two hundred years. Modern nationalism was indeed born on German soil, but it developed wherever conditions sufficiently resembled the impact of modernisation on traditional German society. I do not wish to say that this ideology was inevitable: it might, perhaps, not have been born at all. No one has yet convincingly demonstrated that the human imagination obeys discoverable laws, or is able to predict the movement of ideas. If this cluster of ideas had not been born, history might have taken another turn. The wounds inflicted on the Germans would have been there, but the balm which they generated, what Raymond Aron (who applied it to Marxism) has called the opium of the intellectuals, might have been a different one – and if this had happened, things might have fallen out otherwise. But the idea was born: and the consequences were what they were; and it seems to me to show a certain ideological obstinacy not to recognise their nature and importance.

Why was this not seen? Partly, perhaps, because of the 'Whig interpretation' so widely disseminated by enlightened liberal (and socialist) historians; the picture is familiar: on the one side, the powers of darkness: church, capitalism, tradition, authority, hierarchy, exploitation, privilege; on the other, the *lumières*, the struggle for reason, for knowledge and the destruction of barriers between men, for equality, human rights (particularly those of the labouring masses), for individual and social liberty, the reduction of misery, oppression, brutality, the emphasis on what men had in common, not on their differences. Yet, to put it at its simplest, the differences were no less real than the generic identity, than Feuerbach's and Marx's 'species-being'. National sentiment, which sprang from them, fell on both sides of this division between light and darkness, progress and reaction, just as it has within the communist camp of our own day; ignored differences assert themselves, and in the end rise against efforts to ride over them in favour of an assumed, or desired, uniformity. The ideal of a single, scientifically organised world system governed by reason was the heart of the programme of the Enlightenment. When Immanuel Kant, who can scarcely be accused of leanings towards irrationalism, declared, 'From the crooked timber of humanity no straight thing can ever be made', what he said was not absurd.

I have one more suggestion to offer. It seems to me that the thought of the nineteenth and early twentieth century was astonishingly Europocentric. When even the most imaginative and the most radical political thinkers of those times speak of the inhabitants of Africa or Asia, there is, as a rule, something curiously remote and abstract about their ideas. They think of Asians and Africans almost exclusively in terms of their treatment by Europeans. Whether they are imperialists, or benevolent paternalists, or liberals and socialists outraged by conquest and exploitation, the peoples of Africa and Asia are discussed either as wards or as victims of Europeans, but seldom, if ever, in their own right, as peoples with histories and cultures of their own; with a past and present and future which must be understood in terms of their own actual character and circumstances; or, if the existence of such indigenous cultures is acknowledged, as in the case of, let us say, India or Persia, China or Japan, it tends to be largely ignored when the needs of these societies in the future is discussed. Consequently, the notion that a mounting nationalism might develop in these continents was not seriously allowed for. Even Lenin thinks of national movements in these continents solely as weapons against European imperialism; and of support of them only as likely to accelerate or retard the march towards revolution in Europe. This is perfectly intelligible, since he and his fellow revolutionaries believed that this was where the centre of world power lay, that the proletarian revolution in Europe would automatically liberate the workers everywhere, that Asian or African colonial or semi-colonial regimes would thereby be swept away, and their subjects integrated into the new, socially emancipated international world order. Consequently, Lenin was not interested in the life of various communities as such, in this respect following Marx, whose pages on, for example, India and China, or for that matter Ireland, expound no specific lessons for their future.

This wellnigh universal Europocentrism may at least in part account for the fact that the vast explosion not only of anti-imperialism but of nationalism in these continents remained so largely unpredicted. Until the enormous impact of the Japanese victory over Russia in 1904, no non-European people presented itself to the gaze of western social or political theorists as a nation, in the full sense of the word, whose intrinsic character, history, problems, potentialities for the future, constituted a field of study of primary importance for students of public affairs, history, and human development in general. It is this, as much as anything else, that may help to explain this strange lacuna in the futurology of the past. It is instructive to bear in mind that while the Russian Revolution was genuinely free of any nationalist element, even after the Allied Intervention – indeed, it is fair to describe it as wholly anti-nationalist in character – this did not last. The concessions which Stalin had to make to national sentiment before and during the invasion of Russia by Hitler, and the celebration thereafter of the heroes of purely Russian history, indicate the degree to which the mobilisation of this sentiment was required to promote the ends of the Soviet state.

It would not, I think, be an exaggeration to say that no political movement today, at any rate outside the western world, seems likely to succeed unless it allies itself to national sentiment. I am not a historian or a political scientist, and so do not claim to offer an explanation of this phenomenon. I only wish to pose a question, and indicate the need for greater attention to this particular offshoot of the romantic revolt, which has decisively affected our world.

A Bibliography of Isaiah Berlin

Henry Hardy

Maurice Bowra once wrote of Isaiah Berlin: 'Though like Our Lord and Socrates he does not publish much, he thinks and says a great deal and has had an enormous influence on our times.'[1] Bowra's belief that Berlin rarely ventures into print has been widely held, but it does not fit the facts. He has published a great deal on a wide variety of subjects, but most of his work is of essay length, and has appeared in (sometimes obscure) periodicals and symposia, or as occasional pamphlets; much of it has been long out of print; and little has hitherto been collected in book form.[2] This probably explains the common underestimate of the bulk of his writings. My hope is that this bibliography, together with the four volumes of *Selected Writings*, will set the record straight.

It is likely that the list is not quite complete: though I have conducted explorations on many fronts, my searches have not been exhaustively systematic.[3] I shall be grateful for notification of errors or omissions.[4] But I do not think anything important is missing. I have

[1] In a letter to Noel Annan. See Noel Annan, 'A Man I Loved', in Hugh Lloyd-Jones (ed.), *Maurice Bowra: A Celebration* (London, 1974), p. 53.

[2] Until the present selection, only items 112 and 148 below, apart from collections in translation.

[3] For an informal account of how this bibliography came to be compiled, and of the genesis of the whole project of which it forms a part, see Henry Hardy, 'Editing Isaiah Berlin's Writings', *British Book News*, January 1978, pp. 3 and 5.

[4] I should like here to express my gratitude for help already received: Isaiah Berlin has patiently answered almost endless questions; and I have been assisted on individual points by William Beaver, Andrew Best, Michael Brock, Hugo Brunner, Kensington Davison, Victor Erlich, John Fuggles, Samuel Guttenplan, Robert Hazo, Lord Head, Arthur Lehning, Jeremy Lewis, Aileen Kelly, Anthony Kenny, Robert Kocis, Bryan Magee, Anthony Quinton, Alan Ryan, Hans Schenk, John Sparrow, Galen Strawson, Patricia Utechin and Nicholas Wilson.

excluded interviews (which do not strictly count as writings published by the interviewee), bibliographical details of translations into foreign languages, and a handful of minor items, mainly non-academic letters to the Press.

It may be of some assistance to provide a rudimentary sketch-map for those who are not already familiar with Berlin's work, and wish to sample it in a non-random fashion : it is not always easy to tell from a brief bibliographical entry whether an item is substantial or not, or what its subject-matter is. It is impossible to classify definitively writings which are so remarkably free of the restrictions of conventional subject boundaries, especially since the categories that suggest themselves – in particular philosophy, political theory, history of ideas – overlap so extensively on their own account. One needs a Venn diagram. But failing that, I hope the following is a useful guide.

The contents of the four volumes of *Selected Writings*, listed separately at the end of the bibliography, provide the beginnings of a classification. But each volume lacks, for various reasons, certain items which belong in its category ; and some categories are not represented as such, or at all, in the contents of any volume. So it is worth giving more complete lists here.

The major Russian essays are 30, 44, 56, 57, 63, 76, 82, 108 and 125, most of which are included in *Russian Thinkers* (157) ; also on Russian topics are 27, 46, 65, 67, 68 and 111.

The principal philosophical papers are 20, 25, 35, 36, 54 (with the first part of the introduction to 112), 77 and 93 ; 85 is a more popular article on the nature of the subject. It is somewhat arbitrary to separate these items from those which fall most naturally under political theory, namely 64, 71 (with the second part of the introduction to 112) and 81. Most of the pieces in these two groups are reprinted in *Concepts and Categories* (158).

The main essays in the history of ideas are 37, 38, the introduction to 62, 73, 74, 128, 134, 139, 143, 154, 159, 161 and the studies of individual thinkers : Marx (24 and 78), Montesquieu (58), Moses Hess (75), Vico (79, 99, 114, the bulk of 139, 152, and the more popular 115 and 130), Herder (98), Sorel (121) and Machiavelli (122) ; one might also include here many of the Russian essays mentioned above. Items 79 and 98 are superseded by *Vico and Herder* (148), and the majority of the remaining pieces are included in *Against the Current* (166), the present volume.

There are numerous memoirs of and tributes to twentieth-century figures, mainly scholars and statesmen. All the more substantial pieces in this category are reprinted in *Personal Impressions* (167), so I will not repeat here the list of its contents given at the end of this bibliography.

The principal Jewish studies, apart from 70 and 75, already assigned to other categories, are 43, 84, 118 and 126; there are also 52, 119 and 135.

Finally, there are the musicological items 89, 110 and 124.

Much else, of course, is of interest. In particular, I have not included book reviews in this survey, some of which are essays in their own right. There is no substitute for working right through the bibliography if nothing in a particular area is to be missed. But the selection I have listed comprises the main *oeuvre* at the time of going to press.[1]

Where an item has been reprinted in *Selected Writings*, the title of the relevant volume is given in abbreviated form: *RT* for *Russian Thinkers*, *CC* for *Concepts and Categories*, *AC* for *Against the Current*, and *PI* for *Personal Impressions*.

One of the particular drawbacks of a bibliographical description is that essays or lectures which are published separately are not always readily distinguishable from full-scale books, since both have their titles printed in italics. So it may help to say that items 24, 62, 112, 148, 157, 158, 166 and 167 are books, other italicised items being lectures or essays.

Although, as I have explained, I have not included interviews, some of these are of considerable interest, and it would be unhelpful to withhold their details entirely, in deference to a bibliographical scruple. There is an interview on contemporary affairs with Henry Brandon in *Conversations with Henry Brandon* (London, 1966: Deutsch); on Malraux with Martine de Courcel in her *Malraux: Life and Work* (London, 1976: Weidenfeld and Nicolson), reprinted in the *Partisan Review* 43 (1976), 384–93; and on philosophy with Bryan Magee in *Men of Ideas* (London, 1978: B.B.C.; New York, 1979: Viking).

[1] February 1979. Item 159 came to my notice too late for me to take account of it in the third paragraph of my preface; and I learnt of the translation of items 77 and 81 into Japanese too late even to record it in the list.

1929

1 'Pelican s'en va-t-en guerre: a tale of war and peace', *Pelican Record* 19 (1929), 34–6

1930

2 'Music Chronicle', *Oxford Outlook* 10 (1930), 616–27 (under pseudonym 'Albert Alfred Apricott')
3 'Some Procrustations', *Oxford Outlook* 10 (1930), 491–502
4 Editorial, *Oxford Outlook* 10 (1930), 561–5
5 Review of Ernst Benkard, *Undying Faces, Oxford Outlook* 10 (1930), 628–30

1931

6 'Music Chronicle', *Oxford Outlook* 11 (1931), 49–53 (under pseudonym 'A. A. A.': cf. 2)
7 'Music Chronicle', *Oxford Outlook* 11 (1931), 131–5 (under pseudonym 'A. A. A.': cf. 2)
8 'Oglethorpe University, Ga', *Pelican Record* 20 (1931), 34–40 (unattributed)
9 Editorial, *Oxford Outlook* 11 (1931), 1–2
10 'Alexander Blok', editorial, *Oxford Outlook* 11 (1931), 73–6
11 Translation of Alexander Blok, 'The Collapse of Humanism', *Oxford Outlook* 11 (1931), 89–112

1932

12 'Music Chronicle', *Oxford Outlook* 12 (1932), 61–5
13 'Music Chronicle', *Oxford Outlook* 12 (1932), 133–8
14 Review of Leonard Woolf, *After the Deluge, Oxford Outlook* 12 (1932), 68–70

1933

15 Review of Havelock Ellis, *Views and Reviews: First Series, Criterion* 12 (1933), 295–8

1934

16 'Music in Decline', review of Constant Lambert, *Music Ho!, Spectator* 152 (1934), 745–6

1935

17 'Musiciens D'Autrefois', review of Bernard van Dieren, *Down Among the Dead Men*, *Spectator* 155 (1935), 732; (letter) 906

1936

18 'The Future of Music', review of Cecil Gray, *Predicaments, or Music and the Future*, *Spectator* 157 (1936), 317–18
19 'Obscurum Per Obscurius', review of T. A. Jackson, *Dialectics*, *Spectator* 156 (1936), 888

1937

20 'Induction and Hypothesis', *Proceedings of the Aristotelian Society* supplementary vol. 16 (1937), 63–102
21 'The Father of Anarchism', review of E. H. Carr, *Michael Bakunin*, *Spectator* 159 (1937), 1186
22 Review of Julius Weinberg, *An Examination of Logical Positivism*, *Criterion* 17 (1937), 174–82

1938

23 'The Development of Modern Music', review of Gerald Abraham, *A Hundred Years of Music*, *Spectator* 161 (1938), 489–90

1939

24 *Karl Marx: His Life and Environment* (London, 1939: Thornton Butterworth; Toronto, 1939: Nelson)
  2nd ed. (London, 1948; Oxford University Press; New York, 1959: Oxford University Press); repr. with corrections (London and New York, 1960: Oxford University Press); trans. into French, German, Hebrew and Italian
  3rd ed. (London and New York, 1963: Oxford University Press; New York, 1963: Time Inc.; [Tokyo], 1963: Maruzen); trans. into Dutch, Finnish, Hebrew, Italian, Japanese, Norwegian, Spanish and Swedish
  4th ed. (Oxford and New York, 1978: Oxford University Press; London, 1978: Book Club Associates); trans. into Dutch
25 'Verification', *Proceedings of the Aristotelian Society* 39 (1939), 225–48; repr. in G. H. R. Parkinson (ed.), *The Theory of Meaning* (London, 1968: Oxford University Press); repr. in *CC*
26 Review of Karl Britton, *Communication*, *Mind* 48 (1939), 518–27

1947

27 'The Man Who Became a Myth',[1] *Listener* 38 (1947), 23–5
28 Review of Bertrand Russell, *A History of Western Philosophy*, *Mind* 56 (1947), 151–66

1948

29 'Karajan: A Study', *Observer*, 19 September 1948, 2
30 'Russia and 1848', *Slavonic Review* 26 (1948), 341–60; repr. in *RT*

1949

31 'The Anglo-American Predicament', *Listener* 42 (1949), 518–19 and 538; (letters) 681, 813–14
32 'Mr Churchill', *Atlantic Monthly* 184 No 3 (September 1949), 35–44; as 'Mr Churchill and F.D.R.', *Cornhill Magazine* 981 (1950), 219–40; repr. as *Mr Churchill in 1940* (London, [1964]; John Murray), and in *PI*; trans. into German
33 'Three Who Made a Revolution', review of Bertram D. Wolfe, *Three Who Made a Revolution*, *American Historical Review* 55 (1949), 86–92
34 Review of G. V. Plekhanov, *In Defence of Materialism*, trans. Andrew Rothstein, *Slavonic Review* 28 (1949–50), 257–62; (letter) 607–10

1950

35 'Empirical Propositions and Hypothetical Statements', *Mind* 59 (1950), 289–312; repr. in Robert J. Swartz (ed.), *Perceiving, Sensing, and Knowing* (New York, 1965: Doubleday), and in *CC*
36 'Logical Translation', *Proceedings of the Aristotelian Society* 50 (1950), 157–88; repr. in *CC*
37 'Political Ideas in the Twentieth Century', *Foreign Affairs* 28 (1950), 351–85; repr. in *Four Essays on Liberty* (112, q.v.); trans. into Japanese
38 'Socialism and Socialist Theories', *Chambers's Encyclopaedia* (London, 1950: Newnes), vol. 12, 638–50; revised in 1966 ed. (Oxford: Pergamon), vol. 12, 640–52
39 Translation of Ivan Turgenev, *First Love* (with *Rudin*, trans. Alex Brown) (London, 1950: Hamish Hamilton); illustrated ed. (on its own) (London, 1956: Hamish Hamilton; London, 1965: Panther; Harmondsworth, 1977: Penguin); trans. into Malay

[1] Belinsky.

40 'Russian Literature: The Great Century', review of D. S. Mirsky, *A History of Russian Literature*, *Nation* 170 (1950), 180–3, 207–8

41 'The Energy of Pasternak', review of Boris Pasternak, *Selected Writings*, *Partisan Review* 17 (1950), 748–51

42 'A View of Russian Literature', review of Marc Slonim, *The Epic of Russian Literature*, *Partisan Review* 17 (1950), 617–23

1951

43 'Jewish Slavery and Emancipation', *Jewish Chronicle*, 21 September 1951, 17, 24; 28 September 1951, 17, 19; 5 October 1951, 13, 15; 12 October 1951, 8; repr. from Norman Bentwich (ed.), *Hebrew University Garland* (London, 1952: Constellation Books); trans. into French

44 'Lev Tolstoy's Historical Scepticism', *Oxford Slavonic Papers* 2 (1951), 17–54; repr. with additions as *The Hedgehog and the Fox* (London, 1953: Weidenfeld and Nicolson; New York, 1953: Simon and Schuster; New York, 1957: New American Library); repr. in *RT*; trans. into Italian and Japanese

45 'On Translating Turgenev', review of I. S. Turgenev, *Smoke*, *On the Eve*, *Virgin Soil*, *Fathers and Children* and *A House of Gentle Folk*, trans. Constance Garnett, *Observer*, 11 November 1951, 7

1952

46 'Generalissimo Stalin and the Art of Government', *Foreign Affairs* 30 (1952), 197–214 (under pseudonym 'O. Utis')

47 Review of Benedetto Croce, *My Philosophy*, *Mind* 61 (1952), 574–8

48 Review of Morton White, *Social Thought in America*, *Mind* 61 (1952), 405–9

49 'Dr Chaim Weizmann' (supplementary obituary), *The Times*, 17 November 1952, 8

50 'The Fate of Liberty' (letter), *The Times*, 16 December 1952, 9

1953

51 'Henderson at Oxford: 1. All Souls', in T. Wilson (ed.), 'Sir Hubert Henderson, 1890–1952', supplement to *Oxford Economic Papers* 5 (1953), 55–8; repr. as 'Hubert Henderson at All Souls' in *PI*

52 'Israel – A Survey', in *The State of Israel* (London, 1953: Anglo-Israel Association); repr. in *Israel: Some Aspects of the New State* (London, 1955: Anglo-Israel Association), and as 'The Origins of Israel' in Walter Z. Laqueur (ed.), *The Middle East in Transition* (London, 1958: Routledge and Kegan Paul)

53 'Thinkers or Philosophers?', review of N. O. Lossky, *History of Russian Philosophy*, *Times Literary Supplement*, 27 March 1953, 197–8 (unattributed)

1954

54 *Historical Inevitability*, Auguste Comte Memorial Trust Lecture No 1 (London, 1954: Oxford University Press); repr. in *Four Essays on Liberty* (112, q.v.) and in Patrick Gardiner (ed.), *The Philosophy of History* (London, 1974: Oxford University Press); trans. into Japanese, Norwegian, Spanish and Swedish

55 'Realism in Politics', *Spectator* 193 (1954), 774–6

1955

56 'Herzen and Bakunin on Individual Liberty', in Ernest J. Simmons (ed.), *Continuity and Change in Russian and Soviet Thought* (Cambridge, Massachusetts, 1955: Harvard University Press); repr. in *RT*

57 'A Marvellous Decade', Northcliffe Lectures for 1954; repr. as 'A Remarkable Decade' in *RT*; trans. into Italian

    I '1838–48: The Birth of the Russian Intelligentsia', *Encounter* 4 No 6 (June 1955), 27–39

    II '1838–48: German Romanticism in Petersburg and Moscow', *Encounter* 5 No 11 (November 1955), 21–9

    III 'Belinsky: Moralist and Prophet', *Encounter* 5 No 12 (December 1955), 22–43

    IV 'Herzen and the Grand Inquisitors', *Encounter* 6 No 5 (May 1956), 20–34; repr. as 'Alexander Herzen' in Stephen Spender, Irving Kristol and Melvin J. Lasky (eds), *Encounters: An Anthology from the First Ten Years of* Encounter *Magazine* (New York, 1965: Simon and Schuster), and as introduction to Alexander Herzen, *Childhood, Youth and Exile*, trans. J. D. Duff (Oxford, 1980: Oxford University Press); trans. into French

58 'Montesquieu', *Proceedings of the British Academy* 41 (1955), 267–96; repr. in *AC*

59 'Philosophy and Beliefs' (with Anthony Quinton, Stuart Hampshire and Iris Murdoch), *Twentieth Century* 157 (1955), 495–521

60 'Roosevelt Through European Eyes', *Atlantic Monthly* 196 No 1 (July 1955), 67–71; as 'President Franklin Delano Roosevelt', *Political Quarterly* 26 (1955), 336–44; repr. in *PI*

61 'The Furious Vissarion', review of Herbert E. Bowman, *Vissarion Belinsky*, *New Statesman and Nation* 50 (1955), 447–8

1956

62 (ed. with introduction and commentary) *The Age of Enlightenment* (Boston, 1956: Houghton Mifflin; New York, 1956: New American Library; Oxford, 1979: Oxford University Press)

63 Introduction to Alexander Herzen, *From the Other Shore* and *The Russian People and Socialism* (London, 1956: Weidenfeld and Nicolson; Oxford, 1979: Oxford University Press); trans. into Japanese

64 'Equality', *Proceedings of the Aristotelian Society* 56 (1956), 301–26; repr. in the Bobbs-Merrill Reprint Series in Political Science, No 68812, and in *CC*

65 'The Father of Russian Marxism',[1] *Listener* 56 (1956), 1063–4 and 1077; repr. as 'Father of Russian Socialism', *New Leader* (U.S.A.), 4 February 1957, 14–17

1957

66 'An Episode in the Life of Ivan Turgenev', *London Magazine* 4 No 7 (July 1957), 14–24 (includes translation of Turgenev's 'A Fire at Sea')

67 'The Silence in Russian Culture', *Foreign Affairs* 36 (1957), 1–24

68 'The Soviet Intelligentsia', *Foreign Affairs* 36 (1957), 122–30 (under pseudonym 'L.')

69 (with Miriam Rothschild) 'Mr James de Rothschild: "Grand Seigneur"' (supplementary obituary), *The Times*, 13 May 1957, 15

1958

70 *Chaim Weizmann*, 2nd Herbert Samuel Lecture (London, 1958: Weidenfeld and Nicolson); repr. in *PI*

71 *Two Concepts of Liberty*, Inaugural Lecture as Chichele Professor of Social and Political Theory (Oxford, 1958: Clarendon Press); repr. in *Four Essays on Liberty* (112, q.v.) and in part in Anthony Quinton (ed.), *Political Philosophy* (London, 1967: Oxford University Press); ed. with notes by Kimiyoshi Yura (Kyoto, 1967: Apollon-sha); trans. into Greek, Italian, Japanese, Norwegian and Spanish

72 'Richard Pares', *Balliol College Record* 1958, 32–4; repr. in *PI*

1959

73 *European Unity and Its Vicissitudes* (Amsterdam, 1959; Fondation Européenne de la Culture)

[1] Plekhanov.

74 *John Stuart Mill and the Ends of Life*, Robert Waley Cohen Memorial Lecture (London, 1959: Council of Christians and Jews); repr. in *Four Essays on Liberty* (112, q.v.); trans. into Japanese

75 *The Life and Opinions of Moses Hess*, Lucien Wolf Memorial Lecture (Cambridge, 1959: Heffer); repr. in Philip Rieff (ed.), *On Intellectuals* (New York, 1969: Doubleday), and in *AC*; trans. into French

1960

76 Introduction to Franco Venturi, *Roots of Revolution* (London, 1960: Weidenfeld and Nicolson; New York, 1966: Grosset and Dunlap); repr. as 'Russian Populism' in *Encounter* 15 No 1 (July 1960), 13–28, and in *RT*

77 'History and Theory: The Concept of Scientific History', *History and Theory* 1 (1960), 1–31; repr. in Alexander V. Riasanovsky and Barnes Riznik (eds), *Generalizations in Historical Writing* (Philadelphia, 1963: University of Pennsylvania Press), and as 'The Concept of Scientific History' in William H. Dray (ed.), *Philosophical Analysis and History* (New York, 1966: Harper and Row), and in *CC*

78 'Marx', in J. O. Urmson (ed.), *Concise Encyclopedia of Western Philosophy and Philosophers* (London, 1960: Hutchinson; 2nd ed. 1975)

79 'The Philosophical Ideas of Giambattista Vico', in *Art and Ideas in Eighteenth-Century Italy* (Rome, 1960: Edizioni di Storia e Letteratura); repr. in revised form in *Vico and Herder* (148, q.v.)

80 Review of Henry Vyverberg, *Historical Pessimism in the French Enlightenment*, *French Studies* 14 (1960), 167–70

1961

81 'La théorie politique existe-t-elle?', *Revue française de science politique* 11 (1961), 309–37; repr. in English as 'Does Political Theory Still Exist?' in Peter Laslett and W. G. Runciman (eds), *Philosophy, Politics and Society*, 2nd Series (Oxford, 1962: Blackwell), and in *CC*

82 'Tolstoy and Enlightenment', P. E. N. Hermon Ould Memorial Lecture for 1960, *Encounter* 16 No 2 (February 1961), 29–40; repr. in *Mightier Than the Sword* (London, 1964: Macmillan) and in *RT*

83 'What is History?' (letters),[1] *The Listener* 65 (1961), 877 and 1048–9

1962

84 'The Biographical Facts', in Meyer W. Weisgal and Joel Carmichael (eds), *Chaim Weizmann* (London, 1962: Weidenfeld and Nicolson;

[1] A polemical interchange with E. H. Carr.

New York, 1963: Atheneum); repr. in Dan Leon and Yehuda Adin (eds), *Chaim Weizmann, Statesman of the Jewish Renaissance* (Jerusalem, 1974: The Zionist Library); trans. into French, Hebrew and Spanish

85 'The Purpose of Philosophy', *Insight* (Nigeria) 1 No 1 (July 1962), 12–15; repr. in the *Sunday Times*, 4 November 1962, 23 and 26, as 'Philosophy's Goal' in Leonard Russell (ed.), *Encore*, 2nd Year (London, 1963: Michael Joseph), and in *CC*

86 'Mr Carr's Big Battalions', review of E. H. Carr, *What is History?*, *New Statesman* 63 (1962), 15–16

87 'The Road to Catastrophe', review of Hans Kohn, *The Mind of Germany*, and G. P. Gooch, *French Profiles: Prophets and Pioneers*, *Times Literary Supplement*, 30 March 1962, 216

1963

88 Contribution to Clara Urquhart (ed.), *A Matter of Life* (London, 1963: Cape)

89 'Historical Note', in *Khovanshchina* (opera programme) ([London], 1963: Royal Opera House Covent Garden Ltd); repr. in the 1972 programme

90 'Why are these books neglected?', *Twentieth Century* 172 No 1019 (Autumn 1963), 139–47

1964

91 Contribution to *Meyer W. Weisgal* (New York, 1964); repr. as 'A Generous Imaginative Idealist' in Edward Victor (ed.), *Meyer Weisgal at Seventy* (London, 1966: Weidenfeld and Nicolson)

92 'Felix Frankfurter at Oxford', in Wallace Mendelson (ed.), *Felix Frankfurter: A Tribute* (New York, 1964: Reynal); repr. in *Quest* 1 (1965), 20–2, and in *PI*

93 '"From Hope and Fear Set Free"', Presidential Address, *Proceedings of the Aristotelian Society* 64 (1964), 1–30; repr. in *CC*

94 'Hobbes, Locke and Professor Macpherson', review of C. B. Macpherson, *The Political Theory of Possessive Individualism, Hobbes to Locke*, *Political Quarterly* 35 (1964), 444–68

95 'Portrait of Ben-Gurion', review of Maurice Edelman, *Ben-Gurion: A Political Biography*, *Jewish Chronicle*, 25 December 1964, 7 and 22

1965

96 Contribution to Julian Huxley (ed.), *Aldous Huxley* (London, 1965: Chatto and Windus); repr. as 'Aldous Huxley' in *PI*

97 Contribution to Ian Kemp (ed.), *Michael Tippett* (London, 1965: Faber)

98 'Herder and the Enlightenment', in Earl R. Wasserman (ed.), *Aspects of the Eighteenth Century* (Baltimore, 1965: Johns Hopkins Press); repr. as 'J. G. Herder', *Encounter* 25 No 1 (July 1965), 29–48, and No 2 (August 1965), 42–51; repr. in revised form in *Vico and Herder* (148, q.v.)

99 'Sulla teoria del Vico circa la conoscenza storica', *Lettere Italiane* 17 (1965), 420–31; repr. as 'Appendice sulla teoria del Vico circa la conoscenza storica', *Sensibilita e razionalita nel Settecento* (August 1967), 357–71

100 Review of C. P. Courtney, *Montesquieu and Burke, Modern Language Review* 60 (1965), 449–52

101 'A Great Russian Writer', review of Osip Mandelstam, *The Prose of Osip Mandelstam, New York Review of Books*, 23 December 1965, 3–4

1966

102 Introduction to Marc Raeff (ed.), *Russian Intellectual History* (New York/Chicago/Burlingame, 1966: Harcourt, Brace and World)

103 Preface to H. G. Schenk, *The Mind of the European Romantics* (London, 1966: Constable; New York, 1969: Doubleday; Oxford, 1979: Oxford University Press); trans. into Japanese

104 'L. B. Namier – A Personal Impression', *Encounter* 27 No 5 (November 1966), 32–42; repr. in Martin Gilbert (ed.), *A Century of Conflict* (London, 1966: Hamish Hamilton), and in *PI*

105 'The Great Blood Libel Case', review of Maurice Samuel, *Blood Accusation: The Strange History of the Beiliss Case, Jewish Chronicle Literary Supplement*, 23 December 1966, 3–4

106 'New Ways in History' (letter), *Times Literary Supplement*, 21 April 1966, 347

1967

107 Contribution to Cecil Woolf and John Bagguley (eds), *Authors Take Sides on Vietnam* (New York, 1967: Simon and Schuster)

1968

108 Introduction to Alexander Herzen, *My Past and Thoughts* (London, 1968: Chatto and Windus; New York, 1968: Knopf; ed. and abridged by Dwight Macdonald, New York, 1973: Knopf; London, 1974: Chatto and Windus); repr. as 'The Great Amateur', *New York*

Review of Books, 14 March 1968, 9–18, and as 'Herzen and his Memoirs' in *AC*; trans. into Japanese

109 Comment on Richard Pipes, 'The Origins of Bolshevism: The Intellectual Evolution of Young Lenin', in Richard Pipes (ed.), *Revolutionary Russia* (Cambridge, Massachusetts, 1968: Harvard University Press)

110 'The "*Naïveté*" of Verdi', *Hudson Review* 21 (1968), 138–47; repr. from *Atti del I Congresso internazionale di studi verdiani, 1966* (Parma, 1969: Istituto di Studi Verdiani); repr. in *About the House* 3 No 1 (March 1969), 8–13

111 'The Role of the Intelligentsia', *Listener* 79 (1968), 563–5

1969

112 *Four Essays on Liberty* (reprints of 37, 54, 71 and 74, with a new introduction) (London and New York, 1969: Oxford University Press); trans. into Hebrew, Japanese, Portugese and Spanish

113 Foreword to Michael Yudkin (ed.), *General Education: A Symposium on the Teaching of Non-Specialists* (Harmondsworth, 1969: Allen Lane/Penguin); repr. as 'General Education' in *Oxford Review of Education* 1 (1975), 287–92; trans. into Japanese

114 'A Note on Vico's Concept of Knowledge', in Giorgio Tagliacozzo and Hayden V. White (eds), *Giambattista Vico: An International Symposium* (Baltimore, 1969: Johns Hopkins Press); repr. in *New York Review of Books*, 24 April 1969, 23–6, and in *AC*

115 'One of the Boldest Innovators in the History of Human Thought',[1] *New York Times Magazine*, 23 November 1969, 76–100

116 'Reply to Orsini', *Journal of the History of Ideas* 30 (1969), 91–5 (abstract in the *Philosopher's Index* (1969), 282)

1970

117 Foreword to R. D. Miller, *Schiller and the Ideal of Freedom: A Study of Schiller's Philosophical Works with Chapters on Kant* (Oxford, 1970: Clarendon Press)

118 'Benjamin Disraeli, Karl Marx, and the Search for Identity', in *Transactions of the Jewish Historical Society of England 22 (1968–69)* (London, 1970: Jewish Historical Society of England); repr. in *Midstream* 16 No 7 (August–September 1970), 29–49, and in *AC*; trans. into French and Spanish

119 'Weizmann as Exilarch', in *Chaim Weizmann as Leader* (Jerusalem, 1970: Hebrew University of Jerusalem); trans into Hebrew

[1] Vico.

1971

120 *Sir Maurice Bowra, 1898–1971* (Oxford, [1971]: Wadham College); repr. as 'Memorial Address in St Mary's' in Hugh Lloyd-Jones (ed.), *Maurice Bowra* (London, 1974: Duckworth), and as 'Maurice Bowra' in *PI*

121 'Georges Sorel', Creighton Lecture, *Times Literary Supplement*, 31 December 1971, 1617–22; repr. in expanded form in Chimen Abramsky (ed.), *Essays in Honour of E. H. Carr* (London, 1974: Macmillan), and in *AC*; trans. into Hebrew and Spanish; see also 132

122 'The Question of Machiavelli', *New York Review of Books*, 4 November 1971, 20–32; repr. of part of 'The Originality of Machiavelli', in Myron P. Gilmore (ed.), *Studies on Machiavelli* (Florence, 1972: Sansoni); repr. in the Bobbs-Merrill Reprint Series in Political Science, No 68813; full version repr. in *AC*

123 'Randolph', in Kay Halle (ed.), *Randolph Churchill: The Young Unpretender* (London, 1971: Heinemann)

124 'Tchaikovsky and Eugene Onegin', *Glyndebourne Festival Programme Book* 1971, 58–63

1972

125 *Fathers and Children: Turgenev and the Liberal Predicament*, Romanes Lecture (Oxford, 1972: Clarendon Press; repr. with corrections 1973); repr. in *New York Review of Books*, 18 October 1973, 39–44, 1 November 1973, 22–9, and 15 November 1973, 9–11, as introduction to Ivan Turgenev, *Fathers and Sons*, trans. Rosemary Edmonds (Harmondsworth, 1975: Penguin), and in *RT*; trans. into Japanese; see also 138

126 *Zionist Politics in Wartime Washington: a Fragment of Personal Reminiscence*, Yaachov Herzog Memorial Lecture (Jerusalem, 1972: Hebrew University of Jerusalem); repr. in *PI*

127 Foreword to Friedrich Meinecke, *Historism: The Rise of a New Historical Outlook*, trans. J. E. Anderson (London, 1972: Routledge and Kegan Paul)

128 'The Bent Twig: A Note on Nationalism', *Foreign Affairs* 51 (1972), 11–30; trans. into Spanish

129 'Dr Jacob Herzog', *Jewish Chronicle*, 14 April 1972, 28 and 43; repr. as 'Yaachov Herzog – a Tribute' as preface to 126, and as 'Jacob Herzog' in *PI*

130 'Giambattista Vico', *Listener* 88 (1972), 391–8

131 'History as We Would Like It', *World View* 15 No 7 (July 1972), 16

132 'Sorel' (letter), *Times Literary Supplement*, 14 January 1972, 40

1973

133 'Austin and the Early Beginnings of Oxford Philosophy', in *Essays on J. L. Austin* (Oxford, 1973: Clarendon Press); repr. in *PI*

134 'The Counter-Enlightenment', *Dictionary of the History of Ideas* (New York, 1968–73: Scribner's), vol. 2 (1973), 110–12; repr. in *AC*

135 'A Nation Among Nations', *Jewish Chronicle*, Colour Magazine, 4 May 1973, 28–34

136 'Notes on the Foundation of Wolfson College', *Lycidas* 1 (1973), 2–4

137 'Mr Hamilton Fish Armstrong' (supplementary obituary), *The Times*, 28 April 1973, 16

138 'Fathers and Children' (letter), *Times Literary Supplement*, 12 January 1973, 40

1974

139 *The Divorce between the Sciences and the Humanities*, 2nd Tykociner Memorial Lecture (Illinois, 1974: University of Illinois); repr. in *Salmagundi* No 27 (Summer–Fall 1974), 9–39, and in *AC*; trans. into Italian

140 Contribution to *Arthur Lehning in 1974* (Leiden, 1974: Brill)

141 'Mr C. E. Bohlen: Close Study of Soviet Leaders' (supplementary obituary), *The Times*, 11 January 1974, 16

1975

142 *John Petrov Plamenatz, 1912–1975* (Oxford, [1975]: All Souls College); repr. in *PI*

143 'L'apoteosi della volontà romantica: la rivolta contro il tipo di un mondo ideale', *Lettere Italiane* 27 (1975), 44–68

144 'Performances memorable – and not so memorable', *Opera* 26 (1975), 116–20

145 Presidential Address, *Proceedings of the British Academy* 61 (1975), 71–81

146 Speech at the Official Opening of Wolfson College, Oxford, 12 November 1974, *Lycidas* 3 (1975), 3–6

147 'Sir John Wheeler-Bennett' (supplementary obituary), *The Times*, 13 December 1975, 16

1976

148 *Vico and Herder* (London, 1976: Hogarth Press; New York, 1976: Viking) (revised versions of 78 and 98, with a new introduction)

149 Contribution to John Jolliffe (ed.), *Auberon Herbert: A Composite Portrait* (Tisbury, 1976: Compton Russell); repr. as 'Auberon Herbert' in *PI*

150 'Comment on Professor Verene's Paper',[1] *Social Research* 43 (1976), 426–9

151 Presidential Address, *Proceedings of the British Academy* 62 (1976), 85–94

152 'Vico and the Ideal of the Enlightenment', *Social Research* 43 (1976), 640–53; repr. in *AC* without last section, 'The Workings of Providence'

1977

153 *Sir Harry d'Avigdor Goldsmid, 1906–1976* ([London, 1977]: privately printed)

154 'Hume and the Sources of German Anti-Rationalism', in G. P. Morice (ed.), *David Hume: Bicentennial Papers* (Edinburgh, 1977: Edinburgh University Press); repr. in *AC*

155 'Old Russia', review of Marvin Lyons, *Russia in Original Photographs 1860–1920*, ed. Andrew Wheatcroft, and Kyril Fitzlyon and Tatiana Browning, *Before the Revolution: A View of Russia under the Last Tsar, Guardian*, 24 November 1977, 14

156 Presidential Address, *Proceedings of the British Academy* 63 (1977), 1–11

1978

157 *Russian Thinkers*, ed. Henry Hardy and Aileen Kelly, with an introduction by Aileen Kelly (London, 1978: Hogarth Press; New York, 1978: Viking) (the first of four volumes of his *Selected Writings*, ed. Henry Hardy, comprising reprints of 30, 44, 56, 57, 76, 82 and 125)

158 *Concepts and Categories: Philosophical Essays*, ed. Henry Hardy, with an introduction by Bernard Williams (London, 1978: Hogarth Press; New York, 1979: Viking) (the second volume of *Selected Writings* (see 157), comprising reprints of 25, 35, 36, 64, 77, 81, 85 and 93)

159 *Decline of Utopian Ideas in the West* ([Tokyo], 1978: Japan Foundation)

160 Introduction to *Derek Hill: Portraits* (London, 1978: Marlborough Fine Art)

161 'Nationalism: Past Neglect and Present Power', *Partisan Review* 45 (1978) (forthcoming); trans. into Spanish

[1] Donald Phillip Verene, 'Vico's Philosophy of Imagination', *Social Research* 43 (1976), 410–26.

162 Presidential Address, *Proceedings of the British Academy* 64 (1978) (forthcoming)

163 'Corsi e Ricorsi', review of Giorgio Tagliacozzo and Donald Phillip Verene (eds), *Giambattista Vico's Science of Humanity*, *Journal of Modern History* 50 (1978), 480–9

164 'Tolstoy, Remembered', review of Tatyana Tolstoy, *Tolstoy Remembered*, *New Review* 5 No 2 (Autumn 1978), 3–7.

165 'Mr Nicholas Nabokov' (supplementary obituary), *The Times*, 15 April 1978, 16

1979

166 *Against the Current: Essays in the History of Ideas*, ed. and with a bibliography by Henry Hardy, with an introduction by Roger Hausheer (London, 1979: Hogarth Press; New York, 1980: Viking) (the third volume of *Selected Writings* (see 157), comprising reprints of 58, 75, 108, 110, 114, 118, 121, 122, 134, 139, 152, 154 and 161, and the present bibliography)

1980

167 *Personal Impressions*, ed. Henry Hardy, with an introduction by Noel Annan (London, 1980: Hogarth Press; New York, 1981: Viking) (the fourth volume of *Selected Writings* (see 157), comprising reprints of 32, 51, 60, 70, 72, 92, 96, 104, 120, 126, 129, 133, 142 and 149) (forthcoming)

CHECKLIST OF CONTENTS OF *Selected Writings*

(the numbers refer to the relevant entries in the bibliography above)

157 *Russian Thinkers*

Index

Compiled by Douglas Matthews

INDEX

Hurd, Richard, Bishop, 176
Husserl, Edmund, 254
Huxley, Aldous, 336
Huxley, Julian, 88
Huxley, Thomas Henry, 273

Iambulus, 121
Ibsen, Henrik, 295, 300
ideal, the, 68, 76, 78
ideas, history of, demands of, xvi–xviii; as theme, xix, xlix; as philosophical endeavour, xxii–xxiv; and adoption of familiar values, 333
identity, human, xv, xxxvi; *see also under* Jews; society
Illinois Staats-Zeitung, Die, 246
imagination (*fantasia*), Vico on, xxix, li, 98–9, 104n, 106, 108, 114, 116–17, 124; Hamann on, 166, 176
individualism, Bonald denounces, 24
inner life, xvii, xx, xxix, xxxiv, xlv, 8, 106
Innocent III, Pope, 234
'interested error', xxvi, 1, 163
International Workingmen's Association, 243, 351
irrationalism, historical movements of, 82; German, 162–87; and human actions, 323; *see also* Enlightenment; reason
Isidore of Seville, 103
Israel (state of), 247, 249–50, 252; *see also* Palestine; Zionism
Italy, literature in, 84; 1848 revolution in, 197; Herzen and, 202–3; nationalism in, 230–1, 290, 319, 338–40, 350–1
Itzig, Baron, 278
Ivanov, Alexander Andreevich, 200

Jabotinsky, Vladimir, 258
Jacobi, Friedrich Heinrich, and Hume's doctrine of belief, xxxiii, 162, 171, 178, 181–7, anti-rationalism, 9, 17, 165; on Vico, 119; Hamann influences, 170–1, 174, 180, 182; pietism, 182; on faith, 182–4

Jahn, Friedrich Ludwig, 279, 346
James, William, 302, 319, 324
Jansenism, 2, 147, 306
Japan, 354
Jaurès, Jean, liberalism, 131; Sorel on, 309, 313, 322, 325, 329; on Sorel, 315
Jesuits, 35
Jethro, the priest, 236
Jews, identity question, xxxvii, xxxix, 214, 225, 235–6, 244, 252–7, 259–60, 275, 280; Hess on, xli, 213, 217, 225–7, 231–47, 249–51; conversions and assimilation, 214, 235, 249, 253, 255; Marx's position on, 222, 224, 252, 276–7; reform movement and orthodoxy, 237–8, 244; history, 252–5; emancipation and integration, 255, 257–8, 275; Disraeli's views on, 269–71, 273–5, 277, 279, 285; as revolutionaries, 274; Cicero disparages, 341
Joly, Maurice, 45n
Joseph, the Patriarch, 236
Joseph of Naxos, 254
Josephus, Flavius, 254
Julius Caesar, 44, 52, 149
Julius II, Pope, 59
justice, Machiavelli on, 72; Montesquieu on, 152–5, 161; Kant on, 309; Sorel on, 309; *see also* law
Juvenal, 45, 70, 341

Kaegi, Werner, 29
Kafka, Franz, xlvi
Kalevala, 108
Kalischer, Rabbi Hirsch, 240, 246
Kamenev, Lev Borisovich, 33n, 34n
Kant, Immanuel, on experience, xxii–xxiii; morality, xxviii; attitude to rationalism, 7–8, 19, 165, 180, 186; on individualism and will, 15–16; and hypothetical imperatives, 53; transcendental method, 102; as intellectual organiser, 115; and Vico's ideas, 119;

383